CROSBY, STILLS, & NASH

CROSBY, STILLS, & NASH

THE AUTHORIZED BIOGRAPHY

Text by Dave Zimmer
Photography by Henry Diltz

DA CAPO PRESS

Design by Manuela Paul

Library of Congress Cataloging in Publication Data to come

ISBN 0-306-80974-5

First Da Capo Press Edition 2000

Published by Da Capo Press
A Member of the Perseus Books Group
http://www.dacapopress.com

1 2 3 4 5 6 7 8 9 10——04 03 02 01 00

Contents

Acknowledgments

This book would not exist were it not for the kind support of David Crosby, Stephen Stills, and Graham Nash. They cooperated fully, graciously opened their lives to us, and were always willing to talk or be photographed. Thanks for all of the great moments, guys.

As for our editor, Bob Miller, he proved to be an invaluable friend and guiding light. He believed in the project from the start and was our main ally at St. Martin's. Muchas gracias.

There are many other people who contributed an enormous amount of energy to this project. They each deserve special thanks: Ken Weiss, for his advice and friendship; Mac Holbert, for his heart and insights; Steve Gelber, for getting the ball rolling and for a critical eye down the stretch; Scott Oxman, for his CSN&Y archives and memory; Paul S. Caruso (Museum of Rock Art), for his spirit and enthusiasm; Charlie Blue, for being there when we needed a lift; Kathy Hayes, for landing the deal and getting it right; Joel Bernstein, for his photos and gentle soul; Gerry Tolman, for his loyalty and help backstage; and Ina Shapiro and Lisa Mann for keeping the editorial bases covered.

Warm personal thanks must also be given to: Tod Bottari, for launching the words; Ric Boyd and Tom Lachmar, for turning up the music; Blair Jackson and Regan McMahon, for creating the style; Dennis Erokan, Miles Hurwitz, and *BAM* magazine, for being there in the beginning and making the room; Jane and Edgar Zimmer, for all their love; Tom Stienstra, for sparking the fire; Kay and the girls, for staying strong; Frank G. Scott, for his sincere faith; Elizabeth and Zoë Diltz, for being.

The completion of this book was made possible by a huge team of individuals who donated their time and words to us, in the spirit of CSN. Thanks: Ron and Howard Albert; Gerry Beckley; Michael John Bowen; Kim Bullard; Dewey Bunnell; Gary Burden; Judy Cameron; Gene Clark; Allan Clarke; Cameron Crowe; Saul Davis; Steve DePaul; Jim Dickson; Tim Drummond; Bobby Elliott; Ahmet Ertegun; Cyrus Faryar; Don Felder; Mike Finnigan; Dan Fogelberg; Ben Fong-Torres; Glenn Frey; Richie Furay; David Geffen; Peter Golden; Don Gooch; Bill Graham; Steve Gursky; Bill Halverson; Bobby Hammer; Tony Hicks; Chris Hillman; Pete Howard; Armando Hurley; Jeffrey Husband; Larry Johnson; Stanley Johnston; Paul Kantner;

Danny Kortchmar; Leah Kunkel; Russ Kunkel; Joe Lala; Henry Lewy; Leo Makota; Dewey Martin; Bill Meeker; Joni Mitchell; Leslie Morris; Susan Nash; Martin Perlich; George Perry; Jay Parti; Kenny Passarelli; Charles John Quarto; David Rao; Elliot Roberts; Paul Rothchild; Chris Sarns; Tim Schmit; John Sebastian; Bill Siddons; Grace Slick; William Smith; Michael Stergis; Ron Stone; Dallas Taylor; Peter Tork; Joe Vitale; Jeff Wald and Smokey Wendell.

Also, for additional photography support, thanks: Chuck Boyd, Tom Gundlefinger; the Michael Ochs Archives; Richard Photo Lab; Pete Sherman Photo Service.

Acknowledgments II

Following the publication of the original edition of this book in 1984, we discovered that several individuals' contributions to the CSN story had not been properly acknowledged in the narrative text. We would like to rectify that here. Jeff Wald, as a manager and advisor, helped keep CSN rolling in the early '80s. Elliot Mazer, as an engineer and production guru, captured CSN&Y moments of magic on tape in 1973 and 1974. Engineer/producer Stephen Barncard, who joined the CSN&Y family during the creation of *Déjà Vu* in 1969, has been a group mainstay and key contributor to CSN as well as Crosby and Nash solo and duo projects for over thirty years. Engineer/producer Don Gooch, who poured his heart and soul into Rudy Records, brought his expert hands and ears to many recording sessions, most notably for Nash and C&N projects in the '70s. And, finally, art director and designer Gary Burden, never afraid to follow his creative instincts, has captured the visual essence of CSN and CSN&Y on album covers and in songbooks since 1969.

The preparation and publication of the updated edition of this book was made possible with the help and contributions of a small army of people, most importantly David Crosby, Stephen Stills, Graham Nash, and Neil Young—sincere thanks for sharing your words and ongoing musical magic. Also on board during the process, offering insights, support, or just plain inspiration: Stephen Barncard, Joel Bernstein, Gary Burden, Crazy Horse (Ralph Molina, Frank Sampedro, and Billy Talbot), Cameron Crowe, Marge Falcon Clark, Jan Crosby, Dave DiMartino, John Einarson, David Fricke, Michael O'Hara Garcia, Michael Goldberg, Don Gooch, Glenn Goodwin, Matthew Greenwald, Paul Higham, Robert Hilburn, Steve Hochman, Peter Holmstedt, Alan Jenkins (NYAS), Michael Jensen, Tom King, Pete Long, Francesco Lucarelli, The Lee Shore (Mick Anderson, Dean "Doc" Dunn, Jay Camel, Ernie Osborne, and other CSN fans from around the world who people this online tribe), Jimmy McDonough, Allen McDougall (who should also be thanked for his vivid memories lent to the first edition), Debbie Meister, Bob Merlis, Susan Nash, Scott Oxman, Jeff Pevar, Chris "Hoover" Rankin, James Raymond, Johnny Rogan, Davin Seay, Mike "Coach" Sexton, Steve Silberman, Tom Stienstra, Kristen Stills, Taro, Gerry Tolman, Mike Thomas, Hans van Netburg, Dolf van Stijgeren, Hans Velduizen, and Kenny Weiss. Even though there was not space in this edition to include the full scope of your contributions, we thank you for your generosity of time and spirit.

Also, special gratitude to our families: Claudia and Casey Zimmer, shining lights of support, motivation, and understanding; Elizabeth, Zoe, and Nick Diltz, for continuing to be.

Lastly, you would not be holding this updated edition in your hands were it not for sincere enthusiasm and support from Da Capo Press, past and present, most importantly Andrea Schulz, Michael Dorr, Ruth Jensen, Chris Coffin, Amy Warner, Kevin Hanover, Carmela Carvajal, Rachel Hegarty, and John Radziewicz.

Dave Zimmer & Henry Diltz
October 1999

Foreword
by Graham Nash

I think the subtitle of this book should be "Three-Way Street," because it's definitely like three highways all coming together at a certain juncture. For me to come from the north of England, Stephen from Florida, and David from Southern California and all weave together and create music that gets ourselves off and reaches millions of people and to think we get *paid* for it at the same time . . . God, what a fantasy come true for all three of us!

We've always felt incredibly loved and have tried to honestly express our feelings about what's going on around us. We've always strived to make music that's meaningful. When people come up to us and say that seeing CSN perform has changed their lives or made them think totally differently about the world or encouraged them to get more into music, that's the bonus.

The story of Crosby, Stills & Nash is a complex puzzle to put together and I think Zimmer did an admirable job. This book reads pretty true. Of course, it's all clouded in the lore of people's remembrances. People's memories erode. People see things from different perspectives. But this book is as close to the truth as you're going to get. It's certainly as close to the truth as any writing about us I've ever seen.

Perhaps it was a slight disadvantage for Zimmer to have been so close to what it was that was going on inside CSN. Perhaps he tended to be less abrasive and critical of us out of kindness for people that he knows and loves. I certainly enjoyed talking with him. I think he extracted information very gently and approached this book with a lot of love and a lot of heart, and I'm very grateful for that.

The same thing goes for Henry, a good friend and a fine photographer for the moment that was there, which makes me think about all of the moments that could be in our future. I wonder how it will all end? Since we're still creative beings, who knows what's coming?

Not a lot of people understand the deep commitment that exists between me, David, Stephen, and Neil as friends. We have forgiven one another the most outrageous stuff and still love each other enough to want to make music together. To an outsider, it all must look like madness. But it's been real.

A lot of people, over the years, have concentrated on how much we fight and how much we have failed, because it makes for good press. But one mustn't forget how incredibly popular CSN and CSN&Y have been on the strength of such few records. It's a phenomenon that never ceases to amaze me.

I think we've added some good feeling to the universe. I think that Crosby, Stills & Nash music will last. And I think that generations to come will understand that we were three human beings that tried our best to be as real as possible.

Hawaii
November, 1983

Introduction

Back in 1981, when Crosby, Stills & Nash first learned that we wanted to put together their biography, their reactions were:

DAVID CROSBY: "You mean a book on CSN? Just the *three* of us? It's about time somebody got our story down for the sake of history."

STEPHEN STILLS: "I don't know how you're going to tie it all together. So much has happened in our lives."

GRAHAM NASH: "Boy, it'd sure be a study in relationships."

With their cooperation, over the next couple of years, Henry Diltz and I worked at piecing together the CSN story, one filled with magic, tragedy, pain, and triumph. The process involved hundreds of hours of conversations with Crosby, Stills & Nash, as well as their friends and bandmates, former managers and producers, engineers and roadies, promoters and fans. Ahmet Ertegun, the president of Atlantic Records and an ally of CSN's from the very start, had this to say:

"Crosby, Stills & Nash, their sound is one of the great phenomenons in rock 'n' roll. The music of that group is *legend*. I'm extremely proud to have been a part of it. The only artists comparable, I feel, are the Rolling Stones, Bob Dylan, and the Beatles. I mean, CSN is one of the major contributions to the formation of rock 'n' roll. CSN created the quintessential music of the sixties and what they are doing today is still valid."

Amen. Here is their story.

—Dave Zimmer

CROSBY, STILLS, & NASH

CHAPTER ONE

The Early Years

David Crosby:
The California Dreamer

Hollywood was a new frontier for Floyd and Aliph Crosby. They both came from New York high society and were listed in the prestigious "blue book" social register. Aliph had been a debutante and had gone on to finishing school. Floyd had been a maverick film student amid a clan of conservative, comfortably rich professionals. Shifting from one coast to the other, from a rather stuffy highbrow breed into a potpourri of glamorous risk-takers, sparked in him the creation of new visions.

Floyd became one of the motion picture industry's top cinematographers in the thirties, and eventually won Academy Awards for his work on *High Noon* and *Tabu*. He also made a film about how to shoot documentaries that is still being used at UCLA. Aliph, meanwhile, gave birth to a son, Floyd, Jr., in 1937. Four years later, on August 14, 1941, David Crosby was born.

As he became aware of his senses and his surroundings, David relished the melodious classical music that started filling his ears. Every Sunday morning, his mother would tune in to the morning concert on the radio. Soon, David began planting himself near the tiny speaker and would just listen, for hours. When he was six, David went with his family to hear and see a Los Angeles orchestra perform.

"I saw all of these players doing the same thing, at the same time, making one gigantic noise," says David. "And it really shook me around by the roots. I'd never seen a band before. And watching that symphony, that night . . . it was the most powerful thing I'd ever seen in my life."

Right away, David went home and explored his mother's collection of 78 rpm classical records. David feels that this instilled in him "a strong sense of harmony and melody." Along with these listening sessions, he joined in when his family gathered in the living room and sang and played songs out of *The Fireside Book of Folk Songs*.

"I started harmonizing right away," David says, "as if 'harmony singer' had been stamped in big, bold letters on my DNA. It just seemed so natural. And my mom was a good singer. My dad was fairly musical. He played the mandolin, mostly for chording purposes, like for, 'Eyes of blue, ta-da-da, has anybody seen my gal?' And I still have his mandolin, a little Gibson F-4, a fine instrument."

Floyd, Jr., nicknamed Chip (later known as Ethan), occupied the bedroom next to David's while they were growing up. Chip was a big jazz fan. "And he'd play these records by Gerry Mulligan, Chet Baker, Dave Brubeck . . . *real loud*," David

"I started harmonizing right away." David Crosby (age six) with his dad and older brother, Chip. (David Crosby personal collection.)

recalls, "so I could hear them through the wall. That's how I got into them.

"When everybody else was diggin' 'Blueberry Hill' and 'Blue Suede Shoes,' I wasn't into that shit. I didn't dig Elvis at all. I was listening to late-fifties jazz—*excellent* stuff, man, which led me to John Coltrane."

Whenever David and Chip did the dishes, the two of them would improvise vocal parts together. "That's how I learned to scat sing," David says. "We'd take a song like 'Brother, Can You Spare a Dime?' and scat all over it. We'd sing it like a Dixieland jazz band would play it."

After David had attended University Elementary School in Los Angeles for a few years, in 1950 he moved with his family up the coast to Santa Barbara. There, his mother enrolled him in Crane Country Day School.

"I was a naughty little kid," David says with a smirk. "But listen to this. My daughter [Donovan Ann] just got accepted into Crane, and there's a teacher there who used

to teach at Cate, where I later went to prep school. And this guy told my daughter's mother, Debbie, that for years they used to use me as an *example*. I got thrown out of there my second year. So the schoolteachers started telling all of the kids who got in trouble, 'You better not do that anymore or you'll end up like David Crosby.' Well, this idea backfired on them kinda heavily when I became somewhat known and successful. Then these kids started saying, 'Hey, yeah, man, David Crosby, I can dig being like him.'

"So a while ago, some of these teachers apparently had a meeting and one of 'em got up and said, 'I don't think we should use David as an example anymore. He's obviously a very talented guy and has made a lot of people very happy. So I think we blew it. I don't think we understood him. I think we need to look more carefully at these kids and not just classify them and brush 'em aside. I think if we had tried to understand David, we could have solved his disciplinary problems, helped him, and sped him on his way.' "

David says, "Without exception, I was thrown out of every school I ever went to—Cate, Laguna Blanca, Carpenteria, Santa Barbara City College—I didn't last long at any of 'em."

Rather than for genuinely serious problems, however, David's expulsions were usually prompted by harmless pranks—"mouthing off," note-passing incidents, and failure to attend classes. Between the ages of fifteen and sixteen, which David refers to as "my turbulent years," he was simply more interested in singing, getting laid, and learning about sailing than in sitting through lectures on algebra.

"Once I got a car," David says, "I must confess I spent all of my time and energy trying to get laid. That was the main thing in my life. I wanted girls. I wanted to find out what that was like and do it right away and do it to excess. And I *did*, and I don't regret it a bit.

"I wasn't into alliances in high school," he adds. "When I wasn't with a girl, I was really alone much of the time. I didn't dig the music everyone else did. The only pop music I liked was the Everly Brothers."

David Crosby at sixteen. (David Crosby personal collection.)

Having learned the basics of guitar from his brother, in 1958 David began performing as a solo acoustic folk singer at Santa Barbara "beatnik coffeehouses" like the Noctambulist (a.k.a. the Nightwalker). David revealed the motivation behind this early interest in performing to Cameron Crowe in *Crawdaddy:* "Hey, man, folk singers get laid a lot more often than the other kids in high school. Even if you have to do it in the afternoon on the floor of the coffeehouse . . . I'm never gonna be good-looking enough to be something chicks go after on a

physical level. They have to be crazy enough to like me, to want to fuck me. I'm no Gregory Peck . . . [so] they gotta get into the music somewhat."

While plenty of girls got into David's music, none of his exploits brought him any *money.* Rather than give up music and girls and get a "real job," however, David became a cat burglar. He and a few friends built up a little theft ring. And David, always intrigued by the outlaw way of life anyway, broke into several homes in Santa Barbara before getting caught and arrested.

"And I was convicted," David says. "I deserved to be. But that isn't what really penetrated . . . it was meeting somebody I'd stolen something of tremendous personal value from. I'd stolen the last remaining picture of this woman's old man. There were no others. And I'd swiped it and *lost* it. It was gone. And I felt so badly, looking at that woman's face, man. I thought I was gonna die. I didn't steal things anymore after that."

Instead, at age nineteen, David packed his bags, moved to Los Angeles, and tried to become an actor. "Because my dad was a famous cinematographer, that constituted an in," says David. "Havin' a family tie . . . that's the *only way* to break in, man. If you're just off the street, you can wait around for five years and never get a part.

"So I studied acting for a while from Jeff Corey. But I soon realized that to be an actor, you've got to kiss ass, pretend, *fake* a lot of stuff. I didn't want to be like those people, who seemed shallow and stupid to me."

David gravitated back toward music, broke out his guitar, and started singing at the Unicorn Club (now defunct) on Sunset Boulevard. "God Bless the Child," "Willie Gene," "Come Back Baby," and other blues songs made up his sets. It wasn't long before David became a regular at the Unicorn and gave up acting entirely.

"I loved playin' and singin' so much," he says, "music just eclipsed acting by a mile. Music flat-out just pulled me in."

Stephen Stills: Southern Rebel

The nineteenth-century Stills clan held sway over an enormous piece of land north of Rustin, Louisiana. It was rich and fertile, prime territory by any standards. The Stillses who lived there were proud Southerners, steeped in tradition, and they dug in with a vengeance at the onset of the Civil War. But when General Sherman and his Union troops laid waste to Louisiana, the Stillses were forced to move north.

Illinois and Indiana became the new family stomping grounds and were where, in the thirties, William and Talitha Stills started building a life together. William studied engineering at Southern Illinois University and, at the same time, worked as a booking agent. He helped book big bands all around Champaign, Illinois, and he and Talitha went to as many concerts as they could. This avid interest in music waned somewhat, though, when William accumulated what he thought was enough engineering knowledge, left school, and went to work for Westinghouse. After World War II he got involved in construction and was responsible for building a huge tract-home subdivision in Bloomington, Illinois, one of the first of its kind anywhere. Then, with their daughter, Hannah, and a second child on the way, William and Talitha moved to Dallas, Texas. There, William got involved with the creation of some new tool and die designs. On January 3, 1945, Talitha gave birth to Stephen Arthur Stills.

A short while later, the Stillses were on the move again, back up to Illinois, then back down to Louisiana. Stephen's first memories, not surprisingly, are of being in a car, traveling down the highway toward La Salle. William Stills, an aggressive worker, had "itchy feet" and would shift from place to place, from job to job, making a fortune, losing it, then making it all back again. Besides the construction business, he had great success in lumber, molasses, engineering design, and real estate.

Stephen Stills in Illinois at age two. (Personal collection of Mrs. Stills.)

The single constant in this transient Stills household was music. The records of Bix Beiderbecke, the Dorsey Brothers, Paul Whiteman, Cole Porter, and Leadbelly were played on the family phonograph, and Stephen would listen closely, rocking back and forth on the floor, clapping his hands in time to the shifting beats. Eventually, he got hold of a pair of drumsticks and started experimenting on the family furniture. This led to a confrontation with his father. But instead of being reprimanded, Stephen received a pat on the back and a trip to the local music store.

"My dad told me, 'If you're gonna play music, drums are the best place to start,'" Stephen remembers. "So he bought me a dynamite top-of-the-line set of Slingerland drums when I was only eight years old."

Even though Stephen was an attentive student at Covington Elementary School, he found his priorities shifting with the acquisition of this drum set. He practiced constantly and found a variety of rhythmic ideas; he also started studying piano. "But," says Stephen, "I *hated* piano lessons. My teacher, this very proper lady, had a thing about Brahms, which I could never get into that much. My maternal grandmother was a movie-house piano player and just fabulous. She had the greatest touch and phrasing. She played the nickelodeons during the Depression. And what *she* was doin' was more my style."

Out of this early study, Stephen's own style started to evolve around the middle fifties. And following the birth of Talitha, Jr. (referred to as Ticita), Stephen's younger sister, the Stills family moved from Louisiana to central Florida, where William had a plan to build a tract of luxurious dwellings for retired people or anyone who wanted to get out of the city. At this point, Stephen admits, "I was acting like a complete goon and my mother wanted to turn me into a gentleman." So Stephen was enrolled in Admiral Farragut Military Academy in St. Petersburg.

"For the purpose it was designed for, it was great," Stephen says. "My dad always thought I hated it, but I loved it. It just took a while. Military school is quite an experience, what can I tell you? It taught me honor, developed my character, and helped me become a trouper."

Stephen Stills, sixth grade, Admiral Farragut Academy, St. Petersburg, Florida. (Personal collection of Talitha Stills.)

Stephen had to toughen up fast when he became the victim of some mild hazing activities; however, when pitted against the ringleader of this hazing gang in a school wrestling tournament, Stephen pinned the guy in three seconds flat. All in all, Stephen enjoyed the regimented military atmosphere and marched in the drill team.

Stephen was also becoming proficient on drums, but a couple of incidents pointed him toward another instrument—the guitar. On a trip to Tampa, he encountered an old bluesman, playing on a street corner for nickels and dimes.

"I really believe this guy was Tampa Red," Stephen says. "His skin was mottled, his hair was kinda red, and he was blind. He had an old black Silvertone guitar and played the most dangerous, the *baddest* music I had ever been exposed to. I'd sit down next to him, and I was this scruffy little white kid, but he *talked* to me, showed me how he played slide guitar with a knife. And I think that's where a lot of my love of the blues guitar came from.

Stephen Stills, age fifteen. (Personal collection of Talitha Stills.)

"Then there was Charlie Harris," Stephen continues. "He worked for my father, did everything from repair to farming, and he played the most powerful ragtime you ever heard. I think that's why my dad hired him. And I used to listen to Charlie for hours."

Back in military school, Stephen soon latched on to his roommate's guitar and plunked around until his fingers bled. A friend of Stephen's named Michael Garcia owned a boxful of Library of Congress albums, which Stephen absorbed along with B. B. King, Muddy Waters, and Jimmy Reed records.

After leaving military school and before entering Woodrow Wilson Junior High in Tampa, Stephen spent a summer on his Uncle Sidney's farm. "That's where I learned how to sing loud," Stephen says. "My uncle grew peaches. So I would take this Massey-Ferguson tractor out between the trees and sing as loud and as hard as I could. My aunt said she could hear me from back at the house, *over* the noise of the tractor. That's when I started developing my pipes."

Stephen got his first formal vocal training a couple of years later, when he joined the chorus at St. Leo's Benedictine Monastery.

"I had a very good vocal coach," Stephen says, "so I could sing lead first baritone, lead second baritone, and sometimes attempt a tenor part. We did the Gregorian chant and it was simply enthralling."

Stephen Stills, "A conductor's dream." St. Leo's Prep School, Florida. (Personal collection of Talitha Stills.)

Stephen soon left St. Leo's and headed for Gainesville High. The stigma of being "the new kid" once again didn't bother him too much. In fact, he now looks back on the experience of constant movement as something that provided him with a lot of intellectual stimulation. Stephen was a pretty plucky teenager, so the prospect of always having to make new friends was looked upon with anticipation rather than dread. Stephen was a *musician* and, even then, was always on the lookout for players with whom he could jam.

"Because I wanted to play with everyone, I learned to adapt myself to whatever styles were running around," Stephen says. "I always wanted to fit, so I was always, I guess, a fairly decent mimic. Peter, Paul and Mary, blues stuff—that was pretty popular. And then there was all of this rockabilly shit, fake black music, which I *hated* as a kid. Bill Haley and the Comets were basically jive around my school. And Elvis, after 'Blue Moon over Kentucky,' which I thought was really down-home, he deteriorated into this *schmaltz*, because he was always being told what to do. So we listened to blacks down South. They played the hot stuff, with the rhythm and the time I didn't get really proficient at until later."

While Stephen had sat in on drums for a time with a band called the Radars, he began to devote more and more attention to a cheap Kay hollow-body electric guitar he'd picked up. He started hanging out around Florida frat parties and hooked up with several players, including a beatnik rap artist named Jeff Espina. Stephen's playing and singing, though still raw and basic, caught the eye of drummer Jeff Williams. It wasn't long before Stephen was invited to join Williams's band, the Continentals. Former Eagle Don Felder, who was the lead guitarist in the group, recalls when he first came into contact with Stills.

"Stephen came by this fraternity house, plugged in his guitar, and we thrashed away on E for a while. Then he played 'La Bamba' and a couple of other things. It was real good. And all of a sudden Stephen was in the band. He and I worked out a lot of double leads like Dick Dale and His Del-Tones used to have goin', and it sounded pretty funky.

"We played around Gainesville," Felder continues, "and worked that circuit over and over. One night we played at the Palatka prom. It was one of our best gigs and one of our first 'sleep-overs'—pretty serious stuff for kids in the tenth grade.

Afterwards, somebody got a hold of a bottle of whiskey and me, Stephen, and the other guys went back to our hotel, got drunk, and stayed up all night playin' cards."

Even though Stills was only in the Continentals for about four months, he left a lasting impression. Felder recalls, "He was a little more wild and crazy than the rest of us guys in the band. Stephen was right on the border between genius and insanity. And he was already shedding off the Ivy League, early-sixties button-down-collar stuff and goin' for the gusto. It was refreshing. Stephen was very independent-minded. He had this drive. He was gonna go for it *his* way and be successful, no matter what. For his ability and his attitude, you really had to look at the guy and salute him."

Graham Nash: The English Seeker

In an upstairs room in Blackpool
By the side of a northern sea
The army had my father
And my mother was having me
                    —"Military Madness"

"Totally true," says Graham Nash. "I was born in this upstairs room in a kind of hotel that had been turned into a hospital in an evacuation area. Around Manchester, where my parents' home was, there were bombs dropping, so all ladies that were pregnant were moved outside the city to have their babies. My mother went to Blackpool, which is on the Irish Sea. My father *was* in the army, while my mother was having me—February 2, 1942, in the midst of World War II.

"The first thing that I can distinctly remember, as an actual memory," says Graham, "was being in my crib in Manchester, by a coal fire, playing with a cartoon book and seeing my mother draw the curtains for the blackout—where at night you had to make sure that no light escaped from the house, which could be detected by the bombers."

As peace eventually returned to Europe, things returned to normal in the Nash household as well. "Simple souls," is how Graham describes his parents, William and Mary. "They both slaved hard their whole lives." When William was discharged from the British Army, he went to work in a large foundry. Graham recalls, "Once I bicycled my three-wheel bike to where he worked, and I remember approaching these gigantic doors. When I walked inside, it was pitch dark. I asked where my father was, then turned around and saw a huge slab of molten metal sparking and exploding, quite a sight to a young boy. That's the most vivid thing I remember of my father's work."

At home, Graham spent occasional evenings sitting with his father, whistling melodies of old English folk songs. But there was not a strong sense of music that constantly filled the Nashes' modest Manchester home. Graham explains, "Both my parents worked so hard, from early until late,

they did not have the energy or the time to learn an instrument, to fully explore music."

When Graham started school, at age five, he attended Ordsall Board and, at first, did not have anyone to pal around with. He was quiet and somewhat shy. However, partway into the first term, a new boy named Harold Clarke (better known as Allan Clarke) came to the school. The teacher stood Allan in front of the class and asked, "Now who would like to sit next to this little boy?" Graham was the only one who put his hand up.

"So I sat down next to Graham," says Allan Clarke, "and we started being friends."

"Me and Allan would do early-morning sing-songs," says Graham, "and it just seemed so natural. I honestly don't remember when I realized I could sing. It just never occurred to me that I couldn't."

Graham Nash's first live performance was at a school assembly. He and Allan sang "The Lord Is My Shepherd" in two-part harmony. Eventually, both Graham and Allan joined the school chorus, then the Solford Boys' Club. Says Allan: "Graham

Graham Nash (lower right-hand corner) and Allan Clarke (center) in the sixth grade. (Graham Nash personal collection.)

and I were the only ones that sang. We couldn't understand why people wanted us to sing. But we'd do it and it was fun."

Graham says, "I never took any voice lessons or music lessons. The only training I got was your basic 'do, re, mi, fa, so, la . . .' in school. I wish I understood that musical language better. But I guess it didn't hold me back too much."

In 1953, Graham passed a school exam known as the "eleven plus," which enabled him to graduate to Salford Grammar School. Allan, however, didn't pass. "Not because I was thick," he says. "I was just bad at exams."

"To see me and my best friend separate," says Nash, "it was troubling. Because I was only eleven and had very few friends anyway."

In spite of having to attend different schools, however, Graham and Allan established a strong musical bond in their early teen years. Over the next couple of years, they would get together periodically and explore English skiffle music and American rock and blues.

"I remember having this small collection of American blues records," says Nash. "They were mostly Big Bill Broonzy ones, and they just *thrilled* me. But I couldn't approach that, and everything I was doing felt so pale and insignificant compared to the depth of that music."

Graham got his first guitar, a cheap acoustic one, when he was thirteen. His dad bought it for him. At the same time, Allan Clarke got his father to buy *him* a guitar. And together, Graham and Allan learned the three chords to "Rock Island Line." "We were amazed," says Clarke, "that we were able to make noises with these things."

One day in the spring of 1955, Allan and Graham were thrashing about and singing when Allan's brother, Frank, suggested, "Why don't you go to this club around the corner and audition?" They

looked at each other, shrugged, and then, the next day, trotted off to the Devonshire Sporting Club.

"I can still remember the damp, beery smell inside this club," says Nash. "And Bill Benny, this local wrestler, auditioned us and he liked us. So we got to play one night."

"We had three numbers down pat," says Clarke, " 'Rock Island Line,' 'Worried Man Blues,' and 'Lucille.' But we'd never done this before in our lives. We still went around in short trousers. So I can imagine what the audience must have thought when they looked up at the big stage and saw these two fourteen year olds with guitars. But it went down really well."

Graham recalls, "When we came offstage, Bill gave us ten bob each and said we could come back tomorrow night. It was a flash to get paid!"

Allan says, "We were still used to getting sixpence a week from our mums for candy. So we said, 'Yeah, we'll be back tomorrow.' "

And for the next several months, Nash and Clarke, calling themselves the Two Teens, not only performed at the Devonshire Sporting Club, but at several other pubs in the north of England as well. Sunday afternoons, weekend nights, then several weeknights, this fledging duo developed.

"We got a lot of jobs," says Nash, "and our price slowly went up to two pounds. The big time! And it *was* to us. Playing music in nightclubs till two or three in the morning was unheard of for a fourteen-year-old guy. My mother would occasionally come by and make sure I wasn't drinking beer, that I had fruit juice. She also wanted to be sure," Graham chuckles, "that I wasn't being molested.

"My parents," he continues, "they were very supportive. They always encouraged me. They followed what was happening with me. They didn't squash my feelings whatsoever, which, I must say, made me flower."

Graham's parents frequently left him on his own in his early teens, mostly because William Nash spent long hours at the foundry and Mary Nash worked as an office administrator for the local dairy. When she was home, Mary often had her hands full with Graham's two sisters, Elaine (born in 1946) and Sharon (born in 1953). Consequently, Graham says, "I was able to go down some roads that might normally be frowned upon by most parents." Far from being a delinquent, Graham does admit, however, that he "got into a lot of mischief, a lot of gangs, a lot of funny stuff."

"We'd get beat up a lot," recalls Allan Clarke, "mainly because other gang members were jealous of what me and Graham were doing. Because we played and sang in nightclubs, we attracted all the girls. So this made us targets for rival gangs, which was a little frightening. It was no fun getting beat up. But we survived. And we also did a lot of normal things—like go to the church dances."

"That was where we met ladies," says Nash, "and that was where we learned to dance and find out about what was going on in the community."

"The best dances were at the Catholic churches," says Clarke. "But they only let Catholic kids in. So, because we were Protestants, we were forced to pass ourselves off as Catholics. We learned our Hail Mary prayers and so got in. It was great, because all the best chicks were Catholic and hung out at the dances."

At one of these functions, Graham recalls, "Me and Allan were halfway across the dance floor when somebody put on 'Bye Bye Love' by the Everly Brothers, with that acoustic guitar opening. It stopped me dead in my tracks. I wanted to be a part of it, I wanted to know how to do that, wanted to know what it was about that musical pas-sage that made me feel that way."

Graham immediately bought all of the Everly Brothers records he could find and, he says, "I'd listen to their songs on the phonograph, and because the two-part harmony was already there, I'd put a third part on top of whatever they were singing. That's how I learned to sing harmony, basically. Don and Phil Everly were my teachers. I think that's where a lot of my feeling for three-part harmony came from. And ever since, it's always been very natural for me to be able to go to some strange place with my voice."

As the Two Teens worked out their own two-part harmonies on such Everly Brothers songs as "Wake Up Little Susie," they expanded their range and improved their vocal quality. Graham and Allan also began wearing flashy coats and slacks and became a real *act*. At the same time, they were still young kids. And when the Everly Brothers came to Manchester for a concert, the Two Teens were pressed up against the stage and going nuts right along with the rest of the crowd. They waited outside in the pouring rain until four in the morning to get the Everly Brothers' autographs.

"They took the time to sign autographs and just talk to us," says Graham. "And that impressed me greatly. They didn't have to do that. They could have gone straight to their hotel rooms but they stayed and they were gentle, not off-putting, weren't drunk out of their minds. They inspired me to get more into music."

Just as Nash was beginning to move ahead musically in late 1958, his father became trapped in a tragic situation. He had purchased a camera from a friend at the foundry. Somehow the police caught wind of the transaction, cornered William Nash, and explained to him that the camera was stolen property. When William refused to tell the police from whom he had bought the camera, he was thrown in jail for a full year.

"My family was shattered," Graham says. "It was a tense time. I had to quit school to get a job to help support my family. Money was badly needed at that time."

Fortunately, Graham had little trouble finding work at the engineering firm where Allan had been working for several months. At two pounds five shillings a week, it was a solid job. However, the Two Teens earned almost that much in one night! Working and playing music occupied all of Graham's waking hours for some time.

To escape this nonstop cycle, Graham and Allan once went away to a weekend holiday camp. There they entered a musical competition and qualified for the finals—to be held on Monday, which was a workday for them. They decided to skip work in favor of the contest and ended up winning the competition with a two-part-harmony version of Conway Twitty's "It's Only Make Believe" (later recorded by the Hollies). The thrill of victory dwindled, though, when Graham and Allan returned to work the next day and got called out on the carpet by their boss. Clarke recalls, "For some reason, Graham was retained, but I got fired. So I went to work at the mill and became a laborer."

Nash subsequently lost his job, as well, a short time later, for playing rock 'n' roll records at the company Christmas party. But rather than join Allan at the mill, Graham took a civil service exam and got work with the post office. "It was then considered spectacularly cool to work at the post office," says Graham. "And my mother was proud because I finally had a *real job*."

Of course, to Graham, his nightclub gigs with Allan were infinitely more important than his job, and he never allowed the energy he directed toward his music to wane. Nash explains, "With every job I ever had as a teenager, it caused my day to go something like this: I would get up around seven-thirty, be at work by nine, work till five, go home, get picked up by Allan and the lads, then drive anywhere from ten to a hundred miles to a gig, play three or four sets, come home at around four in the morning, go to sleep, then get up at seven-thirty and start the whole thing all over again.

"Me and Allan's goal," says Graham, "was to be able to just play music and not have to get up in the morning." They also decided, at this stage, to change their name from the Two Teens to the Guytones. "We figured we weren't little teenagers anymore," says Nash, "even though we were still sixteen or something."

In addition to undergoing a name change, it was inevitable that Nash and Clarke would eventually expand beyond a duo. Yet they were so enthralled with the Everly Brothers that the idea of actually forming a whole band came from another source. Pete Bocking, a local guitarist, came to the Nash home one night, electric guitar in hand. "Pete Bocking," Nash sighs. "Very weird man. He was bald at twelve. Lived with his mother. All he did was play guitar all day and all night. Consequently, he could play all the hip solos. He could be Buddy Holly, Bo Diddley, Chuck Berry. He could be *everybody* rolled into one."

Before that night in early 1960 was over, it was decided that Bocking would join forces with Nash and Clarke. Henceforth, they were known as the Four Tones. Six months later, bassist Butch Jeffries and drummer Joe Abrahams joined up, and the Four Tones became a real band. Clarke recalls, "Skiffle music had died down and everyone was coming into bands, getting into rock 'n' roll. It was a natural evolution for us, and we started playing places like the Two Jays, the Three Coins, the Twisted Wheel. We got a *reputation*. And a lot of people came to see us. We played a lot of noontime gigs, too. That's when all of the local agents turned out to check out the bands."

Meanwhile, Graham lost his job at the post office for counting the day's receipts in the presence of a person who was not an employee—Allan Clarke. In order to maintain a flow of money into the Nash household, Graham got another day job at a tailor shop owned by Michael Cohen (who later became the Hollies' first manager).

It was during Graham's aprenticeship as a tailor that his father was released from prison in late 1960. "He was never the same," says Graham. "He'd caught pneumonia while in prison and he also had lost his honor and his spirit." William Nash never fully recovered from his term in prison, and died a year later. Graham, on the road when he was notified of his father's worsening condition, failed to make it back in time for some final words at his dying father's bedside. To this day, that is one of Graham's only regrets.

While watching his father slip away, Graham had seen a vision of what his life was and what it might be. "I could see what it was to escape from the routine, the cycle that my father and his father had been a slave to," Graham says. "When I was growing up, we were coming off the back of the Victorian era, where you were trained to be an apprentice, to have a trade in your hand, to work in the mills or the factories, to retire, and then die. I didn't want to do that. So not only was rock 'n' roll a great opener of my soul, but of my *life!* Rock 'n' roll was the great escape for me."

"Rock 'n' roll saved our asses," says Allan Clarke.

Crosby: Traveling Folk Days (1961–1962)

David Crosby gained an early dose of inspiration while playing at the Unicorn nightclub in Los Angeles. It was there that he met a venerable folk musician named Travis Edmundson, once a part of the folk duo Bud and Travis. David says, "He influenced me a great deal and allowed me to hang out, like an apprentice. I'd 'hawk his changes,' as we used to say. And he actually put the first song I ever wrote on a record of his. But you'll never find the record, so you'll never be able to find out what that song was and I'm not tellin'," David giggles. "Travis was also the first person ever to give me a joint, which was really a wonderful thing for him to do. I've got to thank him a million times for it. We were drivin' down the freeway, I took a toke and just went to heaven. I thought, 'This is for me!' "

One night, in the spring of 1961 after playing at the Unicorn, David went back to his small Hollywood apartment and found a surprise waiting for him. "I walked in," he remembers, "and the girl I was going with at the time, Cindy her name was, she said, 'Dave, uh, we're pregnant.' And I said, 'Gee, well, far out, I'm gonna go down to the market and get some milk. I'll be right back.' Well, I went to Arizona."

Then David hitchhiked to Colorado, played the coffeehouse circuit there for a few months, and met a couple who owned a '57 Ford Fairlane 500 convertible. Together, they decided to drive all the way to New York.

"The Bitter End had just become the Bitter End in sixty-one," says David, who was almost twenty at the time. "And I used to go there every Monday night for open mike. I also played the Cafe Rafio. Dylan was around then, and at first I didn't dig him at all. I thought he couldn't sing his way out of a paper bag. I didn't dig his sense of humor. I couldn't understand it. But after a while, I saw he was a great writer.

"And me, I played some of the grubbiest places—five bucks was a big night. Saturday night was five bucks. So, as you might well imagine, I didn't have that much money for food, so I lost a lot of weight—which was good. I lived in this tiny apartment with five other people and it was a very good time.

"I was still coming off school, you know? So the street just stepped on my head. The streets of New York make a great survival school. Everybody who is at all serious about life should go through it."

David soon worked his way right into the Greenwich Village street stream of artists and came into close contact with folk singer Fred Neil. "Now Freddie," David says, "he taught me more about guitar playing than anybody. He's the one who taught me this weird style of mine, where I use my flatpick and my fingers at the same time."

Armed with this extra guitar-playing element, David decided to explore the regions north of New York. He hitchhiked across New Hampshire, Vermont, and Maine, all the way to Toronto, Ontario. It was the middle of summer, so every night," says David, "I just slept by the side of the road and poured about half a gallon of 6-12 bug repellant on myself."

When David came back to New York as the summer of 1961 was waning, Fred Neil and some other people were talking about heading to Florida. "This one girl was just chattering away about how warm it was, about how there were sailboats, plenty of jobs, plenty of girls," David recalls. "Along about the time she said 'sailboats,' I was headed for the Greyhound bus terminal."

In Miami, David entered a phase of his life he describes as "one of the most fun times I've ever had, man." A couple of David's friends worked at Castle Boat Rentals and had permission to take the sailboats out at night for free. David soon learned the location of every reef and sandbar in Miami Bay. He also played some music in coffeehouses, first alone, then with his brother, Chip—whom David had lured

to Florida. Chip brought along a musician friend of his named Bobby Ingram. As a "loose unit," these three folkies left Florida, bound for America's heartland, in the spring of 1962.

"We split up in Omaha," David says. "And I went to Chicago. That's where I met a great old blues singer named John Brown. We hung out for a while. I also went to see Coltrane at this club on the South Side, and Elvin Jones, his drummer, scared me out of the room. During 'Trane's set, everyone would take solos. And when Elvin started in, the other people onstage wandered off and gave him room. He was the most powerful drummer I'd ever seen. He backed me up against my chair, down the aisle, into the men's room, against the wall. And while I was standin' there, Coltrane walked in with his sax . . . blleepp, buuda, laaaa, wheeee, wop! He'd never stopped playing when he left the stage and came into the men's room, I think, 'cause he liked the echoes. He melted me right into the trashcan. He never knew I was there, I'm sure. He just kicked the door open and *flew!*

"I tell ya. I learned a lot of my guitar chords from Coltrane's piano player, Mc-Coy Tyner. And with all of the suspensions, inversions, and cross-chordings he had, it was impossible to get those sounds out of my hands on the guitar in normal tunings. So I started experimenting with open tunings, real weird ones. It was like having a rocketship in my pocket."

The urge to return to California came with the onset of the fall of 1962. But instead of heading back to Los Angeles, David decided to check out San Francisco. He lived at first in North Beach, then moved out to the *Charles Van Dam* houseboat in Sausalito, with rising folk musician Dino Valenti.

"Dino and I had a coffeehouse upstairs and a high-school dance hall downstairs," David says. "We'd cruise through those young girls like sharks through an ocean full of sailors."

Dino and David would also often head to lush Sausalito parks with fellow folkies David Freiberg and Paul Kantner, form a circle on the lawn, and pass around joints, songs, and guitars. "We had to be in a circle," says David, "so we could smoke without anybody seeing us. If the police showed up, we'd always just ditch the grass."

Producer Paul Rothchild was trying to track down Dino Valenti around this time. One of Valenti's songs, "Get Together," had perked Rothchild's ears. Arriving in Sausalito, Paul asked after the whereabouts of Valenti and was told, "Go to the *Charles Van Dam* and ask for Crosby." Rothchild remembers, "I get on this houseboat and I'm walking down this hallway that's pitch black. And I call out, 'Is David Crosby in here?' And the voice answers, 'Yeah, man, in here.' So I walk through these curtains and David is propped up on these pillows and the first thing he says is, 'Hey, we're smokin' aspirin, wanna hit?' That was my first introduction to David Crosby."

Life on the *Charles Van Dam* took on a dreamlike air, filled with music, sex, and philosophical discussions. "We'd all just read *Stranger in a Strange Land*," says Paul Kantner. "We were very idealistic teenagers hustling for unity and oneness in the world."

Stills: High School/Latin America/New Orleans (1960–1964)

Meanwhile, down in Florida, Stills was not getting quite so ethereal. But he was certainly trying to sample new experiences. When Stephen thinks about where his early creative motivation came from, he says, "My dad always saw to it that we pursued our imaginations and our art. My sister Ticita is an artist, my sister Hannah is a sculptress, and I became a musician, because he saw to it we had room to expand. He never *said* anything or gave us a lick of credit, but he provided the foundation. Of course, my own experience inserted a little more connected drive and considered ambition. If I wanted to do something, I'd just think about it and analyze how to make a dream a reality."

In the middle of high school, though, Stephen was still sorting out his options. "I had all this imagination, you see, and was, well, a bit troublesome." At Plant High in Tampa, where Stephen went after leaving Gainesville in 1960, his after-school activities ran from bagging groceries to working at a racetrack ("My dad made me quit, but not before I learned some stuff.") to running with four gangs—the criminals, the jocks, the car freaks, and the musicians. "We knew how to get nuts in the South," Stills says. "And, boy, could we *drink*. We could always score some booze, 'cause someone always had a parent who was an alcoholic and wouldn't miss a bottle of gin or vodka. Then I'd always borrow a car, and some of the stuff we did was right out of *American Graffiti* and I was like the Dreyfuss character."

"I was a bit worrisome to a few teachers who thought I had any brains," Stills says. He had demonstrated good academic ability, yet, "like my father," he admits, "I just studied what I liked and what I thought I would need." At Plant High, Stephen's main goal was to be student director of the 125-piece school orchestra. He had graduated from last- to third-chair snare drummer and was working with the faculty conductor on arrangement charts. Then Stills ran into a little bad luck. It seems he was in the habit of stashing books he didn't need for homework in whatever empty, broken locker he could find. One time, however, he put his books into a locker that already contained two books owned by another student. Without thinking or looking closely, when Stephen retrieved his books, he picked up the other student's as well. The dean of students didn't believe this tale, accused Stephen of stealing the books, and barred him from leading the school orchestra. Bill Williams, the faculty conductor, tried to help, got nowhere, then admitted, "I don't know, Stephen, I guess he figures you're just one of those hellions, and wants to use you as an example."

Stephen was heartbroken and turned down a token offer to lead the ROTC thirty-piece band. No, Stephen wanted to conduct "the big group" or none at all. And when the dean of students stood firm, sixteen-year-old Stephen quit school and headed to Latin America—where the rest of his family had moved earlier in 1961.

San Jose, Costa Rica, was a beautiful city filled with art, culture, and music; "It's like a little Paris," as Stephen describes it, and the Stillses settled there for the next couple of years. Stephen attended Colegio Lincoln, along with a lot of American State Department children. Says Stephen, "That's when a lot of my English and Spanish came together. My mother used to sit down at the dinner table and quiz me on word meanings and spelling. She was very into the language part of things. So was my Aunt Veda, who taught me a lot and ended up teaching history at Southern Illinois."

Stephen excelled in English and history, but found math and the sciences "a crushing bore." He adds, "The only thing I got out of physics was . . . it taught me how to calculate navigation and to shoot pool."

The music of San Jose, mostly Latin and jazz styles, intrigued Stephen greatly. He frequented a hotel where an ensemble played that featured bassist Palá White and keyboardist Pibe Hine. Stephen recalls,

"Palá was a gentle soul and he taught me the underpinnings of Latin music. He taught me positions on the bass and that little anticipated beat, before the downbeat, which influences the way I play bass to this day." As Stephen told Anthony Fawcett in *California Rock, California Sound,* "Pibe taught me piano. He had the Errol Garner influence, you know, and he taught me how to get a good spread—from what I first learned when I was eight or nine to playing fifths with my left hand and being able to manipulate octaves."

Stephen spent hours incorporating these Latin and jazz elements into his burgeoning style that, besides blues and folk, also drew from Chet Atkins. He also engaged in a few nonmusical adventures, like building a drive-in. With several school chums, Stephen helped clear the land, erect a screen made of bed sheets, and borrow the projection equipment from the U.S. Information Service.

"In Latin America, there were no cheeseburgers or rock 'n' roll then," says Stephen. "So we invented our own recreation. And the drive-in, it was *tits,* if you will, the most exciting thing that had happened in that place for a long time."

Even though Stephen grew very fond of Latin America, after passing his high-school finals at Colegio Lincoln in December of 1963, he made plans to return to Gainesville so that he could attend the University of Florida. In retrospect, he wonders why he even bothered. "I audited some classes for about six weeks and soon discovered, hey, I studied all of this two years ago. Little did I know that with my SAT and achievement test scores—I had a 770 in history and a 782 in English—I could have gone anywhere. But at that point I also thought, 'What more do I need to learn in a classroom?' So I went back to Latin America and had a tremendous fight with my father about being semi-sensible and using my brains, which led to the further adventures of Stephen Stills in the music business."

The street scene in New Orleans was a vibrant one in early 1964, so Stills had little trouble finding a place to work. The first bar he walked into, the Bayou Room, on Bourbon Street, was looking for someone to tend bar. With ideas of also getting work on the Bayou Room stage, Stephen took the job and remembers, "I worked for a guy with a patch over one eye. And it was up to me to watch the bar nearest the door that led to this strip joint. I had to keep all the farmers from Arkansas from clawing the B-girls. A couple of times, I had to pull out a gun and would hear [in a drunken slur], 'Who is this nine year old with a .45?' But I kept the peace." Stills also kept pestering the owner about singing on stage. His response was, "We don't use singles [i.e., solo performers]."

Enter Chris Sarns, a starving folk singer, who wandered into the Bayou Room with his guitar just after Stephen had made another plea to perform. The owner sized Sarns up, looked at Stills, and said, "Why don't you two guys get together?"

"Stephen was into Dylan and I was into the Kingston Trio and Bud and Travis," Sarns remembers. "So we managed to cook some stuff up. We'd do five sets a night until all hours of the morning and made somewhat of a living. We ate a lot of these cheap little hamburgers."

Stills adds, "This lasted for about six months. I wanted to do some more blues and jazz stuff, but that wasn't the thing to do in a commercial folk house. I sang 'John Riley,' all kinds of horseshit. We'd try to find some interesting ones, but basically it was just lame folk."

One time Stephen did manage to stretch out into some raunchy R&B when he sat in on drums with a band at a black roadhouse bar. This experience was short-lived, because, says Stills, "I really did look like I was about nine."

By mid-1964, Stephen was getting restless in New Orleans. He needed some new turf to explore. And when Chris Sarns took off for the Northeast, Stills needed some new musicians to hang out with. It was then that a vocal group from Yale, the Augmented 7th, strolled into the Bayou Room. They struck up a conversation with Stills and offered him a ride to New York. The next day they were out of New Orleans and heading north, and Stills thought, "Now I'm really going somewhere."

Nash: From the Deltas to the Hollies (1961–1962)

In the early sixties, success as an English rock 'n' roller was a long-shot gamble at best. Cliff Richard and the Shadows were stars, with hit records in Great Britain. But Richard had little company at that point. The Beatles were just starting out and Nash and Clarke were in the process of shifting gears.

"We wanted a change of scene," says Nash. "And around this time we ran into

Graham Nash.

Arthur Fee—local con man, dear soul—and he asked me and Allan to join Kirk Daniels and the Deltas, which was actually several bands in one. Me and Allan became 'Ricky & Dane.' And there was some weirdness about wearing apeman suits—you know, tiger skin over one shoulder. And we had bowler hats. It was pretty weird. But the bass player in this group was Eric Haydock and the drummer was Don Rathbone—who we ended up playing with a lot."

During this "Deltas phase in 1961," Allan Clarke remembers, "We found black American R&B to be very translatable to our particular blend of rock 'n' roll. We did Coasters stuff, Chuck Berry, the Zodiacs, and some standard ballads."

"I sang a lot of love songs then," Nash admits. "But most of them were by other people. I really hadn't started writing yet. I don't recall having a real way with words. I've never considered myself a poet. And as naive as I was then, I got turned on by the lyrics of 'Be-Bop-A-Lula.' That's where I was at."

Amid all of this musical activity, it wasn't long before rock 'n' roll began to interfere with Graham's work at the tailor shop. A choice had to be made. He recalls, "Normally, the pattern is . . . when music begins to interfere with your work, you give up your music and settle down to your desk job or go to the mill. With me, when work meant I couldn't make a gig that was two hundred miles away, I chose to go with music. And I mean we were making as much in one night playing music as I was in a whole week at my day job. So it wasn't hard to see that one was a drag and one was totally wonderful. The choice for me was easy, and it's the best decision I ever made.

"When I told my mother," Graham continues, "she had an uncanny knack for knowing what I really wanted to do. She knew this decision didn't freak me. So it didn't freak her. She always seemed to know that I'd always be okay in this universe. And six months before she died [in 1981], she told me that she'd always had ambitions to go on stage her whole life, even when she was a kid. But she never said anything about it. So I have to believe that when she saw me going for it, she thought, 'I wish I'd gone for it like he's going for it.' "

With a clear commitment made, Nash, at twenty, was determined to work as hard as he could at his music. Beyond the concern of bringing in enough money, Graham says, "The drive for me, initially, was to be part of that magical aura that rock 'n' roll created. There was no message then. The only concern was, 'Do you play good enough to have people come and dance?' "

Ricky and Dane, in the Deltas, did inspire people to dance. But Nash began to feel like breaking away from the clutches of the Deltas' manager, Arthur Fee, toward the end of 1961. So Nash, Clarke, Eric Haydock, and Don Rathbone struck out on their own and picked up lead guitarist Tony Hicks from another band, the Dolphins—a three-piece band that also included drummer Bobby Elliott and bassist Bernie Calvert. In early 1962, Nash, Clarke, Haydock, Rathbone, and Hicks (and later Elliott and Calvert) came to be known as the Hollies.

Hollies, 1962. Left to right: Don Rathbone, Graham Nash, Allan Clarke, ballroom promotor Frank Bell, Eric Haydock, Tony Hicks. (Graham Nash personal collection.)

"We were Buddy Holly crazy," says Nash. "So that's how our name came about. And right away we had this raw, youthful, rock 'n' roll sound. This was exactly what I wanted at that time."

The Hollies gained immediate popularity in the north of England. But in the southern part of the country, around London, they were treated like aliens.

"For many years," says Nash, "those of us from the sticks, from the English midlands and north, were ignored or looked down upon by the people from the London area. All we had to do was open our mouths and it was obvious where we came from. We had what were considered funny accents. And in England, if you don't talk proper or have the right color tie, you don't get anywhere."

The Hollies' first forays into London were tentative. Tony Hicks says, "I can still remember that strong coffee smell in all the London clubs. We used to go in there and order lime milkshakes and hope one of the local London bands would pop in. It was like, if you were from London, you were fuck-all."

The Hollies felt more confident and self-assured on their home turf in northern

Tony Hicks and Graham Nash, 1962. (Graham Nash personal collection.)

England. In the spring of 1962, they began playing lunchtime concerts at the Cavern in Liverpool. Between noon and 2:00 P.M., many of the working people and agents in the area would gather for some early-afternoon entertainment. A year earlier, the Beatles had also played the Cavern, as well as other venues along the northern club circuit.

"It was magic and it was mystifying," says Graham. "All we cared about was having fun and getting laid. I mean, we did *work*, we sweated our balls off. It was a real job, but we also had fun."

Crosby: Venice Days/ Les Baxter's Balladeers/ First Recordings/The Jet Set (1962–1964)

In the fall of 1962, Crosby was having his share of fun with his California buddies in Sausalito, although his career was progressing little. And when a couple of months skipped by, he became curious about what was going on down south, in Los Angeles. Crosby suggested to his gang that they all move down there, and no one voiced any serious objections. Crosby, Kantner, and Freiberg, along with Ginger Jackson, Sherry Snow, and Steven Shuster, shared a house in Venice.

"We kept all of our money in a bowl on the mantelpiece," says David. "We shared everything." And, as he once told *Rolling Stone*, "We never wanted for food, nor smoke, nor a guitar to play on, nor fresh strings. . . . We had a Volkswagen bus, in the classic manner. And we spent most of our time doin' exactly as we pleased, which meant mostly laying around on the beach, goofin' off."

Paul Kantner affirms the obvious. "At this point we never worried much about getting a career together. We were *thinking* about making an intro into show business, but playin' on the beach is about as far as we got."

Kantner and Freiberg eventually moved back up north and started a series of folk clubs, where they performed, gave music lessons, and hung out. Crosby occasionally traveled up the coast to play at clubs like the Tangent in Palo Alto, the Off Stage in San Jose, and the Cabal in Berkeley. But to survive financially, David joined up with a commercial aggregation of folk groups known as Les Baxter's Balladeers. David's group included his brother Chip, Bobby Ingram, and Mike Clough. David always winces at the mention of this portion of his career. He admits that his motivations were more financial than creative. He also says, "We did some good work, but had a shitty name."

Jack Linkletter Presents a Folk Festival, released on Crescendo Records in 1963, features five songs performed by Les Baxter's Balladeers. When David's voice cuts through, one can hear the warm, clear depth he had even then. After this record was recorded, the Balladeers went on a bus tour that crossed paths with the Big Three—featuring Cass Elliott.

"Cass and I got to be best buddies," says David. "We'd get high together and laugh and laugh. One day I passed out in a big plate of spaghetti at this restaurant and she left me there without paying the bill. We'd been up for three days on psychedelics."

Cass's sister, Leah Kunkel, was along for the ride when the Big Three ran into Les Baxter's Balladeers, and she recalls, "They all wore matching red coats. David was so *cute* . . . and he sang like an angel."

But David was not *feeling* like an angel. He didn't enjoy being locked into such highly arranged, slick folk music. His peculiar ear for abstract vocal combinations needed room to move. It was inevitable that he leave Les Baxter.

Crosby was playing an acoustic solo set in one of his old haunts in Los Angeles, the Unicorn, when Jim Dickson walked in. Dickson had produced the Dillards and recorded sundry jazz players at the old Club Renaissance. When he first heard Crosby, Dickson recalls, "His voice sounded so *smooth* and had such a nice quality . . . like a low note on a flute."

Dickson, in association with Eddie Tickner, had just formed a publishing company, Tickson Music, and had access to World Pacific Studios. At the beginning of 1964, Dickson approached Crosby about recording some songs there for a demo.

"I went for it," says David, "because I was anxious to get something going." Talking about Jim Dickson to the writer Johnny Rogan, Crosby once said, "He helped me shape my whole attitude to the world. He instilled in me a healthy cynicism, and at the same time he had a lot of humor. He was one of the smartest men I'd met up until that time. He had a vantage point that none of us had . . . he'd been around show business for years. He already knew what the scams were. He knew the record companies were totally dishonest and unscrupulous and couldn't give a rat's ass about music, which is still true, even to this day."

At the beginning of 1964, Crosby went to World Pacific Studios and, with Jim Dickson producing, recorded Hoyt Axton's "Willie Gene," Ray Charles's "Come Back Baby," and Dino Valenti's "Get Together." (Dino was also known as Chet Power at this time.) Sparse instrumentation was provided by guitarist Tommy Tedesco, drummer Hal Blaine, and bassist Ray Pullman. Pullman later produced "Shindig!" and got the Byrds their first gig on the show.

When Dickson presented a tape of these songs to Joe Smith, a producer at Warner Bros. Records, his response, according to

David Crosby (front left) in Les Baxter's Balladeers, 1963. (Reprise Records publicity photo. The Michael Ochs archives.)

Jim, was "You have no material here and no one is buying that vocal sound." Later, Smith must have regretted this judgment, for "Willie Gene," "Come Back Baby," and "Get Together" all became popular hits. Crosby's versions of "Willie Gene" and "Come Back Baby" appeared on *Early L.A.*, a compilation album released on Forward

Records in 1969, which also featured tracks with Crosby's voice blending with two other L.A. folkies, Jim McGuinn and Gene Clark.

Like Crosby, McGuinn and Clark were just a couple of frustrated folkies, trying to make it in L.A. McGuinn had survived Greenwich Village, backed up Bobby Darin, and gained some experience as a sideman. Clark had been one of the New Christy Minstrels. Together, as an acoustic duo, McGuinn and Clark were creating some nice sounds, but had no real direction.

Crosby, in early spring 1964, was looking for harmony, musical and otherwise. Back on the L.A. folk circuit, he felt like he was retracing his steps; the Troubadour, the Ash Grove, and the Ice House were places he knew all too well. David was getting some encouragement from Jim Dickson, but with the failure of the Crosby demo, the doorway into the record industry was still locked and barred. The only thing David could do was keep playing. He was a regular at the Troubadour Hoots. Also playing there in the early part of 1964 was the Modern Folk Quartet—which included Henry Diltz.

"David came to see us play one night," Henry recalls. "And afterwards, he came backstage and was kind of whining, 'Oh, man, nothing I seem to be trying is working. I wish I could sing like you guys. I wish I could *find* some guys to sing with.' "

A short while later, when Crosby was playing by himself on the Troubadour stage, in walked McGuinn and Clark.

"I really liked how he sang," Gene Clark remembers. "And I turned to McGuinn and said, 'There's the other voice.' And he said, 'No, man, I know David, I remember him in the Village.' But I insisted. 'Listen, believe me, he's got that great harmony voice we've been lookin' for.' "

Later that night, in a stairwell leading up to the office of Doug Weston, the Troubadour's owner, Crosby laid a harmony line over an informal McGuinn–Clark jam. "That sound," David recalls, "rang clear and we were off and runnin'."

As the Jet Set (the name was McGuinn's idea—he was an airplane freak), this trio hooked up with Jim Dickson and cut a couple of tracks, Gene Clark's "You Movin'," and McGuinn and Clark's "The Only Girl."

Dickson managed to engineer a deal for the Jet Set with Elektra Records, which resulted in the recording of one single, "Please Let Me Love You," backed with "Don't Be Long" (a.k.a. "It Won't Be Long"). The single was released under the moniker "The Beefeaters"—supposedly selected by Elektra's president, Jac Holzman, in honor of the British gin. The hastily produced single went nowhere and the Beefeaters disappeared from Elektra's roster.

Even at this early, sputtering stage, however, Crosby was excited. "I could feel the fire building," he says. "I knew we were doin' something kind of unique. The harmony and twelve-string, it was a good marriage, man."

But in order to function as a real band, they needed a drummer. McGuinn spotted a guy walking down Santa Monica Boulevard who looked like the Rolling Stones' Brian Jones. Because of his "cool look," Michael Clarke was recruited to play drums, even though he'd had virtually no experience. During initial rehearsals, Clarke kept time on some cardboard boxes. Crosby, meanwhile, was trying to learn how to play the bass. "He bought a five-string model, thinking it would be easier because it was more like a guitar," says Dickson. "But it didn't matter. He was awful."

Crosby was the first to admit it, and in

the summer of 1964, he gladly gave way to Chris Hillman, a bluegrass mandolin player for the Hillmen, a country-bluegrass band that Jim Dickson had managed.

"They asked me to play bass," Chris says. "And even though I'd never played the instrument before in my life, I jumped at the chance. The folk thing was dying, the Beatles had just been on "The Ed Sullivan Show," and Gene, Roger, and David were creating a vocal sound that floored me."

There was no denying the distinctive quality of this blend. Crosby had already begun to take liberties with his harmony parts and—combined with McGuinn's chimey Rickenbacker electric twelve-string guitar and Hillman's roaming bluegrass-influenced bass—folk rock was springing to life inside World Pacific Studios in Los Angeles.

Stills: Greenwich Village/ the Au Go-Go Singers/ Meets Neil Young in Canada (1964–1965)

On the other side of America, in New York City, Stills was exploring Greenwich Village—where Crosby had been more than two years earlier. The scene in 1964 when Stephen entered it, was brimming with talented performers, all struggling to stay alive. Fred Neil, Richie Havens, Tim Hardin, John Sebastian, Richard and Mimi Fariña, Woody Allen, Lenny Bruce, Lou Gossett, Jr., Phil Ochs, Bill Cosby, Cass Elliot and the Big Three, Richard Pryor, John Hammond, Jr. Stephen is still fond of rattling off the names.

Among this huge roster of entertainers, Stills had his favorites. He once told *Rolling Stone,* "I used to really love Timmy Hardin, and Freddy Neil taught me an incredible amount about playing rhythm guitar,

about playing guitar at all, you know, a lot of the stuff I do with insinuating arrangements with my guitar, all that came from Fred. I could never sing that low, so I could never sing his songs that well, but boy! I mean, Freddy is probably more responsible, Freddy and Timmy Hardin and Richie Havens, are probably more responsible for my style on guitar, along with Chet Atkins, than anybody else. . . ."

Of course, Stephen also kept up his blues and performed for change at basket houses like the Four Winds, the Bitter End, the Night Owl, and the Gaslight. Along this circuit, Stills recalls, "I could never get over all them dudes from Cambridge singin' the blues that I'd grown up with . . . I mean, it's really hard for white kids from the suburbs to get next to Mississippi John Hurt and really *get* him. Dave Van Ronk got close, but John Hammond, Jr., Spider John Koerner, Dave Glover—these guys *got it.* Everyone else was a little too uptown."

Stephen himself admits, "I didn't get that proficient in my blues until later." But he still managed to work the elements into his playing. After one of his basket sets, Stephen ran into a fellow blues folkie from North Carolina named John Hopkins. They became friends, took a small apartment together, and started fooling around with some songs. One bluesy set of changes would later surface in a couple of Stills tunes, most fully realized in a banjo work-out called "Know You Got to Run."

While working with Hopkins, Stills began hearing about a musician in the Village who supposedly, says Stephen, "looked just like me." This person, Peter Tork, had been hearing the same thing. One day they met on the street. Tork says, "We just grinned, shook hands, and said, 'So you're the kid who's supposed to look like me.' And we *did* look quite a bit alike."

Tork, Stills, and Hopkins ultimately formed a trio, with Stephen and John on

Fred Neil joins Stephen Stills, Graham Nash, and Stephen Fromholz onstage at Stills's Madison Square Garden concert, New York City, 1971.

guitars and Peter on banjo. When they broke up in mid-1964, Tork remembers, "Stephen seemed cheerful and confident enough. There was little doubt he was going to do something."

Henry Diltz, who was also playing in the Village in 1964 with the Modern Folk Quartet, remembers, "Stephen was real friendly and you could see he was eager. He was always playing."

"Henry Diltz and the MFQ," says Stills, "had an influence on how I looked at harmony singing. And later, I often felt that they should have been more popular than they were. They were—and still are—great singers, and Henry taught me a lot about playing the banjo. In the Village, I was like a sponge and picked up whatever I could absorb. Of course, I was always developing something on my own at the same time."

Initially, this "something" turned out to be another duo act with his former New Orleans partner, Chris Sarns—who had also come to the Village. " 'I Know You Rider' [a traditional folk-blues song] was our big show stopper," says Sarns. "And I remember hearing one of Stephen's first songs. It had a refrain that went like, 'The bear went over the mountain to see what he could see. It seems he's got the same disease that's affected you and me, that's affected you and me.' "

Ed E. Miller, a musical director and songwriter who had scored a semi-hit with "Don't Let the Rain Come Down," saw Stills and Sarns and offered to build a group around them. This was a vocal group known as the New Choctawquins, which later changed into the Au Go-Go Singers—after Chris Sarns got drafted and Richie

The Au Go-Go Singers, New York, 1964. Richie Furay, sixth from the left. Stills, far right.

Furay arrived on the scene in late 1964 with a couple of friends from Ohio.

"I'd run into Stephen earlier when he was playing with Peter Tork and John Hopkins," says Furay, "and I thought they were really doing it right."

The Au Go-Go Singers, named after the Café Au Go-Go in Greenwich Village, also managed to do a few things right. Says Stills, "That group put a little experience under my belt and got me to remember all of my choir and harmony chops. Jim Friedman, who became the arranger, influenced my vocal technique an enormous amount."

A nine-member vocal group, the Au Go-Go Singers starred in an off-Broadway production, opened for a string of Vaughn Meader dates, toured down to Texas, and even recorded an album, *They Call Us the Au Go-Go Singers*, for Roulette Records (recently reissued). Comparisons with the New Christy Minstrels were unavoidable, because both groups' vocal style and sound were completely parallel. And where the Minstrels had Barry McGuire to add a touch of grain to the polish, the Au Go-Go Singers had Stephen Stills. At nineteen, Stephen's voice already had that bluesy, semi-coarse quality that would later become a trademark of the Buffalo Springfield and Crosby, Stills & Nash.

When the Au Go-Go Singers split up in mid-1965, Stephen wanted to get an electric guitar. He wanted, as he put it, "to be the Beatles." Stephen recalls: "When I saw *A Hard Day's Night* at the Waverly Theater in 1965, I immediately thought, 'Yeah! All of my folk music, all of my blues, all of my Latin music, all of my fingerpicking styles, all of my orchestral sensibilities . . . I could use all of that together and electrify it!'"

Before he followed his impulse, however, Stephen went on a two-and-a-half-week northeastern tour with a group known as the Company (previously known as the Bay Singers, an outgrowth of the Au Go-Go Singers), to explore new regions of Canada. One stop was the Fourth Dimension Club in Ontario, where Stephen and the Company shared a bill with Neil Young and the Squires.

Stephen remembers watching Neil on stage for the first time: "He was doing the same thing I wanted to do . . . playing folk music with an electric guitar. And Neil had such an interesting, intense attitude. That night I thought about forming a group with him, because he wrote such intriguing songs and he played *lead*. I hadn't played electric guitar since high school."

But after the gig, Stephen and Neil didn't talk business. Instead, they piled into Neil's hearse, picked up some beer, and, says Stills, "We had a friggin' ball."

It wasn't until the next day that Stephen assessed the situation. Should he quit his group and get something going with Neil in Canada? Or should he continue his tour, then go back to New York and try to arrange a visa for Neil to come and work in America? Stephen decided upon the latter plan, and Neil supposedly agreed. However, by the time Stills returned to Greenwich Village and persuaded Joe Marra at the Four Winds to sponsor Neil's working visa, everything flipped upside down.

"I had it all set up," Stephen muses. "Then I couldn't find Neil. So I called up Richie Furay and he came around, but he wasn't into being in a band at that time. When I finally did get hold of a phone number in Toronto and called for him, he'd gone back to being a folk singer. This chick, a folk singer named Vicky Taylor, had told him, 'Hey, man, I think you're Bob Dylan.' Neil believed her, broke up his band, and started being a folk singer, playing acoustic guitar in coffeehouses, something I'd already been doin' for almost three years. So that was it . . . Neil wanted to be Bob Dylan, I wanted to be the Beatles."

CHAPTER TWO

Rising to Fame

Nash in the Hollies (1962-1968)
Crosby in the Byrds (1964-1967)
Stills in the Buffalo Springfield (1966-1968)

The Hollies: Hits and Tours in England (1962–1964)

Over in England in 1962, the Beatles' early path was repeatedly crossed by the Hollies.

"I remember playing St. George's Ballroom with the Beatles," Nash says. "John and Paul took me aside and said, 'Listen to this new song we wrote for Helen Shapiro.' Then they sang 'Misery.' And another time at this nightclub, we taught John the words to 'Anna' the night before the Beatles were going to record it."

While the Beatles were on the verge of massive success, the Hollies weren't that far behind. Even at this early phase, Nash explains, "the Hollies had a reputation for doing great business, having a lot of energy and getting kids off righteously. Also, we weren't flaky; we rarely canceled gigs, we always showed up on time and we were well behaved."

This attitude, coupled with the Hollies' dense but bright harmonies, impressed EMI Records' Ron Richards enough for him to travel to the Cavern in Liverpool to catch one of the band's noontime concerts in late 1962. Nash remembers, "I was a notorious string breaker and we weren't rich enough to replace them right away all the time. So the day Ron came to see us play, I had no strings on my guitar. I played rhythm guitar with no strings!"

This didn't seem to affect the fate of the Hollies too adversely, however, because they were subsequently asked to come to London and audition at EMI/Parlophone studios in January 1963. The band played their normal set through twice. The Hollies left London with a record contract.

"We were just wide-eyed and laughing," says Nash. "It was like a miraculous dream!"

This dream came true when the Hollies cut their first records and scored immediate hits with spirited covers of the Coasters' "(Ain't That) Just Like Me" and "Searchin'," Maurice Williams and the Zodiacs' "Stay," and Doris Troy's "Just One Look." These were songs that Graham and Allan had sung since their mid-teens. Consequently, their performances in the studio were injected with pure emotion, rather than careful, self-conscious construction.

Clarke handled most of the lead and melody vocals, while Nash sang high harmony. With the addition of Tony Hicks's voice underneath, the Hollies created some of the most stirring three-part harmony in rock. It was this Nash–Clarke–Hicks triumvirate that would soon come together as a songwriting team.

Graham admits, "The reason we first started writing was not one of great intellectual intent, to reach people's souls. The reason was, there was *money* in it. We realized that every time an A-side sold, there was a B-side stuck to it. And when the sales started mounting up, we wanted a piece of that vinyl sandwich."

At first the results were, says Nash, "Songs like 'The Whole World Over,' our first B-side, a totally naïve little pop song." Consequently, the Hollies' hits were still written by people other than themselves, notably Graham Gouldman (who would later join 10cc), the author of such Hollies smashes as "Bus Stop" and "Look Through Any Window."

In the midst of this consistent commercial roll, the Hollies were at the center of the English "beat boom" and lodged right next to the Beatles for a time. Nash says, "There was no rivalry. It would have been silly. All the bands from the north stuck together, and we *applauded* the Beatles. They opened the door for the rest of us. The Beatles made it respectable to be from the north; and from then on, everyone tried to talk with Liverpudlian accents. It was weird."

In 1964, the Hollies toured all over Europe, and when they pulled into various cities, Tony Hicks says, "We tried to find hotels with fire escapes so we could sneak chicks in. Graham would be getting a Coca-Cola and occupying the geezer at the front desk while we'd scamper through the revolving doors and get upstairs with the chicks."

Graham was never quite as rowdy a reveler as his bandmates. With his gentle charm and warm smile, however, he attracted the attention of many female admirers. During one of the Hollies' shows at a place called the Oasis Club, Graham met a beautiful young woman named Rose Eccles. They lived together for a time, then were married. Graham says, "It wasn't difficult being married and being in the Hollies at the same time. Because Rosie thought it was all a gas; it was an escape for her too. She'd get off at the Oasis and loved traveling with the Hollies wherever we went, at all hours of the night."

The Byrds: "Preflyte"/ "Mr. Tambourine Man"

Throughout 1964, the team of Crosby, McGuinn, Clark, Hillman, and Clarke was intent on grooming their sound. They had been recording nightly at World Pacific Studios for months. Though a lot of the music sounded half-baked, "The Airport Song," written by Crosby and McGuinn, emerged as an engaging piece, but never made it onto a Byrds album. Instead, "The Airport Song" was released in 1969 on *Preflyte*, a collection of songs from these first sessions. Crosby now says, "I don't think that music should have ever been released. We were still *learning*, and you can hear that. Jim Dickson was recording us so we could listen back and hear our mistakes. We were raw."

Having given up the bass, Crosby began concentrating solely on his vocals. But it wasn't long before he took the rhythm guitar out of Gene Clark's hands. David explains, "I had to, because Gene just couldn't keep time, couldn't play on the beat. I'd been playing rhythm guitar in coffeehouses for quite awhile, so it was natural for me. We needed *someone* to keep the beat, because Michael [Clarke] barely knew how to play drums."

Jim Dickson says, "In the beginning, David was very musically intimidated, so he tried to intimidate others. Gene was fine. But David shook his sense of time by telling him he was off. I've seen jazz guys do that to each other. Gene's never been the same guitarist since."

Of course, Gene Clark, along with McGuinn, still carried most of the lead vocals, as well as the songwriting load at the outset. Crosby's main function was that of harmony singer. The importance of this role soon became evident after Dickson worked out a Columbia Records deal for the band, christened the Byrds (again, thanks to McGuinn's fascination with flight), in November 1964. Their first single was a cover of Bob Dylan's "Mr. Tambourine Man," a perfect vehicle for Crosby's harmony. Some of the instrumentation was supplied by session players, on the advice of Dickson. "He didn't think we were strong enough on our instruments to cut it," says Crosby.

Jim Dickson, 1967.

David also admits, "Dickson was the one that convinced us to sing Dylan songs. He knew him and got a test pressing of 'Tambourine Man' before it was out. We weren't sure about the song, but Jim got us to try it, and it worked."

When "Mr. Tambourine Man" was released in April of 1965, it rocketed to the top of the charts. Crosby says, "I remember the day it went on the radio. We were driving along in this old '56 Ford station wagon we'd bought from Odetta, and damned if it didn't come on KRLA right when we were listening. And they played it three times in

a row, man! We went crazy! We pulled over to the side of the road. We were jumping up and down, pounding each other on the backs, yellin' and screamin'. It was just ecstasy."

The Byrds paid a visit to one of Crosby's old buddies, Paul Kantner, who was on the verge of getting the Jefferson Airplane off the ground. "Having a record on the radio was a really big deal," says Kantner. "When David and the Byrds came to visit us in San Francisco, they left their car parked out front and, naturally, it being Turk Street, all of their equipment and their suits got ripped off. In a way, though, this set them free, because I don't think they ever went back to wearing those Beatles suits."

Casual "do your own thing" clothes became the Byrds' standard stage attire, and seemed much more compatible with their emotional, fluctuating live sets. Jim Dickson remembers watching Crosby perform at one of the band's first live shows. "He tried to wiggle like a rock 'n' roller, but he didn't know how to wiggle, because David was still basically a folk musician. And folk musicians don't wiggle."

Chris Hillman adds, "With the Byrds, you never knew, from night to night, how the shows would go. Some were great. Some were just terrible."

The Byrds managed to deliver a series of peak shows at Ciro's, on Sunset Boulevard, and this club became the band's favorite nest. It also was where Bob Dylan first dropped in for a listen.

"Dylan could have been a real shit to us," says Crosby. "But he liked us. Maybe he felt an obligation to come by, but we didn't care. We were still starvin' kids and Dylan was, well, *Dylan.*"

In the wake of "Mr. Tambourine Man"'s universal success, the Byrds dipped further into Dylan's bottomless bag of material. "It wasn't just because we'd had a

Bob Dylan onstage with the Byrds at Ciro's, Los Angeles, 1965. (The Michael Ochs Archives.)

big hit with one of his songs," insists Crosby. "We all dug him then, saw he was a great writer and we were probably a better interpreter of his songs than he was."

On *Mr. Tambourine Man*, the Byrds' first album, no less than four Dylan songs were covered. But, unlike the single, the whole *band* played on this album. "Columbia wanted us to use studio guys again," says Crosby. "But we threatened to quit if they were gonna make us do that."

As for band originals, Gene Clark dominated the songwriting, with his "I'll Feel a Whole Lot Better" emerging as the best of the lot. That Crosby was not involved with lead singing or songwriting at this stage was not the result of repression. "David just didn't have the authority to be the lead singer," says Jim Dickson, "on enough kinds of songs. So it wasn't so much a matter of not wanting him to sing lead. The material just wasn't right for him. And as for his own songs, writing never came easy for him."

Crosby admits, "From the start, I was mostly into harmony. That's what I dug. That's what I was best at. And most of the

time Gene and Roger would be on the melody, so I had all this space, I could shift around between the third and the fifth intervals. I came up with some weird, beautiful shit, man. It was great fun."

Stills: From New York to California/Early Songwriting/the Monkees/Reunited with Furay (1965–1966)

Stephen Stills was not having a great deal of fun in New York in August of 1965. Neither Neil Young nor Richie Furay wanted to join a band with him. Stills says, "I desperately wanted the job of bass player in the Lovin' Spoonful, but I was just too shy to push for it." While contemplating his future, Stephen discovered that his mother had left his father in Latin America and was now living in New Orleans with his sister, Ticita. He wanted to go down there and give them support. He was also thinking

29

about giving California a shot, because, says Stephen, "I was listening to the radio and heard the Byrds. The sound of their electic guitars and voices made me think that L.A. was the place to be if I wanted to rock 'n' roll."

Rather than take off for the West Coast alone, however, Stephen called his mother and sister to see if they were interested in joining him. They were, and a whirlwind trip from New York to New Orleans to San Francisco ensued. Stephen had thought that the San Francisco Bay area, rather than Los Angeles, might be where his mother and sister would want to settle, and he was right. Stephen himself, on the other hand, still felt that L.A. held the key to his musical future. However, before leaving San Francisco, Stills saw the Jefferson Airplane and the Great Society perform. He immediately fell in love with Grace Slick's voice, but, he explains, "She was married to the drummer, the band was terrible, and I was just too shy to ask her if she wanted to get some good musicians and form a *real* band."

Once he was in Los Angeles, Stephen thought that maybe he should have approached Grace, because the hub of the music industry was not easy to crack into alone. He had just begun to write some songs that he felt "were personal statements and had something to say." "Four Days Gone," written about a draft dodger, was one. "Sit Down, I Think I Love You," a fairly direct love song, was another. Using a borrowed tape recorder, he practiced arranging his music and made some rough demos.

"Because I was starvin'," Stills says, "I sold 'Sit Down, I Think I Love You' and a couple of other things to Chuck Kaye [then connected with Screen Gems–Columbia publishing]. He was hustling just like everyone else in L.A., but who knew? I mean, I now have a guy [Ken Weiss] who is the publisher for my company [Gold Hill Music]. No one will ever again *own* what emanates from my pen. What I create out of the thin air is *mine*."

In the fall of 1965, however, the couple of hundred dollars he received for selling the songs allowed him to pay the rent on a small apartment and buy a few meals, while he attempted to form a group with Van Dyke Parks—"a fine mind and rapier wit," Stephens says—and though the combination didn't work out, Parks ended up persuading a group he was producing, the Mojo Men, to record one of Stills's songs, "Sit Down, I Think I Love You." It became a fair hit the following year, but because Stephen had sold the song's publishing rights, he never saw any writer's royalty money.

"I just couldn't keep anything going," Stills admits. After his aborted association with Van Dyke Parks, he put together a short-lived folk duo called Buffalo Fish with bass player Ron Long (another refugee from Greenwich Village). Together, they hit the Southern California folk circuit in late 1965, playing mostly folk and blues standards. One night, when they hit the Golden Bear, in Huntington Beach, Peter Tork was working in the club's kitchen.

"I was between gigs," says Tork, "washing dishes and jerkin' beer at the Golden Bear, when all of a sudden I hear this voice coming from out in the club. I look and it's Stephen, who I hadn't seen since leaving New York."

Over beers, Stills and Tork renewed their friendship and Buffalo Fish became a trio, with Tork adding some vocal support and comedic touches. But after a few more times around the circuit, Buffalo Fish spread apart. In January 1966, Stephen heard about a casting call for a new television program. The premise of the show was a sanitized version of *A Hard Day's Night*. Bert Schneider and Bob Rafelson, who were putting the show together for NBC television, had been scouring Hollywood, searching for musicians who looked good and could take direction. Stills tried out for a part. And while the story has often been told that Stephen failed a screen test because of a recessed front tooth, he now says, "That wasn't true. They could have fixed my teeth. What I really wanted to do was write songs for the show. But I found out that I'd have to give up my publishing and that they already had a pair of staff writers in [Tommy] Boyce and [Bobby] Hart."

While Stills decided not to get involved with this production, when the casting director asked him, "Do you know anyone who looks like you who might be interested?," Peter Tork came to mind immediately.

"I got this frantic call from Stephen," Tork says. "And he gave me the whole story and I went, 'Yeah, sure, Stills,' and hung up. He called me right back and said, 'Man, you really ought to get your ass down here.' So I did, finally, got the part, and so began my career with the Monkees."

After this episode, Stephen drove back up to San Francisco to visit his mother and sister. Meanwhile, in New York City, Richie Furay, Stephen's old Au Go-Go Singers comrade, had encountered Neil Young walking through the Village, toting a guitar. Richie invited him up to his apartment, and Neil played him a slew of new songs he had written, one of them being "Nowadays Clancy Can't Even Sing." "I recognized Neil's talent right away," says Richie. "He taught me 'Clancy,' and I started playing it at the Bitter End hoots."

When finances got tough, Furay went up to Hartford, Connecticut, to earn some cash. But he soon got the urge to play more music, and decided to write a letter to Stills. "I sent it to his dad in El Salvador," Richie says. "That's the only address I had on him. But the letter came back to me with postage due. It was one cent short! So I sent it out again with the right postage, and waited to hear."

By the time Stills received Furay's letter—which had been forwarded to San Francisco—he had hooked up with a freelance producer and advisor named Barry Friedman (later known as Frazier Mohawk). Word that Furay was looking for work couldn't have come at a better time; Stephen, on Friedman's advice, was looking to put a band together and wanted another singer to build around.

"I didn't want to be the only lead singer," Stephen says, "because I didn't want to just be out there alone. I wanted some harmony, another voice. So I called Richie and said, 'Hey, come out to California. I need you to sing in this new group I've got together.' I didn't really have a group yet, but I figured Richie might not come if he knew it was just me. So I lied a little."

Furay went for the bait and recalls, "When I got to L.A., there wasn't anything happening. Stephen was living in this tiny little apartment on Fountain Avenue. It was really frustrating. There were a couple of times when I wanted to check out early. But Stephen still had this drive and enthusiasm that kept me there."

Little did Richie and Stephen know that their destiny would soon be altered by the occupants of a long black hearse, motoring across America, headed for California.

Buffalo Springfield: Born in Hollywood (1966)

Fate on the Street

The outlook was grim. Two months into 1966, Stills and Furay had failed to find any suitable partners who could fit into a band with them. Even Stills's unshakable optimism was beginning to weaken. Could their careers be dying right in front of them in the middle of the music capital of the world? Where else could they go?

Equally frustrated were a pair of Canadian musicians—Neil Young, the elusive folk rocker whom Stills had never been able to find, and Bruce Palmer, a bassist who had been playing with Young in Ricky James and the Mynah Birds. After cutting a couple of tracks for Motown, the band had blown up when lead singer Ricky James Matthews got picked up for desertion from the U.S. Navy. In the middle of this catastrophe, Young and Palmer decided to stick together, sold most of the Mynah Birds' equipment, and set their sights on the Promised Land—Los Angeles, California.

Without any visas or working papers, Neil and Bruce bombed down into the

States inside a hearse nicknamed "Mort" or "Clancy" (Neil was fond of nicknames. He once named every chicken in his mother's henhouse). When the hearse reached L.A., it was early March 1966. Neil had heard Stephen was now living there, but had little hope of locating him. So Young and Palmer decided to just "take in California." In Hollywood, this long black hearse drew more than a few stares. And a couple of those stares happened to belong to Stills and Furay.

"We were in this white van," says Furay, "stuck in traffic on Sunset Boulevard. I turned to brush a fly off my arm, looked over into the other lane, and saw this black hearse with Ontario license plates going in the other direction. Then Stephen looked across and said, 'I'll bet I know who that is.' "

Somehow, Furay then engineered one of the most amazing illegal U-turns ever

Dewey Martin with drum head, 1967.

Buffalo Springfield, 1967. (Photo by Ti Stills.)

attempted and pulled up behind the hearse. "Yeah, that's Neil," said Stephen. With a combination of horn-honking and arm-waving, he and Richie managed to get Neil to pull his hearse into a supermarket parking lot. It was there that the four young musicians shared their frustrations about making it in the music business. On Stills's suggestion, they drove over to Barry Friedman's house and got totally ripped. An extended jam ensued, in which Richie and Stephen played Neil their arrangement of his song "Nowadays Clancy Can't Even Sing." That was the kicker. They made plans that night to form a group.

They started rehearsing with a drummer friend of Stephen's, Billy Mundi. Something didn't quite click, though, and when he had the chance, Mundi moved on to join forces with an L.A. folk group, Mas-

ton and Brewer. At the same time, drummer Dewey Martin had been let go by the Dillards, who had decided to shift back to bluegrass. When Dewey caught wind of the opening in Stills's band through Jim Dickson, he was skeptical at first. Dewey had previously played with such top professionals as Carl Perkins, Roy Orbison, Faron Young, and Patsy Cline.

"I hadn't auditioned in years," says Martin. "I was used to just getting a job and going to work. But I didn't have anything going, so I lugged my drums over to this old house on Fountain Avenue. They were paving the street, I remember. And there was this steamroller out front with a big sign on the side that read BUFFALO, SPRINGFIELD. When I walked into the house, the guys were already talking about taking that as a group name, and I thought, 'Yeah, what a great name—Buffalo Springfield.' "

Stills remembers, "Neil and Barry (Friedman) had stolen a Buffalo Springfield sign off the steamroller for Barry's house. They put it up. We all looked at it on the wall and a light went off. That's how we came up with the name."

Dewey Martin, originally from Canada, immediately had something in common with Neil and Bruce. Stills warmed up to Martin after he learned of his credentials, and they started playing together. With an eight-song repertoire that included Stills's "Sit Down, I Think I Love You" and "Pay the Price," and Young's "Clancy," the Buffalo Springfield prepared for their first gig—which finally took place at the Orange County Fair Grounds, in San Bernardino, in late March 1966.

Before the Springfield attracted any real attention, the band was staying together at the Hollywood Center Hotel. They subsisted on a diet of peanut butter, hot dogs, bologna, mayonaise, mustard, and white bread. Occasionally they'd splurge for a hamburger. During this phase, Stephen was reviving his creative engine, writing songs and sharpening his guitar licks. Dewey Martin, however, was not used to starving, and remembers sitting on a bench in the middle of Hollywood, thinking about the Springfield and wondering, "What am I doing here?"

The Hollies: Recording with the Everly Brothers/Tours in Europe/The First Trip to America (1966)

Early in 1966, the Hollies had an opportunity to not only meet their mentors the Everly Brothers, but to record an album with them as well. Called *Two Yanks in England*, this Everly Brothers LP, on Warner Bros., featured a young session guitarist named Jimmy Page (pre–Yardbirds), eight Nash–Clarke–Hicks songs, and sparkling Hollies harmony. Graham recalls the experience: "It was just a total thrill. To go from 1958, waiting in the pouring rain for the Everly Brothers, to '66 and being in the studio and singing on the same mike as Phil Everly, was a mind-blower for me—mind-blowing—one of the real high points of my life!"

The Hollies' live shows in 1966 featured some great examples of live rock harmony. Yet the bulk of the band's audience didn't seem to be listening. Instead, they were *screaming*, often louder than the Hollies were playing.

"We did almost an entire tour," says Nash, "and I'm convinced we never got heard once. The girls kept on screaming. It was just the thing to do. And I admit we deliberately tried to provoke them. Most groups had one thing that would really start the audience going. With the Beatles, it would be the 'ooooohs' or the shakin' of their mop heads. Mick Jagger, he'd clap his hands. Us, if we wiggled a leg or reached forward to touch a girl's fingertips, the volume of the screams would be unbelievable. We did an early tour with the Stones, and it was insane, just insane."

But this was Europe. The Hollies had yet to set foot in America.

"I remember rubbing my nose against the music-store window in Manchester and looking at the instruments from *America*. These were things one sent away for, if you got them at all. But you never really thought about getting on a plane and actually *going* there."

But Nash's childhood wonder turned to nervous anticipation when he and the rest of the Hollies were in Heathrow Airport in the spring of 1966, about to journey to America for the first time.

"You've got to understand," says Nash, "that we were incredibly jazzed to go from Manchester to London. Amplify that ten times, and you've got an idea of how we felt when our visas came through and they said, 'You leave for New York at four o'clock.'"

The Hollies were in a virtual daze through the entire flight. And when the plane touched down at Kennedy Airport, there was a limousine waiting for them. "It was one of the longest cars I'd ever seen in my life," says Graham. "It was *so* long, we spent at least ten minutes laughing before we got in."

Driven directly to the Paramount Theater, the Hollies became part of one of the more interesting bills in musical history: Little Richard (with Jimi Hendrix on lead guitar), Shirley Ellis and the Vibrations, King Curtis, and the Paramount Dancers. The Hollies performed "Rockin' Robin" and "Here We Go Again." Nash says, "We were used to playing several forty-five-minute sets. But after two songs here, that was it."

The next day, while the Hollies were investigating the streets of New York, they drew more than a few sidelong glances. "I suppose we looked like these weird punks of today," says Tony Hicks. "We'd stopped wearing our suits when we came to America. And I remember Graham had on one of those big furry hats and long black boots—he looked like a Russian cossack. I had on a big, white, frumpy coat and a big Stetson hat. I thought we looked all right, but we'd get these weird comments from Americans, things like, 'Take a bath,' right on the street."

Such reactions merely amused the Hollies, however, who were still in awe of New York and the American dream. "I tasted a brand-new life," says Graham. He mingled with a potpourri of musicians and discovered, he says, that "people were really interested in what I had to say. Because we were part of the whole British Invasion, Americans wanted to know how we made records. They wanted to know what energy they could pick up on. Whereas, in England, if you didn't know John and the lads, you weren't anybody.

The Hollies, New York City, 1966.

"I remember the Hollies were staying at the Holiday Inn on Fifty-seventh Street," Graham continues, "when the doorman called and said, 'There's a guy here who says he's Paul Simon.' And I thought, Paul Simon! 'I Am a Rock' [which the Hollies covered]. I didn't know Paul. Yet here he was. He wanted to talk and learn. We got together, we shared ideas. Paul and Arthur [Garfunkel] ended up showing us a lot about making records."

With this experience dancing in his head, Nash and the rest of the Hollies returned to England. But it wasn't long before they flew back across the Atlantic, this time bound for Los Angeles, California.

The Byrds: In England/ "Turn! Turn! Turn!"/ "Eight Miles High" (1965–1966)

In spring of 1965, the Byrds had journeyed, for the first time, from Los Angeles to London. The band's reception had been less than pleasant; audiences there were already skeptical of the tag, "the American Beatles." Tired and ill, the Byrds performed in a casual, offhand manner and were duly slaughtered by the British fans and press. However, on this trip, the Byrds also hung out with the Rolling Stones and the Beatles for a time.

Meanwhile, back in the States, Sonny and Cher scooped the Byrds with a cover of Dylan's "All I Really Want to Do." Also, other seminal groups—such as the Mamas and the Papas, the Lovin' Spoonful, and the Turtles—were latching on to the new folk-rock sound that the Byrds were popularizing.

When the Byrds returned to L.A., it took them a while to put any new material on the market. There were many fruitless marathon sessions. Fights broke out in the heat of recording. Crosby was often involved.

Once, Dickson had David down on the floor and was choking him. Another time, Michael Clarke took offense at a remark, got up, and slapped Crosby in the face. Chris Hillman recalls, "David just had this knack for causing trouble. He was like Peck's Bad Boy. He was insecure, like everybody else. But if anything frightened him, he got belligerent."

Dickson says, "I was always on the side of the guy who was getting picked on. Once, the Byrds threw Crosby out of this meeting and I went and got him. I told the guys, 'No Crosby, no group. If you can't include each other, you can't include the audience.' "

When the Byrds' second album, *Turn! Turn! Turn!*, finally came out in December 1965, their audience was ready and waiting. The title track became the band's biggest single ever, rising to the number-one position on the charts at a fast clip. Beyond this commercial success, however, the album showed no extraordinary progression by the Byrds. There were a couple more Dylan songs, more writing from Clark, McGuinn's "He Was a Friend of Mine," and a Crosby–McGuinn collaboration, "Wait and See." But David Crosby was only then getting ready to fly.

In early 1966, LSD and the sound of the sitar helped spawn a brand of music called "raga rock." Crosby and the Byrds were one of the first to experiment in this direction. And no song exemplified this sound more effectively than the Byrds' "Eight Miles High," conceived by McGuinn, Clark, and Crosby.

"We first cut the song at RCA studios," says Crosby, "with Dave Hassinger [a producer]. It was fantastic! The song just took off. But we'd done it secretly, without Columbia's approval. So they made us redo it with union nerds. The record company slapped our hands if we tried to touch the board. It was a shame. The version that got released wasn't nearly as good."

Nonetheless, "Eight Miles High" rose into the Top Twenty, despite a rash of radio station boycotts, sparked by the song's drug connotations. This didn't hurt the Byrds all that much; if anything, it helped fuel their image. What did upset Crosby, however, was the subsequent release of Paul Revere and the Raiders' "Kicks."

"It was a dumb anti-drug song," says

The Byrds in New York City. (The Michael Ochs Archives.)

Crosby, "a falsely adopted stance. With 'Eight Miles High,' we were talking about something very near and dear to our hearts."

The flip side of "Eight Miles High" was "Why?"—credited as a McGuinn–Crosby song. But David claims, "It was all mine. That was one of the first songs I ever wrote that I really liked. It was *saying* something and questioning." And musically, "Why?" brought Crosby's developing vocals up front.

This musical turn was suited to Crosby's personal and stage image. He often shrouded himself in a green suede cape and strode about with a flamboyant air, unabashadly praising the use of LSD and marijuana. He was the "rebel character" in the Byrds. And, as Gene Clark once said,

"Who else could be Lawrence of Laurel Canyon?"

Crosby also threw himself more seriously into songwriting. However, as Jim Dickson observed, "Songwriting wasn't David's forte. It was a painful process for him. He'd come up with these pretty changes and melodies, then clutch up on the words. This was when Gene was just spittin' them out."

Because Gene Clark had been the principal writer of most of the Byrds' early originals, he became rich on publishing royalties. His cohorts, though not poor, scrambled to catch up. Dickson says he believes "McGuinn started going for songs because of the publishing money, rather than going for the best songs." Clark, meanwhile, graciously stepped aside when any

David Crosby of the Byrds. (Photo by Chuck Boyd.)

controversy arose. But that didn't remove him from the fray. Suddenly he started getting criticized for missing beats on the tambourine.

"David," says Dickson, "put Gene on edge. He was making the devil's sign behind him on stage and was anxious to be number two in the group."

Crosby says, "I had nothing against Gene personally, and never set out to hurt him. I liked him a lot. But he couldn't keep a beat. His tambourine playing was driving me crazy."

By the spring of 1966, Clark was out of the Byrds. A fear of flying escalated to the point where he exited a plane right as the Byrds were set to take off for New York. Clark admits, "At the time, I had this phobia about flying. I'd get claustrophobic and just have to get out. And I was having a nervous breakdown. But I didn't really intend to leave the Byrds. I just needed to go somewhere for a break."

But when Clark departed, the other Byrds didn't wait around. Crosby, in particular, entered into a particularly creative phase that rode into the Byrds' third album, *Fifth Dimension*. His "What's Happening?!?!" was an expansion of jazz-rock

ideas, and centered by Crosby's admission (with an audible chuckle on the record), "I don't know how it's supposed to be. No one, has the key to the instruction booklet."

Buffalo Springfield: Helped by the Byrds/The First Recordings (1966)

In Hollywood, the five members of the Buffalo Springfield were having trouble getting anything to click at the start of the summer of 1966. They had no steady live work. They had no money. All they had were songs and equipment.

But the fortunes of the Buffalo Springfield changed rapidly after Chris Hillman of the Byrds came by for a listen. "I thought the Springfield was just great," says Chris. He got caught up in the raw energy they projected, and thought about managing them—"for about two seconds," he says. "I mean, I had enough going on with the Byrds, and I was so young. What did I know about managing?" Nevertheless, Hillman persuaded Elmer Valentine, owner of the Whisky A Go-Go, to give the band a shot. This resulted in an all-important six-week stay at the Hollywood club. One night Hillman brought David Crosby to see the band play.

"He didn't like 'em," says Chris. David says, however, "I don't know, man, all I can remember is Stephen and Neil cookin' real good on guitars. And I liked some of their harmonies. I knew they had something right away."

The Buffalo Springfield became the new challengers, and, says Hillman, "The Byrds were still king of L.A. then. The Springfield should have made us work harder. But instead of meeting the challenge and getting down, we just went, 'Ehhh, we're the Byrds.' "

Catching Fire

Hungry for recognition, the Buffalo Springfield performed with a bold intensity and fire at the Whisky. News about this "hot new group" quickly spread all over Los Angeles. Fans started lining up around the block outside the Whisky and, even more important, other musicians, such as the Mamas and the Papas, Barry McGuire, and Sonny and Cher came to check out the Springfield. What happened next, Neil Young later described best in his song "Don't Be Denied":

The businessmen crowded around
They came to hear the golden sound
There we were on the Sunset Strip
Playing our songs for the highest bid

Dunhill Records set the advance-money ante at $5,000. Warner Bros. raised the action to $10,000. Then, thanks to Charlie Greene and Brian Stone (who had previously pumped life into Sonny and Cher's career and then set up a publishing arrangement with Buffalo Springfield), Ahmet Ertegun, president of Atlantic Records, came to check out the scene and immediately offered the Springfield a con-

Buffalo Springfield, Santa Monica, California, 1967. (Left to Right: Richie Furay, Stephen Stills, Neil Young, Bruce Palmer, Dewey Martin.)

tract with Atco (an Atlantic subsidiary label) and a $22,000 advance. The band went for it.

"I loved the Buffalo Springfield immediately," says Atlantic Records president Ahmet Ertegun. "There was something about how Steve and Neil worked off of each other. And all of the members became very dear to my heart."

One of the first songs the Buffalo Springfield recorded was Stills's "Go and Say Goodbye." Chris Hillman says, "I remember when Stephen was writing that. I showed him a mandolin lick from an old bluegrass song, 'Salt Creek,' and Stephen added in a variation of that in 'Go and Say Goodbye.'" It stands as one of the first examples of what would later be branded "country rock."

Though it was known as the band's first single, "Go and Say Goodbye" would later be relegated to a flip side in favor of Young's "Nowadays Clancy Can't Even Sing." But before this bit of maneuvering occurred, the Springfield took off on a series of concerts, for which they were paid $125 per show to open for the Byrds. There were other bills, with Johnny Rivers, among others; and, at the Hollywood Bowl, the Buffalo Springfield opened for the Rolling Stones.

"The first six months that we were together were the best," insists Furay. "Everybody enjoyed each other, *depended* on each other. We had these tunes, we had this desire, the shows were magical."

Stills agrees: "I remember that first week at the Whisky and the gigs we did with the Byrds. We could really *smoke!* That band never got on record as bad, and as *hard* as we were. Live, we sounded like the Rolling Stones. It was great."

In addition to having this powerful sound, the Buffalo Springfield also projected quite a colorful onstage image. Stephen took to wearing a vest and cowboy

boots, and often resembled a duded-up frontiersman. Neil, with his Comanche war shirt, long raven-black hair, and raindance-like spasms while playing lead guitar, was the Hollywood Indian. Furay wore his paisley Nehru jackets and took wild duckwalks across the stage. Palmer stood back, underneath his monk's cap. Martin flailed away on his drums, with his ruffled ties flashing. The guys in the Springfield were distinctly unique and perfect candidates for fame. All they needed was a hit song.

According to David Crosby, he was responsible for first getting the Buffalo Springfield on the radio. It seems David had been in England, hanging out with the Beatles, when they played him an advance

Charlie Greene, 1968.

tape of "A Day in the Life." Before returning to Los Angeles, Crosby was able to get a copy of this tape, which also happened to have on it a bizarre comedy routine, "I'm Freakin' Out on Acid," created by Paul McCartney's brother, Michael, a.k.a. Mike McGear.

David says, "I played 'A Day in the Life' for Stills, and he fuckin' fell out and told his managers, Greene and Stone, about it. Well, these guys hired this girl to come and fuck me and swipe the tape. After that went down, Greene and Stone went to KJH and told 'em, 'We'll give you a tape of some new Beatles stuff if you'll play the Buffalo Springfield's 'Nowadays Clancy Can't Even Sing.' I'll be damned if KHJ didn't go for it. They played the Springfield, then they played the Beatles tape and thought 'I'm Freakin' Out on Acid' was the Beatles, too. The fools. But that's how the Buffalo Springfield got on KHJ!"

Even at this early stage, it was clear

that Stills's lyric ideas were fairly literal, compared with Young's more ambiguous images. Stephen himself admits, "Although my words were okay, being a fairly decent English student, back in the Springfield days, Neil's lyrics were far superior to mine. His songs were like poems, in a way, while I usually got right to the point."

This was certainly the case with most of Stills's songs that made it onto the first Buffalo Springfield album. The rest of the songs—all Young's—were moodier, generally darker reflections. Though Furay failed to get any of his compositions onto the first album, he did handle lead vocals on two of Young's.

Richie Furay, 1967.

"I think they [Stills and Young] had me sing a couple of Neil's songs just to appease me, to keep me satisfied," says Richie. "Because I had all the songs that made it onto the second album written when we were recording the first one. But Stephen and Neil were very strong, they had good songs, and they recognized, I think, that a lot of my talent and ability lay in my voice."

"Stephen and I would sing a lot together," Richie continues. "We patterned ourselves after Lennon and McCartney. We did a lot of unison stuff. We were heavily influenced by the Beatles and wanted to be the next big thing."

The Buffalo Springfield might have had a better shot at that lofty throne had they hooked up with a producer who knew how to transfer the *real* Springfield sound onto tape. This failure, Stills has admitted, "virtually destroyed the band." He and Young mixed a mono version of *Buffalo Springfield* that had a bit more *bite*, but most of the public would hear the stereo version produced by the band's managers,

Greene and Stone. On most of the songs, it sounded like the guts had been ripped out of the band.

Denied the opportunity to re-record the album, the Springfield also had to wait until January 1967 to see it in the stores. In the meantime, the band scored a three-night stand at Bill Graham's Fillmore West, in San Francisco.

"I *loved* the Buffalo Springfield," says Graham. "And Stephen and Neil's guitars really drove that band."

Ralph Gleason, a music critic for the *San Francisco Chronicle* at the time, probed even deeper in a review of one of the Springfield's shows. He focused on Stills.

"I think I owe Ralph Gleason my career," Stephen says. "He had an understanding of what I was going for that even I didn't have. He recognized how I was arranging the show. And I *was* trying to apply all of the skills and tools I'd learned in school about craftsmanship and musicianship. We were just a bunch of folkies, for

Stephen and Neil at the Big Kahuna's Luau, Malibu, 1968.

chrissakes . . . so I tried to organize every-thing in the manner of a good ensemble. Ralph understood this and let a lot of people know how thoughtful the Buffalo Springfield's music really was."

The Hollies: Visit L.A./Nash Meets Crosby (1966)

Freedom Found

In June of 1966 when the Hollies made their first sojourn to Los Angeles, they were not prepared for what they saw around them—palm trees, swimming pools, glittering boulevard lights, acres of sandy beach. "There was no question," Graham says, "about me being mystified by the place. I mean, the telephone rang just like in the movies."

On this visit, the Hollies were scheduled to appear at a press party arranged by Imperial Records (the band's American label in 1966). It was a typical industry function, with most everyone either exchanging forced pleasantries or attempting to make an influential contact. Graham felt a bit uncomfortable in this situation and was taken off guard by a smallish, congenial "man about town" named Rodney Bingenheimer (currently one of Los Angeles's most popular new wave disc jockeys on KROQ).

"I was just standin' there," Graham says, "and this funny-looking little guy, Rodney, comes up to me and asks, 'What are you doin' after the party?' I didn't know. I was new in L.A. Then Rodney says, 'Do you want to go hear the Mamas and the Papas record?' Now, at this point, for all I knew, he could have been planning to mug me. But I went with the flow and took him up on it. I wanted to check out Michelle Phillips, 'the beautiful one.' But at the ses-sion, I totally fell for Cass. Her sense of humor and her mind *floored* me."

Later, Graham went up to Cass's house and he says, "She opened my mind to opening my life. Cass showed me many wonderful things in a very gentle way. She was the person who introduced me to grass. I'd always been curious. And I'd smoked a little hash. But never grass. So when Cass and I got high, I'll never forget it. I remember we went down to a coffee shop on Sunset Boulevard, had breakfast, and I kept thinking, 'This is a *banquet!*' And I also realized that marijuana was a key, a key to unlocking the way one sees oneself and everybody else and situations and the world as it is. So, yeah, right away, Cass became a very pivotal being in my universe."

She was also a strong emotional and creative ally of David Crosby's. Before the Hollies left L.A., Cass devised a plan. She wanted to take Graham up to David's house without any "formal introductions." A musical matchmaker if there ever was one, Cass was curious as to how David would relate to Graham "the man" versus Graham "the Hollie."

Cass Elliot and Graham Nash. Lunch at the Café Figaro garden, New York, 1966.

Crosby recalls, "Cass brought Graham over and she didn't tell me who he was. I spent hours with the guy. We talked and I liked him a lot. He seemed like a real sharp dude. And he and Cass seemed very fond of each other. So later on, after they'd left, I called over to Cass's and Graham answered. So I said something like, 'When you came by, it was great, man. You're obviously making Cass really, really happy. So all I gotta say is *thanks*, whoever you are, masked man!' The next day Cass told me it was Graham Nash and I went 'Ahhhh! Another master harmony singer.' 'Cause I'd heard the Hollies' records, man. And I loved Graham's harmony *way* up there."

Graham was equally impressed with Crosby's vocal work with the Byrds. But before they could compare notes, Graham was on a plane with the Hollies, bound for England.

"After being in Los Angeles, I think going back to England was slightly drab for Graham," says Allan Clarke. And Graham admits, "Of course I thought Los Angeles was cool, but I was also still interested in taking what I'd learned and expanding within the Hollies."

Inspired by Cass, inspired by Crosby, inspired by the wide-open musical and cultural landscape he'd just found, Graham attacked his songwriting with a new vigor and steered the Hollies into some untested territory. He was anxious to raise the band above "the singles machinery" and infuse more experimental elements into the Hollies sound.

Graham succeeded in doing this with a lot of the music on *Evolution* (called *Butterfly* in England and released in 1967). "Carrie-Anne" worked particularly well. Graham says, "I sang all the choruses, then we decided to take one verse each. A nice, fun record. When we played it live, we used a tape of the bass part and the steel-drum solo. We'd be in rhythm with the tape, then the bass player would turn off and the steel-drum solo would come sailing out of nowhere! It was very effective. We had orchestras on tape, trumpets on tape . . . people

didn't know where the fuck this stuff was coming from. We blew a lot people's minds."

Crosby was astounded by the Hollies' experiments. When the Byrds journeyed to England in late 1966, Crosby paid Nash a visit. "David was staying in a place called the White House, which he thought was pretty funny . . . and I invited him over to where Rose and I were living," says Graham. "He must have stayed for four or five days. But when he wasn't Byrding, I'd by Hollie-ing. Except this one afternoon, I went with David to a press conference, and he was one of the first persons I'd ever seen stand up to a reporter. I mean, the Hollies had been browbeaten into going along with whatever the media wanted—'stand there, talk now, tell us everything'—not Crosby. At this conference, this reporter asked him some personal question and David said, 'What the fuck has that got to do with you?' There was a deathly silence. Then David carefully explained that one doesn't ask personal questions of a total stranger. It was brilliant, but something I had never had the balls to do. It was then I began to realize that Crosby and I treated people a lot differently. I can tolerate a lot, while David suffers fools not at all."

During the early stages of this budding Crosby-and-Nash friendship, Graham admits, "Crosby fascinated me. I'd never met anybody like him. He was a total punk, a total asshole, totally delightful, totally funny, totally brilliant, a totally *musical* man. And I enjoyed his company."

Former Hollies publicist Allan McDougall recalls, "Once I took David and Graham to this Hollies reception at Village Records. I didn't know Crosby, really. But here we were in this London hackney carriage, clipping along. I looked over at David and he was lighting up a hash pipe, then he hands it to me. And I remember thinking, 'What a guy, what a *guy!*' "

The Byrds: "Younger than Yesterday" (1967)

Crosby Spreads His Wings

"David was more of a leader in the Byrds than McGuinn was," says Chris Hillman. "He always projected real well on stage. He was an extrovert and had a lot of guts—which sometimes meant he could be an arrogant jerk."

"Very fiery, with a lot of drive, David had that," says Jim Dickson. "The energy amazed me. He seemed to be sort of lazy at first, but he really had tremendous resources once he got going."

With the release of *Younger than Yesterday* in early 1967, it was obvious that Crosby had grown as a writer and as a singer. "Everybody's Been Burned" unveiled a more relaxed and fuller vocal style than David had shown before. Built on an unfolding Crosby rhythm progression, the song's E-minor drone hinted at the wealth of chords and melodies that Crosby would begin to cover.

" 'Everybody's Been Burned,' " says David, "was most characteristic of what was to become my style. Pretty changes, an unusual feel and flavor—plus good words." The emotional gamble involved with risking your heart and your being in a relationship is dealt with in the song's final verse: "I know all too well how to turn / How to run, how to hide behind a wall of blue / But you die inside if you choose to hide / So I guess instead I'll love you."

Crosby could melt ears with such sentiments. He could also, in the next moment, become strange with a song like "Mind Gardens," an atonal, wandering song-poem that the rest of the Byrds would just as soon have seen omitted from *Younger than Yesterday*.

"It was a total struggle to get that song on there," David says. "McGuinn, to this day, still hates the song. He told me, 'It doesn't have rhythm, meter, or rhyme.' I told him, 'Who cares? There are no damn rules!' The lyrics were a cop on Shakespeare. I did that on purpose. And the music was me with my twelve-string, recorded backwards. I liked the song because it stretched the senses. It was intended to encourage the breaking down of walls, which is what I did with the song."

Buffalo Springfield: "For What It's Worth"/ "Stampede"/ Neil Young Quits (1967)

With the dawning of 1967, Stills had also begun to expand his writing, by reporting on what he saw around him. Along with most of the other kids in Los Angeles, he often wandered down to the Sunset Strip. As L.A. radio personality Rodney Bigenheimer once described it: "The Strip was like Las Vegas with flowers at all hours." This was certainly the case in 1966 and 1967. Hundreds of kids hung out along the sidewalks, around the Whisky a Go-Go and Pandora's Box (the latter, long since torn down). Several of the more conservative business owners in the area complained to the L.A. police about "all of these dirty, long-haired kids chasing away my customers." A confrontation between the kids and the police seemed inevitable. And one night, following a series of "incidents," the police roared onto the Strip in force. Stills recalls the scene. "I'd just come from Latin America after being caught in Nicaragua . . . when I saw the Sunset Strip riots . . . all the kids on one side of the street, all the cops on the other side. In Latin America, that meant there would be a new government in about a week."

Disturbed by this incident, Stephen went home and got out his guitar. In the middle of plunking out some ideas, he heard a knock on the door. It was David Crosby. With David as an audience of one, Stephen continued to experiment with his guitar.

Crosby says, "I remember him going"—then he mimics a guitar sound—" 'brrrrang, bump, ba, de, da, brrrrang, bump, ba, de, da.' And I told him, 'That's a great lick, man.' Stephen said, 'Oh? You really think so? It's part of this new song I've got going called 'For What It's Worth.' "

When the rest of the Springfield heard the song, the whole band marched into the studio and cut it immediately. Jim Dickson remembers, "Greene and Stone were producing the song, and on the line, 'What a field day for the heat,' they had a cymbal crash covering up the word *heat* so they wouldn't get in trouble with the police. That's how scary things were in those days. But I told Charlie [Greene], 'Look, this is a hit record, leave the word in.' "

Well, *heat* stayed in "For What It's Worth," and the song itself enjoyed some pretty hot chart action, climbing to number seven on *Billboard's* Hot 100. This commercial explosion forced Atlantic to re-release the first Buffalo Springfield album with "For What It's Worth" as the opening track, bumping off Stills's "Baby Don't Scold Me" (thereby making the first pressing of *Buffalo Springfield* a collector's item).

Riding the crest of what was to be their commercial peak, the Springfield landed a ten-day stay at Ondine's in New York. Otis Redding sat in at several of these shows. This was in April of 1967, when the band also recorded a new prospective single, Young's "Mr. Soul"—respectfully dedicated to the ladies of the Whisky a Go Go and the women of Hollywood. It was during these sessions for "Mr. Soul" that the band decided to can Greene and Stone as their

producers and managers. Dewey Martin recalls, "Charlie Greene got so upset, Neil had to give him some Valium to calm him down. But these guys had to go. We didn't need the extra hassles they caused. We had enough problems to deal with."

The most immediate concern, at that point, was Bruce Palmer, who had been busted for posession of marijuana in New York and deported to Canada. So that the Springfield wouldn't blow an appearance on "The Hollywood Palace," the band's new manager, Dicky Davis, sat in on bass. Then came Bobby West (Love's bass player), former Squires bassist Ken Koblum, and ultimately Jim Fielder—once a member of Frank Zappa's Mothers of Invention. None of these replacements adequately captured what Palmer had added to the Springfield.

Stills explains, "He had a style with the bass. He had a Bill Wyman kind of Motown feel put underneath everything, and it made it work for me." Stills also once explained to Michael Watts in *Circus*, "His [Bruce's] relationship to me and Neil was the focal point of the group. He was the focus that balanced Neil and me."

Bruce's absence from the stage, then, might partially explain an increase in the number of flare-ups between Stills and Young. Their guitar battles had always been fiery, and their contrasting styles—Young's brittle, staccato wrenchings against Stills's bluesier, more fluid phrasings—made for intense, effective call-and-response sessions. In the middle of a short tour in early 1967, however, it became open warfare on stage—the cowboy versus the Indian. Dewey Martin remembers one incident when, he says, "Things got pretty hot on stage, and when Neil and Stephen got into the dressing room, they started swinging at each other with their guitars. It was like two old ladies goin' at it with their purses."

Stills now attributes such behavior to "being young" and to the fact that "Neil

Cover for *Stampede*, the Buffalo Springfield album that never came out.

was trying to arrange some stuff, which was my trip, and I was getting more into lead guitar, which he thought was his trip. So things got intense for a while."

During such madness, the Buffalo Springfield managed to put together a collection of recordings aimed, supposedly, toward a second album, tentatively titled *Stampede*. The band even posed for a cover shot that aptly reflected the mood of the Springfield at that point. In front of an old Hollywood Western movie set, Stephen is staring straight ahead, a cigarette in his mouth, looking like a hard-ass; Furay's attention is down the road; Dewey, caught with his mouth open, looks confused; Neil is a bit apart from the scene, with his eyes closed; and there is a guy down in front, taking a siesta behind a big black hat. Stills says, "That was Dicky Davis. Bruce was still gone."

But Bruce was around for the recording of some of these *Stampede* outtakes, many of which surfaced several years later in bootleg form. Stills's "So You Got a Lover," "Neighbor Don't You Worry," and "Come On (Here)" were great takes, as were several early Neil Young songs—recorded *sans* the rest of the Springfield.

"I think Neil always wanted to be a solo artist," Furay says. "And I can't hold that against him. It just seems there may have been a different way to make that point clear, rather than just not show up."

With a prestigious appearance scheduled with Otis Redding on "The Tonight Show," and Bruce Palmer just back in the fold, Neil made his first exit from the Buffalo Springfield. Stills reflects: "The Carson show was like 'The Ed Sullivan Show' at that time. It was an important show to be on in 1967. We were playing our best ever. But Neil quit the night before we were to leave for New York. It was sheer self-destruct."

But in the wake of Young's departure and the cancellation of the Carson appearance, Stills managed to keep the Springfield chugging along by enlisting the services of guitarist Doug Hastings (formerly with an obscure San Francisco band, the Daily Flash). This version of the Springfield managed to pull off a few interesting shows, but with an apearance at the Monterey Pop Festival at hand, Stills began wondering if the current Springfield lineup needed an extra element.

CHAPTER THREE

Looking for New Partners

Crosby: The Rebel Byrd / Jamming with Stills / With the Springfield at Monterey (1967)

Crosby, in the late spring of 1967, had grown increasingly restless, and now looked like a rebel itching to *rebel*. He'd sprouted a radical mustache that drooped down over his lips. His hair now curled down to his shoulders. He often wore Borsalino or cossack hats. More than ever, Crosby stood out from the crowd. He was also discovering that all of his musical impulses didn't necessarily have anything to do with the Byrds. He explains bluntly, "I was bored as hell with the Byrds, man. They were holding me back. They weren't letting me grow. They didn't dig my stuff. It was a burn, man."

David Crosby had grown increasingly restless.

Crosby was able, however, to share a lot of his expanding energy with Stephen Stills. During the creation of Stephen's "Rock 'N' Roll Woman," Crosby came up with the repeating lick that echoed, in altered shape and feel, the heart of his own "Renaissance Fair." There was more musical trading back and forth.

David recalls, "People kept telling Stephen, 'Ah, you're just like Crosby, just a little punk.' But he wasn't like me at all. He was just feisty and a fine player."

Stills relates, "I remember hearing all of these horror stories about what an arrogant asshole David was. But when I met him, I found he was basically just as shy as I was, and making up for it with a lot of aggressive behavior. I recognized the symptoms, because I was like that myself."

It was only natural, then, for Stills to think of Crosby as Monterey Pop approached. Crosby could provide the additional "muscle" the Springfield needed. Neil Young still had not returned, so David recalls, "Stephen asked me if I would sit in with the Springfield at Monterey, and I said, 'Hell, yes, I'll do it.' So I sang with the Byrds; then, for a grand total of forty-five minutes, I was in the Buffalo Springfield."

This, of course, caused all kinds of resentment within the Byrds. Hillman says, "Yeah, we got upset, because one just didn't do that then. We were competitive kids and it seemed like David was telling us, 'Hey,

Soundcheck at Monterey. Left to right: Dewey Martin, David Crosby, Richie Furay, Stephen Stills.

Crosby performs with the Buffalo Springfield at the Monterey Pop Festival, 1967.

look at me, I can play wherever I want.' "

During the Byrds set, Crosby inflamed the situation further during the opening of "He Was a Friend of Mine." David aggressively denounced the validity of the Warren Report, then turned right around and praised the benefits derived from taking LSD. This blatant political/acid rap infuriated McGuinn. He took it as a personal affront and things were never quite the same between McGuinn and Crosby again.

Stills: With Hendrix at Monterey/Malibu/On the Road with the Monkees (1967)

At Monterey Pop, besides the Byrds and the Buffalo Springfield, the Who, the Jefferson Airplane, Otis Redding, and Big Brother and the Holding Company performed. But the entire three-day affair, June 16, 17, and 18, 1967, was stolen by a young guitarist named Jimi Hendrix. *Everybody,* fans and musicians alike, was enthralled by this vibrating maniac who pulled howling, screeching wails and crashes from his electric guitar—then set it down on the stage, sprayed lighter fluid on it, and set it afire. Probably more intrigued than anyone was Stephen Stills. Amid the fire and the flash, Stills saw a devastating blend of rock-blues-jazz lead guitar. Backstage, Stephen struck up a friendship with Hendrix and they agreed to rendezvous back in L.A., at Peter Tork's house in Laurel Canyon.

Stills, Hendrix, and drummer Buddy Miles all ended up at a beach house in Malibu, which the Springfield had just rented. Stephen re-creates the scene: "I set up my big amps, we took some acid and just *went.* We played quite literally for twenty straight hours. We must have made up fifty songs. But there was no tape runnin', no nothin'. We just played for the

ocean. Brucie [Palmer] eventually showed up, and, a little while later, so did the sheriffs. They came to the door and asked, 'What's the deal?' And I said, 'Did you get a call?' 'No,' they said, 'we were just curious. This area is usually very quiet and, you know, we were curious about who was playing.' I told 'em, 'Well, there's me and a guy from Chicago and a guy from Seattle and we're just playin' blues and stuff.' And they said, 'Oh yeah? Well, I know what you're thinkin', but would it be okay if we parked across the street and listened?' I shrugged. So the guy said, 'Don't get paranoid because we're out there. We don't care what you're doin'. We just want to listen. And if one of our sergeants shows up, someone'll sound a siren, which means just cool it for a few minutes.' So me and Hendrix jammed with the sheriff's protection! And that night I really started to learn how to play lead guitar."

In August 1967, when the Buffalo Springfield crossed paths with the Monkees in the Midwest, Stills discovered that the Monkees' opening act was Jimi Hendrix.

"Jimi was my guru, man," says Stills. "Nobody could play guitar like that cat. Now, when I caught up with him on the Monkees tour, I proceeded to follow him around. Some people thought we were fags or that I was a groupie. But, hey, it wasn't like that at all. It was like I was going to music school, learning how to play lead guitar."

After one of these Monkees/Hendrix shows, a jam session took place that had to be one of the most unique ever. Peter Tork recalls, "We were in this hotel room. Jimi and Stephen were sitting on these beds facing each other, just flailing away on acoustic guitars. In between 'em was Micky Dolenz, slapping his guitar like, *'slap, whacka, slap, whacka, slap.'* And all of a sudden Micky quit. Then Stephen and

Stephen Stills, 1967.

Jimi stopped and Stephen said to Micky, 'Why'd you stop playing?' Micky said, 'I didn't know you were listening.' So there's one for ya—Hendrix, Stills, and Dolenz."

On stage with the Springfield a while later, though, Stills had difficulty cutting into the "magical zone" with his leads, and wasn't spurred on by guitarist Doug Hastings. The absence of Neil Young could not be ignored. Dewey Martin says, "Stephen woodshedded and got to be a damn hot guitar player. But without Neil, the Springfield wasn't the same. We were used to getting a solo from Neil and a solo from Stephen. That was the unique thing we had goin' for us, the two lead players trading back and forth."

Young never really fit back into the Springfield. He began recording his own tracks, some with producer Jack Nitzsche and some with various members of the band. This obviously changed the chemistry of the Springfield. The eager, innocent drive and enthusiasm the band once projected was nowhere to be found.

Nash: Drifting from the Hollies (1967)

Meanwhile, the Hollies were undergoing some changes of their own—thanks to Graham Nash. Ever since he'd visited New York, and then Los Angeles, Nash's approach to songwriting had begun to change. While on tour with the Hollies in Yugoslavia in 1967, Nash recalls, "I wrote one of my first *real* songs, 'King Midas in Reverse.' I mean, I'd obviously written many songs before that, but this was one of the first ones that really came out of the *inner* me. It wasn't simply manufactured. I was in my hotel late at night when I wrote it, and I'm still not sure I understand it. I don't know if I'm King Midas or the gold or the dust."

The rest of the Hollies weren't sure, either. Graham's creative turn was pushing the band in a more ethereal, psychedelic, complex direction, to which neither Allan Clarke nor Tony Hicks was willing or able to contribute. Nonetheless, all of the Hollies songs from this period still read "Nash–Clarke–Hicks" on the writing credits. Graham admits, "This was beginning to bother me, because I was really working hard writing a lot of songs on my own, then not getting full credit for them. We'd set up this writing partnership that made anything any one of us wrote automatically credited to the three of us. It was a totally ridiculous situation."

All was not well with Graham's marriage at this time. He explains, "Things started mounting up over petty things, little jealousies." Consequently, he welcomed the chance to make another trip to America

Graham tries out a new song on his fellow Hollies. Left to right: Allan Clarke, Bob Elliott, Tony Hicks, Bernie Calvert, Graham Nash. (Photo by Don Paulsen, The Michael Ochs Archives.)

with the Hollies. On a Greyhound bus tour, Graham wrote a song called "Stop Right There," which, he says, "expressed these feelings that I had about my marital problems. Cass was on tour with us. She loved being on the bus, hangin' out with the lads. And she, around this time, introduced me to acid, which opened me up a great deal more.

"I was beginning to see that what was happening in my marriage was the equivalent of my relationship with the Hollies. I felt resistance. I felt a little bored. There was a lack of forward motion and it was hard to move ahead because of such an attachment to the past. And because, with the Hollies, this *thing* we'd created was so heavy with hits."

Crosby: Byrd Spats/At Home in Beverly Glen/Fired from the Byrds (1967)

Hits were the last thing on Crosby's mind in the summer of 1967, as he began going through more radical changes with the Byrds. "It just wasn't any fun anymore," David says. "Because the spirit wasn't there, man. We were playin' like the fuckin' *canaries*, not the Byrds."

Hillman agrees. "The band simply wasn't cutting it on stage. And the Byrds were never that consistent live, anyway. The Buffalo Springfield was stronger when they played live. And there just wasn't even any comparison when we started really messin' up. We did some pretty childish things."

In the middle of a Crosby song, Hillman might take a drag on a cigarette and let a few bass beats go by. Or, if David was taking an inordinate amount of time to tune up, Hillman would announce, "Ladies and gentlemen, the David Crosby Show." David began to play carelessly, as if his mind was somewhere else, which it was. He says, "It was hard to put on a consistent show, when *nobody* wanted to be there."

Still, Crosby tried to work within the framework of the Byrds, and pushed hard for the release of a new song of his called "Lady Friend." To this day, he is still proud of the brass break he inserted in the middle of the track. Released only as a single, backed with the forgettable McGuinn–Hillman collaboration, "Don't Make Waves," "Lady Friend" was a commercial failure and served as a prelude to what was to come.

Amid the turmoil he was experiencing with the Byrds, David often sought refuge in his secluded home in Beverly Glen, a wooded region west of the Hollywood Hills. Here, Crosby would sink back into his

Paul Kantner, 1970.

leather couch, with his twelve-string in his lap, and calmly explore. A frequent guest was Paul Kantner.

"David was real ongoing and searching," says Kantner. "He was always finding new things. And, unlike most L.A. musicians, David joyfully went around and *showed* everybody his latest lick. In L.A., most players used to hide their hands, playing in clubs, so people wouldn't steal their licks. David was very unlike that, which was probably one of the reasons we got along well."

Kantner goes on, "And David was not only surrounded by nubile girls, but *intelligent* nubile girls. Anybody could get average nubile girls, with a gram of cocaine. But intelligent nubile girls were another matter. David always had a lot of intelligent friends who happened to be girls. It wasn't that sort of L.A. cocksman approach."

Grace Slick describes what she saw on one of her visits to Crosby's home. "It seemed like David's house was completely made out of this fantastic wood. And everything inside was either wood or

Grace Slick, 1970.

leather—*no plastic*. There were a couple of ladies running around with hardly any clothes on, all tan and blond, with perfect figures, serving sliced oranges and stuff. David was talking about this perfect weed he'd just gotten. And he and Paul were playing on these perfect wooden acoustic guitars, this perfectly wonderful new song David had written. And he was looking so happy, with his goddamned Borsalino hat on. And I know, you're probably thinking, 'Oh, come on, things weren't really like that.' But with Crosby, yeah, they were. To me, at that time, he was one of those pure, loving, natural guys. He loved the planet. He loved life. And I was mightily impressed by that."

McGuinn and Hillman, however, were completely perplexed by David's activities. They were not supportive of his new songwriting direction, which was yielding such compositions as "Laughing"—written, says David, "for George Harrison about his devotion to the Maharishi. Nobody can tell me they know the answer."

Crosby, then, was naturally skeptical of McGuinn's faith in Subud, a spiritual organization that sparked his name change from Jim to Roger.

At a Byrds session in October 1967, David walked out in the middle of the recording of "Goin' Back." He gave no reason. He just left. Crosby later admitted he was upset because the Byrds had rejected a new song he'd written called "Triad"—a lyrical scenario about a ménage à trois. Chris Hillman says, "David has always said we didn't like 'Triad' because of its moral implications. That's not true. We just felt it was a lousy song."

Grace Slick disagreed. "When David came over to RCA studios and played it for us," says Grace, "we loved it. Because, you know, I had seen him have successful relationships with two women at the same time, and it worked. The two women liked each other just fine. Most of my best female friends, to this day, I've gotten to know because we had the same boyfriends. So that ethic David was singing about holds true for me too."

McGuinn and Hillman did not relent in their refusal to record "Triad," however. In fact, one afternoon, the two of them roared up to Crosby's Beverly Glen home in their two Porsches, jumped out, walked right into David's living room, and said, "Crosby, you're through! You can't write, you can't sing, you're an asshole, and we'll do better without you." Crosby responded, "Well, if that's the way you want it, but I think it's a waste of a bunch of great music." McGuinn and Hillman weren't listening. They had already turned on their heels and were out the door, having performed one of the more dramatic firings in history.

Crosby was startled by the abruptness of the dismissal, but he wasn't caught totally off guard. "I was no little angel then," he admits. "I was certainly difficult by anybody's standards. It was only because I wanted to get my music out, I *needed* to get my music out. But it obviously wasn't meant to be with the Byrds."

Chris Hillman says, "Perhaps we should have handled it a bit differently. But we just couldn't work with David anymore, and he'd led us to this manager who was robbing us. It was not the best of times, and David was just restless. He saw the end coming before the rest of us, and he was looking for new things to do."

Crosby: Sailing in Florida / Meets Joni Mitchell / Returns to L.A. (1967–1968)

Crosby's Royal Scam

More than anything, Crosby now relished his freedom. He no longer had to stifle the spontaneous musical strangeness and political outcries that had contributed to his dismissal from the Byrds. Still, he had been fired so summarily that his ego was still a little tender, and he was periodically haunted by Roger McGuinn's last words to him. Not that Crosby had any serious self-doubts about his musical abilities. He simply felt he had been given a bum rap and was determined to prove McGuinn wrong.

David still believed "Triad" was a great song. Grace Slick and Paul Kantner thought it was a great song, and the Jefferson Airplane recorded it on their *Crown of Creation* album, with help from Crosby on guitar and in the arranging stages.

In the midst of this activity in November of 1967, Crosby heard about a sixty-foot schooner for sale in Florida. He had always been a lover of the sea, and figured,

"Twenty-two grand for a sailboat like that is outright theft, man. As soon as I heard about it, I thought, 'There's my boat.' "

Before leaving L.A., however, Crosby hit upon a "royal scam." "You see," he says, "even though McGuinn and Hillman had thrown me out of the Byrds, I was still technically under contract with the Byrds' label, Columbia. But I wanted my complete freedom. I did not want to be on that label anymore. So I came up with this theory that if I made myself look totally valueless, Columbia would let me go."

Crosby wrote a letter to Clive Davis, then president of Columbia Records. The missive was brief and to the point: "My music's all dried up. I don't have it anymore. Please let me out of my contract." Upon receiving this, Davis immediately phoned Crosby.

"I see here you're asking to be let free. Why should I do that?" Clive asked.

Crosby responded. " 'Cause I'm quitting the business. I don't want to have anything to do with it anymore."

Apparently this exchange wasn't enough to persuade Davis, so he contacted Roger McGuinn, who reiterated, "Crosby's through." After hearing this, Davis got back in touch with Crosby and told him, "Okay, David, we'll terminate your contract." Crosby just smiled and thought, "They *bought* it. They let me go for free." He laughed all the way to Florida.

When he arrived in Coconut Grove, Crosby immediately paid the $22,000 for his sailboat, christened *The Mayan*. And while learning to be a good sailor, he spent hours on the deck, making up tunings and patterns on his twelve-string guitar.

Although David missed his Canyon friends, he was enjoying his sabbatical from the bustling L.A. scene. It gave him some time to fool around with ideas on his own and to bask in the Florida sun. He got a rich bronze tan and stopped taking drugs.

At night, he would occasionally wander inland. One early evening, David stepped into the Gaslight South coffeehouse in Coconut Grove. He was immediately struck by a slender blond woman, sitting on stage singing and strumming an acoustic guitar.

"Right away I thought I'd been hit by a hand grenade," Crosby says. "Her voice, those words . . . she nailed me to the back wall with two-inch spikes. I went up to her afterwards and said, 'You're incredible.' She said, 'You really think so?' "

Joni Mitchell.

The young folk singer was Joni Mitchell. And, as David says, "I promptly fell in love with her and we started a little romance."

"It was a radical change in his life," recalls Joni. "He'd left the Byrds, he'd taken on this boat, and he was in very good health. He was a very impressive sailor. He'd take this boat out in the open water and up canals. I remember one time going to visit somebody, and David took this schooner and double-parked it like a Volkswagen. I was very impressed with the way he handled that thing.

"And David's temperament was . . . I used to call him Yosemite Sam, because of his long mustache and red hair, you know? He was a colorful kind of pirate type. But he was twinkly. His eyes always looked like

David Crosby and Joni Mitchell.

star sapphires and they always had fire comin' out of 'em."

Peridots and periwinkle-blue medallions
Gilded galleons spilled across the ocean
    floor
Treasure somewhere in the sea he will find
    where . . .
Like a promise to be free
Children laughing out to sea
All his seadreams come to me
                                    —"The Dawntreader"

"That was the 'hello, David, I love you' song," says Crosby. Joni admits, "Yes, David can claim that one. At the time, he was thinking about what to call his boat. The name of it, when he purchased it, was *The Mayan*, which he kept. But I liked *Dawntreader*, which comes from a children's fairy tale about a boat that sails off the edge of the earth—assuming that it's flat—and goes on some beautiful trip. That was my suggestion. And the music of 'The Dawntreader' curves and undulates like a boat on water."

With many more brilliant songs in her repertoire, Joni was planning to head to Los Angeles "to escape the grayness of New York, and because California was sending out beacons." Crosby, by this time, was anxious to go back to L.A. himself. So the decision to leave was easy.

"Joni was so good," says David, "that I wanted to toss her in everyone's face. 'Ha, give me a bad rap, try *this*.' And Joni was fantastic, man. Everyone knew the minute they heard her that she was something special."

But when Joni signed a record deal with Warner Bros., Crosby was worried that some outside producer was going to ruin her, so he offered to handle the production chores himself. Joni admits, "David kind of came in as a conservationist. When he said he would produce me, the record company was confident that he would produce a folk-rockish thing, since that was his background. But all along, David was planning to perpetuate a hoax and preserve the beauty and intimacy he liked in my music. He understood my music and was very sympathetic toward my vision."

Another individual who was keeping a close watch on Joni's vision was Elliot Roberts, her manager and close friend. They had hooked up in New York a couple of years earlier. Now, in January of 1968, out in L.A. with Crosby, they were experiencing a whole new lifestyle. Elliot remembers, "David was my inspiration when I first came to California. He really was. I lived on David's floor for a while, and he was my idol. He had style, he had a lot of class. Of all of the guys—Stephen, Neil, Graham—David was the one I was close to when I first came here. He gave me my first hit of sinsemilla. David was like the guru of experience. We were all *new* in L.A. David was *from* here. He knew who was cool to know, where it was cool to go. He was like a guru to everybody involved with the late-sixties scene. David was into being a rebel when no one else had the balls. David was out there spitting on people and being an asshole for no reason . . . he just did it. And everybody looked to David to see what was happening. He was a great captain in those days. He just *took* it. Some guys couldn't

Elliot Roberts, 1971.

handle that pressure, but he could and it was great."

Meanwhile, the Buffalo Springfield was in the studio at Sunset Sound, right next door to Joni, David, and Elliot. "I knew Neil from the old folk days in Canada," says Joni, "and when I heard 'Mr. Soul' on the radio, it was like, 'There's my friend on the airwaves, man.'" A joyful reacquaintance took place between Joni and Neil at Sunset Sound. Elliot remembers, "Joni had told me, 'You've got to meet Neil, he's hysterical, you guys will love each other.' So we hung out after the Springfield sessions. But the next day I moved in with Stephen and Buddy Miles. Stephen had just taken a house and he said, 'Live with me, man. No problem.' So I moved in. A day later, Buddy Miles took over my room. But it wasn't too long after

that, I started working with the Springfield and found out what was going on with that band."

Stills: "Buffalo Springfield Again" / Stills in Charge / Young on the Edge (1967–1968)

Rumbles from the Herd

Buffalo Springfield Again had been released in December 1967. Even though it was a vastly more mature work than the first album, Richie Furay explains, "On the second record, we'd drifted off into a lot of our own things, and a lot of overdubs were used. The first time, we just set up in the studio and played live, with a four-track going."

From a band *unity* standpoint, it makes sense to all play at once, in the same place, but from a *quality* standpoint, individual members can often create better tracks alone. On *Buffalo Springfield Again*, Stills proved for the first time that he could really build songs. The finest example of this was "Bluebird" (originally titled, according to Stills, "The Ballad of the Bluebird"). The liner notes exaggerate: "GUITARS—Steve, Neil & Richie—all 11,386 of em'." But "Bluebird" does explode with a barrage of metallic acoustic and electric fretwork. All Stephen remembers about laying down the guitar parts is "me and Bruce Botnick [an engineer] together, very high, working our asses off." Stills credits Botnick and Jim Messina with instructing him about the studio process. Later, Stephen would go on to run every aspect of recording sessions singlehandedly. In the Springfield, he was an eager student.

The diversity of music on *Buffalo Springfield Again* was an accurate representation of the different directions the band was pulling in. "Every guy had *his* songs, *his* studio time, and *his* frame of mind," says Dewey Martin. To complicate matters, Bruce Palmer had exhibited some more bizarre behavior—beyond living in a tree house and taking up the sitar—that had a direct effect on Stills. Once, in New York, Palmer had his bass volume set way too loud. When, after repeated requests, Bruce wouldn't turn it down, Stephen punched him into the drums. At a gig in San Jose, Bruce started griping about how long it took Stephen and Neil to tune up between songs. Eventually, Palmer dropped his bass and walked off stage. Rather than stop the show, Stills simply picked up the bass and directed the rhythm section for the rest of the night. A couple of weeks later, this situation resolved itself when Palmer was busted for possession of drugs again, and deported to Canada. Jim Messina came out of the engineering booth to become the Springfield's new bassist.

To maintain some semblance of order in the band, Stills tried to be, as he has put it, "the boss cat." This move didn't surprise Furay, who explains, "I always looked at the Springfield as Stephen's band. It was really his vision, and he had the musical direction it took." Dewey Martin adds, "We always used to say, 'Steve's the leader, but we all are.' We never let Stephen have the full title of leader." Nevertheless, it was obvious that Stills was the leader of the Buffalo Springfield, and if he hadn't adopted a take-charge attitude, no one else in the band would have picked up the ball.

During early 1968, Stills not only tried to keep hold of the reins of the Springfield, but he also hung out and jammed often with Duane Allman (then playing in a band called the Hour Glass). And when Stephen stopped in to check on Crosby's sessions with Joni Mitchell, he ended up strapping on a bass and cutting a track on her "Night

Stephen Stills, 1967.

in the City." Buffalo Springfield road manager Chris Sarns recalls, "Stephen was a workaholic, and he'd drive me pretty hard. But he never asked me to do anything he wasn't willing or able to do himself. And he never pushed anybody as hard as he pushed himself."

But even Stills's efforts weren't injecting life back into the Springfield. Elliot Roberts provides an overview: "It was a hard period. Stephen thought the Springfield was his band, but Neil had all of these great songs. I'd hang out with Neil up at his house and he basically already had a lot of the songs that showed up on his first two or three solo albums. Yet Stephen and Neil had tremendous respect for each other. I think that's why the Springfield stayed together as long as it did. But it was just a matter of time before it had to break up."

Young once discussed the final days of

the Springfield with Cameron Crowe: "I just couldn't handle it toward the end. My nerves couldn't handle the trip. It wasn't me scheming for a solo career, it wasn't anything but my nerves . . . I was going crazy, you know, joining and quitting and joining again. I began to feel that I didn't have to answer to, or obey, anyone. I just wasn't mature enough to deal with it. I was very young. We were getting the shaft from every angle, and it seemed like we were trying to make it so bad and getting nowhere."

Stills adds, "There was this desperation to make it that kind of chewed at us. . . . I could definitely see the end coming . . . we had too much fame and no money."

Nash: Conflicts in the Hollies / Nash Meets Joni Mitchell in Canada / With Crosby and Stills in L.A. (1968)

Thousands of miles away from this mess in L.A., in early 1968 inside a small recording studio in London, England, Graham Nash was trying out a new tune on the Hollies. Slowly picking a simple guitar part, he opened up his throat and sang, "And when I return I will kiss your eyes open / Take off my clothes / And I'll lie by your side . . . " When Graham ended this tune, "The Sleep Song," there was a moment of silence. Then Allan Clarke piped up, "We can't bloody sing that filthy stuff. What is this shit?"

Nash was stunned by the reaction, and came back at the band with charges that their plan to record an album of Dylan songs was sacrilege, especially since the arrangments, according to Nash, "were coming out like Las Vegas rave-ups."

This disagreement wasn't resolved, but ceased when everyone but Nash headed off to a local pub to have some drinks. Graham stayed behind in the studio and continued to practice a batch of new songs he was working up, including "Marrakesh Express' and "Right Between the Eyes."

"I had been contemplating doing a solo album," says Graham. "But the Hollies frowned on such a venture. They didn't feel you could be a person *and* a member of a band. Their attitude was, 'You can't go making solo albums and be a member of this bloody group. What in the bloody 'ell are ya tryin' to do?' Totally closed-minded thinking."

Amid this frustration, Graham says, "I was the only one who smoked dope in the band, and it was obvious that this contributed to the giant rift that was developing between us. Once you start becoming more self-aware, more deeply aware of surroundings and feelings and the heightening of all your experience levels, which marijuana did for me then—and LSD, to a certain extent—you also become more open and eager to experiment.

"The other guys in the Hollies were not into smoking. They were still the five-pints-every-night lads, and would end up scrapping, a little drunk. So the more dope I smoked and the more beer they drank, the deeper the rift between us became."

When the Hollies came to North America in February 1968, Graham was edgy and felt that his creativity was being stifled, but he carried on like a trouper. As the Hollies were arriving in Ottawa, so was Joni Mitchell, who had finished her record with Crosby and was back on the club circuit. After the Hollies' concert, both Graham and Joni happened to end up at the same radio station promo party at a Holiday Inn.

Nash recalls, "I walk into this room, get myself a Coca-Cola, and I see this woman sitting in the corner. She's got long blond hair and bangs, is wearing a blue-gray silk dress, and she has a large Bible on her knee. And the manager of the Hollies, Robert Britton, whispers in my ear, 'I want to introduce you to this person.' And I said, 'Please don't bother me now, I'm checking out this lady. I'm really interested in who the 'ell is sittin' in the corner.' He said, 'Well, if you'd just shut up for a second, that's who *I'm* talking about, *too*. This lady's name is Joni Mitchell. She's a friend of David Crosby's and she wants to talk to you.' So I walk over and say, 'So *you're* Joni Mitchell,' because David had played me some of her material and you don't have to be a fuckin' genius to realize she's one of the greatest talents on the planet. . . . So I struck up a relationship with Joni and she took me back to her hotel room and played me some songs."

Joni remembers the incident a little differently. "I didn't have a Bible on my knee," she says. "But I can see how Graham might remember it as that, because it was actually a large black antique photo album with gold edges, and it had a music box inside it, with three melodies. You wound it up with a key on the side. All of the melodies were brief little ditties, Irish or something. And at the end of every one, there'd be one note, kind of like a period, completely outside of the key that the song was in. So it would go, 'dee, daa, de, de, da, da, *deeent!*' We played that music box over and over that night, just listening for and laughing over this one stray note."

When Joni first observed Graham at this point, she says, "Superficially he was very British Mod, you know? The night I met him, I think he had an almost tuxedo-like thing on, the way the Hollies performed. Offstage, he wore these ankle-length black velvet coats and yards and yards of pink chiffon, almost foppish, like the way Jagger and a lot of the British bands dressed at the time.

Graham Nash, New York City, 1966.

"I thought Graham was very gentle, soft-spoken, and kind, with a certain degree of rock 'n' roll arrogance mixed in."

Joni's tour leapfrogged back to Los Angeles, and the Hollies were also headed in that direction. All the while, Graham was thinking about this fantastic new lady that he'd met. He also began to wonder about his California friends, David Crosby and Cass Elliot. As soon as the Hollies hit the West Coast, Nash made a point of looking up Cass and the rest. "Cass was the catalyst," says Graham. "She was the person who'd know, straight off, where everything was happening and where everything stood."

Things were loose and unsettled, as Nash soon discovered. Crosby was just hanging out. John Sebastian was hanging out. Cass was trying to keep the Mamas and the Papas alive. Stills was doing the same thing with the Buffalo Springfield.

When Crosby took Nash over to meet Stills, Graham remembers, "He was playing on this upright piano, and I think he was playing '49 Reasons.' Normally in my life, I've been a fast picker-upper of whatever's being laid down in front of me. But Stephen was a slightly different case. I saw no hint of how far out he could be physically, psychically, and musically. It was a gradual process of finding out."

Stills says, "Graham was such a *gent*. You couldn't help but love him. And he was obviously a great singer."

Graham Nash, New York City, 1966.

Nash proved this once again when the Hollies played a free show at the Whisky on February 14, 1968. Stills and the rest of the Buffalo Springfield, as well as Crosby, Sebastian, and the Mamas and the Papas all turned out. "We were stoked, man," says David. "Here was this cat who could really

sing. Graham could *really* sing. It sounded, sometimes, like he'd swallowed a trumpet!"

After this show, Nash was escorted down Sunset Strip by Crosby and Stills. Then they piled into Stills's Bentley. Crosby and Nash were in the back seat, Stills up front. As the three passed a few joints back and forth and exchanged stories, a subtle chemistry sparked between them. Finally, Stephen looked back at Crosby, gestured toward Nash, and said, "Which one of us is gonna steal him?"

Stills: Buffalo Springfield's "Last Time Around" (1968)

Crosby was ready to steal Nash immediately, but Stills, determined to drive the Springfield a while longer, backed down and watched Nash head back to England with the Hollies. Perhaps Stephen should have followed his initial instincts with Nash, because the Buffalo Springfield was fading fast.

On the final Springfield tour, Furay and Messina talked about forming a country-rock band together (they later founded Poco). Back in L.A. only Dewey Martin maintained some kind of hope for the Buffalo Springfield. But these hopes were dashed when, following the recording of Stills's "Uno Mundo," everybody gathered for an informal jam in Topanga Canyon and the session was raided by the police. Moments after Dewey Martin had left, two girls arrived with a healthy stash of marijuana. So everyone in the house was arrested—everyone, that is, except Stills. He had managed to leap out a bedroom window and scramble up the hill to road manager Chris Sarns's house, where he called a lawyer. Legal entanglements dragged on for several weeks. Then came a few more ragged live shows. After the Springfield's final show in Long Beach on May 5, 1968, the band was officially laid to rest.

"I hated to see the Buffalo Springfield break up," says Ahmet Ertegun. "But it was inevitable, at that point, because Steve and Neil had very different ideas about which way they wanted to go."

In the wake of the band's demise, a final Buffalo Springfield album was compiled by Richie Furay and produced by Jim Messina. Called, appropriately enough, *Last Time Around*, this LP is dominated by five strong Stills songs: "Four Days Gone," one of Stephen's best ever, "Pretty Girl Why," a gentle lover's plea, "Special Care," dominated by angry protest against social injustice, "Questions," which turned up again more than a year later as the second half of "Carry On" on Crosby, Stills, Nash & Young's *Déjà Vu* album, and "Uno Mundo," a lively Latin rocker that brings to the surface, for the first time, Stephen's Central American roots. The sum total of all this musical diversity on *Last Time Around* screamed out, "Stills, you can go anywhere."

Stills: Heads East / More Jams with Hendrix / Judy Collins / "Super Session" (1968)

According to Mac Holbert, a long-time friend of Stills and current Crosby, Stills & Nash tour manager, "If you put Stephen out in the middle of the desert at midnight, within an hour he'd have a guitar, a bottle of Jack Daniel's, and someone to jam with." Stephen himself admits, "Music has always been the most enduring part of my life. I've never been without it. And I've never lost the fire for it."

Even the agonizing demise of the Buf-

Stephen Stills and Peter Tork, South Dakota Indian reservation, 1967.

falo Springfield did not cause Stills to stop and take a break. In search of some more adventure and new challenges, Stephen left Los Angeles behind when the spring of 1968 turned hot. His first stop was New York and he immediately looked up Jimi Hendrix. When the infamous guitar war between Hendrix and Johnny Winter took place at the Scene, Stills was on bass.

"Winter was into the whole gunfighter syndrome, taking it seriously," says Stephen. "He tried to play so fast and couldn't relax. The only person Jimi was connected with was me. But I was so drunk I could barely see. After a while, Jimi leaned over and nudged me with his guitar, then he literally moved my hand on the bass. I was a fret off! I was cookin' in A-flat, but Hendrix was playing in A. I nearly died of embarrassment."

While in New York, Stephen also spent quite a bit of time with Judy Collins, with whom he lived for a while. Stephen toured with Judy, backing her up on guitar and bass, and played on her album *Who Knows Where the Time Goes?* "I'd be hanging out with Judy one day and Jimi the next," says Stills. "It was absolutely crazy."

Things got even crazier when Stephen got a call from former Blood, Sweat and

Tears leader Al Kooper. It seems Kooper had an idea for a "super session" album. When he was deciding who should be involved, Stills's name came to mind.

"It was one of those middle-of-the-night 'Hey, wanna come down and jam?' calls," says Stephen. "And I thought it'd be fun. The drummer, Eddie Hoh, was an old friend of mine. So I went for it."

Ensconced in the studio with multi-instrumentalist/vocalist Kooper, bassist Harvey Brooks, drummer Hoh, and keyboardist Barry Goldberg, Stills let his licks run wild. There was no pressure. He just dug in and played, particularly on a version of Donovan's "Season of the Witch."

"I wasn't signed with anybody at the time," says Stephen. "So it was a piece of cake for Al to have me on there. I just played my ax. And that was the first gold record I ever got."

In a bizarre twist of fate, shortly after *Super Session*, Stills was offered the lead singer spot in Blood, Sweat and Tears, a position previously held by Kooper. "I was flattered," Stephen says, "but I graciously declined. I didn't want to be in another big group yet."

Instead, Stills raced from session to session and played with quite a potpourri of artists. He and Duane Allman teamed up and got funky on wah-wah guitar with the

Queen of Soul, Aretha Franklin. Stephen hooked up with an old friend from Greenwich Village, Joan Baez, and added some subtle acoustic flourishes to her songs. Then one night, in the studio with Hendrix, Buddy Miles, and John Sebastian, he backed up some of Timothy Leary's poetry ("You Can Be Anyone, This Time Around" and "I've Been Around the World in My Brain, I've Settled Evolutions, No Pain"). At this time, Leary was campaigning for governor of California. Whenever things got too wild in New York, though, Stills and Hendrix would just split.

"We'd rent a limo and throw a bunch of guitars and amps in the trunk," Stephen says. "Then we'd go up to Connecticut and we'd just look for clubs and look for a good rhythm section. Then we'd go in and take over the places. Money wasn't a problem. We'd always be carrying about two or three grand in our pockets, so we could close the doors and have a private party."

Crosby: Solo Demos / "Wooden Ships" (1968)

Building Up

By March 1968, Crosby had finished producing Joni Mitchell's album and started thinking about getting a deal as a solo artist. He was particularly eager, because he was not in the best of financial shape and the government was threatening to take away his boat. Paul Rothchild remembers, "David kept knocking on my door, saying, 'Come on, man. You gotta help me. I've got to get something going *now*.' I soon realized that David always writes best when he's in trouble."

Crosby, Rothchild, and engineer Doug Botnick entered Hollywood Recorders on March 28. David sat down on a stool, put

Stephen Stills and Jimi Hendrix.

his twelve-string guitar on his knee, cleared his throat, and began singing. Over the next couple of hours he unveiled a batch of exciting new songs. Crosby's voice sounded warm and clear as he scatted around open-tuned chords throughout "Song with No Words" ("Tree with No Leaves")—released more than two years later on his first solo LP. He played "Games" and "The Wall Song" (no words yet)—both later to be included on the first Crosby and Nash album. He added a certain Byrdsian twang to "Laughing"—including simulated cymbal crashes with his voice. But perhaps the most startling piece of music he pulled out of his bag was a complicated series of chord and melody shifts that exploded into a rush of humming and guitar-flailing. This was a large chunk of what would ultimately become the music to "Wooden Ships."

"Wooden Ships" . . . Free and Easy

Crosby's periodic flights from Los Angeles in the spring of 1968 led to his own wooden ship, *The Mayan*, docked in Florida. "I've always loved sailing, but I've never been into racing," Crosby once said. "My favorite thing is to lie around in a pretty lagoon with a bunch of naked people and fall over the side and swim and goon about."

That was pretty much the scene when Paul Kantner and Grace Slick flew in for a

The Mayan. **(From the David Crosby collection—Photo by Bobby Hammer.)**

visit. Grace remembers, "Here was David's natural wood boat and all of these natural, perfectly shaped blond nude women with big boobs and tans, serving watermelon and diving into the ocean. I was impressed, but I was real skinny and all white from being in the studio with the Airplane, so I was too embarrassed to take my clothes off. I was there for three days, and it was like watching a movie that I wasn't a part of."

Grace and Paul made Crosby a part of *their* movie once, however. Kantner explains, "We spiked David with some acid cookies out in the middle of the Atlantic and he spent the entire afternoon face down on this little key."

Amid the fun and games, Crosby did manage to create some music on his boat, including "Lee Shore." He also completed the music for "Wooden Ships," which had been bouncing back and forth between him and Kantner for several months. The lyrics came about when the two of them met in Florida with Stephen Stills, who was down from New York.

"We started talking about how bad things were getting," Crosby says. "And we thought if the country kept going in the direction it was going, that it would be intolerable and we weren't at all sure if we could stay here. Then we hit upon the idea of these wooden ships that would take the people who thought like us away from all this madness. This turned into a theme for a song. I'd been writing some new music and a few words. Stills came up with a verse, Kantner wrote two or more verses, and here was this tale that was like a science fiction movie."

Wooden ships on the water, very free
Easy you know the way it's supposed to be
Silver people on the shoreline let us be
Talkin' 'bout very free and easy.

"Wooden Ships," the song, remains a stirring anthem. Kantner chose not to receive a writing credit because of legal entanglements he was experiencing with his publishing company. He later recorded it with the Jefferson Airplane, however.

"Apocalypse songs are always good food for thought," says Kantner.

But Grace Slick adds, " 'Wooden Ships' was from a very young and idealistic point of view . . . 'Oh, after the bomb, I'm gonna sail away on my wooden sailboat and go eat berries on this goddamned island' . . . Sure you are, you and all your radiated friends that are turning green."

Such dark thoughts wouldn't come until later. Filled with thoughts of this magical escape plan, Stills headed back to Jimi Hendrix and Judy Collins in New York. Grace and Paul hit the road with the Jefferson Airplane. Crosby, meanwhile, decided it was about time to check out what was going on back in Los Angeles.

Crosby: In Laurel Canyon / "Long Time Gone" (1968)

Canyon Trips

When David Crosby swooped back into Laurel Canyon in late May 1968, he was very aware of the strength to be derived from living free and in close contact with others. He was also coming to the realization that musically he wasn't ready to become a solo artist just yet. David admitted to himself, "I need some people to sing parts with, man." He went on to explain, "I'd been pretty well convinced by Jim Dickson that maybe I could sing lead in some fashion or another, but that my strongest suit was singing harmony with somebody else. So that's what I was lookin' to do."

Joni Mitchell, David Crosby, and Eric Clapton trading songs in Cass Elliott's backyard, Laurel Canyon, 1968.

He wasn't the only one. After the Lovin' Spoonful broke up, John Sebastian began intellectualizing about "life after groupdom." Cass Elliott was floating following the demise of the Mamas and the Papas. So Crosby spent hours singing and talking with Cass and John. And one afternoon, Eric Clapton from Cream came to the canyon and he and David got together with Joni Mitchell and sang until sunset.

But then, on June 6, 1968, Sirhan Sirhan gunned down Bobby Kennedy. Crosby watched the news reports flash onto his TV screen. His mind began churning up thoughts: "What's happening to this society? Is there any hope in sight?" Troubled and confused, he couldn't go to sleep that night and began to commit words to paper: "You know there's something going on around here that surely won't stand the light of day . . . And it appears to be a long time before the dawn." By morning he'd finished a new song, "Long Time Gone."

"The whole thing just smacked me in the face," Crosby says. "I saw a man, Bobby Kennedy, who I thought was someone who hadn't been bought and sold, someone who wanted to make some positive changes in America. And I believed him. Then I saw this man killed and 'Long Time Gone' was my reaction to that. I was angry."

David's anger was soon assuaged by a new love, Christine Gail Hinton. A slender beauty, she and David fell into a blissful

"David and Christine." (Photo by Bobby Hammer.)

David Crosby in Peter Tork's pool, Los Angeles, 1969.

relationship that inspired the song "Guinnevere." "Christine and I spent so much time lying around naked," says David, "that one morning I got up, jumped in my Volkswagen bus, drove down to Peter Tork's house, got out, walked through the living room, and went and lay down by the pool before I realized I hadn't put any clothes on."

David Crosby.

Stills: Back in L.A. / Reunited with Crosby (1968)

Stephen Stills came back to Los Angeles in July 1968 with a handful of new and half-finished songs. Among these were three musical fragments that dealt with an aspect of his fluctuating relationship with Judy Collins. Many of the words had been pulled from a rambling poem Stephen had written. The music grew out of a group of acoustic guitar patterns that worked together in what Stills has called "the Bruce Palmer modal tuning." One morning he fit everything into place, flailed the opening guitar licks, and sang, "It's getting to the point where I'm no fun anymore, I am sorry. Sometimes it hurts so badly I must cry out loud . . . I am lonely . . ." The words and music of "Suite: Judy Blue Eyes" streamed out into the air for the first time.

Of the song, Stills once explained to Martin Perlich, host of *Singer Songwriter:* "I was trying to say something to her [Judy Collins] about how disassociated her life was. She was always trying to do so many things and was so intense about it. Was she a folk singer? Was she in show business? Yadda, yadda . . . She was real confused about it. And I was just trying to help her out a little bit. [There's] not much more I can say . . . except I really love her."

This feeling broke through into several other songs as well. "You Don't Have to Cry," a sprightly folk tune, worked as a direct plea for love and sanity. The germ for

the composition was planted, Stephen has said, "after I'd written this love letter. Even though the letter never made it to the mailbox, the message definitely got sent through this song."

Stills roughed early versions of his songs in the studio by himself. "Whenever Ahmet [Ertegun, president of Atlantic] would give me some studio time," Stephen says, "I'd usually go in for a few hours."

"After the Springfield broke up, I decided I would throw my lot in with Steve Stills," says Ahmet. "Because Steve was kind of the driving force in the group, I knew that he would come up with something great."

As an experiment, Stephen once recorded a version of Traffic's "Dear Mr. Fantasy." He sang every part and played every instrument himself. The finished product (which remains unreleased) has been heard by few people. David Crosby is one of the lucky ones and he told *Rolling Stone,* "Goddamn, man, it made Traffic look like a bad second band at the Whisky. I mean, it was tight shit."

The same could be said of the original demo version of "49 Reasons," recorded on an eight-track machine, with Bill Halverson engineering, at Wally Heider's Studio III. Stephen overdubbed a "backwards guitar," bass, keyboards, drums, and vocals. Again, he played everything.

To give himself a bit more flexibility,

Stephen started looking for a drummer. John Sebastian suggested Dallas Taylor, formerly with a band known as Clearlight. Stills remembers, "Dallas just called me up and said, 'Listen, man. I play my ass off. You gotta hear me.' I went, 'Hey, all right, sure.' He came over and he was great."

Together, Stills and Taylor demoed some songs and jammed. As Stills once told Michael Watts in *Zig Zag*, however, "One day, we suddenly realized a drummer and a guitarist do not a band make."

Stephen briefly hooked up with former Traffic guitarist Dave Mason, but, says Stills, "He wanted to be a solo. What could I say?"

"I really needed another element," Stephen continues. "And then I thought about Crosby and said to myself, 'Now there's a pro. That guy thinks just like I do.'"

A short while later, Stills and Crosby got together. "It's funny," says David. "Not a whole lot was discussed. But the minute we started playing together again, I knew we were gonna be hot shit. We started playing 'Long Time Gone' and I could hear something was happening."

Stills agrees. "The chemistry that bubbled between us is something that neither one of us had experienced in a while."

"Stephen, man," Crosby gushes. "Here's a guy who's always loved to play music, with his whole heart and soul. He eats it for breakfast, rubs it in his hair. Stills, man, the cat plays music twenty-five hours a day! And knowing me, isn't that just the kind of guy I'd want to hang out with?"

Crosby and Stills: "The Frozen Noses" (1968)

Crosby and Stills quickly became inseparable. "We would get up around midday or so," David says, "trot down to one of the places on Sunset, and grab some shitty breakfast. Then we'd get high and start playing' guitar and singin'. And we would play guitar and sing *all day*, until we couldn't stand up, until we'd fall down, exhausted. Then we'd go to sleep, get up, and do it all over again. That's how we got so damn tight."

One afternoon, while Crosby and Stills were singing away in Cass Elliott's backyard, they decided to commit some songs to tape. So they pooled all of their guitars and amps, loaded them into Crosby's VW bus, rolled down the Canyon and into Wally Heider's studio in Hollywood, and began recording. The engineer for these sessions, Henry Lewy, recalls, "Right away they started doing everything themselves. They were like little geniuses. At one point, Stills was playing drums, then guitar, then organ. I'd seen other multitalented people before, but none as equally adept at every instrument."

Stills tracked in six different guitar parts on "Long Time Gone" alone. Crosby spruced up the atmosphere with some rhythm guitar swipes, then concentrated on his vocals. The only other musician involved was Jefferson Airplane bassist Jack Casady.

"Ol' Thundercrunch, I used to call him," says David. "But when he came in and played the bass part for 'Guinnevere,' it was like the most lyrical thing he ever recorded. It worked almost like another voice in there."

Henry Lewy agrees: "I just sat there with my mouth hanging open when 'Guinnevere' came together. The music, the words, and those harmonies. I'd been working with the Mamas and the Papas. So I knew good harmonies. What Crosby and Stills were doing was somehow sweeter. It was a joy to see these two . . . very amiable, in complete harmony, working away, creating some miracles."

"Guinnevere" and "Long Time Gone,"

two of Crosby's finest, joined Stills's equally impressive, previously demoed "49 Reasons" on an acetate. Several copies were produced for distribution to certain record companies. However, Crosby recalls, "B. Mitchell Reed [the late L.A. disc jockey] got ahold of one of 'em somehow. God knows how it happened. And he started playing the songs on the radio. He introduced 'em, 'Now here's some music by a local group called the Frozen Noses.'" David giggles, "Stills and I were just starting to become cokeheads at the time, so the name Frozen Noses was, well, it spoke for itself. I remember telling B. Mitchell Reed to stop calling us that. I mean, it didn't do a hell of a lot for our reputations. But the music was sounding so good, man, we could have been called anything and it wouldn't have really mattered."

CHAPTER FOUR

Crosby, Stills & Nash (1968–1969) The First Union

Crosby, Stills & Nash: The Sound Is Born in Laurel Canyon (1968)

Crosby and Stills had put something together that excited both of them. Their tight vocal blend would be at the heart of many of Cass Elliot's swimming-pool sing-alongs. Nightly, all of the Laurel Canyon folkies between bands would shed their clothes and spend hours soaking in Cass's pool. "It was consistently kept at 98.8 degrees," says Sebastian. "You'd get in there and want to pee in under four minutes. It was terrific for becoming psychedelicized, staring up into the stars, and singing."

John Sebastian, 1969.

Sebastian's own pool was the site for several of these "liquid jams." Once, David, Stephen, Sebastian, Cass, Paul Rothchild, and designer Gary Burden congregated at Sebastian's. Everyone jumped in the water except Stills, who plopped down on the edge of the diving board, started picking his guitar, and broke out two songs, "Helplessly Hoping" and "You Don't Have to Cry." Moonlight gleamed on Stills's Martin guitar while he and Crosby harmonized through the rising steam. Sebastian and Cass joined in. Afterwards, Sebastian suggested, "You know, Stephen, you really need a high voice to get over you, so you can sing the melody." Everyone bobbed in the water and thought for a moment. Then Sebastian continued, "There are two great high harmony singers in the world right now. One of them is Phil Everly. The other is Graham Nash."

Back in England, Graham was still desperately trying to dissuade the Hollies from recording an album of Bob Dylan songs. He also had separated from his wife and was now living with Larry Kurzon, a friend working for the William Morris Agency's British interests. In light of these developments, Nash's life was unstable as the summer of 1968 wore on.

After a particularly heated argument

with the Hollies, Graham stared blankly at the band he'd grown up with. He felt utterly frustrated that his new songs and ideas were not being listened to. Later, alone in a coffee bar near the studio, he started thinking once again about his friends back in Los Angeles.

"I wanted to sing with Graham as soon as I heard 'King Midas in Reverse,' " says Crosby. "It was definitely in my mind to do that. I sent him a tape of 'Guinnevere' and 'Long Time Gone.' But I didn't think he'd really leave the Hollies."

"We thought such an idea would be preposterous," says Stills. "The only person who knew how unhappy Graham was was Cass."

Cass was the only member of "the Laurel Canyon Gang" with whom Graham had shared his deepest feelings. Both over the phone and in person, he opened up to her and let everything pour out. So it's not surprising that Cass was the main person Nash thought of when the Hollies situation and his marriage went awry. She would provide support and might offer some insights Graham hadn't thought of. So, in July 1968, he decided to take a short vacation trip to Los Angeles. Twenty-four hours later, he was there.

As soon as he saw Cass Elliot's smiling face, Graham knew he'd made the right decision. Laurel Canyon felt like home, and

Cass Elliot, Los Angeles, 1968.

all of his troubles back in England seemed so very far away.

In just a few days, Crosby, Stills & Nash would sing together for the first time. The circumstances surrounding this event have, with the passage of years, become Hollywood folklore. The only consistently reported *fact* is that, yes, these three voices did come together in a living room in Laurel Canyon for the first time in the summer of 1968. Whose living room? It depends who you talk to. Crosby has always insisted it was Joni Mitchell's. In a couple of early interviews, Stills remembered it as being Sebastian's (as did John himself). Now Stephen says it was Cass's. Nash vacillated between Cass's and Joni's; now he says it was Cass's. Paul Rothchild says, "I tell ya, it was Sebastian's, all the others were after the fact." Bill Chadwick of the Monkees' show says, "Man, I was *there*. It happened at Doug Weston's." Elliot Roberts stands firm: "I remember it as being Joni's." Ron Stone (who now lives there), agrees. Unfortunately there were no tape recorders, no news reports. No one even kept a definitive journal! So who's right? Joni Mitchell, ever the diplomat, says, "They're *all* right."

For the sake of poetic setting, one hopes it was Joni's place. She describes it as "a little house, kind of like a treehouse. It was green, had a rural feeling to it, and was built into the side of a hill on Lookout Mountain Road. So when the trees spread out, the branches were right at the windows. Birds flew in and nested. It was a charmed little place, built by a black jazz piano player in the twenties as a weekend project. It had a kind of soulfulness and was full of knotty pine, which was kind of our interior anthem at the time. That was hippie heaven, with a little rustic fireplace and a good feeling.

"Sometimes people would drop in singularly, or sometimes a group would congregate. There would be nights when every-

Joni Mitchell playing her dulcimer on the front steps of her house in Laurel Canyon, 1970.

body sat up and played acoustic music and swapped songs. Everyone was particularly fertile."

Wherever it was, it seems that Crosby and Stills were singing together one afternoon in the company of Nash, Joni, Cass, Sebastian, and Rothchild. As Crosby and Stills continued to harmonize on each other's songs, Nash cocked his head and listened. But he didn't sing or say a word. Then they sang Stills's "You Don't Have to Cry."

"Sing that again," Graham requested.

Crosby and Stills shrugged and ran through the song again.

"Please, play it once more," Nash said.

And for the third time, the song was performed.

Nash closed his eyes for a moment, opened them, then asked, "Play it . . . *again.*"

David and Stephen looked at each other, then at Nash. They all giggled. Then Stills put his head down and plucked the intro on his guitar. The first line rose up, "In the morning when you rise . . ." Crosby and Stills's harmony chimed together and, simultaneously, over the top of the blend, came Nash's high cry. When this three-part harmony arched up, it hung in the air and everyone in the room froze. What was that sound? Crosby, Stills & Nash raised goose pimples on themselves.

"I hear bells," said Nash, laughing.

Crosby started chuckling. Stills started "You Don't Have to Cry" again. On into the night, the trio locked voices and sang and sang and sang—oblivious to anyone around them.

"It was scary," says Crosby. "But once we knew what we had, you could not pry us apart with a crowbar. We knew we'd lucked onto something so special, man. We could hear it plain as day."

But Stills recalls, "Even though we knew the combination was a winner, David and I didn't really think it could happen. I remember we were talking about it as we drove home after that first time and David was saying, 'No, man, Graham would never do it, the Hollies have been together forever . . . but, boy, what a sound!' So we didn't dare approach him and came to the conclusion that we'd get Cass to ask him. We were just too afraid."

But as it turned out, Crosby and Stills had little to worry about. Nash says, "The minute I heard how our voices sounded together, I was physically and musically linked with David and Stephen from then on."

Crosby, Stills & Nash in Gary Burden's backyard, Hollywood, 1969.

Joni Mitchell recalls, "The feeling between them was very high, almost amorous, you know? There was a tremendous amount of affection and enthusiasm running back and forth among them. And the sound . . . it was so fresh. *They* were fresh. Part of the thrill for me being around them was seeing how they were exciting themselves, mutually. They'd hit a chord and go, 'Whooooaa!' then fall together, laughing."

John Sebastian says, "Although I'd been impressed with Graham's range, Crosby's harmony sense, and Stephen's sort of bluesy quality, I don't think anything could have prepared me for how this particular trio of voices blended together. The sound was magical, otherworldly harmony, like nothing I'd ever heard before."

"For the next several days," says Paul Rothchild, "they hit the road and played all the hippest houses in L.A. They threw their shit up the flagpole to see if anyone would salute. Well, not only did people salute, they fell down on their knees! At that point, Crosby, Stills & Nash could have started a religion."

"They'd hit a chord and go, 'Whooooaa!' then fall together, laughing," remembers Joni Mitchell.

CSN: Nash Leaves the Hollies / CSN Record for the First Time (1968)

When David, Stephen, and Graham eventually dropped back down to earth, they had to face the reality of uniting as a band. This would take some doing. Crosby and Stills were as free as tomcats. Nash, on the other hand, was still technically in the Hollies and signed to EMI/CBS. "In my mind," says Nash, "I had already left the Hollies."

But he needed to tell them. On the flight back to England, Nash says, "I felt both elated and sad. I was sad that my personality was not strong enough to move the Hollies in a way that I thought we should go as a band. But I was *elated* that I'd heard what me, David, and Stephen could do. Once you hear something like that—it's taken me mere microseconds to hear beauty my whole life—I saw that CSN sound so fast it was absolutely silly."

Of course, when Graham related all the particulars of his visit to Los Angeles to the Hollies, they were shattered. Allan Clarke, Graham's mate since grade school, felt the worst. "I took it as a personal thing," Allan says. "I'd always thought we'd be together the rest of our lives. I relied a lot on our friendship. So I felt bad. I was in a state of shock."

"When Graham left," Clarke told *Circus* in 1972, "I thought, 'What the hell are we gonna do?' He's the spokesman, the leader, the trendsetter . . . he was trying to bend things his way and we were going for it, but we were too slow for him. He was always ahead of me; he always has been, right from the beginning, when we first started off. He was the guy who would go on stage and say, 'Hello, folks, you gotta clap,' and I'd be going, 'Oh, don't say that.' I was always behind him, like two years be-hind Graham, but I always got to it eventually."

But Nash was not interested in waiting, in view of his new musical discovery. To the Hollies, his other friends, and the British press—who had yet to hear what CSN sounded like—Nash seemed to be acting like a fool.

Graham responded, "Wealth and fame can only be so important in the face of musical magic."

Having communicated this message, Nash also set in motion a divorce from his wife. The ties that bind would all be severed, he was starting a brand new life. Between final commitments with the Hollies and divorce proceedings, Nash flew back to Los Angeles for a brief rendezvous with Stills and Crosby. They locked voices again, and the magic was still there. They *hadn't* been dreaming. To make doubly sure, it was decided they would head into the studio.

"But I've only got another day," said Nash.

"Wait a minute," said Crosby, "Paul Rothchild's at the Record Plant in New York. If we leave now, we can make it there by morning."

They took the red-eye flight from L.A. to New York. And at 10:00 A.M., a taxi carrying Crosby, Stills & Nash arrived at the Record Plant. With Paul Rothchild already inside, busy readying the board, CSN filed into the studio and went to work, recording "Helplessly Hoping" and "You Don't Have to Cry."

"I experimented with doubling their voices," says Rothchild. "They were afraid it was going to sound too Association-y. But the effect was great. Stephen played bass, guitar, and piano. And instead of drums, we put on a tambourine and guitar whacks. Great sound."

Nash says, "I think the version we got of 'In the Morning When You Rise' [a.k.a. "You Don't Have to Cry"] was better and had more life, in my opinion, than the one that got on the album."

This album was still far off, though. Nash was not out of the Hollies yet, and as soon as the sessions with Rothchild were completed, Graham was en route back to England. Under less than comfortable circumstances, Nash recorded another song with the Hollies, called "Listen to Me." Meanwhile, Stills told Ahmet Ertegun about "this great new sound" that the CSN amalgam had stumbled upon. But no written commitments were made.

With Nash over in London with the Hollies, Crosby was getting nervous. He was worried that tradition and old ties might cause Nash to reconsider his decision to go with Crosby and Stills. In the middle of this concern, David called Graham in England and said, "Hey, man, we don't want to wait any longer. Stephen and I are gonna come over as soon as we get some cash." While Crosby said this, Stills walked into the room, pulled out his wallet, and spread twenty-five one-hundred-dollar bills on the floor. Crosby and Stills were in England a day later.

Two benefits, one with Pete Townshend and Tiny Tim, and another, sponsored by Princess Margaret, were the final live appearances the Hollies made with Graham Nash. During this period, Crosby says, "Me and Stephen weren't taking any chances. That's why we went to England. We didn't want to let the Hollies get their hooks back into Graham. Boy, Allan Clarke was really giving me the stink-eye. He was definitely thinking, 'Yankee, go home.'"

Crosby, Stills & Nash, February 1969.

But a course was already set. On December 8, 1968, Nash was in the Hollies. The next day he joined forces with Crosby and Stills.

CSN: Together in London on Moscow Road (1968)

"We Are Not a Group"

They were together at last, but they were not yet calling themselves Crosby, Stills & Nash. That particular name combination would not come until about halfway through the recording of the first album. At this early stage in England, they were just known as "these three lads." Crosby went so far as to say, "We are not a group, just an aggregate of friends."

Graham Nash elaborated upon this idea to a British reporter: "The essential difference between us and a typical group is the commitment involved. We don't want to feel as if we have to be in a certain place at a certain time, or arrange our lives to suit anybody but ourselves. If one is into something groovy, and something groovier comes along, one should go and do that. We have all paid our dues. . . . Now we want to try something different."

In December 1969, *Rolling Stone* asked Crosby to describe the sound. He responded, "There's a whole bunch of it that just don't make it with words—its like trying to describe fucking."

Moscow Road

"We were eager, young, and *hungry*," says Stephen Stills. "All we needed to do was get it right. So we figured we'd stay in England for a while, stay away from everyone we knew in the industry. The English

have a lot more respect for people's privacy."

David, Graham, and Stephen took a small apartment together in London, on Moscow Road. "You should have tasted the great bread and hot chocolate they had in this store next to us," says Crosby.

Nash recalls, "What David *really* wanted was this sign that hung in the window near the butcher's counter. It read, 'All Joints Must Be Re-Weighed at Time of Purchase.' David wanted that sign *badly*. So one day I went up to the butcher and said, 'I'll have four pork chops, that piece of lamb roast, a half-pound of liver—and that sign.' I managed to pry it out of the guy, bought it, and gave it to Crosby. Made him a happy little bear."

Close bonds developed among the three while they traded songs and experimented with harmonies on into the wee hours of the night. "We just didn't want to stop singing," says Stills. But a downstairs neighbor felt a little differently. Crosby remembers, "We were playing real loud at four in the morning when we got this very dignified, kind, and reserved note from a neighbor. It read [David adopts a prim English accent], 'It *would* be nice . . . if you could play just a little more quietly at four in the morning. Because, you see, I have to get up at five in the morning to get to work. So if you could please try and turn down, just a *little* bit, it would be nice.' We saved that note for the longest time."

Crosby, Stills and Nash managed to avoid eviction and, says Graham, "We were so high on hash half the time, we were just floating." There was a two-track recorder in the building, but none of the three singers can remember if they actually committed anything to tape. "Some of that time's a bit of a fog," says Nash.

What he does remember, however, is the presence of the Beatles. "They had recorded the White Album *[The Beatles],*"

Graham says. "And when we heard McCartney do 'Blackbird,' we flipped and learned it right away. That song was made for our three-part."

After one of their interactions with the Beatles, Stills penned a song called, "The Doctor Will See You Now Mr. L." for John Lennon. Nash laments, "We didn't record it. And none of us can remember it now. All I can recall is the last line, which was, 'And I'll take some horses and ride off into the sunset.' It may sound pretty hokey, but it was a great piece of cinema. A lost gem, perhaps."

But this trio had plenty of other songs that were being rehearsed to perfection. "Suite: Judy Blue Eyes," "Helplessly Hoping," "Guinnevere," "Lady of the Island," "Wooden Ships," "Marrakesh Express," and "You Don't Have to Cry" were among them. "When we could sing an album's worth of songs top to bottom," says Stills, "we invited George Harrison over to listen, to see if the Beatles' Apple label might be interested in us. After we finished he went, 'Wow!' Then he turned us down! The English attitude toward American musicians was a lot more competitive than I expected. 'Flippin' Yanks, tryin' to steal our thunder, eh?' And little ol' naïve Stephen from down there in Florida was just tryin' to be friendly. A little encouragement from our limey mates wouldn't have hurt."

Nash talked to Harrison about this in 1983. And Graham says, "George told me he'd heard us on tape, but I don't remember making any tapes in England then. We *could* have. But, anyway, George tells me, 'It's damn lucky CSN didn't end up on Apple, because things were so totally chaotic, you would have been swallowed up in the bullshit.' So I guess the luckiest thing that ever happened to CSN is that we didn't end up on Apple."

Crosby says, "Everything that should have happened for us *did* happen. We knew what we had. And we knew we were gonna knock everybody on their asses."

CSN: Christmas in L.A. / Rehearsals in Sag Harbor, New York (1968–1969)

Winter Harmony

Crosby, Stills & Nash were cocky as hell when they flew into Los Angeles a few days before Christmas in 1968. And it was a happy emotional time for each for them. Graham was rekindling his relationship with Joni Mitchell. David was falling deeper in love with Christine Hinton. And Stephen basked in the glow of knowing that he might have found, at last, "the best band in the world."

One night, everyone gathered at Gary Burden's house, made Christmas cookies, and sang carols while decorating the tree. "Silent Night," Silver Bells," and "What Child Is This" were magnificent when delivered by Crosby, Stills, Nash, Mitchell, Elliot, and Sebastian. Leah Kunkel, Cass Elliot's sister, says, "Hearing the Christmas choir was so special. It's a memory I will always treasure."

January 1969: New York was covered with snow. The city was peaceful, and this suited David, Graham, and Stephen just fine. They had decided once again to leave Los Angeles behind to get ready for some "official" recording sessions. John Sebastian had found them a house, a few down from his own in Sag Harbor, a sleepy artists' community on Long Island—the perfect place to rehearse and create without distraction.

"Another reason we were there is because I wanted to be close to Judy [Collins]," says Stephen. "I mean, I *loved* her, but that relationship was already beginning to fall apart."

"We had purpose, we had great spirit and we had these voices," says Nash. Beyond that, they had a couple of acoustic guitars. What else did they need? According to Graham, "Nothing. I thought it was going to be an acoustic album. It had started out that way. But Stephen had other ideas."

When Stills and Crosby, then eventually Nash, had worked on John Sebastian's solo album a few months earlier, many of the tracks had included the rhythm section of bassist Harvey Brooks, drummer Dallas Taylor, and keyboardist Paul Harris. Stills wanted to see how this same group would work behind CSN. "It was a little weird," Nash recalls, "but interesting."

John Sebastian recalls, "I knew that Stephen wanted a drummer who wouldn't mind being lost in the mix. It was going to be that kind of record. And I knew Dallas had worked for me. I figured he'd work for them."

Sebastian was right. Living room rehearsals raged for a couple of weeks and Taylor was the only player, other than CSN, who fit into the sound. Nash still admits, "We were feeling our way. I remember it snowing like hell and we'd be inside next to a beautiful crisp fire with lots of wood. A fine time. We were getting it."

Dallas Taylor. Rehearsal at Stephen's house, 1969.

"I was worried they were taking too long," says Sebastian. "I thought they might blow it and peak before ever getting into the studio."

Graham, David, and Stephen weren't worried, however. In fact, they even wrote some new songs in Sag Harbor. Nash wrote "Teach Your Children" there. Crosby wrote "Almost Cut My Hair." He explains, "The whole polarization of the country was

David Crosby, Hollywood, 1969.

starting to happen. And it had gone from 'Hey, are you a boy or a girl?' to 'Goddamn hippies, let's *kill* 'em all.' That was pretty intense."

CSN: Find Managers / Sign with Atlantic Records (1969)

The pregnancy was over. Cabin fever was setting in and "the boys" were ready to move. All they needed was a manager and a record deal.

"My agent friend, Larry Kurzon, had heard us," says Nash, "and he wanted to manage us. Paul Rothchild wanted to be our producer and wanted points. That was early on."

Crosby remembers, "We ended up going with David Geffen, because we were in a shark pool and needed a *shark*. But even

Elliot Roberts and David Geffen at Lookout Management office, Los Angeles, 1971.

though we knew David was smart and would do a good job, I never thought he was that nice a guy and I didn't trust him all the time. So we needed an insurance policy. A watchdog. That was Elliot Roberts. I knew him from working with Joni and I knew he'd look out for our best interests. Elliot was more of a *mensch*. So he balanced things out."

Nash agrees: "Elliot became an incredible translator of our madness. He had an ability to oversee us and keep us from our own worst behavior. Of all of the people around us in those early days, Elliot was the one who kept us together. He was a

Elliot Roberts with CSN, 1970. "He had an ability to oversee us and keep us from our own worst behavior."

street manager, a scoundrel, bright, funny, an honorable man."

Roberts says, "I believed I had the wave of the future. Joni's first album was successful, not in sales, particularly, but in an artistic, creative way. Neil was going to happen. The Crosby, Stills & Nash sound was magical and I was of the school that believed everyone was getting Airplaned and psychedelicized out. So here I was representing all of these singer/songwriters and that sound hadn't quite blossomed yet. But I thought I had what would be that sound's strongest elements. And I knew it would just be a matter of time before I ruled the world."

Toward that end, Geffen and Stills hit upon a plan that culminated in CSN signing with Atlantic. "We were morally committed to Ahmet from the start," says Stills. "He was really like the Mother Superior of this group."

"Steve called me," remembers Ahmet, "and said that he was working with this trio—made up of himself, David Crosby, and an English singer from the Hollies. He said they were terrific-sounding and I'd be very excited by them. They were out in Long Island somewhere. When I first heard the Crosby, Stills & Nash demo, I thought they were very similar to the Everly Brothers, but better. It was a three-way harmony as opposed to a two-way harmony. And it still had some of the feeling of the Buffalo Springfield, but augmented. I knew they were going to be great."

But before CSN could sign with Atlantic, a deal had to be struck to free Nash from his EMI contract in England and Epic in America. In addition to a few financial shifts, Nash was traded by Epic (a CBS subsidiary) for Richie Furay, still under contract to Atlantic. The rationale behind this exchange worked in both parties' favor. Nash needed to be with Crosby and Stills on Atlantic in order to get an album off the

Crosby, Stills & Nash, West Hollywood, 1969.

ground; Furay, just starting Poco, felt good about being on a label, Columbia, that had a solid reputation in the country field. So, after one of the most unusual business deals in recording industry history, Crosby, Stills & Nash were finally on Atlantic and ready to record.

CSN: The First Album (1969)

Rain was falling in Los Angeles when Crosby, Stills & Nash came back to town. It was February 1969, and muddy streams of water flowed down from the canyons. It was a time to be indoors. And that was where David, Graham, and Stephen were going to be for awhile, inside Wally Heider's studio on the corner of Cahuenga

and Selma in Hollywood. Bill Halverson, the studio manager, remembers, "I saw their name come up on the schedule and I put my thumb on it. I'd done that eight-track with Stephen. I knew all of their backgrounds. So

Bill Halverson, 1969.

I asked to become their engineer. It was agreeable with them. It was agreeable with Atlantic.

"I didn't know what I was getting myself into until the first night. They all showed up in Crosby's VW bus. I asked them what they wanted to do. They said, 'Tonight we're going to sing and play acoustic guitars.' Stephen sat right down and

Recording vocals on "Marakesh Express" at Wally Heider's studio, Los Angeles, 1969.

played guitar for about seven minutes and that became the basic track for 'Suite: Judy Blue Eyes.' "

When Halverson put a microphone on the Crosby, Stills & Nash vocal blend for the first time, he says, "It was amazing what their voices did together. The tightness was incredible. I don't think any of us were quite prepared for the power that came out of that blend. They would lean together around one mike and get takes with such ease."

"What a joy those sessions were," says Crosby. "We got a lot of air mixes [locked-in harmonies]. Very often we'd walk in and get a song on the first try. Graham's 'Lady of the Island' was like that. I sang that nice little fugue in the middle on one pass."

Of that song, Nash reveals, "The islands in question are Ibiza and Long Island. It's about two different women. It's a song for two ladies meshed into one. Warm . . . gentle feeling."

While the recording of Stills's "49 Bye-Byes" was coming together (it began as two songs—"49 Reasons" and "Bye-Bye Baby"), former Hollies publicist Allan McDougall dropped by for a listen, accompanied by Elliot Roberts and Ahmet Ertegun. McDougall remembers, "I was in rock 'n' roll heaven. And when the boys harmonized on the line 'bye-bye baby,' I went, 'Oh, good Christ,' and I don't think my nipples have softened since."

"There was a lot of happiness in CSN at that time," says Ahmet. "When they were making that first record, it was very joyful meeting and working with them. I loved the boys, the boys loved me, and the whole thing was very, very . . . it was really one of the most wonderful experiences I've had in the record business."

More friends arrived. Cass Elliott, John Sebastian, and Joni Mitchell were among them. "They'd come in," says Nash. "We'd sing and always blow 'em away. When they'd leave, they'd be like zombies."

It was not a perpetual party, however. Stills quipped at the time, "For two bucks a minute, we don't have time to socialize."

Stephen took this project very seriously. He knew right from the beginning that he was going to be responsible for most of the complex instrumental tracks. Crosby was a solid rhythm guitarist, but had never played much lead. Nash was simply an adequate acoustic guitarist, Taylor a dependable drummer. So it was left to Stills to create and execute all of the bass parts, the lead guitar, most of the finger-picked acoustic and complex rhythm guitar, and

says. "And I was just trying to get the best out of everyone's songs. So they let me run with it. There were no egos. Everyone was surprisingly cooperative. We worked together and still gave each other room. I've never felt such support since."

"Stephen felt very comfortable with CSN right away," says Elliot Roberts. "He was easily the heaviest of the musicians and knew, 'Hey, I've got two guys who will listen and who are great.' It was ideal for Stephen."

"Sometimes," says Nash, "Stephen just needed to work by himself. He'd say something like, 'Listen, didn't you say you were

Stephen Stills as "Captain Manyhands."

all of the organ. Crosby and Nash immediately dubbed Stills "Captain Manyhands."

"I hadn't found anyone who could play these parts like I heard them," Stephen

going to get a burger?' And we would leave."

It was under such circumstances that Stills came up with the lead guitar that flies over "Marrakesh Express," and the spiraling guitar (recorded backwards) in "Pre-Road Downs." After a long, frustrating attempt at injecting more life into "Long Time Gone," everybody called it a night—except Stills and Dallas Taylor. As the studio clock clicked away—3:00 A.M., 4:00 A.M., 5:00 A.M., 7:00 A.M.—Stephen worked with maniacal intensity, recording new bass, organ, and guitar parts for a brand-new chorus section. By 8:00 A.M., Stills had "the track" and staggered home, exhausted, but satisfied.

Ten hours later, Stephen came back to the studio and unveiled the *new* "Long Time Gone." Crosby and Nash were startled. "Captain Manyhands does it again!" shouted Graham. David was already on his way into the recording chamber, where he unleashed an aggressive vocal that was unlike any part he had ever sung before. In Ellen Sander's book, *Trips*, Crosby described the experience: "I finally found my voice. Five years I've been singing and I finally found a voice of my own. Every time I sang a lead part with the Byrds, I choked up, because I was so scared. But these two loved me enough to let me find my own voice."

During the playback of his vocal on "Long Time Gone," he couldn't suppress a loud chuckle. His mustache quivered. His eyes glimmered. "Nice work, Fat Bear," said Nash. "Your turn, Razor Throat," shot back Crosby. And out into the studio went Graham to crest the chorus with a high harmony that sliced through the air, clean and sharp.

"Those first album sessions got to levels of unbelievable connection," says Nash. "When you find someone that you're psychically linked with, it's a fortunate thing. When you find *two* people like that and you're in the same room with them, it's *scary*. There's a certain look in the eyes. We got really out there. It got to the point

David Crosby awaiting cue.

where we would make mistakes deliberately, because one knew the other two were going to make the mistake and wanted it to sound the same. Unbelievable stuff like that happened."

Whenever anyone *really* hit a clinker, Bill Halverson says, "They'd throw an 'air pie' at whoever did it, laugh, then move on." One night, however, the emotional level in the studio suddenly got tense and no amount of joking around seemed to help. So road manager Chris Sarns, Christine Hinton, and a couple of other friends went out and came back with some *real* cream pies. When CSN walked out into the studio to try another vocal pass, they got bombarded. Cream and crust flew everywhere. This snapped the tension, and everybody laughed except Stills. He was pissed because he happened to be wearing a wolf-fur coat, and he sat down in a corner and

Graham Nash. ". . . a high harmony that sliced through the air . . ."

It's a good thing they didn't have some domineering producer around. If there were ten hands on the console, so be it. That's the way it was. I was flying by the seat of my pants a lot of the time. Nash had some production experience. Stephen was real intent on learning how to mix."

Stephen Stills adds his part.

furiously tried to wipe the cream off the fur.

"Loose times," says Crosby. "We loved each other a lot, man. And we'd get so high. I cannot tell a lie. We used to smoke a joint and snort a line before every session. That was a ritual."

Crosby also made a habit of coming up with spontaneous vocal outbursts between takes. "Sounded like Russian to me," says Halverson. It was more like "Crosbian." What earthly language does this resemble? "Whoopa-a-mess-a-hooga-hoffa-a-messi-goush-goush." That bit of insanity made it onto the CSN album between "Suite: Judy Blue Eyes" and "Marrakesh Express." "When David was feelin' really good," says Graham, "we just let him fly."

Through all of this, Halverson sat back behind the mixing board. He says, "It was a process of giving them freedom to create.

"Halverson," says Stills, "taught me all I know about the electronic processes of production. I'd record something and he'd say, 'Balance it.' He understood that sometimes only Stephen Stills can tell what Stephen Stills hears, ya dig? And some of the guitar tones on that first album, we used to giggle about how *fat* we got 'em. How many other albums in 1969 had guitar tones like that?"

"Stephen switched guitars a lot," says Halverson, "and he always knew how to get the right sound for the right spot."

It was Halverson's job to capture this

on tape. Once, however, he remembers, "Stephen had smashed his fingers in a minor car accident, so he was having trouble with this bass part. When he finally got it, I didn't record it. When Stephen found this out, he walked over and put his foot through a door. I went back five years later and there was still a patch over the hole Stephen had made."

"When any of us lost it or when it got totally crazy," says Nash, "we turned to our alter egos, 'the Reliability Brothers.' They were always *on*. CSN in phantom form. I can remember yelling, 'Hey, the Reliability Brothers, man. We can fuckin' do it.' Then there'd be some great take. We must have over a thousand tapes that begin, 'Reliability Brothers, take . . . '"

The Reliability Brothers, Fat Bear, Captain Manyhands, Razor Throat . . . who were these guys, really? What was it going to say on the album cover? "We definitely wanted to use our own names," says Crosby. "We'd decided that. Because we didn't want to be locked into roles. We didn't want to be replaceable parts. We wanted the freedom to pursue solo careers. Also, we were proud of ourselves and didn't want to get lost behind some dumb band name."

"We were tired of playing behind animals," says Stills. "This project was *ours*."

But what about the order of the billing? "I left the room when that was being decided," says Crosby. "To me," says Nash, "Crosby, Stills & Nash was the only combination and order that rolled off the tongue. It had nothing to do with whose name was first or last. We just needed a combination with its own meter, its own rhythm that would be easy for people to latch on to. Crosby, Stills & Nash was it."

And these three guys really were the band. Dallas Taylor drummed, came up with some ideas, and worked on production. Jim Gordon played the drums on "Marrakesh Express." Cass Elliot sang in the middle of the bridge of harmonies on "Pre-Road Downs." But that was it. Everything else was CSN. Consequently, it was possible for these three eager characters to wander into somebody's living room and virtually *perform* the album right there on a couch. Nash remembers, "We would sit people down and say, '*Listen*.' And then we would sit down and play 'Suite: Judy Blue Eyes' right in front of them, *great*. And we would follow it with 'Helplessly Hoping,' 'You Don't Have to Cry,' 'Marrakesh Express,' 'Right Between the Eyes,' 'Guinnevere,' 'Long Time Gone.' By the time they'd sat down and listened to this hour of music, they were *on the floor!* We used to play deliberately to blow people away."

When CSN paid a visit to Modern Folk Quartet singer Cyrus Faryar's farm, he recalls, "I'd just painted this big old piano I had pink. And when CSN stopped in, they were jacked up to the max. They'd just come from the studio and David said, 'Wanna hear our record?' and they performed it for me! I fell on the floor. David, of all of them, seemed most thrilled with it all. With that sound—so enthusiastic, clear, and concise—they could pay off a lot of spiritual debts."

With album sessions winding down, CSN could see the whole take shape. They kept trying to get "Blackbird" down, but finally decided to go with just their own material. The night before they were to complete final mixing, Crosby, Stills & Nash huddled together and listened to their work. As track after track unfolded, they'd laugh, clap, and sigh. They were like happy little kids who had just finished a school project. But when the tape ended, Stills said, "Hey, guys, uh, could we do 'The Suite' over again?" Crosby and Nash exchanged startled glances, then laughed. In the next six hours, CSN succeeded in recording "Suite: Judy Blue Eyes" all over again. "Then," says Nash, "we listened to the two versions back to back and ended up using the original one. It was just better. And we didn't want to fuck with greatness."

Crosby, Stills & Nash were also concerned that the album cover should reflect the intimacy and the special quality of the music. It had to look natural. It had to look real. While driving around Hollywood with album cover designer Gary Burden, Graham Nash spotted an old abandoned house near the corner of Palm Avenue and Santa Monica Boulevard. "That's it," they both agreed. Later, CSN met Burden and photographer Henry Diltz there, and the album cover was shot. "The couch, the house, the palm tree—it was all there. Nothing was added," says Diltz. (Later, though, Dallas Taylor's face was stripped into the back window.)

When the proofs of these original shots came back from the lab, it was discovered that the *order* was wrong. The guys were sitting on the couch as Nash, Stills, and Crosby, rather than CSN.

"So we went back to reshoot the cover," says Burden, "but the house had been torn down! All that was left was a pile of rubble

Nash, Stills, Crosby, and the old house on the first album cover, West Hollywood, 1969.

Limo ride to Big Bear to photograph inside spread of album jacket in the snow. Left to right: Henry Diltz, David Crosby, Joni Mitchell, Graham Nash, 1969. (Photo by Gary Burden.)

at the back of the lot. Even the palm tree was gone! Graham went, 'Whooa, this is pretty cosmic. The hatman has been here and is telling us you don't get a second chance!' "

More photos were taken for the inside-cover spread at Big Bear, a mountain lake resort east of L.A. There were patches of snow about and, in the right order, Crosby, Stills & Nash bundled together in fur parkas, glazed by the light of the setting sun. They looked like pioneers. And, in a musical way, they were.

The year 1969 was one of turmoil in popular music. The Beatles were on the verge of breaking up. Eric Clapton, having been proclaimed God by his legions of fans, was out of Cream and looking toward Blind

Faith. Jimi Hendrix had left the Experience behind and was in search of his Band of Gypsys. Jimmy Page was beginning to define the early stages of heavy-metal rock with Led Zeppelin. More than any individ-

Joni and Graham.

Stephen rode shotgun.

ual performer, the electric guitar sat uneasily on the throne of rock. Where would a rush of acoustic harmony land in the middle of this climate?

After Ahmet Ertegun had called in producer Tom Dowd to make sure the vocals on the CSN album were prominent enough, the tapes were finally taken to the mastering plant. Meanwhile, Crosby headed off to his boat in Florida, Stills hung out with Mickey Hart (of the Grateful Dead) for awhile, then went to his cabin in Colorado, and Nash accompanied Joni to Philadelphia, where she was playing a concert. Photographer Joel Bernstein, only seventeen at the time, remembers, "Joni and Graham were in the dressing room and sang 'Our House' together at the piano. It was something, hearing that. I remember that version in my head more than the one Graham eventually recorded."

After Joni's show, Joel says, "We were in this taxi and Graham goes, 'Can I borrow a dollar?' I gave him one, then he laughed, 'It's funny. Today I can't even afford a taxi, but tomorrow I'll be a millionaire.' "

This prediction was not far from the truth. When *Crosby, Stills & Nash* was released by Atlantic the last week of May 1969, public reaction was swift. The album rose rapidly up the charts, and Nash's

"Marrakesh Express," the single, took off, followed by a shortened version of Stills's seven-minute, twenty-two-second "Suite: Judy Blue Eyes."

When former Eagle Glenn Frey first heard the CSN album, he says, "It struck me as being very American, even though I knew Graham was English, but the *sound*, man, it was like this massive 'ahhhhhhh!' coming from the heartland. And I'm telling ya, everyone who was playing in a power trio wished they could sing like those guys."

"It was a step back to honesty," says Paul Rothchild. "Crosby, Stills & Nash were the honest kids from down the block

David Crosby.

who hung out on the beach. . . . I have to give an enormous amount of credit to Stephen for the sound of that first record. And his music was touched by an ethnic source. Everybody was listening to old Delta blues singers and Stephen's voice echoed that. His voice sounded like it had

Stephen Stills.

already been brutalized by bottles. When Willie [Graham Nash's nickname] joined in, all of a sudden that high tenor got on top of that. But it wouldn't have worked so well if David weren't holding down the bottom. David always brought a certain feeling, a certain noncommital honesty to the music. Crosby, Stills & Nash—one of those wondrous pieces of alchemy."

Jimi Hendrix remarked in *The Superstars*, "I've seen Crosby, Stills & Nash burnin' ass. They're groovy. Yeah. Western sky music. All delicate and ding-ding-ding-ding."

Rock 'n' roll critics loved Crosby, Stills & Nash at this point. *Rolling Stone* ran a particularly glowing review, containing endorsements such as, "They do what they please—singing a short blues phrase be-

Graham Nash.

Crosby in limo to Big Bear.

tween cuts, performing their multi-melodies with a grand sense of their own uniqueness, throwing in clever bits, engaging in musical conversation, combining songs. . . . They are in complete control of all they do and the result is an especially satisfying work."

"We felt like we'd really won, man," Crosby says. "And everybody was on our side." Within this triumph, only one question remained: how were Crosby, Stills & Nash going to take this album on the road?

CHAPTER FIVE

Crosby, Stills, Nash & Young: And Then There Were Four (1969)

Crosby, Stills, Nash & Young: Neil Young Joins Up / Getting Set for the Road / First Live Performance (1969)

"I didn't want us to be another Simon and Garfunkel," says Stills. "That's what David and Graham were pushing for, but I went, 'No, no, no, *no!*' I mean, the harmonies and the acoustic guitars were part of the show, but not the *whole* show. We needed to rock too."

Nash admits, "I wanted to do a CSN acoustic tour, sure. Because we'd already knocked people on their asses singing with two acoustic guitars. Some of my fondest memories are when we played for our friends in their living rooms. In that sense, making the album was kind of an anticlimax for me. I was ready to go out there, just us acoustically, and bring back that living room atmosphere. But Stephen wanted to rock 'n' roll. And he was right, we needed to do that."

There was no getting around the fact that they would have to add to the trio configuration, then. Dallas Taylor was an obvious choice for the drummer's spot, because he'd just spent almost two months in the studio with the group. A bass player needed to be found. However, another guitarist was not originally sought.

"I wanted to get a keyboard player," says Stills. "And my number-one choice was Stevie Winwood. He's the first guy I thought of. So Dallas and I went over to England, ran into Keith Moon and Chris Wood, then went trudging out—knee-deep in mud—to Winwood's house. But he just didn't want to know."

A while later, in New York, Stills approached former Paul Butterfield Blues Band keyboardist Mark Naftalin. But once again, Stephen admits, "I could never pin him down." It was Ahmet Ertegun who finally suggested recruiting Neil Young.

"One evening I had Stephen and David Geffen up to my house for dinner," Ahmet recalls. "Afterwards, I played them some old Buffalo Springfield songs. One of them was 'I Am a Child.' And I said, 'We ought to add Neil to CSN. There's something about Neil Young that goes with this.'"

"But, Ahmet," Stephen cried, "he's already quit on me twice. What do you think's gonna happen this time?"

After some discussion, Stills agreed to propose the idea to Crosby and Nash. Back in Los Angeles, a meeting was held and an unlikely dissenter emerged.

"I was against Neil joining at first," says Graham Nash. "I felt a little threatened, because the three of us had made this *thing* of CSN, this album, this image, this *sound*, and I felt afraid that it was going to change.

"After having been through the turmoil of the Hollies, I thought, with CSN, 'Wow! Finally there's something stable here.' So I definitely felt a little shaky about Neil, which had nothing to do with my opinion of his music, which was very high."

When Stephen approached Elliot Roberts (manager of both CSN and Neil Young at the time), more resistance cropped up. "I didn't know if it was a good idea," says Roberts, "because Neil had already started playing with Crazy Horse and had recorded *Everybody Knows This Is Nowhere*. So I didn't know if Neil would feel the need to be in another band."

"At this point," says Stills, "I was thinking, 'If I'd only had a little more time to find a keyboard player like I wanted in the first place.'"

But the push for Young was already in motion. He'd heard the music on *Crosby, Stills & Nash*, and, says Stephen, "The vocals just killed him. So I went up to his house and we talked about being *brothers*, about being a little older and about how we should be able to play in a band together."

When Crosby and Nash accompanied Stills on another visit to Young's, as David once said in an interview in *Crawdaddy*, "He [Neil] played 'Helpless,' and by the time he finished, we were asking him if we could join *his* band."

Since Buffalo Springfield, Young had

Neil Young.

steadily been developing his own career and had already recorded two solo albums: *Neil Young* and *Everybody Knows This Is Nowhere* (with a trio of musicians known as Crazy Horse). Why, in July 1969, did Young then make the decision to join forces with Crosby, Stills & Nash? As Neil once told *Rolling Stone*, "Playing with Stephen is special. David is an excellent rhythm guitarist and Graham sings so great . . . shit, I don't have to tell anybody these guys are phenomenal. I knew it would be fun. I didn't have to be out front. I could lay back. It didn't have to be me all the time."

Young would later admit that joining Crosby, Stills & Nash really put his name in the public eye. This blast of exposure lit a fire under Neil's entire career. However,

Crosby, Stills, Nash and Young, Los Angeles, 1969.

Graham Nash reveals, "There was talk at first of it still being Crosby, Stills & Nash when Neil joined. But he said absolutely no way. And I came to see there was no sense in not including his name. He was going to be a partner." At the same time, Neil stated, "Before I joined Crosby, Stills & Nash, I made it clear to both sides that I belong to myself."

How large a role Neil would play in Crosby, Stills, Nash & Young was not known at first. Stephen says, "It looked like Neil and I could go back and forth between guitar and keyboards; we were gonna have that flexibility." Stills also said in *BAM* magazine, "And I really wanted a musical *foil*. I wasn't quite confident enough in my lead playing to carry the whole thing, which, in retrospect, is kind of silly."

Crosby says, "Neil added a little bitter to the sweet." As David once explained, "When Neil Young walks into anything, I don't care if it's a bathroom, things change."

This expanding mothership was nearly full, but Stephen still had not found a bass player. While visiting Judy Collins in Colorado, he had run into a young bassist named Kenny Passarelli, who was eager to play. But, Stills recalls, "He was just *soooo* young, I thought Hollywood would completely freak him. But I should have brought him right then." Instead, Stephen turned to his old Springfield bassist, Bruce Palmer. He rehearsed with CSN&Y for a couple of weeks, during which they recorded a version of Terry Reid's "Horses Through a Rain Storm." However, says Nash, "When we went to New York and rehearsed at the Cafe Au Go-Go, it was decided that Bruce was not going to fit in." Crosby explains, "Bruce Palmer was into another instrument and his head was not where it should have been."

Back in Los Angeles, Young's old partner, Ricky James Matthews (now known as Rick James), recommended a young Motown bassist named Greg Reeves. At nineteen, Reeves had already been working for

Greg Reeves.

three years as a session man. His bass work appears on the Temptations' "Cloud Nine." Nash remembers, "Right away, Greg was just a kick-ass bass player. There was never

CSN&Y with Bruce Palmer (middle) and Dallas Taylor (right) in costumes, pre- *Déjà Vu*, Los Angeles, 1969.

Stephen drove the old army truck up the hill to where the light was best.

Double put-on in the field above Stephen's house.

Dallas Taylor and Greg Reeves with CSN&Y, Los Angeles, 1969.

Neil Young.

Stephen Stills.

CSN&Y rehearse in Stills's backyard, Los Angeles, 1969.

Graham Nash.

a question of searching for the right groove with him. Greg was *there* and created a groove we could count on."

Crosby, Stills, Nash, Young, Taylor, and Reeves rehearsed at Peter Tork's spacious mansion—rented by Stephen—atop a hill in Studio City. The living room became the *playing* room. Stills also wanted to set up outside. Crosby argued, "We can't play outside, man. The cops'll come." Robert Hammer captured this disagreement between Crosby and Stills on film. And when David left and Stephen started playing, sure enough, the police showed. Rehearsals moved back indoors.

"It was the West Coast version of Sag Harbor," says Nash. "People were everywhere, sleeping on the floor, in closets, and we were in the middle, getting ready for the road."

John Sebastian was at the edge of these rehearsals and remembers, "The mood of the band was changing radically at that point. People were being made aware of the potential of Crosby, Stills, Nash & Young, and in some ways it wasn't a good thing. Rather than *thinking* about how it's all going to be, it's better to just do it. Graham and I seemed to share this kind of populist, working-musician attitude and I saw that he was and continues to be the moving force in that organization."

But Nash says, "We were still investigating a whole new novelty we'd created, and there was a virginity about it. We didn't know what to expect when we hit the stage for the first time."

Stills remembers, "David Geffen and I lived together for a time and began plotting the future of CSN&Y. I ended up having dinner with a guy from the Chicago Auditorium and sold him on CSN&Y for the basic price of $10,000. This was for a never-before-seen group! Geffen and I were aghast

John Sebastian at Stills's house.

peak. All told, the concert ran nearly three hours. And up in "the cheap seats," a young musician named Dan Fogelberg watched the action onstage through binoculars.

"I'd been playing electric guitar in this

Crosby, Stills, Nash & Young with Taylor and Reeves.

at our panache."

On August 16, 1969, CSN&Y did in fact perform at the Chicago Auditorium. It was their first live performance ever. Enlivened by the spirit of experimentation, CSN&Y traded songs back and forth, building from an acoustic opening to a raucous electric

band," says Fogelberg. "I was really influenced by the Buffalo Springfield and when I heard about this show with Crosby, Stills, Nash & Young, I had to go. I had to be there. So there I was, in the Chicago Auditorium, high on psychedelics, watching Joni Mitchell and CSN&Y through binoculars.

This girl who was sitting next to me was copying down all of Joni's guitar tunings. I was real impressed myself and the day after the concert, I went out and bought a Martin acoustic guitar. Seeing Joni and CSN&Y like that had an effect on my whole career."

Backstage, after this show, David Crosby was not aware of the impact their music might have made on the audience. He was simply charged up by the fact that they had performed without any serious mishaps. "We did it, man," he squealed. "We made it through the show, and without a net."

CSN&Y: Woodstock (1969)

The Age of Aquarius was ripe and about to blossom across Max Yasgur's farm at White Lake, New York. On August 15, 16, and 17, 1969, more than 400,000 "young people" funneled toward this site for a "music and arts fair." Toting backpacks and bearing plenty of mind-altering drugs, everyone sensed that it was a time to be yourself *and* be together. No other group on the bill at the Woodstock Festival epitomized this feeling more than Crosby, Stills, Nash & Young.

The first day of the festival, however, CSN&Y cooled their heels in New York's La Guardia Airport. A Mohawk Airlines service representative had never heard of Crosby, Stills, Nash & Young, so David was biting the guy's head off. Stills, meanwhile, was on the phone chartering two private planes that would take everyone within a few miles of the festival. The rest of the trip would be by helicopter.

"At the airport," says Crosby, "we kept hearing all of these news reports that it had gotten completely out of hand, that there were a million people, that it was very tense, that they didn't know whether to call the National Guard or drop flowers."

In view of this alleged chaos, Joni Mitchell was in a New York City hotel room with Elliot Roberts's assistant, Ron Stone. Joni says, "It was decided between Geffen and Elliot that I wouldn't be able to get out in time to make my appearance on 'The Dick Cavett Show,' which was ridiculous, because the boys did make it out and ended up being guests with me on the show [everyone except Nash, that is, who was not an American citizen and didn't have the proper permit]. But I was the *girl* of the family and, with great disappointment, I was the one that had to stay behind."

By this time "the boys" were crammed into helicopters that were swooping toward the festival in the middle of a driving rainstorm. "I thought we were gonna die," says Elliot Roberts. "When I looked down," says Crosby, "I'd never seen so many people in one place in my whole life."

Somehow, the copters managed to land safely and the band staggered around for a few minutes on wobbly knees. Then they got impatient when their lift to the stage area was late in arriving. Roberts says, "I went with Neil and Jimi Hendrix in this stolen pickup. Neil hot-wired it, then drove the truck with Hendrix on the hood. Jimi Hendrix was the hood ornament! And we were all tripping on mescaline or something. It was just insane!"

When CSN&Y finally congregated backstage and their equipment arrived, Stills was screaming, "Keep the guitars out of the rain, man. Out of the rain!"

In front of the stage, the audience stretched out in all directions, in loose clusters, on blankets and between pools of muddy water. Peoples' systems had not only been affected by the elements and whatever drugs were making the rounds, but by an endless onslaught of music as

Woodstock crowd.

well. The Who, Jimi Hendrix, Santana, Ten Years After, Arlo Guthrie, Jefferson Airplane, Joan Baez, Richie Havens, John Sebastian—it went on and on. And while most of the crowd knew what to expect from most of these artists, there was a special sense of anticipation and uncertainty about Crosby, Stills, Nash & Young. The album, *Crosby, Stills & Nash*, had leapt toward the Top Ten, and that *sound* had everyone intrigued. And with a look at the album cover, the communal hippie mind flashed and thought, "Hey, man, these guys look like pretty regular dudes." That "come on in and have a listen" aura seemed genuine. And when Neil Young, with his shaky voice and patched jeans, settled onto the couch with CSN, everyone just went, "Yeah, right on," and waited to see what would happen.

At 3:00 A.M., Crosby, Stills & Nash finally wandered out onto the Woodstock stage with their acoustic guitars. Surveying the crowd, Stephen spoke up: "Hey, man, I just gotta say that you people have gotta be the strongest bunch o' people I ever saw. Three days, man! Three days! We just love ya, we just love ya, God knows . . . tell 'em who we are."

Nash mumbled, "They'll *hear* who you are."

Crosby echoed, "They'll all know if you just sing . . . *hell*-0 . . . 49, 65, hike!"

And with that, CSN ripped into a rough but emotionally charged "Suite: Judy Blue Eyes." At the song's end, applause from the crowd flew toward the stage in staggered bursts. Stills acknowledged, "Thank you. We needed that." Crosby explained, "This is our second gig." Stills elaborated, "This is the second time we've ever played in front of people, man! And we're scared shitless!" This bit of vulnerable honesty draw another chorus of cheers.

"We *were* scared shitless," said Crosby, fourteen years after Woodstock. "Because standing right behind us was the entire music business in this big semicircle. The

Graham Nash and David Crosby on stage at Woodstock, August 1969.

Airplane, Hendrix, the Who, every record company president—all these people waitin' for us to land on our noses or fly. And of course, we landed on our noses. Everybody was extra excited, playing over their heads, trying extra hard. So yeah, we were nervous. But what made us nervous was the scrutiny of the people behind us, not the ones in front of us."

Grace Slick, who was among this crowd, says, "CSN—CSN&Y—it was their show. Well, maybe not their show, but their *time*. They represented the Woodstock sound, whatever that was or is."

When the amps were wheeled out on

Neil Young at Woodstock.

stage for the CSN&Y electric set, there were some hassles with some of the cameramen, because Neil Young did not want to be filmed. "I never understood why Neil didn't want to be a part of that," says Nash. "It was like he didn't want to be *connected*. But when you're playing in front of four hundred thousand people, those are trips you better think about before you pull 'em."

But this bit of tension went unnoticed by the crowd. Jerry Hopkins, in *Festival*, described CSN&Y at Woodstock: "They became like musical rocketships, filling the night with light and luminescent vapor trails."

While these fireworks were raging at Woodstock, Joni Mitchell was still camped out in her New York hotel room. "The deprivation of not being able to go," says Joni, "provided me with an intense angle on Woodstock. I was one of the fans. I was put in the position of being a kid who couldn't make it. So I was glued to the media. And at the time I was going through a kind of

Stephen Stills at Woodstock.

Jefferson Airplane and San Francisco contingent on the Woodstock stage, first afternoon. Left to right: Paul Kantner, Jack Casady (headband), Grace Slick, Spencer Dryden (hat), Country Joe McDonald (headband), Bill Graham.

born-again Christian trip—not that I went to any church, I'd given up Christianity at a very early age in Sunday school. But suddenly, as performers, we were in the position of having so many people look to us for leadership, and for some unknown reason, I took it seriously and decided I needed a guide and leaned on God. So I was a little 'God mad' at the time, for lack of a better term, and I had been saying to myself, 'Where are the modern miracles? Where are the modern miracles?' Woodstock, for some reason, impressed me as being a modern miracle, like a modern day fishes-and-loaves story. For a herd of people that large to cooperate so well, it was pretty remarkable and there was tremendous optimism. So I wrote the song 'Woodstock' out of these

feelings, and the first three times I performed it in public, I burst into tears, because it brought back the intensity of the experience and was so moving."

After Woodstock, when CSN&Y rendezvoused with Joni, Graham recalls, "We were enthused tremendously about what had just gone down. And she, in talking to the four of us, got such a depth of feeling for it, she was able to write a song about Woodstock and she wasn't even there! And as soon as I saw her writing it, I said, 'Oh God, what's this?' And it was such a great song, the whole *feeling* of the song . . . it pinned exactly what had happened, in terms of being in a wheel in something turning. As soon as the four of us heard it, we wanted to do that record so bad. And we did."

CSN&Y: The Greek Theater in L.A. / Big Sur (1969)

Woodstock had been front-page news, so Crosby, Still, Nash & Young were accorded a heroes' welcome when they opened a five-night stand at the Los Angeles Greek Theatre on August 25. David Crosby says, "Before the first show, I remember the excitement of being up at Tork's house, with just me, Stills, and Nash getting into Stephen's 600 Mercedes short limousine. I was drivin', smokin' a joint, and we were laughin' our asses off blastin' down the hill to the Greek Theatre. There was heavy traffic around the place, so I drove up over the curb, onto the lawn, and past the line of people all the way down the block. What a great time, man."

Ron Stone, 1970.

"CSN&Y was the most radical thing the Greek had ever had," says Ron Stone. "So the people who ran the place were real uptight, because CSN&Y was a politically oriented group. I even had trouble getting Joni into places. So, in a lot of ways, by playing in concert-hall situations, they stepped out into the unknown and helped break ground for everybody else."

Following an opening acoustic set by Joni, CSN&Y took the stage at the Greek and were magnificent. Playing on an oriental rug that covered the coldness of the concrete, "they held public porch," as it was aptly put by Charles John Quarto, a poet and friend of the band. Outdoors, on a hot summer night, the setting was idyllic. Crosby, Stills & Nash's harmonies streamed out on "You Don't Have to Cry," "Blackbird," and "Suite: Judy Blue Eyes." Crosby and Nash sent shivers through the crowd on "Guinnevere." Stills bowed his head over his acoustic guitar and seemed the picture of the solitary bluesman while crying "4 + 20." Young carried this further, during his solo spot. Then the energy shifted in the middle of the electric set, when Stills and Young stormed up against each other, creating sparks with their guitars.

"At their best," says Joni Mitchell, "Neil and Stephen had a beautiful staglike duel going onstage; and it was quite pretty to watch. It was like watching two very good long-distance runners pair up and pace each other."

Of CSN&Y's electrical performance, Paul Kantner says, "I think some of their desire to be real crazy electric rockers came from San Francisco. It had that sort of looseness you can get away with if you're from here. But it's not something you learn. You just *do* it. And when it works, it works. Crosby, Stills, Nash & Young's electric music, to me, was never as fully realized as the acoustic set. Because their acoustic music was so perfect, any little imperfection in the electric music was very noticeable."

Clearly, CSN&Y was a band that snapped through musical boundaries and careened ahead with a free spirit. Elliot Roberts says, "We're talking about a bunch of guys who were really out on a limb, on the edge, night after night."

However, Roberts goes on to say, "CSN&Y took a minimum number of gigs. We discussed certain exposure points and took the ones that were important. We knew the money would be there down the line, so that never came into play."

They performed at Woodstock for a grand total of $10,000. Later they passed up a chance to appear on "The Hollywood Palace" in favor of offering their services for free at the Big Sur Folk Festival with Joni, John Sebastian, Joan Baez, and others. Many of the high moments from this two-

Crosby, Stills, Nash & Young with Taylor and Reeves up at Stephen's house, Los Angeles, 1969.

day affair, held in mid-September 1969, were captured in *Celebration at Big Sur*, a film produced by Carl Gottlieb, a longtime friend of Crosby's. Footage of "Sea of Madness" and "Down by the River" show CSN&Y in excellent form. At the same time, the cameras also caught Stills almost coming to blows with a drunken spectator who was heckling the band about their fur coats and fancy guitars.

"It pissed Stephen off 'cause we were playin' for free," recalls Crosby. "So he put his guitar down and went after the guy. I kept saying, 'Peace, love, kick his ass, peace, love . . .' Then a lot of people intervened. It was a weird scene."

Stills recalls, "I was going to push the guy into the pool, which was about forty degrees. That would have cooled him off quick. But David, over the mike, said, 'Stephen, you can't push that guy in the pool!' At that point, the guy turned on me and the resultant altercation took place. I was surprised, to say the least, to discover while viewing the film years later, how long I was nice to the guy. I was just trying to tie him up so he couldn't swing. It was when someone pulled us apart that he clipped me and I took him out, at a non-violence festival, yet!"

Before playing "4 + 20," Stephen told the audience, "You know, we think about

"They'd always get you high." Santa Barbara concert, 1969.

. . . like the guy was saying, we look at these fur coats, fancy guitars, fancy cars and say, 'Wow, man, what am I doin'?' You know, so when somebody gets up and freaks out like that, it kind of strikes a nerve and you end up right back in that old trap, and where that guy is at is in that same trap and that's gettin' *mad* about something. And that ain't nothing, you know, and I had some guys to love me out of it and I was lucky. We gotta just let it all be. 'Cause it all will be however it's gonna."

"CSN&Y knew how to talk to an audience," says Joni Mitchell. "Their music and the camaraderie on stage was genuine. It always seemed like the real McCoy to me. A very good-feeling band, they'd always get you high."

Graham and Joni (1969)

All during Crosby, Stills, Nash & Young's rise, Graham Nash and Joni Mitchell were building their relationship. When not in the studio or on the road, they lived together in Joni's small house on Lookout Mountain Road in Laurel Canyon. It was this place that Graham immortalized with the lines, "Our house is a very, very, very

fine house, with two cats in the yard, life used to be so hard. Now everything is easy, 'cause of you."

"The first night we spent together, I felt very warm and felt like I'd really found a home," says Graham. "I'd left the Hollies successfully, I'd left my country successfully, CSN was becoming like a dream. A good time. And Joan and I had a great love affair. A very, very positive experience. I had never been with a woman like Joan. I had never been so much in love. I had never been so unsure of myself. I had never been so fragile. A lot of people think I'm strong, but how it looks on the inside is a different picture sometimes.

"And how could I *not* love her? We had the ability to make each other laugh and not take each other too seriously. I was as different from her as she was from me, which created an interesting union. People used to say Joan and I would light up rooms when we walked in."

Both Graham and Joni were enjoying creative peaks in 1969. While he was recording with David and Stephen, she was painting the self-portrait for her second album cover, or huddled over the piano, writing such songs as "Rainy Night House," "Ladies of the Canyon," and "Morning

"**Now everything is easy 'cause of you.**" Joni and Graham, 1969.

Morgantown." On the drive out to Big Bear to shoot the inside photo for the first CSN album, Joni was between Graham and David in the back seat, writing out the words to "Willy" (a variant of Graham's middle name, William).

Joni writing the words to "Willy," her song about Graham, in the limo to Big Bear, 1969.

Graham says of the song, "Just to know that by my presence and by my actions I can provoke a song such as 'Willy' thrills me and makes me a little uncomfortable, because she's laying it out there. And I can remember the specifics . . . I can remember looking out the window at the moon, I remember talking about hearing wedding bells too soon. I remember all those incidents that came together to form that song. So it's pretty scary."

By the fall of 1969, Graham and Joni were beginning to drift apart, he says, "Because there was a lot of hesitancy on Joan's part and on my part to really commit to a relationship. A lot of the past reared its head. And when you have two intensely creative people living in the same house, it can get uncomfortable sometimes. And I was beginning to spend long hours away from her with CSN and CSN&Y, so there was some distance created, and someone like Joan thrives on attention, as well she should. One must *nurture* relationships. So, I'm afraid, with the slings and arrows of this society, my relationship with Joni gradually crumbled. . . . But just to have been a part of that woman's life thrills me beyond belief. We have had a deep, deep relationship. She is an incredibly special woman. I have incredible respect for her."

CSN&Y: Egos Clash at the Fillmore East (1969)

Cracks in the Foundation

Amid the ups and downs of Joni and Graham's relationship, CSN&Y headed to New York for a series of concerts at the Fillmore East in September of 1969. The term "super group" was now being used to describe this aggregation. Crosby would respond, "We're four individuals playin' together, don't call us a group and don't call us super." But when they hit the Fillmore stage and reached one fantastic peak after another, CSN&Y certainly *seemed* like a group, and their performances were super. In the center portion of "Suite: Judy Blue Eyes," when Stills sang, "It's my *heart* that's a-sufferin', it's a-dyin'," he shot up into his falsetto range on the word *heart* and sent the entire auditorium into ecstasy. At night's end, after an excursion through

CSN&Y warming up backstage.

every form of acoustic and electric music, Crosby, Stills, Nash & Young left the crowd with some "wooden music," a new, then untitled song Stephen had written for the movie *Easy Rider*. Four voices wove together on the lines, "Find the cost of freedom, buried in the ground / Mother Earth will swallow you, lay your body down." A few seconds of dead silence preceded an outpouring of cheers and applause, directed toward the four men, arm in arm, standing at the center of the stage.

Bob Dylan showed up for one of these Fillmore shows and, naturally, CSN&Y were anxious and excited about his presence. Nash remembers, "Our concerts have always been pretty flexible. And when we did our acoustic set, Stephen wanted to do an extra song on his own. We said, 'Fine.' But Stephen ended up doing *three* extra songs and it was a drag because it interrupted the flow of the program. We *all* wanted to impress Dylan, but Stephen took advantage of the situation and, during intermission, I told him that what he did was a drag. And I remember him standing in front of me with a can of Budweiser. And while we were talkin', Stephen was gettin' so pissed, he was *crushing* the can in his hand and beer was foaming all down his arm."

Stills insists, "I got hung up and forgot who was there. I remember thinking when Graham got mad, 'What an egocentric prick.' "

Ron Stone says, "When I came into the

dressing room, the band was breaking up before my eyes. Finally, Elliot walked in and became the focus of all of their anger. He shrugged. 'Fine, break up. But let's finish the show. If you're gonna break up, what's a couple of hours?' "

"They'd been off the stage for forty-five minutes," recalls road manager Leo Makota, "and I was standing in front of their door when Bill Graham walked up with a note that read, 'Your audience awaits you.' They went on and played one of the greatest shows they'd ever done. That's what always amazed me about them. They could be at each other's throats, then turn around and immediately make such great harmony on stage."

After the final song of the last Fillmore date, the audience would not leave. Everyone in the place held up lighted matches and screamed for more. Graham Nash says, "We were in our dressing room and Bill Graham tried to bribe us into doing another song by stuffing hundred-dollar bills underneath our door. Neil kept saying, 'More, more!' Then Bill threw in a whole fistful. Neil scooped, 'em up and said, 'Hey, let's go out and give these to the audience.' And I said, 'Whoa, wait a minute. We're in New York, the crowd's excited. You can't go throwing hundred-dollar bills off the stage. You'd probably cause a riot, a real bad scene.' So we went out and gave 'em more music."

CSN&Y: Tragedy Strikes in Marin (1969)

In San Francisco, the last week of September, Crosby, Stills, Nash & Young were looking forward to a four-night engagement, October 2–5, at the Winterland Auditorium with their old friend John Sebastian. Casual rehearsals took place at Crosby's new home in Novato, several miles north of San Francisco Bay. Earlier in 1969, David had sold his Beverly Glen home in L.A., because, he says, "One afternoon I was up on Mullholland Drive, a view site if there ever was one, and I couldn't see the valley floor because there was so much smog. I knew then it was time to move."

His Novato home, surrounded by a grove of trees and thick foliage, served as a perfect refuge for Crosby and Christine Gail Hinton. On September 30, they were lazing about near the pool with a few other members of the CSN&Y clan. Nash recalls, "It was early afternoon. And we were thinking about what to have for a late breakfast. There were a couple of nice-looking naked ladies in the pool. Everyone was relaxed. Then Christine walked up and handed me three joints she'd rolled. She had on a leather coat and said she was going to take the cats to the vet. She said she'd be right back."

Ten minutes later, while Christine was driving Crosby's VW bus toward the vet on Diablo Avenue, one of the cats sprang out of passenger Barbara Langer's arms and sank its claws into Christine. This caused her to swerve into the path of an oncoming school bus. A head-on collision occurred and Christine was killed instantly.

"David went to identify the body," says Graham, "and he's never been the same since."

Right after the tragedy, Crosby slipped into a state of shock. The CSN&Y/Sebastian Winterland dates were canceled. With Nash by his side, Crosby headed for his sailboat, then New York, then London. "I needed to do something to keep from going completely out to lunch," David says. "I stayed with him," says Graham. "I drank as much as he drank, I went wherever he went. David was in a bad way and we forged a deep, deep friendship there."

"We went to my boat," says Crosby, "and I know this sounds kind of corny, but I

David and Christine. (Photo by Bobby Hammer.)

wanted to bury her at sea. Christine, she was a shining light, man."

When Crosby and Nash rendezvoused with the rest of the band in Los Angeles after this whirlwind flight from emotional pain, David was still in no condition to perform. CSN&Y did, however, make an appearance on Tom Jones's TV show. "I'm afraid so," says Nash. "I have videotape evidence of Tom Jones singin' the lead on

'Long Time Gone.' It was incrediby weird. 'You stand there. No, wait—here. We need to block this out.' It was because of that experience we didn't do television for the next ten years."

The memory of "This Is Tom Jones" faded quickly, however. In spite of all that had happened in the past couple of weeks, Crosby, Stills, Nash & Young had an album to complete.

CHAPTER SIX

Crosby, Stills, Nash & Young: Déjà Vu and the Road to Freedom (1969–1970)

CSN&Y: Recording "Déjà Vu" (1969)

The gloom of lost love hung over CSN&Y's recording sessions in October 1969. Music became an escape from pain rather than an expression of joy. Besides the death of Christine, Nash's relationship with Joni was on the brink of disaster. Stills and Judy Collins seemed as though they had split for good. Young was not enjoying the best of times with his wife. "Music was all we had," says Stills.

At Wally Heider's in San Francisco, Joni Mitchell patiently taught the band "Woodstock." It would prove to be one of the few songs that was recorded with everyone in the studio at once. "Stephen sang the shit out of it," Young once told Cameron Crowe. "The track was magic. Then, later on, they were in the studio nitpicking. Sure enough, Stephen erased the vocal and put another one on that wasn't nearly as good."

Stills explains, "Not exactly. I replaced one and a half verses that were excruciatingly out of tune."

Young did a fair amount of additional work on his own songs after the band had provided a basic recording. "I was a little resentful of Neil taking his tracks out of the studio," says Nash. "I was a junkie for music and I wanted to be there to see all of those overdubs go down. But with Neil's stuff, I loved the end result. When I heard 'Country Girl,' what could I say? There was no point in getting uptight, because it was beautiful."

When Bill Halverson took over the engineering duties from Russ Gary, the scene in the studio was scattered. "Neil never seemed like a part of the group," says Halverson, "and it was rare to see everybody in the studio at once. Unlike the first CSN album, the feeling was not comfortable. There was a lot of making it up as we went along. And a lot of times they were simply not ready to record. They'd be hangin' out at someone else's session."

The Jefferson Airplane was in the studio at the same time, and Stills ended up playing some organ on their *Volunteers* album. Also, Jerry Garcia of the Grateful Dead dropped in and eventually added a steel guitar lick to Nash's "Teach Your Children." "It started out as a slightly funky English folk song," says Graham. "But Stephen put a country beat to it and turned it into a hit record."

Teach your children well
Their father's hell
Will slowly go by
And feed them on your dreams
The one they pick's
The one you'll know by

"That was as up and communicative as we could get," says Nash. "We were all at each other's throats. There were many late-night sessions. When we'd finish at three in the morning, Stephen had developed a habit of continuing until eight, which made the crews late and made *him* late, which made the sessions start late the next day. And it went later and later . . ."

Road manager Leo Makota says, "I had to stay there until Stephen finished, because we had to tear down the equipment every morning so this other band could come in at noon. One night, David and Graham left at around midnight. Stephen and Halverson were trying to get these two songs. I fell asleep on this couch and woke about 3:00 A.M. and Stephen and Halverson were fairly drunk and excited because they'd just finished 'Carry On.' "

"We didn't have an opener for the album," says Nash. "And I've always been the member of this band that's been into programming. We needed something like the 'Suite,' something that was instantly identifiable as CSN or CSN&Y. When Stephen

David Crosby.

came up with 'Carry On,' I knew we had an opening tune."

David Crosby had somehow managed to "carry on" throughout these sessions, and when it came time to record "Almost Cut My Hair," he unleashed an emotional scream that seemed to release every bit of anger and frustration he'd been holding inside. By far the roughest track CSN&Y ever recorded, "Almost Cut My Hair" also stands as one of the most *real*.

In contrast to this one-take outburst, Crosby's "Déjà Vu" took nearly forever to record. One estimate is one hundred hours. Stills explains, "The first section went fairly quickly. David was so charged with scattered energy, he was like a downed wire

Graham Nash.

"The first time I saw a sailboat, I knew how to sail it," David says. "I knew how to sing harmony without ever taking lessons. My imaginative level has always been stronger than my rational one, which led me to believe that my life, *people's* lives, may be all previously constructed. When a person dies, I think the identity goes away, but the energy gets recycled. So I think the law of conservation applies."

The idea of déjà vu carried over into a concept for the album cover. In conjunction with art director Gary Burden and photographer Tom Gundelfinger, CSN&Y, Taylor, and Reeves "went back in time." "We tried to look like we thought our ancestors might have looked one hundred years ago," says Nash. So, after visiting a costume store, they congregated in Crosby's backyard. Each member had been transformed: Crosby into Buffalo Bill Cody (complete with rifle), Stills into a Confederate soldier, Nash into a peasant laborer, Young into a cagey gunfighter, Taylor into a desperado, and Reeves into a servant. Gary Burden used an old camera and processing technique to further simulate a Civil War–era photograph, but the shot eventually used on the *Déjà Vu* cover was actually taken with a Nikon and then doctored. A "pasted on" photo added an additional step to the cover art process and, with the special textured jacket, *Déjà Vu* became one of the most expensive album covers in history.

People were beginning to wonder if CSN&Y would ever finish the album to slip into the *Déjà Vu* jacket. Stills was annoyed by this situation and says, "Getting that album done was like pulling teeth." In *Zig Zag* magazine he once explained, "It was just four cats recording their own tracks . . . [so] it wasn't any fun anymore, with all the bickering and fighting going on." Stills later elaborated, "It went from Neil having *his* tracks and David having *his* tracks to, 'That was *my* idea, man, not *yours*.' Silly

bouncing around on the pavement. Dallas and I kept waiting for some coherency to his playing. The downbeats weren't the same from one verse to another. Nash, in the [recording studio] booth, understood our frustration. So we just wore David down, until he was so tired he quit thinking and played the second half with some consistency. Graham then winked at me and told David to run along home, that we'd go at it again tomorrow. Well, that night, we edited 'Déjà Vu' together and David was amazed we'd gotten such a great take. We didn't have the heart to tell him."

Crosby's statement, "We have all been here before," grew out of his personal experience with déjà vu.

The *Déjà Vu* group during album cover session. (Photo by Tom Gundelfinger.)

shit like that. And someone came up with the game, 'I'll kill it if it wasn't my idea.' When that shit started, I just cleared out."

To keep his sanity, Stephen would sometimes go to the racetrack. "Working with horses would clear my head of all that brouhaha," he says. "Breezing a horse at just about dawn is one of the biggest thrills you can imagine. It's all quiet and you're just going like a bat out of hell, close to thirty or forty miles an hour. That would give me a different, more immediate sense of reality that I would consequently take back to work. But this was a double-edged sword, because I'd be so centered, so in touch and clearheaded, I'd get annoyed real quick if there was any bullshitting around. I could only take so much of the marijuana mentality when I wanted to just go to work."

As he did on *Crosby, Stills & Nash*, Stephen put in more studio hours than any other member on *Déjà Vu*. He figures the album took about eight hundred hours to complete. Ron Stone says, "Fun in the studio with CSN&Y was hearing one phrase played 460 times in a row." Of course, there was the occasional "quicky." No one felt the need to add anything to "4 + 20," which Stills had recorded on acoustic guitar in July. "It was just too perfect to touch," says Nash. When Stephen's voice clutched up right before the line "embrace the many-colored beast," that moment of vul-

nerability said as much about Stephen Stills as did the words of the song.

Neil Young's "Helpless" ached with the kind of emotion that everyone in the CSN&Y camp was feeling. Crosby says one of his favorite moments on the whole album occurred when he invented the "moving oooohs" that CSN harmonize on behind Young's frail cry. In his *Decade* liner notes, Neil wrote: "Recorded in San Francisco about 4:00 A.M. when everybody got tired enough to play at my speed."

By mid-November 1969, CSN&Y was ready to run—out of the studio. Nash describes the climate: "It ran from total elation to . . . I ended up crying one night, as a matter of fact, during those *Déjà Vu* sessions, out of total frustration. We had so much to give, and because there was so

Stephen riding. "Working with horses would clear my head."

much bullshit in the way, we were truly in danger of seeing it all just turn to a piece of shit."

Nash continues, "We were all staying in this goddamned Caravan Lodge motel . . . and Neil had these two bushbabies in his room—Harriet and Speedy. They were jumping around, my bathtub was overflowing, it was *nuts*. I swear, I thought I was in a Fellini movie."

Neil with his pet bushbaby at the Caravan Lodge Motel.

CSN&Y's movie finally changed reels when the band shifted from the studio to the concert stage. On November 13–16, they finally played the previously canceled dates at Winterland in San Francisco. A week later, they began the longest tour any of them had ever been on.

CSN&Y: The "Carry On" Tour (1969–1970)

Honolulu, Denver, Salt Lake City, San Antonio, Phoenix, Altamont, UCLA, Sacramento, Pittsburgh, Cleveland, Chicago, and Detroit—Crosby, Stills, Nash & Young hit all of these places in less then a month. Aptly called the "Carry On" tour, this bit of roadwork marked the first time a rock 'n' roll act had played so many arena shows in such a short time. This was before packaged tours, before realistic travel time was calculated. Leo Makota also reveals, "We were one of the first bands to carry all of our own sound reinforcement and lighting equipment. And while a lot of bands had three microphones up on stage, CSN&Y used *twenty-one*. We had to air-freight massive amounts of equipment every night, and at the shows we used a wagon for all of the amplifiers, electric guitars, and drum risers. When the acoustic set was over, we'd just strike the stools and roll out the wagon. Everything was plugged in and tuned. We never failed to get a round of applause."

That CSN&Y, on December 6, played at Altamont "was a very carefully hidden fact," says Graham Nash. "We let the Rolling Stones take that one. That was your pedestal, Mick."

Stills remembers, "David and I pushed for us to do that gig. But I sensed real danger the minute we got there. I was literally flinching on stage and had a horrible feeling someone was going to shoot Mick. When we finished our set, I started barking orders and picked up two guitars. David picked up two. And with Neil's wife, Susan, between us, we carried all of the above to the chopper on a dead run. Dallas and Cros understood completely and moved right out. We cleared the area in ninety seconds flat. The others were a bit nonplussed, but followed. After our Pauley Pavilion gig [at

Crosby, Stills, Nash & Young at Balboa Stadium in San Diego, December 1969.

UCLA] that night, the tension caught up with me and I got the whirlies on the way to the dressing room. It was an embarrassing end to a day best forgotten."

Before a break for Christmas and some more tinkering on *Déjà Vu*, one of CSN&Y's finest concerts ever took place December 21, outdoors at San Diego's Balboa Stadium. By early January, they were on the road to Houston, but their equipment was

Graham Nash.

Greg Reeves.

David Crosby.

Electric set.

Graham having a cup of tea behind the amps. (Far right: Elliot Roberts, manager.)

Neil tuning up. (Left: Leo Makota).

Stephen warming up before the concert.

CSN tuning in their harmony before a concert.

when our stuff arrived, we unloaded our own amps and guitars and put on a *fantastic* show, man."

For Graham Nash, all of this cross-country touring held an unforgettable magic. "It was all very wonderous," he says. "You must understand that I was not only seeing it through the eyes of someone from another country, but this was brand-new success at a different level. I began to see the effect CSN&Y was having in terms of its rhythm within the age."

Was it still possible to get close to the Garden of Eden in 1970? CSN&Y were determined to try. By early February they had managed to spread their harmony all over America and into Europe. CSN&Y's last show of the tour was in Copenhagen. Leo Makota recalls, "It was obvious everybody needed a break from each other for a while. There were no major conflicts goin' on. In fact, we all got together after the last gig, found out we had a lot of leftover tour drugs, and gave 'em to a community of American draft dodgers staying in Denmark."

On that note, Crosby and Nash headed down to England, but stayed there only a short while before taking off for Crosby's boat in Florida. Young flew back to Los Angeles to dive into another solo album and a tour with Crazy Horse. Stills, meanwhile, decided to plant some new roots in England.

Stills: Moves to England / Records First Solo Album (1970)

"I wanted a complete change," Stephen says. "California was just getting too nuts."

Initially staying at the Dorchester Hotel, then in a small apartment in London, Stills adjusted to British life right away. "I had a sense of living abroad from growing

snowbound en route. Crosby remembers, "The four of us sat down on the edge of the stage and, using the house PA, told everyone, 'Hey, our gear got caught in a snowstorm. It'll be here in forty minutes. If any of you want to leave, we'll give you your money back.' Well, they all stayed and up in Latin America," he says. "I took England on as itself, rather than being 'the ugly American' in a foreign country."

One of the first friendly faces Stephen encountered belonged to Ringo Starr. The two of them drove out to Ringo's Brookfield House—a 350-year-old Tudor mansion in Elstead—formerly owned by Peter Sellers

Brookfield House, Elstead, Surrey.

and before him, Spencer Tracy. Because Ringo grew tired of making the commute into London from southern Surrey, the estate had been vacant for a while. But after some discussion, Stills rented Brookfield House (he ended up buying it for $250,000). Surrounded by twenty acres of lush greenery and several ponds, with ducks, geese, and other wildlife, this brick-and-beam manor was a perfect refuge for Stills—a good hour-and-a-half drive from the hustle and bustle of London.

"Brookfield House was a magical place," Stills says. "There were ghosts. And I had wonderful bursts of creativity there."

By late February, Stephen had written close to twenty new songs. It was then that he decided to go into the studio. About this idea of making a solo album, he said at the time, "It's sort of been stirring up inside me for a couple of years now. I've just been waiting for the right amount of songs, and the right kind of songs. Which is to say non-group songs."

So Stills, then, was the first of the CSN "aggregation of friends" to test the strength of the mothership. The plan, right from the start, had been to split off and do solo projects whenever one felt like it. CSN, then CSN&Y, were supposed to piece back together in the same manner. This was a progressive ideal that no other group had attempted.

Recording at Island Studios in London, first with Andy Johns, then with Bill Halverson engineering and co-producing, Stills rounded up an all-star roster of musicians, including Ringo Starr, Eric Clapton, and Jimi Hendrix.

"Jimi and I burned," says Stills. "We must have jammed for five days. We cut a bunch o' things, and a lot of 'em are still in hiding." "Old Times Good Times" is the only one that has made it out so far. Another track of Stills's was called "White Nigger." This would doubtless have been included on an album the two guitarists were thinking of doing together. "Jimi thought we were starting on it when he came in to play on my record," says Stephen. "It was all planned. We were *gonna* do it. But he died."

As fiery as the Stills–Hendrix interactions were, just as explosive was the pairing of Stills and Eric Clapton. At one point in early March 1970, both of them were working on their first solo albums right next to each other at Island Studios, and it was only natural that Stills and Clapton should wander into each other's sessions. One night, Stephen cut a lot of the bass parts, played some guitar, and sang background harmonies on several of Clapton's songs, including "Let It Rain." After tracking in some lead guitar, Eric jumped over to one of Stills's songs, "Go Back Home."

Clapton, on playing with Stills: "He's one of the first pickers I ever met that I could really pick with."

Stills, on playing with Clapton: "Eric's my brother . . . we've been through the same changes, fought the same battles, and

Stephen Stills at Island Studios, London, 1970.

later. But everybody loved me doing it solo acoustic so much, I put it on the record.

" 'Black Queen,' " Stills continues, "was written rather quickly, and I used the card-game metaphor to explain the capriciousness of this woman. In poker, when you're trying to fill out a straight flush with a black queen . . . it has a habit of showing up in the nastiest places, you know?"

During twenty-five sessions in twenty-seven days, Stills cut an astonishing number of songs. It's no wonder that, right after this stretch, he told British journalist Ritchie Yorke, "I've considered calling it [the album] *Stephen Stills Retires.*"

Once again, Stills had recorded and overdubbed many different instruments himself. He told Yorke, "I guess you might

Stephen Stills at the Island Studios board with Bill Halverson, London, 1970.

we're both just coming out of the other side." In 1974, Stills told Ben Fong-Torres, "He taught me fluidity necessary for that style of nicely constructed blues guitar."

Stephen says that in 1970, "Eric and I got into a tequila-drinking bout that led into a two-and-a-half hour jam on the song 'Tequila.' We could afford to trash around with our studio time then." On this particular night of "trashing around," Stills also managed to cut a mean version of Robert Johnson's "Crossroads" and his own "Black Queen"—this one ending up on the album and dedicated to Jose Cuervo tequila. "That's because," says Stephen, "I was *real* drunk when I cut it. And that was just meant to be a demo for me and Eric or me and Jimi to work from and play electrically call them manufactured records, but I certainly don't look at it that way. It's the way the first Crosby, Stills & Nash record was made, it's the way I made several records with the Buffalo Springfield . . . and it's also the way Paul McCartney has done his album. I don't think there's anything to be said for or against doing everything yourself. It's only whether it makes it that matters."

This Stills solo material was definitely making it. The catchiest, most overtly commercial track that came out of these sessions was "Love the One You're With," a syncopated rock shuffle with Latin underpinnings, notably Stills's steel drum and the bass parts played by Calvin "Fuzzy" Samuels.

A Jamaican bassist, Samuels had been gigging around London in a reggae band when Stills discovered him and invited him down to his sessions. The Stills–Samuels combination became the center of several songs. And the chemistry was right in a way that Stephen would not soon forget.

Crosby and Nash: Sail Away (1970)

Out in the gulf of Mexico, a long way from the heat of Stills's sessions, Crosby and Nash were lazing on David's sailboat. For Graham, the experience was a particularly nurturing one. "It had an effect on my life, *totally*," he says. "I'd never been on my own, and I decided that I needed to just go and be alone for a while. And I know that's a hard thing to do with four other people on a sixty-foot boat, but as far as not dealing with the other areas of my life, I was relatively alone."

Graham and David often stood watch in shifts and, says Crosby, "I've never seen anybody pick up navigation faster than Nash did." Besides Leo Makota, who went

on board for a while, and another crewmember, the only other beings present were of the oceanic variety.

"I saw some *incredible* stuff," Nash says. "The most mindblowing thing was seeing an eighty- to ninety-foot blue whale come within fifty feet of us. It had a blowhole about six feet across, and to feel the power of a monster like that, with a couple of dozen dolphins swimming around in its wake . . . that's basically where 'Wind on the Water' came from" (This was a song Nash later wrote about whales being tragically slaughtered by man.)

By the time *The Mayan* docked near San Diego, Crosby and Nash had also been transfixed by a school of dolphins swimming in tandem. "They looked like fifteen-foot-long bullets of phosphorescence," says Graham. "And we also saw a beach walk away from us that was actually made up of solid crabs."

Such sights had also thrilled Crosby, but his thoughts invariably wandered back to memories of Christine. Losing her had left a huge void in him. On the boat, he would often stare out at the waves for hours on end. Once David got on dry land again, he set about filling his inner void the only way he knew how—with music.

CSN&Y: United in L.A., Divided in Chicago (1970)

When *Déjà Vu* hit the record stores in March of 1970, the album had already shipped two million copies. The freshness that *Crosby, Stills & Nash* had evoked in the summer of 1969, the harmony and the explosiveness that CSN&Y had created at Woodstock and on countless other stages— these were not things people easily forgot. And *Déjà Vu* managed to combine the sparkle of the first record with the rawness of the live shows, as difficult a task as that proved to be. Because these guys wrote and sang with whatever personal feeling they had to draw on, all the pain, the joy, the hurt, the peace, the love, the anger, the *frustration* that went on within their lives during the making of *Déjà Vu* came out in the grooves and demanded attention.

Although a CSN&Y tour was being mapped out to support this record, "the boys" were not quite back together yet. David and Graham were working their way up the coast of California on *The Mayan*. Stephen had flown into Los Angeles from England to sing on Neil's *After the Gold Rush* album; unfortunately, right after that he fractured his wrist in a car accident in Laurel Canyon. So Stills ended up spending

a good part of April "healing and relaxing" in Hawaii with Henry Diltz.

Henry Diltz and Stephen Stills in Hawaii, North Shore, Oahu.

Stephen in Hawaii playing pool with his wrist in a cast, 1970.

When rehearsals finally started in the last couple days of April, a crisis occurred almost immediately. Bassist Greg Reeves was fired. "We had to do it," says Crosby, "because Greg suddenly decided he was an Apache witch doctor. He just flipped right out, man, and none of us wanted to argue the point with him."

Nash adds, "Greg also wanted to sing some of his songs on the CSN&Y show, which I thought was ludicrous, *only* because the songs weren't great. We'll sing any song if it's great, but *not* just because it happens to be written by our bass player. So we had to let Greg go."

Of course, this created a major problem. A CSN&Y tour was set to begin in a couple of days, and suddenly they had no bass player. Who could possibly jump in and learn the songs in forty-eight hours? Stills thought of someone who just might be able to do it—Fuzzy Samuels, the young bassist he'd worked with in England. The rest of the band agreed it was worth a try. A few phone calls and several hours later, Fuzzy was in Los Angeles.

"He looked great," Nash remembers. "He walked in wearing this tan suit, a bowler hat, and roller-skate shoes with no skates on the bottom. Right away, he picked up the parts and sounded great."

Fuzzy Samuels.

But Crosby remembers a forboding question that came up during rehearsals: "We were set up at the old Warner Brothers studio on the soundstage where they'd just shot *They Shoot Horses Don't They?* Some of the set was still up. And the funniest thing is . . . we were playing kind of tensely, not getting on too well, when I noticed, at the far end of the room, in four-foot-high letters, 'HOW LONG WILL THEY LAST?'

"We all looked at each other and laughed, just as Bill Cosby walked in with a bullwhip. He said, 'Hey, all right, play me "Melancholy Baby."'" Then he cracked the whip. 'All right. Hop to it.' We laughed our asses off. But at the end of rehearsals, I still remember seeing those letters, 'HOW LONG WILL THEY LAST?'"

When CSN&Y opened this tour in Denver, it looked like they might not last through the whole show. The band was under-rehearsed and the electric set was ragged, except for several of Stills's songs—which Fuzzy Samuels had the bass parts

CSN&Y rehearsal on Warner Brothers soundstage with Johnny Barbata and Fuzzy Samuels.

down pat on. "Because Fuzzy had been working on my solo album with me in England," says Stills, "it's obvious that he'd know my songs better."

This reasoning seemed logical enough. But the fact that Stills's material dominated the show caused no small amount of tension.

"I was browned off by the monster dominating force Stills was at the time," says Nash. "I don't mind being guided, but he was being preposterous."

"It was a matter of professionalism," Stephen says. "They were not into being arranged. So I had to cop out. It wasn't me trying to dominate anything. I was just trying to act like a pro and carry on in the middle of a difficult situation."

The situation became even more difficult when Neil Young walked off stage in the middle of a song toward the end of the show and refused to come back for the encore. According to Dallas Taylor, "Neil thought I was fucking up his songs on pur-

Stills tuning up, 1970 tour.

pose. But that wasn't the case at all. Fuzzy was missing notes because he didn't know the songs. And I could never play Neil's stiff grooves. He never told me what he wanted. I always got pegged for not liking Neil. But I really tried to get to know him. I could just never understand him. And after this Denver show, I was outside the dressing room door when I heard Neil say, 'Either Dallas goes or I go.' "

Several hours before CSN&Y were scheduled to play Chicago, Dallas was out of the group. A little while after that, *everybody* was out of the group.

"We broke up in Chicago," says Nash. "We couldn't relate to each other on a rational level. When we can't do that, we can't play. So we all flew home."

Everyone, that is, except Stills, who had already left for the soundcheck when the decision to pack it in was made. Leo Makota recalls, "We were tearing down the equipment when Stephen walked in and said, 'What's goin' on?' We told him there wasn't going to be a show and that everyone had left. He said, 'There is too gonna be a show tonight, even if I'm the only one who plays!' "

But the Chicago Auditorium had not agreed to present a Stephen Stills solo show. It was either CSN&Y or nothing. Stills gives his version of what led up to the cancellation: "I had a fucked-up knee and was in a thigh-to-ankle cast. So I was bouncing around on crutches, with ten pounds of plaster on my leg. The other guys were fat, rich, and lazy stars, filled with an inflated self-image that precluded rehearsing with the new bass player.

"After that aborted soundcheck, at one amazing meeting, I watched Neil, David, Graham, Elliot, and God knows who else smoke an ounce of weed and blow off a seven-million-dollar year, purportedly because I was being a showboat. If a voice of reason could have cleared that fog, we would have realized our full potential and CSN&Y would be mentioned in the same breath with the Beatles and the Stones. We also would have become rich enough to get really creative. But I was the biggest fool. I thought the managers would come up with some strength. They didn't. So we all lost, right there, that day, to indulgence. We lost it all."

CSN&Y: "Ohio" (1970)

On May 4, 1970, four students were killed by National Guardsmen at Kent State University in Ohio. As news of this tragedy flooded the media for days afterward, Young and Crosby were holed up with Leo Makota inside a small house in Pescadero—a tiny coastal community thirty miles south of San Francisco. The horror of the Kent State killings sparked angry conversation. Neil Young finally got up, went off by himself for a while, and came back with a new song, "Ohio."

Neil Young, 1970.

Not much time passed before Young and Crosby headed for Los Angeles and rendezvoused with Stills (in from England), Nash, Fuzzy Samuels, and a new drummer

named Johnny Barbata. Crosby had suggested Russ Kunkel, but Stills and Nash wanted Barbata—formerly of the Turtles. Barbata was in. So a hastily regrouped CSN&Y, with yet another rhythm section combination, recorded "Ohio" at the Record Plant. It was an emotional session, and at the end of the take, Crosby burst into tears.

Young expressed his feelings about "Ohio" on his *Decade* liner notes: "It's still hard to believe I had to write this song. It's ironic that I capitalized on the deaths of these American students. Probably the biggest lesson ever learned at an American place of learning. My best CSN&Y cut."

"Ohio" *was* Young's best CSN&Y cut, if for no other reason than that it caught these four individuals *together*, live in the studio. It's a shame CSN&Y couldn't have recorded more songs like that. It's an even worse shame that it took a national tragedy to make them record this one.

CSN&Y: "The American Beatles" (1970)

If the public had had any say in the matter, Crosby, Stills, Nash & Young would never have parted. This was particularly true in the early summer of 1970. *Déjà Vu* had catapulted up the album charts, and "Teach Your Children" was a smash single and was about to be joined by "Ohio" (backed with a live take of Stills's "Find the Cost of Freedom").

It was during this period that CSN&Y seemed like the American Beatles. The impact, the power, and the "star quality" of CSN&Y had not been approached by any other American group. Sure, Creedence Clearwater Revival had unleashed a remarkable string of hits, but did that band ever walk out on a stage and get a standing

The audience was there to listen and CSN&Y were there to share. Santa Barbara concert.

ovation before uttering a sound? No. CSN&Y inspired such a reaction at *every* show. But it wasn't the kind of frantic, wild screaming that would intrude on the music. CSN&Y also had the ability to *calm* a crowd, and to get its respect. The audience was there to listen, and CSN&Y were there to share.

No other band in the history of rock 'n' roll has ever been able to carry on a conversation with an audience like CSN or CSN&Y. The raps between songs were as much a part of their show as the music, sometimes. There have never been any barriers between them and the people they have sung to. "We've always gone through our changes publicly," says Nash. "And in our words are pieces of our lives that people can look at and maybe find something they've also experienced or passed through."

On stage in 1970, CSN&Y also exuded a definite charisma, an aura that was not all musical. Like the Beatles, CSN&Y projected as four individual spirits. The stage

personalities, the presence, and the *look* of these characters were unique. Young, with his sunken-eyed stare shooting out from behind long black strands of hair, loomed to one side of the stage like a captive renegade. Stills floated out front more often, standing with his back straight like a country gentleman, striking hard poses while soloing, or loosening into a pained bluesman at the mike. Nash was the gentle, personable English hippie, who always charmed the crowd with his good nature. Without a doubt, it was Crosby who centered the team on stage. By his own admission, he was "the group mouthpiece." David also, at this time, coined a visual image that pretty much became the international archetypal hippie look—a long mustache brushed down over the lips, long, frizzy hair grown to the shoulders, and a frontiersman's buckskin jacket, with fringe flying.

"I really tried not to look at myself very closely," Crosby says. "Otherwise, you can become you *watching* you, instead of you

being you. So I just wore what I wanted to, felt like I wanted to, and did whatever I pleased. I smoked joints, snorted coke, played, sang, talked a lot, and just had a good ol' time."

This was an attitude adopted by legions of CSN&Y fans, who saw Crosby as someone who was openly thumbing his nose at traditional values and institutions and, at the same time, earning a lot of money within the country's economic structure. So Crosby became a role model for rebellious teenagers. And he, along with Stills, Nash, and Young, was unabashedly idolized.

"I believe we definitely got treated to the 'hero syndrome' by a lot of people," says Nash. "Not that that's good, not that that's bad, it just happened. . . . We were like little folk heroes in a way. We were doing it for everybody out there, for every musician that felt the way we did. When they saw us up there, they say *themselves*. It was a very interesting thing that happened between the artist and the audience, a very close symbiotic relationship."

Leo Makota says, "When I was out with CSN&Y in 1970, I could see how the crowds just *loved* those guys. There were never any problems. They were always well behaved. And after the shows, the crew would be loading equipment into the trucks and a lot of people would still be in the parking lot, singing CSN&Y songs."

This was *after* shows. During the actual performances, the crowds showed an astounding amount of enthusiasm. "If you get twenty thousand people all projecting, *emphatically*, the same thing toward the stage, the energy is immense," Crosby says. "And when it hits you, it's *big!* It comes in waves. You can almost see it. A big place, a hot night, a special moment, then that fuckin' surf . . . whooosh! It breaks on you, shakes you around, man, and the feeling is *righteous!*"

A five-night stand at New York's Fillmore East, June 2–6, 1970, found

David Crosby, somewhere on the road, 1970.

"When they saw us up there, they saw *themselves.*"

CSN&Y well rehearsed, fiery, and the recipient of just such crowd reactions. Photographer Joel Bernstein remembers, "The day after I graduated from high school, I went to see CSN&Y in New York. In the afternoon, I came across Graham, who had just split up with Joni a few minutes before, and he was completely devastated. He wrote 'Simple Man' that day and played it for the first time at the Fillmore East. I took a photograph of him playing it that was used on the back of his *Songs for Beginners* songbook."

Later that same day, Joel paid a visit to Neil Young's hotel room. "Neil played me an acetate of 'Ohio,' which hadn't been released yet, and he was writing 'Southern Man,' " says Joel. "For a kid one day out of high school, it was quite an afternoon."

CSN&Y: Political Voices (1970)

With the addition of Young's "Ohio" and "Southern Man" to CSN&Y's "political/protest set," which already included Crosby's "Long Time Gone," Nash's "Chicago," and Stills's ranting medley of "49 Bye-Byes," "For What It's Worth," and "America's Children"—the overall effect became that of a huge wrecking ball pounding against America's darkest political and societal elements. To some, these songs and the accompanying raps may have seemed like excessive proselytizing. Graham Nash admits, "We're all punks and we're all big-mouths. That's basically what it was and still is. I saw Bobby Seale get chained and gagged and bound and put on the witness stand. And everyone goes, 'Here, now we're going to have a fair trial.' That was total bullshit and that's where 'Chicago' came from, which I actually wrote to Stephen and Neil . . . 'Won't you please come to Chicago, just to sing?' And when Crosby witnessed the incredible societal impact of the Kennedy assassinations and wrote 'Long Time Gone,' when Neil saw four kids get gunned down in cold blood by the National Guard, when Stephen saw the Sunset Strip riots . . . this stuff just smacked us in the face, and it's fair to react when that happens. We've never believed in proselytizing, but we can't ignore what hurts us and angers us."

"I don't believe you can get out there and tell people what to believe," Crosby says. "And we never did that. I never said, 'I've got God's phone number . . . this is the Way.' We *did* offer an alternative set of values to the young people of this country, which is the only way to fight a government as strong and powerful as ours. We've always tried to reach the children."

In 1970, Crosby delivered one of his definitive raps in front of a film crew documenting CSN&Y. The film, shot and produced by Larry Johnson, Gary Burden, and David Meyers, never came out in its entirety, but Neil Young used parts of it in his film *Journey Through the Past*, released in 1973.

"I mean, man, on one side you've got a set of values that's doom, death, degradation, and despair, being dealt off the bottom of the deck by a gray-faced man who hates ya. And on the other side you've got a girl, running through a field of flowers, man, half-naked and high and laughing in sunshine. Now you offer those two alternatives to a child, and a child is too smart to make that mistake. It's not gonna go for that gray-faced dude with the cards."

Bill Graham says, "Crosby, Stills, Nash & Young were one of the first groups to not only sing out, but *speak* out. They were one of the first groups to rap and sometimes over-rap between songs. David and Stephen sometimes forgot it was a forty-five and not a seventy-eight. But those guys were the leaders of a whole socioeconomic movement."

"We were for a time on the point, so to speak, of that whole movement," admits Stills. " 'For What It's Worth' was me going, 'Pssst. I think we're in trouble.' The troops in 'Nam took it as their marching song. It became the theme song for the entire Third Marines for a while. From then on I was kind of *known* for that. Everybody

David Crosby.

was looking for a political message in everything I wrote, like I was running for the Senate at twenty-four. I said, 'Hang on, wait just a minute. I do not know the rules of the Senate.' "

But Stephen and the rest of the band knew how to reach the people. Ron Stone expounds: "Crosby, Stills, Nash & Young were the radical spokesmen for a generation. They were the voice of the underground. They said things on record and on the radio that every kid was saying about what was going on. They were a mirror for the audience's souls."

CSN&Y: The End of the Road (1970)

When CSN&Y went back to Los Angeles for some concerts at the Forum,

Laura Nyro experiencing CSN sound close up, Los Angeles, 1970.

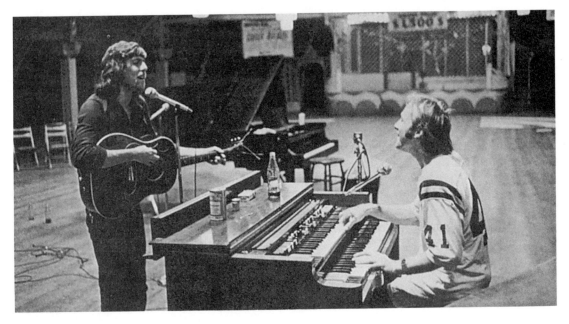

Rehearsal on the *They Shoot Horses Don't They* set.

CSN&Y with Taylor (left) and Reeves (right), Los Angeles, 1969.

June 26, 27, and 28, the emotional level of the shows was swinging back and forth like a crazy pendulum. During the acoustic portions, when different configurations serenaded softly, the vibes was still pure "peace, love, and togetherness." However, in the heat of the electric set, Stills and Young were flying neck-and-neck. " 'Southern Man' was the best of the conversation pieces," says Stills, "but it really was the only one that was dependable. It was slow, there was room to fuck up . . . but the unfortunate reality was that it was *Neil's* song, therefore he paid more attention. We never got that kind of commitment and interaction going in some of my pieces or some of David's or Graham's. 'Carry On' could have been so much better, but you

have to play fast and pay attention and do all the things I was doing in 'Southern Man.' You have to imitate each other. You've got to pick up what the other guy was playing and play it right back at him and not insist that what you made up was cooler.

"Overblowing is a forgivable sin and easy to correct. All it takes is a gentle reminder from someone *conscious* that, 'Hey, you two are stepping on each other. Pay attention. Be cool. And remember that this guy is not your enemy.' Overblowing is also the province of the young, excited musician.

"The attendant managers and various functionaries, for all their 'tsk, tsk' remarks, actually *got off* on all that destructive competition between me and Neil, and would, in fact, goad us on. They'd take one or the other of us aside and say something to the effect of, 'That asshole is stomping all over your songs, your vocals, everything! You're better than him! Show him!' A good manager would have approached the situation with prudent reality, taken us both into a private room and given us a forceful reminder that we were on the same team, that we were being equally disrespectful to each other and were equally to blame."

Ron Stone, at the edge of the stage for these shows, says, "Stephen and Neil squared off a lot. They'd end up blowing through each other's songs. Stephen would take a lead part and blast right through one of Neil's vocals. Then Neil would turn up and blast through Stephen's vocals. Then the whole thing would end up in complete disarray. They'd go into the dressing room and try and kill each other."

In contrast to this situation, Ron Stone remembers, "If you stood in proximity to David Crosby for more than fifteen minutes, you'd contract something called the Crosby Virus. His smoke was so devastating, you'd be unable to finish complete sentences for two or three hours afterwards. I tried to stay away from David whenever I had any real business to attend to."

Nash confirms, "Yeah, we smoked an insane amount of marijuana on the road. No wonder some of that time seems a little blurry now."

Since Fuzzy Samuels was from Jamaica, one might expect him to have spent the whole tour in some kind of ganja cloud. But Ron Stone says, "The last night of the tour, Fuzzy told us that he took *acid* every single day of the tour. He was so frightened, he stayed high the whole time. We just thought he couldn't talk."

When the CSN&Y tour did finally end, in Minneapolis, July 9, everybody got together and had a huge poker game. Lots of

Crosby rolls one.

135

End-of-tour dinner in Minneapolis hotel suite, 1970. Left to right: Neil Young, Mrs. Young (Neil's mother), Fuzzy Samuels. Johnny Barbata, Ron Stone, Stephen Stills, Graham Nash, Henry Diltz (in mirror), Dan Campbell, Leo Makota, David Crosby, Elliot Roberts, Charles John Quarto.

money changed hands. But with regard to the immediate future of CSN&Y, no hand revealed what was in the cards.

CSN&Y: "Cowboy Movie" (a.k.a. "The Break-Up of the CSN&Y Gang") (1970)

"I saw the splintering of CSN&Y coming from day one," says Elliot Roberts. "It was a combination of four very strong songwriters, very strong individuals. And I knew it would just be a matter of time before Neil just had too much to do on his own."

In July 1970, Young added the finishing touches to his *After the Gold Rush* solo al-

bum and was ready to launch his solo career again. At the same time, Stills had brought the tracks for his first solo album to Los Angeles and invited a chorus of friends into Wally Heider's to overdub some harmonies. Among them were Crosby, Nash, John Sebastian, Cass Elliot, Rita Coolidge, Priscilla Coolidge Jones, and Claudia Lanier.

During these sessions, Stephen fell head-over-heels in love with Rita Coolidge, but these feelings were destined to be unrequited. "Nash took Rita away from Stephen so fast it was absurd," says Crosby. "One second she was with Stephen, the next minute Nash. He walked into the room, blinked once, bent his finger, and *bam!* . . . she ran to him. That's sort of the way it always was with Nash. He could have any of 'em he wanted and was able to

Elliot and Neil at Lookout Management; Nash and Geffen in background.

take any of our old ladies or any others he pleased, because he was the best lookin', the Englishman, debonnaire."

Graham says, "With Rita, it was just a matter of two guys falling in love with the same girl. No big deal. But it created a whole fuckin' scene. Stephen was very upset. But I never crocked my finger or *stole* Rita. That's simply not true. We fell in love with each other and went to Stephen to explain the situation, but he wouldn't listen. In fact, he spit at me."

Stephen offers his thoughts: "Nowhere in my experience, limited though it was to the Southeastern United States, Latin America, and the Wabash River Valley, had I ever seen anyone go about snaking a buddy's girl with so little discretion. It simply wasn't done. Not only did the situation not arise, but *never* did one just blithely intrude upon the romance of a mate, no matter how one-sided or foolish that attachment might be, and carry on as if there was no more to all of this than cutting in at a dance. Humiliated as I might have been at how badly I misread the lady's feelings that she could be so easily distracted, I was absolutely mortified by how public it all was.

"This paragon of civility, whose friendship I cherished, caused me to feel like a public spectacle, allowing something private that should have remained between us to become fierce gossip before I had the faintest idea of what was afoot. That ain't cool in the gang.

"Part of the beauty of being in a group, a team, or any other intimate aggregation, is that no matter what you might be going through among yourselves, there is shit that just don't go out of the family, *ever*. Whatever I think about my partner today, however badly I might want to kill him, nobody else besides his ol' lady and the other partner even opens his *mouth* about him in front of me, let alone has an opinion, never mind laughs at him. That's my partner you're talking about. Do it in front of me and I'll break your fucking face, freeze you out of this scene so fast your backstage pass will fall off, shove that in-the-know smirk of yours so far up your ass your teeth will come out backwards. I hope that's clear. *That* is the big fucking deal."

David Crosby distilled the collage of events that occurred in July 1970 into a song called "Cowboy Movie." A colorful look at human nature, it unfolds as a Western/outlaw scenario built around "the story of the CSN&Y gang"—with each member given appropriate aliases and personality traits.

Fat Albert (Crosby) narrates and sets a scene of revelry: "Me and my good partners . . . we were ridin' back to have ourselves a party, to celebrate the robbing of the train"—the completion of the CSN&Y tour. This mood quickly dissipates with the arrival of Raven (Rita Coolidge). Young Billy (Neil Young) remarks, "Something here ain't exactly right." A series of confrontations follows between Eli (Stephen Stills)—"He's our fastest gunner. He's kinda mean and young and from the South"—and Duke (Graham Nash)—"He's our dynamiter." They both want Raven—who Fat Albert suspects might be "the law." She was.

"In actual fact, the law I was thinking

of was the law of averages," says Crosby, who provided the insights for the above interpretation. "I was thinking of a higher law than human law." David adds, "Human lives don't grow in parallel courses. They are constantly converging and diverging. That's always been the case with us guys. And 'Cowboy Movie' happens to be about one of those times when our lives were destined to follow different courses for a while."

When CSN&Y did in fact scatter in July 1970, Stills was not quite as philosophic about the situation as Crosby. He was openly upset. Stephen explains, "I just wish we could have held it together a little longer. But there were petty ego jealousies going on. Nash and I weren't talking. Neil wanted to be on his own. I had my solo album to finish. But we *still* could have done that *and* kept CSN&Y going. But we threw it all away for very fallacious reasons, I can see now. I mean, we were standing on the verge. And all of the freedom we wanted for our personal careers would have still been available to us. But we couldn't put the trivia going on between us aside and we became, I believe, very cavalier with our careers."

CHAPTER SEVEN

Solo and Duo Careers: Passing Ships on the Water (1970–1973)

Crosby: Moored in Marin/Records First Solo Album (1970)

David Crosby's career shifted into a solo mode in late summer of 1970. Living on his boat, docked at Sausalito harbor in Marin County, David began preparing his own album. Nightly, he would head into Wally Heider's studio in San Francisco. Although most of the music being recorded was his, he explains, "I don't think it's right to call it a solo album, because I got an awful lot of help from a lot of my friends." Jerry Garcia, Phil Lesh, Mickey Hart, and Bill Kreutzmann from the Grateful Dead, and Paul Kantner, Grace Slick, Jorma Kaukonen, and Jack Casady from the Jefferson Airplane were part of this community of musicians, which also included Joni Mitchell, Graham Nash, and Neil Young.

"It was cross-pollination at its best," says Crosby. "Everyone wanted to share some of their music."

Called *If I Could Only Remember My Name*, this album was imbued with myriad

Paul Kantner, Marin County, 1970.

David Crosby and Phil Lesh.

textures and musical colors, led by Crosby's vocals and modal, open-tuned twelve-string guitar. Garcia added lead guitar phrases; Casady wandered freely with his bass; Joni sang harmony, and Neil squeezed out some of his most frail-sounding cries. This was spontaneous ensemble playing that worked.

"When I was recording 'I'd Swear There Was Somebody Here,' I was thinking about Christine a lot," says Crosby. "It's the best requiem I could have sung for her."

David Crosby.

The album was dedicated to Christine Gail Hinton and, in that light, there is a certain spirituality that comes to a head in "Laughing," a philosophical "revelation" of sorts: "And I thought I'd seen someone / Who seemed at last / To know the truth / I was mistaken / It was only a child— laughing—in the sun / Ah! In the sun."

Concurrent with the recording of *If I Could Only Remember My Name*, Paul Kantner was assembling many of the same musicians and leading them on board the Jefferson Starship (the name that Kantner used for this musical flight *before* changing the Jefferson Airplane into the Starship). Much of what came out of these sessions made it onto Kantner's *Blows Against the Empire*. Crosby's presence cannot be missed, particularly throughout "A Child Is Coming," written by Crosby, Slick, and Kantner. Equally evocative are the vocals and words of "Have You Seen the Stars Tonight?" a Crosby–Kantner collaboration.

"These sessions," recalls Grace Slick, "were like, 'Uh, do you wanna play guitar on this one?' 'No, man, I have to go to the bathroom.' 'Okay, David, you wanna play?' 'Sure.' Whoever felt like doing something *did* it. Parts interchanged, *people* interchanged."

Graham Nash mixed the entire second side of *Blows*. He remembers, "They asked my opinion and I just jumped right in. Grace, Paul, David—they let me do whatever I heard. I was searching for this kind of environment when I came to America. And when I was mixing in the studio, our imaginations were running rampant. We were creating virtual kingdoms with music."

"The combinations that happened on these records," says Kantner, "will probably never happen again."

Kantner, Jerry Garcia, and Crosby.

Nash: Life with Rita / The Pained Artist / "Songs For Beginners"

In Los Angeles, watching the summer of 1970 slip away, Graham Nash divided his time between a bungalow (shared for a time with Charles John Quarto) at the ex-

Graham and Rita Coolidge.

clusive Sunset Strip Hotel, the Chateau Marmont, and a house in the Hollywood Hills, where he lived with Rita Coolidge.

"My time with Rita was a very high time," says Nash. "She was very easy to be with, very funny. We shared a lot in common. She came from an equivalent background in the South to mine in the north of England. I wrote a lot of my first solo album, *Songs for Beginners*, when I was with Rita."

But Graham admits, "There was also a period when I wanted to retreat. I went to the Chateau Marmont for two nights and stayed four months. I used to enjoy playing the pained artist. I had a little Wurlitzer piano in one room. I'd order room service and only come out at night. I wrote a lot of tunes there . . . like 'Stranger's Room,' 'Southbound Train.' But it got boring. I don't like being by myself that much."

And, in fact, Nash amassed an army of friends to help him record his first solo album. He rounded up Johnny Barbata, Fuzzy Samuels, Rita Coolidge, David Crosby, Phil Lesh, Jerry Garcia, Dave Mason, bassist Chris Ethridge, and the vocal section of Clydie King, Vanetta Fields, Shirley Mathews, and Dorothy Morrison.

Early in the sessions, however, as Bill Halverson recalls, "One night I told Graham, 'If it continues on like this, you're going to have an album that's a cure for insomnia.' Graham stormed out and, as it happened, that was right when I had to go to England to work with Stephen. So Larry Cox, the Jefferson Airplane's engineer, came to finish the album. And when I heard the five tunes I'd recorded with Graham, which were pretty down, with the five that Larry had done, which were up, *together* they made a nice album."

Songs for Beginners (released in June 1971) does work because it blends Nash's sensitivity (most clearly on "Sleep Song," "Wounded Bird," and "Simple Man") with more forceful statements, such as "Chicago," "Military Madness," and "Better Days."

"I thought Graham had made the best solo album of anyone in the band at that particular time," says Elliot Roberts.

Elliot Roberts and Graham Nash at Elliot's ranch, 1971. (Left: Johnny Barbata.)

Nash himself says, "I was very proud of *Songs for Beginners* because it stretched my awareness of who I am a bit further. It helped me gain more self-confidence and allowed me to come in contact with many fine players and singers."

In reference to the LP's title, Nash explains, "It was a beginning, my first solo album. But also, *beginning* means songs for people who *act*, begin things. Because people think a lot, but then don't act on their thoughts."

Graham was acting on his thoughts and, toward the end of the recording sessions, he bought an old Victorian house in the Haight-Ashbury district of San Francisco. "I saw this house," Nash says. "I walked in and looked out at the backyard, which was glowing with a fabulous sunset. At that moment I said to myself, 'This is my new home.' "

Stills: Changing Partners and Places (1970)

In August 1970, Stills was searching for some peace and once again turned to horses as a means of blowing off steam. He also, apparently, turned to some chemical means of escape and, on August 14 (Crosby's twenty-ninth birthday), Stills was arrested on various drug possession charges. "I took responsibility for everything," Stills told *Circus* in 1972. "I got a fine, which was hefty enough, but fair within the law. And that ended that trip."

Stephen Stills.

But Stephen's trip had really only begun. At the end of August, he flew in a Learjet to his cabin near Gold Hill, Colorado—where he stayed for more than a month. Fuzzy Samuels, Dan Campbell (a

Stephen and Dan Campbell, Denver Airport, 1970.

friend and adviser), and Henry Diltz were there most of the time with Stills. Many casual, late-night jam sessions ensued, with Stills on guitar or piano, Fuzzy on bass, and Diltz added some percussion by shaking a jar filled with peanuts. During the day, there were a couple of rock-climbing expeditions. But this serene atmosphere changed one afternoon. The September 18 entry in Henry Diltz's journal reads: "Today in Stephen's cabin we learned on the old wall phone that Jimi Hendrix was dead. Stephen was quite shaken."

"When Jimi died," Stills once said, "I almost quit the business." Stephen is still convinced that Hendrix's life might have been saved. "The people around him weren't on top of it," Stephens says. "He

Stephen Stills.

Stephen in the snow at dawn sitting for his first solo album cover photo, Colorado, 1970.

was runnin' with a strange crowd then." Stills dedicated his first solo album to James Marshall Hendrix.

In addition to this Hendrix dedication, Stills's first solo album also featured a poem on the back cover, written by Charles John Quarto. Called "A Child Grew Up on Strings," the verse accurately portrayed Stills's ability to carry on with his music despite an occasional need to withdraw into his shell like a turtle, the central metaphor in the poem.

On September 22, snow fell in the Rockies, and Stills, at dawn, walked outside his cabin, guitar in hand, and posed for his first solo album-cover shots.

"Stephen wanted the purple giraffe in every picture," says Diltz. "He was trying to send a message to someone."

Stills never revealed to whom, and by early October he was back in London.

When *Stephen Stills* was released a month later, it was an instant success and went gold (500,000 units sold), thanks to the hit single, "Love the One You're With." By this time, Stills was deep into another recording project, employing the services of Fuzzy Samuels, Dallas Taylor, drummer Conrad Isadore, Eric Clapton, guitarist Nils Lofgren, and the Memphis Horns.

"During these sessions, I was going after getting a real performing band together," Stills says. "It was obvious that CSN&Y was still scatterbrained, so it was time to get together *my* show. Chicago [the group] had just come out and there were a lot of people trying to utilize horns. I made an attempt at doing the same thing with the Memphis Horns. I was trying to do what Otis Redding did. But the unfortunate thing was, I was kind of categorized as an acoustic guitar, voices, really meaningful, poetic, folk singer type. But I wanted to play some R&B, man!"

But Stephen also went where his obvious strengths lay—folk-blues acoustic guitar—particularly on "Word Game," a song written by Stills in a five-minute torrent after viewing a TV special on South Africa. "We recorded enough music for a double album," says Bill Halverson.

Stephen also ventured out of the studio. "I met a lot of people who shared my kind of views on music," Stills says. "They took their music seriously. They wouldn't get so loaded or self-involved that they couldn't stop and clarify a change. They were much more dedicated to their work, if you will, constantly trying to improve. When they jammed, they *practiced*. Whereas in California, you'd smoke the most powerful marijuana you could find and play one chord for an hour . . . *boring!* So I was interested in learning all I could in England. I played with much more serious people. Doris Troy would stop and show me how to sing. She showed me a lot of scales

Stephen leading the Memphis Horns, Island Studios, London, 1970.

Stephen with Peter Sellers and John the gardener at Brookfield House, Sellers's former house and gardener.

Stephen sitting in with the Rolling Stones during their 1970 Amsterdam concert.

and techniques. She taught me how to sing notes I might have been slurring before. So this was a time of real growth for me."

In the fall of 1970, Stephen played with bassist Jack Bruce, Buddy Miles, Eric Clapton, Jimmy Page, and Buddy Guy in a film later released as *Supershow*—featuring Stills on electric versions of "Black Queen" and "Crossroads." Stephen also dropped in on a Rolling Stones concert in Amsterdam and sat in on keyboards. When he ran into Peter Sellers in London, the two went back to Brookfield House together and actually "jammed" for a bit in the music room. Later, Stephen appeared as a guest on a couple of British television shows and

traded guitar riffs with Frank Zappa at a London nightclub. Is it any wonder Stills came to be known as one of the world's most active jammers?

A nonmusical adventure, an attempt to rendezvous with Steve McQueen—who was shooting a movie in Paris—involved renting a long Mercedes limo, boarding a ferry, and traveling to France, only to discover that McQueen had already left. It was a $30,000 "lost weekend" that Stephen says, "I'm still paying for." A companion on this trip was Anthony Fawcett, a British art critic who, along with Diltz, spent a lot of time with Stills during this period. "Anthony was wonderful," says Stephen. "He was always more than happy to do anything to help out. And he and I shared a world that you don't often share with people. He knew his onions about art. We'd have these marvelous conversations and poke around obscure art galleries."

Stills's devotion to horses did not wane in England. In fact, he had some stables on the grounds of Brookfield House and ended up buying two thoroughbreds, Major Change and Crazy Horse.

Stephen in his kitchen with Allan McDougall, Mark Volman, Anthony Fawcett (background), and his prized bottle of Tabasco sauce—hard to get in England.

me from going off the deep end at certain points in my life."

This period in England was not one of those times when he edged toward the deep end. True, he maintained a whirlwind pace in the studio and had his share of adventures. But he never shifted into a crazed mode. Stephen was just on a high creative roll. And by mid-autumn both Crosby and Nash were in England and stopped in for a visit. Crosby added some harmony to Stills's solo tracks. Then, at one point, all three singers harmonized on "As I Come of Age"—a song written by Stills after he wrecked his Ferrari.

"It was a catalyst to thoughts," says Stills, "about being led kicking and screaming into adulthood."

Stephen riding Major Change.

"The thing about horses," Stephen says, "is that they *demand* your attention, so you have to forget about whatever else is going on in your life when you're with 'em, particularly if you're in a training process. I think working with horses definitely kept

CSN&Y: "4 Way Street" (1971)

With the dawning of 1971, a CSN&Y regrouping was rumored to be in the works. This talk increased when, in February, Atlantic released *4 Way Street*, a CSN&Y double-record live set, culled from several of the summer 1970 shows. Nash and Stills devoted the most attention to the project, but they were often off in different places, doing different things. Consequently, Bill Halverson explains, "I sort of became a runner between the guys to make sure there was enough of everybody in there. I think I finished that album twenty times before they all said, 'Okay, put it out.' " To a man, they all now seem to regret its existence.

"It's because we were too proud to loop [overdub]," says Stills, "which I thought was really jive. You've got to be the Mills Brothers in Carnegie Hall not to have to

CSN&Y backstage on the road, 1970. (This photo is the frame following the one used on the inside of the *4 Way Street* album.)

Graham and friend at Stills's house in Elstead, Surrey.

loop a little. . . . My feelings about live albums are that as long as you get the live *feel*, if there's some out-of-tune singing, cheat! I mean, the hell with it, we were not in tune on that second chorus. So let's lay in that second chorus and nobody will know the difference, which they *don't*. Then Crosby goes, 'No, man, it's gotta be *pure*, man.' I thought that record was bad."

Periodic out-of-tuneness notwithstanding, *4 Way Street* roughly simulated the structure of CSN&Y live shows in 1970—first, some group acoustic numbers, then solo and duo turns, following intermission with group electric, then an acoustic close. The high moments on this record were Crosby's "Triad" and "Lee Shore" (not previously on any other official release); Nash's "Right Between the Eyes" (also unreleased); Young's "Southern Man" and "Ohio"; and Stills's "Love the One You're With." There was enough CSN&Y magic on *4 Way Street* to appease fans who were eager for another tour.

The chances of CSN&Y sharing a stage together in early 1971 seemed remote at best. Young's *After the Gold Rush* had been a success and Neil was in bed following a back operation. Crosby was working with Carl Gottlieb on a film called *Family*. Nash had produced a poetry album for Charles

John Quarto and was working in the studio with a band called the Fool. Stills, meanwhile, was in the middle of recording his second album, working with Ringo, the Small Faces, and, he says, "God knows who else."

4 Way Street could not have been more aptly titled.

Stills: "Stephen Stills 2"/The Drunken Memphis Horns Tour (1971)

Stephen had been looking for a change of scene, and Ahmet Ertegun suggested Florida. Engineers Ron and Howard Albert were in Miami's Criteria Studios in February of 1971 when late one night—2:00 A.M., actually—Stills ambled in the door carrying a guitar. "We didn't know he was coming," says Howard Albert, "and we were in the middle of making a Johnny Winter live album. Luckily there were two of us, 'cause Stephen wanted to start right away. That first night we cut an acoustic version of 'Relaxing Town.' "

Over the next several months, one marathon session after another resulted in the completion of *Stephen Stills 2* (released in July 1971). The album featured the moderate hits "Marianne" and "Change Partners," as well as tracks filled with horns, acoustic and electric guitars, piano, and plenty of rhythm sounds. A good many of the songs were intensely personal statements and demonstrated Stills's willingness to pour his heart out into his music.

Even though Stills's ambitious explorations were filled with sincere expression and soul, certain "poison pens" ripped his work to shreds.

"I was still kind of a kid in this racket," Stephen says. "So, boy, it was real hard when anything I tried that wasn't what was expected of me was called horseshit. I was

Charles John Quarto in limo with Graham and David somewhere in the Midwest, 1970.

148

trying to grow up and just try some new things, then I'd get *slammed*."

This, of course, didn't foster a great deal of self-confidence when Stills began a fifty-two-date American tour in July 1971, backed up by Dallas Taylor, Fuzzy Samuels, keyboardist Paul Harris, guitarist Steven Fromholz, and the Memphis Horns. This was Stephen's first solo tour and he had no clear idea what to expect when he flew into Seattle for opening night.

"I was booked into the city three months after Boeing was closed," Stephen muses. "So when I played this fifteen-thousand-seat auditorium, three thousand people showed up. I was *mortified*. So I got blind drunk and was suitably horrid."

This set the tone for the rest of the tour. "I got real *torn*, man," Stills admits. "A lot of the time I'd hit the stage drunk and would end up singing sharp and playing flat. I'm not very proud of that tour. But, in addition to some insecurity, I'd lost a *woman* and did what millions of American men have done for generations—you lose a woman, you pour yourself into a bottle. So I was not in the best of shape. I thought my charts were pretty good, though, and there were some shows the crowds just adored, like my performance at Madison Square Garden. But Bangladesh happened three days later and all of the New York critics were living in George Harrison's hallway. My show didn't even get reviewed. And when I donated my stage, sound and lighting system, *and* my production manager to George, he didn't just not invite me to play, he didn't mention my name, I never got a thank-you note. I got so upset, I went to Ringo's room, got *real* drunk, and just sat there barking at everybody, 'Thoosshhh asssholes.' My feelings were just real hurt and I wanted to make everyone else as miserable as I was."

Toward the end of the tour, when Stills and the Memphis Horns hit Cleveland, across town the Flying Burrito Brothers

Stephen Stills, Madison Square Garden concert, New York City, 1971.

were finishing up a show. Chris Hillman, then the Burritos' lead singer and driving force, recalls, "I was as bored with the Burrito Brothers as David had been with the Byrds. And I was broke. So, when I saw

Stills/Burritos pre-Manassas band at the Hollywood Bowl. Left to right: Lala, Berline, Taylor, Perkins, Hillman, Samuels, and Stills.

Stills was in town, I went to his show and it was obvious *he* was ready to get into something else. We talked afterwards, and a week later I got a call from Stephen. He said, 'Meet me in Miami.' "

Elliot Roberts and Graham Nash watching Stephen's Madison Square Garden concert.

Stills wanted Hillman to bring along Burrito guitarist Al Perkins and fiddler Byron Berline. Down at Criteria Studios, Stephen had been visualizing a concept album that would group together rock, folk, Latin, country, and blues. This didn't require any brass tracks, so, with his tour just over, Stephen sent the Memphis Horns packing. Retained were Dallas, Fuzzy, Paul Harris, and a young percussionist named Joe Lala. Formerly with Pacific Gas and Electric and Blues Image, Lala had been hired by Stills in the middle of the tour as a backup vocalist.

When this Stills–Burritos amalgam congregated in the studio, something clicked almost immediately. Rehearsals flowed right into recording sessions. And one night, after cutting a vampish blues-rock jam called "Jet Set," Stephen herded everyone into the control room and announced, "Hey, men. We're gonna be the best band in the world and make a million bucks."

Crosby and Nash: Pair Up in Detroit / Harmony and Comedy (1971)

In the summer of 1971, Crosby and Nash teamed up and carried on the spirit of the original CSN "living room days." Without banks of amplifiers or an extensive entourage, David and Graham simply hit the road with their acoustic guitars and voices.

"We hung out a lot and got off so much together, the combination of me and Nash had to happen," says Crosby.

Nash agrees: "We'd both finished solo albums and we'd done this 'Winter Soldier' benefit for Vietnam Vets Against the War in Detroit, just the two of us. We found out we could do it. We were pretty relaxed, pretty funny, there was a lot of good music, and we got people off righteously."

Playing medium-sized halls throughout America, C&N were able to present an entertaining, musically varied two-hour show that included a liberal dose of CSN favorites such as "Wooden Ships," "Teach Your Children," "Our House," and "Guinnevere," as well as solo/duo material like Nash's "Southbound Train" and "Immigration Man," and Crosby's "Games" and "Laughing." The heart of these concerts proved beyond a doubt that the real har-

Crosby and Nash in concert.

151

monic strength of CSN or CSN&Y lay in the vocal cords of Crosby and Nash.

What was equally striking about these C&N shows was the constant comedic repartee the duo established. David and Graham became the Abbott and Costello of rock. More than actual rehearsed routines, however, their dialogue consisted of spontaneous between-songs raps. An example:

NASH: We must have the best gig in the entire world . . . it's true! . . . We sit here . . .

CROSBY (in a whisper): Blabbermouth!

A VOICE FROM THE CROWD: Get loose!

NASH: Hang loose?

CROSBY (giggling): Loos*er*! If I get a lot looser, I'm gonna forget which finger is on the guitar.

NASH: What guitar? There's a good joke.

CROSBY: I did that one night at the Fillmore. In the old Fillmore Ballroom one night, it was one of the few times I tried to play behind acid, and the strings got the size of ropes! (Howls of laughter from the audience.) Song? What song? Ohhhhh! It was very loose. It was too loose.

NASH: Lautrec.

CROSBY (after a pause): Lautrec. I *knew* you were gonna say it. You couldn't resist it.

NASH: No, it's because you did that on purpose just to trigger my psychological reaction to that remark you made.

CROSBY: Trick you! Haaaa! (Giggles.)

NASH (deadpan): He's got me exactly where I want him.

The above exchange can be found on the popular Crosby and Nash bootleg album, *A Very Stony Evening*, recorded in 1971 at a concert in California. It's one of many interactions that fall between the songs.

"That night," Nash remembers, "David

David Crosby.

had a 104-degree fever, was on antibiotics, and was totally spaced. We nearly canceled the concert. But David figured he could go on and was *so funny*. I guess he was really relaxed . . . And that line, 'He's got me exactly where I want him,' I got that from my father."

While in Los Angeles around this time, Nash was the best man at former Hollies publicist Allan McDougall's wedding. What happened in the courtroom was—well, Allan tells the story:

"We just did it front of the judge," says Allan. "Graham showed up in his best jeans and denim shirt. And needless to say, during the ceremony Nash dropped the ring, which caused everyone to look at his feet. He had on one brown boot and one green boot. Graham just laughed, 'I've got another pair just like it at home.' And when he signed the register, this old Jewish judge looked at the signature and said, 'Nash, Nash . . . are you famous?' Graham went, 'Well, sort of, I guess, yes.' Then the judge said, 'Are you the writer?' Graham said, 'Yeah, I write a bit.' Then the judge blurted out, 'Well, I'll be damned. Ogden Nash in my courtroom! I've admired your work for years!' "

Meanwhile, David Crosby was making good on a promise to help out a young songwriter named Jackson Browne. David had boosted Browne a year earlier, in an interview with Ben Fong-Torres: "I think Jackson Browne is one of the probably ten best songwriters in the country . . . the cat just sings rings around people and he's got songs that'll make your hair stand on end."

David had originally planned to produce Jackson, but this plan evolved into Crosby singing all of the harmonies on Browne's debut album. Nash joined in on harmonies for the recording of the single, "Doctor My Eyes." Later, Browne wrote a song for Crosby called "For Everyman."

"Jackson listened to 'Wooden Ships,'" says David, "and he called me on it being an elitist attitude. He said, 'What about the guys who can't escape?' And I said, 'Well, fuck 'em.' He said, 'That's not cool,' then wrote 'For Everyman.' He was right, of course, I eventually saw that. You've got to stick around and fight. Because there are people out there who can't fight for themselves and you can't just leave them to the meat grinder."

CSN&Y: A Brief Coming Together (1971)

By the late summer of 1971, Atlantic was beginning to wonder if the idea of CSN&Y had been deserted by its four principals. They had, in fact, congregated a couple of times at Neil Young's new Broken Arrow Ranch near La Honda, in the Santa Cruz Mountains. However, no full-scale CSN&Y recording took place. Instead, various other configurations supported a few of Young's songs on his fourth solo album, *Harvest*. Crosby and Nash sang backup on "Are You Ready for the Country?" Stills and Crosby can be heard on "Alabama." And Stills and Nash harmonized behind Young on "Words." But this was only a brief CSN&Y shot.

Atlantic and the public were anxious to see the four back together, and a couple of live reunions did occur in September 1971, in Boston and New York. Billed as Crosby and Nash shows, they developed after an hour or so into CSN, when Stills walked on, guitar in hand, having flown up from Miami. A little while later, there appeared the fourth piece of the puzzle—Neil Young, who had just finished *Harvest* and was in the process of shooting footage in the South for his first film, *Journey Through the Past*.

Neil Young at his Broken Arrow Ranch, La Honda, California.

Playing only acoustically, Crosby, Stills, Nash & Young traded off songs like old college roommates exchanging stories at a corner bar. The magic hadn't died. And a few weeks later, at the Berkeley Community Theater, another partial grouping took place. This time it was Crosby, Nash & Young, prompting an obligatory cry from the balcony—"Where's Steve?"

Stills: Miami Marathons/ "Manassas Junction" (1971–1972)

Striding around Criteria Studios in Miami with an electric guitar slung over his shoulder, Stills was flying. He'd been up for two days and had laid down eight new tracks. Says Chris Hillman, "I quickly saw that here was a guy who could go all night and then some. Then he got us all involved in the same pace."

Stephen Stills.

"The longest session was a hundred and six straight hours," says engineer Howard Albert. "I can't tell you what we did. All I know is that I was there."

On the rare occasions when anyone actually went to a hotel, rather than sleeping on a studio couch, Stills would often get them out of bed. Ron Albert recalls, "We'd

taken a break after an eighty-hour streak. I was in my room, had just fallen asleep, when the phone rings. It was Stephen, saying, 'Hey, I'm sorry, I know you're tired, but there's this idea I've got for this song that I want to get on tape before I forget it.' "

"Those marathons got pretty crazy sometimes," Stills admits. "But it was just a matter of keepin' the fire lit. When you get onto something, you want to track it down. We broke a lot of new ground doin' that."

"It was always search and find," says Hillman.

What they found were several different realms of music—rock, pop, country, bluegrass, Latin jazz, blues, and folk—that were combined and played with a lot of spirit. Songs like "The Treasure," "Johnny's Garden" (written for Stephen's gardener at Brookfield House in England), and "It Doesn't Matter" (co-written by Stills, Chris Hillman, and Rick Roberts) were among those recorded.

Bill Wyman and Stephen Stills at Island Studios, London, 1970.

In the middle of these sessions, Rolling Stones bassist Bill Wyman stopped in for a visit and helped Stills write "Love Gangster."

"Fuckin' Bill Wyman wanted to quit the Rolling Stones to join us," says Dallas Taylor. "I got this from Bill Wyman himself. But he said, 'You guys never *asked* me.' "

Manassas at Stephen's house in England. Left to right: Paul Harris, Joe Lala, Chris Hillman, Dallas Taylor, Fuzzy Samuels, Stephen Stills, Al Perkins. (CMA publicity photo from the collection of Dave Zimmer.)

Stills says, "I nearly jumped off a bridge when I found out about this."

By late 1971, however, Stephen and his merry band were an exclusive club. And with a double album's worth of material in the can, all they needed was a name. This problem was solved when Stephen, an avid student of the Civil War, took the band on a tour along the East Coast. One stop was Manassas, Virginia. A photograph was taken of the band standing beneath a sign at Manassas Junction. When the film was developed, Manassas came into view as their official name.

That taken care of, Stephen flew everyone over to England with the intention of rehearsing for the road. Chris Hillman recalls, "We were all staying in Stephen's Surrey house, but we didn't rehearse much. Stephen had just had a knee operation. It was cold and foggy every day. I think we rehearsed there four times over a two-month period."

Stills says, "It was a little more than that. But all I know is that it cost me an arm and a leg. I was supporting everybody. Joe Lala himself drank almost $10,000 worth of wine. He drank a case of 1947

Cheval Blanc without knowing how expensive it was."

By the release of *Manassas*, a double album, in May 1972, the band had managed to get tight enough to take on the world. Manassas played all over Europe, Australia, and America. The shows generally ran close to three hours, with an opening rock set, then Stills playing solo acoustic, Hillman and Perkins on bluegrass, then Manassas country, more Manassas rock, and an acoustic finish.

"It was built off the Flying Burrito Brothers format," says Hillman.

Stephen reflects, "Manassas was such a terrific band. It really had some structure and reminded me of the Buffalo Springfield at its best. Manassas could play *anything*. We used to drive people nuts playing that whole first side, top to bottom. We played the *edits* we'd done in the studio!"

Howard Albert says, "I tell ya, Manassas was one of the greatest *and* most underrated bands of the seventies. That double album, along with Eric Clapton's *Layla*—which me and my brother both worked on—stand as the most *important* and best albums we've ever been a part of."

"Atlantic could have really swung with Manassas," Stills insists. "But they were so wrapped up in CSN&Y, they couldn't find a handle on what Manassas could stand for, even though it was right in front of them. God knows, I thought I really gave 'em the ammunition with that double album. But Ahmet was always required to ask, 'When is *the group* getting back together?' Hell, I didn't know. But everybody was always blaming me for the fact that CSN&Y was apart—even though, at the time, Neil had a big hit with *Harvest*, and David and Graham were in the middle of a duo thing. So I got fairly intense about carrying on with my own trip. I was fed up with having the responsibility of being the leader in a group that would rebel at the first sign of leadership. It was insane."

Crosby & Nash: First Duo Album / Nash and Young's "War Song" (1972)

Crosby and Nash were working together with consistency toward the end of 1971. They scotched a plan to release a live album featuring the CSN&Y Boston and New York onstage reunions. Instead, they went into the studio together as a duo for the first time and recorded an obscure Joni Mitchell song, "Urge for Going."

"It wasn't quite just me and David," says Graham. "When we were in there gettin' ready to sing, David Geffen walked in, straight toward the mike, put the headphones on, and said, 'Roll the tape!' Halverson rolled the tape and I told him, 'Hit that red button!' So we have a tape of Geffen singin' the verses and me and Crosby singin' the choruses. A great track! We were gonna put it out as a single for Christmas in 1971."

That record never did get released. But Crosby and Nash returned to Wally Heider's studios in Los Angeles and San Francisco in early 1972 and cut a whole album, *Graham Nash/David Crosby* (released in May 1972). Some familiar faces helped out, including a couple of Grateful Dead members, the Section (drummer Russ Kunkel, bassist Lee Sklar, guitarist Danny Kortchmar, and keyboardist Craig Doerge), and guitarist Dave Mason.

Nash remembers, "On my thirtieth birthday (February 2, 1972), I dropped a huge quanity of acid with Dave Mason and tried to eat this huge Italian meal at Venessi's in San Francisco. It was hysterical. Then I went into the studio to try and mix Crosby's 'Where Will I Be?'—a spacey track to begin with. I felt eight miles deep and came up with some pretty strange ideas . . . 'Is that a cowbell on there?' Pretty weird. But that album, with 'Southbound Train,'

Crosby and Nash recording session at Wally Heider's in Los Angeles, 1972. Left to right: Lee Sklar, Russ Kunkel, David Crosby, Danny Kortchmar.

'Page 43,' 'Immigration Man' . . . all very emotional songs."

Crosby agrees. "My 'Where Will I Be?' and 'Page 43' combination, I'm real proud of that. And my other stuff on there is sufficiently strange."

Nash included a fifty-eight-second live experiment called "Black Notes" (recorded in Carnegie Hall while Nash was waiting for Stills to walk on). "With this song," Graham says, "I tried to deal with overcoming and starting anything, especially piano playing. I started to just bash anywhere on the black notes, not using any white notes, and wrote this little song right on the spot. And if anybody could see me on stage at Carnegie Hall, just thumping with my arms and elbows on the black notes and making up a song, they should have realized that they could play and they could write songs, because I'd just done it."

Graham Nash/David Crosby was dedicated to "Miss Mitchell." Nash explains, "We both owed Joni a deep spiritual debt, because she was very supportive of me and David. She was a real catalyst in a lot of ways."

Even though this record was not a commercial smash, it provided the impetus for some more Crosby and Nash live work. And since most of the songs were acoustic, they still felt no need to put a backing band together. Neil Young did show up at one of the duo's San Francisco shows, and midway through the summer of 1972, when Nash and Crosby were on individual breaks, Young wrote a new tune called "War Song." Inspired by the assassination attempt on George Wallace, it was antiviolence and antiwar. Before recording it, Young called up Nash. Together they recorded the song at Neil's ranch with the

David Crosby at Wally Heider's, 1972.

Graham Nash at Wally Heider's, 1972.

Stray Gators (bassist Tim Drummond, drummer Kenny Buttrey, and steel guitarist Ben Keith). It hit the streets as a single, billed as "Neil Young, with Graham Nash."

"He could have just put it out as a Neil song," says Graham. "It pleased me that he gave me credit."

A seemingly insignificant gesture, it did, nevertheless, make it easier for Young to ask a favor of Graham and David a few months later.

CSN&Y's Rising Offspring: The Eagles and America

In the absence of any new CSN or CSN&Y material on the market in 1972, a couple of new groups who had been heavily influenced by the CSN sound entered the fray. The Eagles, hatched in Los Angeles, and the band America, formed by two mili-

tary brats in England, made no efforts to deny their inspirations.

"Hey," says former Eagle Glenn Frey, "the first day I was in California, I saw David Crosby on the porch of the Canyon Store in Laurel Canyon. He had on his brimmed hat and his cape. I was struck by how small he was. Because in my mind, David Crosby was this *giant!*

"So I took seeing him like that as kind of an omen for me. And I later saw Crosby hanging out at the Troubadour and went up to him and told him I dug his stuff and I kept sayin', 'I hope I'm not botherin' you.' And he said, 'No, man, I don't mind.' He could have just told me to scram.

"And Crosby always had the best pot. When J. D. [Souther] and I were playing at the Troub five and six nights a week, a couple of young coyotes, two 'soon-to-be's,' we'd spot some of Crosby's girl friends. And this one girl had a stash of David's pot. And

Eagles, 1972. Left to right: Don Henley, Bernie Leadon, Randy Meisner, Glenn Frey.

we'd think, 'Well, we don't wanna rip off the Cros,' but one night this girl said, 'I happen to have some grass here I got from David.' She rolled one up. J. D. and I took about two tokes and we were *gone*. I thought, 'No wonder they can write such great songs!' "

When the Eagles were just coming together, Frey says, "Anybody who wanted to get anywhere in the L.A. scene in the early seventies just picked up the CSN album and went, 'Hmmm. Here's who the managers are. Here's who took the photos.' Then you'd go for it."

Sure enough, the Eagles signed on with Elliot Roberts, got a record deal with David Geffen's new Asylum label, and had Henry Diltz shoot their album cover out in the desert. And in 1972, the Eagles scored an immediate hit with "Take It Easy," a Frey–

Jackson Browne composition that oozed CSN-like harmony.

America took a similar route up the music-biz ladder. They got a record deal with Warner Bros. (Neil's label), signed a management agreement with Elliot Roberts, and when America's debut album came out in 1972, it not only screamed "CSN&Y" but on the single, "Horse with No Name," Dewey Bunnell's vocals sounded so much like Neil Young that thousands of music fans were convinced that America was Young's new group.

"I didn't intentionally try and imitate Neil," says Bunnell. "But it's true that he and Crosby, Stills & Nash were huge influences on us. I mean, there's no getting around that."

Throughout America's career, and even as recently as 1983, with their hit "You Can

America at Elliot Roberts's ranch, 1972. Left to right: Dan Peek, Gerry Beckley, Dewey Bunnell.

Do Magic" (written by Russ Ballard), the echoes of CSN have remained.

The Eagles, too, one of the most successful groups of the seventies, repeatedly looked to CSN&Y and acted accordingly.

"When CSN&Y started all of their solo trips, I remember Henley and I instructing ourselves, 'Man, we'll never do that. We gotta stick together,'" Frey says. "Of course, we immediately turned around and made some changes in the band, but they were for the better. When we got Don Felder, then Joe Walsh into the group, I thought, 'Yeah, now we've got like a Stills–Young lead guitar combination here.' And that freed me up to be the Crosby guy, who plays rhythm guitar and talks to the crowd between songs—which David's always been really good at."

How did the genuine articles react to all of this?

Graham Nash responds, "I didn't react at all. It was complimentary and flattering and it was obvious that part of the change we helped give music was being manifested in [these] groups . . . not imitating our sound, but being affected by it enough to want to do it *their* way. Dewey [Bunnell, of America] specifically told me at one point that they wanted to make an album like the first CSN album—not that they wanted to copy it, but they wanted to make a thing that was as powerful as that. And that's a great thing to instill in people, to inspire them to do things like that."

Stills: Manassas "Down the Road"/Cooling Out in Colorado (1973)

The Stills inspiration that had once fueled CSN was running Manassas from

"**Running Manassas from city to city.**" Stephen and Fuzzy, 1972.

"**Stephen was always very generous with his money,**" says Chris Hillman.

city to city as the fall of 1972 approached. The pace of this roadwork was maniacal at times, and Stills admits, "I think for a while there, ICM [a booking company] said, 'Let's just put a harness on this guy and get fifteen percent.'" Chris Hillman remembers, "We had a charter plane and Michael John [Bowen, Stills's manager at the time] had all of the luggage numbered . . . Stills number one, Dallas Taylor number two, me number three . . . it was very organized, like we were in the army or something. And Michael John had been a sergeant in the Green Berets in 'Nam.

"Stephen was losing money on these Manassas tours," Hillman continues, "because he was covering the whole overhead. Finally one night I told him, 'I may be cutting my own throat, but you're paying us too much. We're making more money

than you are.' He had a million guys on the road who were all just kissin' his ass. Stephen was always very generous with his money. Probably *too* generous. He gave me a 1939 Lloyd Lord Gibson mandolin when I joined up with him, and he was always giving away stuff."

One thing Stephen did not give away, however, was his Brookfield House in England, which he sold for a one-hundred-percent profit. This financial coup came at the same time that Stills's personal life took a turn for the better. After a Manassas show in Paris, he met and fell in love with French singer/songwriter Veronique Sanson.

"She says she fell in love with me immediately after hearing me play the banjo," Stephen says. They would marry in April of 1973.

Before this, Stills persisted in maintaining a round-the-clock schedule with Manassas, on the road as well as in the studio. This resulted in the production of another album's worth of material, written not only by Stills, but by Chris Hillman, Fuzzy Samuels, and Dallas Taylor. Stevie Wonder even sang one track, but much of this music was shelved. "There was a lot of sloppy playing going down" says engineer Howard Albert. "We'd say, 'Hey, Stephen, that's not good enough.' And he'd say, 'Next song.' We finally had to leave because our opinions weren't being listened to."

Down the Road was completed at Caribou Ranch Studios in Colorado, with engineer Jim Guercio, and at the Record Plant in Los Angeles, with Bill Halverson, and released in January 1973. The best songs that came out of this work were "Pensamiento," a Stills Latin shuffle with original Spanish lyrics, and a Stills–Hillman folk-country lament called "So Many Times." The title track is the roughest thing Stephen ever committed to vinyl.

"I short-circuited there for a while," Stephen admits. "Things were moving too fast. I got a little crazed. Too much drinkin', too many drugs. What can I say?"

After settling a paternity suit in California on December 22, 1972, which proved he had fathered a child, Justin, by a woman named Harriet Tunis a couple of years earlier, things settled down a bit for Stills. He spent Christmas in Colorado and reflects, "When I was growing up in the Southeast, I hated the humidity and was totally addicted to air conditioning. I discovered that in Colorado there was air conditioning outside all the time, and I loved it.

"Also, in Colorado, I met some real down-home people who had no particular illusions about who I was. To them, I was just Stephen. I liked that. It helped me sort out a few things and brought me back to an understanding that there's more to this life than just rock 'n' roll. I began to paint; I was a Rocky Mountain rescue volunteer, as well as an auxiliary fireman."

Crosby: New Byrd Tracks (1973)

David Crosby was free in the fall of 1972. He'd just completed some more touring with Nash and was contemplating beginning another solo album when the

Crosby and McGuinn in the studio again, Wally Heider's, 1972.

phone rang. It was Crosby's old nemesis, Roger McGuinn. For a couple of weeks, four-fifths of the original Byrds had been helping their old producer Terry Melcher record an album. When Crosby's name came up—bingo!—the idea of a reunion lit up in everybody's mind.

Following a few record-company business shuffles, the original Byrds did in fact enter Wally Heider's in November and cut an album for David Geffen's Asylum label. The finished product was not a knockout, however. Crosby sang lead on three tracks. His "Laughing," originally written for the Byrds, was reworked, but did not compare favorably with the version already re-

Byrds reunion recording session: Crosby, McGuinn, Clark, and Hillman.

Byrds at the Troubadour bar, 1972. "David used to be ferocious. Now he's nice," said Roger McQuinn.

corded on *If I Could Only Remember My Name*. More successful, on this Byrds LP, was David's interpretation of Joni Mitchell's "For Free," but Chris Hillman explains, "We were all afraid of stepping on each others' toes."

Right after the recording in 1972, however, Crosby told *Rolling Stone*, "The impression I was left with more than anything else was how much everyone, particularly Gene and Chris, had grown. I had a wonderful time doing it, working with all of them. Stress that. I dug it a lot."

McGuinn even chimed in, "David used to be ferocious. Now he's nice."

This renewed friendship between Crosby and McGuinn led to talk of a duo album. However, it never got beyond David's contributing some harmonies to Roger's first solo LP. Also, the possibility of an actual Byrds tour was discussed. This degenerated into an attempt, more than a year later, to put the Byrds, the Buffalo Springfield, and Crosby, Stills, Nash & Young together on a huge "super bill" at the Los Angeles Coliseum. Alas, this concert—which would have involved quite an elaborate game of musical chairs—never materialized and the original Byrds were grounded once again.

CHAPTER EIGHT

The Road Back to CSN&Y (1973–1974)

Crosby, Nash & Young: Faithful Friends Don't Fade Away (1973)

While David, Graham, and Stephen were involved in their own ventures, Neil Young was keeping pretty busy himself, and rising up the commercial ladder as a solo superstar. In 1972, his "Heart of Gold" single had been a smash. However, success drifted toward the back of Neil's mind on the eve of a three-month-long arena solo tour, when he was forced to fire former Crazy Horse guitarist Danny Whitten—who was hopelessly trying to kick a heroin habit. Whitten was finally given fifty bucks and a plane ticket to Los Angeles. A matter of hours after arriving in Southern California, Whitten used the money for some heroin, overdosed, and died. Young proceeded with his tour, but delivered one ragged, reckless show after another. When his normally high-pitched whine became a hoarse croak, Young called up Crosby and Nash.

"I was ready to help a friend in need," says Nash, who was not in the best of shape himself. The first part of 1973, his girl friend at the time, Amy Gossage, was murdered by her own brother. "Tragedy was written across Amy's every action," Graham says. "Her loss affected me deeply,

because she had been a big part of my life. Her brother ended up doing time, but only three years! I felt helpless and really empty."

Crosby was also struggling with some personal pain in early 1973. "At the time," Crosby once told writer John Rogan, "my mother was in the hospital, dying of cancer. I needed the music. It's my major magic. It's the one thing to hang on to when things get crazy. It was the only thing to hang on

Neil Young at his ranch in Northern California.

to when Christine died, and it was the only thing to hang on to when my mother died."

So, when Young's call for help came, Crosby and Nash went on the road with him. This CN&Y combination stayed together for the last nineteen dates of the tour. Because it was Neil's show, David and Graham worked as vocal harmonizers, rhythm guitarists, and cheerleaders. This support improved Young's shows, although, as can be heard on *Time Fades Away*—a live album from the tour, released in 1973—an edgy roughness remained.

More than anything, this *Time Fades Away* roadwork succeeded in bringing the three friends closer together. Once again, they realized that there was strength in numbers.

Stills says, "I was always curious about why I was never called." But by the spring of 1973, Stephen had married Veronique Sanson and taken a sabbatical from Manassas. A couple of months later, he did receive a call from a couple of his old mates and Crosby, Stills, Nash & Young were on their way to Hawaii.

CSN&Y: The "Human Highway" Leads to Maui (1973)

"Sure," says Graham Nash, "the big forces that be were putting pressure on all of us to get back together. But they couldn't make us do what we didn't want to do. You must remember, at this time, we were incredibly cocky fuckers and sure of ourselves. We thought we were hot shit. So what brought us together in 1973 came out of a giant fog of psychic and musical connections between the four of us, some unspoken, some spoken.

"After we finished Neil's tour, it just happened that one of us would be thinking about the other when . . . the phone would ring. It also happened that all of us had been planning to take summer vacations in Hawaii. So the timing seemed right and we all had good songs we'd been kind of saving for CSN&Y."

Hawaii was an ideal setting for putting some music together. Rehearsals moved back and forth between David's boat and an old beach house that Neil was renting on the island of Maui.

"Right away," says Nash, "Neil's 'Human Highway' seemed like the perfect umbrella song for an album."

A tale of feelings lost and found, this song signaled a coming-together of sorts. And "Human Highway" was just one of many songs the four artists brought to the islands.

"We knew we had an album," says Stills. And it was decided, after these Hawaiian rehearsals, that they would shift back to California to record. On their last day on Maui, Crosby, Stills, Nash & Young gathered on the beach near Neil's house. Nash had Stills's Hassleblad camera. There was one unexposed frame left.

"In the last ten minutes of sunlight," says Nash, "I got everyone together, focused the camera, set the time exposure—with no meter—placed the camera in the sand, and ran into the picture."

A friend named Harry Harris clicked the camera.

"This is the new CSN&Y album cover!" cried Stills.

Such an optimistic comment proved premature, however. When CSN&Y rendezvoused back at Neil's ranch a couple of weeks later, the energy had dissipated. Several songs were recorded, including Young's "Human Highway" and Nash's "And So It Goes" and "Prison Song," with Tim Drummond on bass and Johnny Barbata on drums. Then bickering began over whether CSN&Y should tour or finish an album. They ended up doing neither, and

CSN&Y on Maui—*Human Highway* album cover never used. (Photo by Harry Harris, from the collection of David Crosby.)

left Young's ranch completely vexed with one another.

"That spaced us out for a while," says Nash. "Because it's hard—you get so high with the prospect of doing a great album that the temptation to just put up with other people's bullshit is great. But this just turned to a piece of shit."

Stills explains, "Nobody could take criticism from their partners. It was silly."

CSN&Y: Combos Fall and Rise / Nash's "Wild Tales" (1973)

The drug overdose of former CSN&Y equipment manager for guitars Bruce Berry didn't help to foster a climate of harmony in the fall of 1973. Neil Young, who took Berry's death the hardest, pieced

CSN&Y and friends.

together another band (including the remnants of Crazy Horse), did some recording (later released as part of *Tonight's the Night*), and planned a tour. Then Young performed at the grand opening of the Roxy nightclub in Los Angeles. Graham Nash served as the opening act.

Stills, meantime, returned to Colorado, only to find that drummer Dallas Taylor had slipped deeper into heroin addiction.

Also, Fuzzy Samuels had left to pursue a personal project. Rather than fold Manassas right then, Stephen got in touch with bassist Kenny Passarelli, already working with Joe Walsh and Barnstorm. To solve this conflict of interests, Stills got Walsh to open for Manassas on a short Eastern tour, and Passarelli played in both bands. By all accounts, these shows had their share of peaks and valleys. CSN&Y drummer

Felder and Stills at Lake Tahoe, 1981. (Michael Stergis middle background.)

Johnny Barbata had even briefly joined Manassas in case Taylor got too weak to perform, although Barbata ended up playing on only one song.

Right as this Manassas tour ended, however, Crosby and Nash were in the process of putting their first electric band together and quickly nabbed Barbata, along with bassist Drummond and guitarist David Lindley. This combination played several shows on the East Coast before Lindley came down with the flu, forcing him off the tour and back to L.A. Standing in the wings was Don Felder, the Florida guitarist with whom Stills had played years earlier in the Continentals.

"I'd been playing lead guitar for Crosby and Nash's opening act, David Blue," says Felder. "And when Lindley got sick, Graham asked me if I'd fill in. I jumped at the chance. I saw the Hollies when they came to Florida in the sixties and I'd been a big fan of Nash's for a long time. So, in a couple of hours, Graham taught me the entire set in his hotel room."

Felder performed admirably with Crosby and Nash, but he never told them about his teenage days with Stills. It came out when the C&N show hit Denver. Waiting backstage was Stephen Stills.

"David and Graham couldn't believe Stephen and I had played together in high school," says Felder. "It blew their minds."

Crosby, Stills, Nash, and Felder gave a one-shot performance that blasted into the night, then disappeared. Crosby and Nash had a tour to complete. Stills had some unfinished business with Manassas.

Fuzzy Samuels had returned, so Stephen wanted to launch one final tour. Everyone was committed to other projects in the late fall—Hillman, in particular, to the ill-fated Souther–Hillman–Furay Band. But no one objected to a Manassas sendoff.

"We all loved that band," says Hillman. "In terms of musicianship, I don't think I've ever been in a better one. It's true that Stephen didn't let some of the other guys do much, at times, but it was Stephen's ballgame. I'm sure he relied on me for some direction, but I was a helper, one of the guys . . . it would have been fun to do some more work with Manassas."

Dallas Taylor adds, "But I think everyone in the band realized they'd better start lookin' out for themselves. Because as long as the possibility of CSN&Y existed, Manassas never had a chance."

And the possibility did seem to exist when Manassas played a couple of shows at Winterland in San Francisco, in early October 1973. In the middle of Stills's acoustic set, Crosby and Nash walked on. A little while later, out came Neil Young. "I could *smell* a CSN&Y reunion," says Chris Hillman. Backstage, Stephen did have a powwow with CN&Y, but no decisions were made.

Graham Nash had grown frustrated at his partners' lack of commitment. So, when the last CSN&Y attempt had turned to dust on Neil's ranch, Graham started on an alternative course. When he wasn't on the road with David, he was busy piecing together a solo album in a studio that he'd built in the basement of his San Francisco home. The name of this studio, Rudy Records, has an interesting story behind it.

"Rudy," says Nash, "was a Doberman pinscher that belonged to my friend Leo Makota. And back in 1969, before I'd met Leo, he was living in Florida with Rudy. Well, in the spring of that year, Crosby went down to Florida to spend some time on his boat. And while he was standing near the harbor one day, this big dog jumps up on him and starts licking his mustache. That dog was Rudy. Leo says that Rudy'd never

jumped up on anybody like that before and figured it must have been the marijuana scent on David's mustache that did it. So anyway, Rudy introduced Leo to David, then David introduced Leo to CSN&Y. Leo became our road manager for a time, he helped me with my affairs when I needed him and he helped me build my studio. And all of this was because of Rudy, who's since passed away. So naming my studio after him was a tribute to a great dog."

But many of the songs that Nash was working on in Rudy during the fall of 1973 were in memory of another being that he'd lost.

"The murder of my lady, Amy [Gossage] had stimulated a lot of dark feelings in me," says Graham. "A lot of them came out in the songs that I was writing. Amy was such an incredible spirit, such an incredible flame, such an incredibly creative talent, her loss affected everything I did."

When this Nash solo album, *Wild Tales*, was released in December of 1973, it sold poorly, rose to only #34, then quickly fell away. Backing players such as drummer Barbata, bassist Drummond, lead guitarist David Lindley, acoustic guitarist Joel Bernstein, and David Crosby (on harmonies) infused the record with a lot of feeling. But the black-and-white cover photo showed a long-bearded Nash looking totally lost, near a book bearing the title *Goodbye Baby and So Long*. The back cover, a Joni Mitchell water color portrait of Nash, evoked a similar mood. Graham admits, "It was a pretty stark-looking album cover that may have put some people off. But that's where I was at that time in my life."

Nash took the commercial failure of *Wild Tales* hard and didn't discover until much later that Atlantic had not serviced the record properly. In a 1980 *BAM* magazine interview, he assessed the situation. "I'd spent three years thinking it was my basic failing, and to find out later that there was an actual move afoot to quell the record was an astounding fact to find out."

Ahmet Ertegun says, "When an album doesn't make it, it's only because the public doesn't react. With *Wild Tales*, the public didn't react. The record was serviced to radio stations. All record companies want to maximize sales. That's the only way they can stay in business."

Whatever the reason for *Wild Tales's* poor showing, in December of 1973, Nash was still in the dark and appreciated the support of his partners. When Nash and Crosby played an electric concert at the San Francisco Civic Auditorium a couple of weeks before Christmas, Neil Young wandered out during the acoustic set and stayed on stage the rest of the night. "Only Love Can Break Your Heart," "Déjà Vu," "Pre-Road Downs," "Almost Cut My Hair," "Military Madness," "Ohio"—the three artists brought out their best and delivered a powerful dose of electric harmony. At 1:00 A.M., a happy audience floated out of the hall singing "Teach Your Children," while, behind the curtain, Crosby, Nash, and Young slumped down on folding chairs, exhausted but smiling.

CSN&Y: The Anatomy of a Reunion (1974)

"No one's saying no," is how Stephen Stills responded to questions about the possibility of a CSN&Y reunion in February of 1974. Yet he and his three cohorts had still not decided exactly *when* they were going to "do it again." Individual projects continued to fall across the path leading to a reunion.

Stills had almost completed another solo album, tentatively titled *As I Come of Age*, and was hitting the road with a new band that featured guitarist Donnie Dacus (formerly with Veronique Sanson's group

in Paris), bassist Kenny Passarelli, drummer Russ Kunkel, keyboardist Jerry Aiello, and percussionist Joe Lala. Young was in the studio once again, cutting his sixth solo album, *On the Beach*, when he was visited by David Crosby, who dropped in to add rhythm guitar lines to "Revolution Blues." But both Crosby and Nash, who had done separate solo acoustic tours in the East, were talking about going out alone again. Were CSN&Y slipping down a four-way drain?

"That's crap," Crosby said at the time. "I can't deny we've butted heads a lot. I can't deny our egos got in the way of some great music. But there are also times when we just need to stretch out on our own."

This seemed like one of those times. And the experience, particularly for Crosby and Nash, helped strengthen their self-confidence. In March 1974, Nash told *Rolling Stone*, "The next tour I'm doing is going to be a Graham Nash tour. I need to take a step into who it is I am or who it is I'm going to be, because ever since the Hollies and then Crosby, Stills, Nash & Young, I've always been in a band. I never really knew whether they were coming to see me or the others. Recently, I went out with my acoustic guitar totally alone and was able to move people. It was thrilling for me to realize that, and it fills a space in me that has made me much more reasonable to deal with. I have a much calmer outlook on things, because now I don't have that insecurity."

But it was during this period that another call came for CSN&Y. Stills had been on the road a month. The shows were relaxed affairs. In fact, one night his band dared him to do his acoustic set in an Afro wig. "He said, 'Five hundred bucks if I do it,'" remembers Russ Kunkel, "and the son of a bitch went out there and did it. Played his whole acoustic set in an Afro wig, and the audience didn't say a word. They were so into listening to Stephen, they didn't care what he wore."

Several of the acoustic and electric songs from this tour made it onto *Stephen Stills Live,* an Atlantic album mixed by Tom Dowd. "He was a mentor of mine," says Stephen, "when I was learning how to engineer in the studio." And as great as some of the performances on this live album sounded, this did not overshadow the lure of CSN&Y. Through several phone calls, Stills learned that Young had almost finished *On the Beach* and that both Crosby and Nash were free and talking about solo tours. Elliot Roberts accused all four men of "pissing in the wind" and set about the business of arranging a reunion. From the stage of the Chicago Auditorium in early March, Stills shouted to the crowd, "Folks, CSN&Y are gettin' back together this summer for a big tour, and we'll make another album in the fall." Of course, this news was greeted with loud whoops and cheers.

"Every one of us had had some degree of success alone," says Stills. "But none of us had come across as a playing unit with the solidity that we had together. Also, I'd gotten married, my son Christopher was being born, and my financial situation was starting to get a little strange. I'd been thinking about getting a group together with Eric [Clapton], but no solid commitments came out of that English scene. So, when I talked to Neil, I said, 'Come on, let's press the bet.' And once we talked it over with management and Bill Graham, it was decided, 'If we're gonna do it, let's take it to the max, the *n*th degree, you know?' And there was the feeling we could sell an outdoor stadium tour, something the Stones hadn't even tried yet. So CSN&Y wrote 'the plan.' And no one has done anything since except to equal what we set down in 1974."

Bill Graham confirms, "CSN&Y did the first real stadium *tour.* We'd done a big Bob Dylan and the Band tour, but that was inside. With CSN&Y, we booked thirty-five dates; twenty-seven were outdoors."

When news of this tour spread, people began wondering how the CSN&Y acoustic sets would sound in front of ninety thousand people, some of them a half-mile away from the stage. "I wasn't happy about the logistics," says Crosby. "I knew the sound was probably going to suck." In that light, some charged that CSN&Y had only regrouped for the money.

"We always wondered why nobody ever asked the Stones these questions," says Stills. However, he had already admitted that his finances were a problem. Later, he joked to Cameron Crowe, "We did one for the art and the music, one for the chicks. This one's for the cash." Stephen followed the comment with a laugh, but some people wondered about the motives behind it all.

"We did it because we wanted to," says Stills. "And we knew the music would be great." This became a pat answer. And when each member of the outfit explained his own moments of torture when the music *didn't* happen, the fans gave them the benefit of the doubt, because they wanted just to hear and *see* Crosby, Stills, Nash & Young together on stage one more time.

CSN&Y: Rehearsals at Young's Ranch / "Practice Makes Perfect" (1974)

Where was that *noise* coming from? In the Santa Cruz Mountains, in groves of redwood, eucalyptus, and oak trees, a new sound was shattering the silence. Crosby, Stills, Nash & Young were tuning up on a huge redwood stage that had been constructed on Neil's ranch. It was late May, eleven in the morning, and the sun was out and glancing off the metal of guitars and amplifiers. What a way to rehearse for a stadium tour!

CSN&Y rehearsal at Neil's ranch, 1974. (Photo by Joel Bernstein.)

Everyone was in high spirits. One potentially difficult moment had already passed when the group was deciding who should make up the rhythm section. Stills had recommended Kenny Passarelli for bass, but Crosby and Nash wanted Tim Drummond. Drummond got the nod, along with drummer Russ Kunkel and percussionist Joe Lala. The lineup was set.

Rehearsals progressed smoothly, as everyone relearned parts they'd let get rusty and introduced ideas no one had ever heard before. At high noon one day, Joel Bernstein took a photo of everyone on Neil's stage. Later in the summer, he took another shot of CSN&Y in a stadium filled with ninety thousand people. Someone fused the two shots together and blew them up to poster size. Large print in quotes between the images read PRACTICE MAKES PERFECT.

It was an attitude shared by everyone in the band. Stills was the one who was most pleased about this dedication to precision.

"The first times we went out," Stephen says, "it was really pretty sloppy. Everything we played was *cool*. There was that atmosphere, and the fact that we were simply *there* was enough. Unfortunately, when that happens, you can get real lazy. So it was a long time comin' that we actually went out there and really worked. You can't walk on stage fried or drunk or any of that shit. It's not cool. You're cheatin' the crowd. It was like we used to take off, but then sometimes we'd forget where we came from and get lost trying to find our way back. In 1974 we reintroduced that exploratory element, but, for Neil and me especially, there was some form, from which we could fly and on which we could land."

Playing in the heat of the day became an exhilarating experience for the whole band. "Everyone had their amps on ten [maximum volume]," says Tim Drummond. "The hills around where Neil lives would be full of people sittin' there listening, while our music just shot up from the tops of these trees."

Not all of this music floated into the atmosphere, however. At various points the band would set up inside Neil's Broken Arrow Studio at night and cut some tracks. The most memorable of these was a still-unreleased song called "Little Blind Fish."

"David wrote some changes and the 'little blind fish' part," says Nash. "Neil wrote the next part. Then I wrote a part that goes, 'Hold on, boys, hold on, I'm comin'.' Stephen wrote the last part. And this is the *only* song that CSN&Y all had a hand in writing."

It's a shame that it never made it to vinyl, because it was a good vehicle for CSN&Y's solid harmony, as well as for their individual vocals. Relaxed and happy, CSN&Y might have recorded a whole album in June 1974, but their minds at that time were focused on the course at hand— the biggest tour any rock 'n' roll group had ever undertaken.

CSN&Y: Into the Stadiums (1974)

Time magazine reported the 1974 return of Crosby, Stills, Nash & Young in this way: "Their performances were fueled by dueling egos. Musical infighting built up the excitement they generated, but it also made breakups inevitable. Now, with half a decade gone, perhaps the mightiest U.S. supergroup of all is back together: Crosby, Stills, Nash & Young, whose pungent lyrics and soft-edged counterpoint to acid rock made them a primal force in popular music."

In *Rolling Stone*, Ben Fong-Torres wrote: "Minutes after Crosby, Stills, and Nash, and then Young hit the stage for the first concert of their reunion tour, it was clear that no other group ever had a chance of replacing them while they were apart— not America, not Bread, not Poco, not the Eagles, not Seals and Crofts, or Loggins and Messina, or Souther, Hillman, and Furay. Not even Manassas or the reunion of the original Byrds."

CSN&Y did not let anybody down when they launched into "Love the One You're With," the first of some forty songs, spread over three and a half hours. Ostensibly a warmup gig, their Seattle show, held July 9, 1974, didn't come off that way. Crosby got so involved in his performance that he blew his voice out. The cobwebs were swept away all in one night. Fong-Torres reported: "At 1:37 in the Pacific Northwest, with the monorail long out of commission and several hundred people suddenly needing rides, Crosby, Stills, Nash & Young wove together into a four-man hug. They had overdosed, and the next

CSN&Y at soundcheck, Seattle, 1974. (Photo by Joel Bernstein.)

night would be a disaster. But they had proven that they were in it, more than anything else, for the music."

This held true when CSN&Y moved into stadiums for the first time, July 13 and 14, at the Oakland Coliseum. Also on this bill were the Band, Joe Walsh and Barnstorm, and Jesse Colin Young. It was one of the most delicious rock menus ever created. Filled with anxious anticipation, many of the more than forty thousand fans who would file into the stadium each day slept in their cars on nearby side streets in hopes of landing a plot of grass in front of the huge stage.

By the time CSN wandered into view, it was nearly six o'clock. But the sun-drenched crowd showed no signs of fatigue and broke into wild, celebratory war

whoops. It was as if "the boys" had never been away. Crosby, with his halo of wild long hair and his bushy mustache intact, spouted greetings into the microphone and reclaimed his position as the group spokesman. Nash, with an unruly full beard and looking more gaunt than usual, danced back and forth like a kid who'd just been given a new bicycle. And Stills, wearing a Washington Redskins football jersey, strapped on his Firebird electric guitar, then stalked toward the edge of the stage, bulkier and more imposing than ever before, and ripped into the opening rhythm of "Love the One You're With."

"There was a couple right in front of the stage," remembers tour accountant Bob Hurwitz. "And when 'Love the One You're With' began, they started to . . . well, fuck to the music. I swear. And when someone pointed them out to Crosby, that's all he talked about for *days* afterwards."

When Young came out from the side of the stage during the second song, "Wooden Ships," some people in the audience hardly recognized him. He'd sheared off his long hair, but kept his long black side burns, and he peered over the neck of his big Gretsch White Falcon guitar from behind reflector shades. For the next three hours, Young and CSN left no fan favorite unplayed. "Carry On," "Teach Your Children," "Ohio," "Long Time Gone," "Suite: Judy Blue Eyes," and "Almost Cut My Hair" were all delivered with renewed enthusiasm. Also, there was a batch of new songs, the best of them being Crosby's "Carry Me," Nash's "Grave Concern," Stills's "First Things First," and Young's "Pushed It Over the End."

During the "wooden music," Crosby hushed the audience. Ron Stone, at the side of the stage, says, "All you could hear were people breathing." A few moments later, CSN launched into "Blackbird." Then Young came out and they did "Human Highway," "Long May You Run," and "Only Love Can Break Your Heart." Solo stints followed. Then came another electric set and an acoustic encore. But the audience still wasn't satisfied until CSN&Y trooped back out and played "Love the One You're With" for the second time, after which Stills clutched his throat as if to say, "We've given you all we physically can."

When Crosby thinks back to the 1974 tour, he says, "I didn't dig playin' stadiums. That was Neil and Stephen's trip, especially Stephen's. He was into being bigger than the Stones. Bigger than *everybody*. But

CSN&Y at the Oakland Coliseum July 15, 1974. It was as if "the boys" had never been away. (Photo by John Gravilis.)

the music suffered, I feel. When we got into the electric set, Neil and Stephen started competing on guitar simply by turning up. We clocked 'em once and they got up to 135 decibels. So Nash and I were unable to sing harmony. It was a drag."

"That competitiveness," says Stills, "was yet another manifestation of other people goading us on. Proper monitors would have helped. But Crosby's Alembic twelve-string was the loudest mother-fucker you ever *heard*. Half the time Neil and I would have to turn up to hear past the bastard, who was between us. When we stood in the middle of the stage, there was nothing to hear but David's overexcited rhythm."

Crosby denies that his volume forced Stills and Young to turn up, but he did begin to refer to the CSN&Y stadium tour as "The Doom Tour." "When half the audience couldn't see us," says David, "how could we do them justice with music they could only hear if the wind blew right? But somehow we managed to get a lot of people off. They were really with us, man."

A testimony to this was the Atlantic City show, performed in the midst of a driving rainstorm. "We were advised not to go on," says Nash. "But we looked out and saw seventy thousand kids sitting there, waiting on us. There was no way we were going to let them down. So, despite the rain, we went on and played our hearts out. We never felt so loved."

This devotion translated into an audience eager for a new CSN&Y record, or *any* CSN&Y product. Leslie Morris, an assistant to Elliot Roberts at the time, recalls, "I called Atlantic and suggested that they re-release Graham's *Wild Tales*. They refused."

Instead, Atlantic issued a CSN&Y "greatest-hits" package called *So Far*. It included the single versions of "Ohio" and "Find the Cost of Freedom," but beyond those songs, nothing was on there that CSN&Y fans who owned *Crosby, Stills & Nash* and *Déjà Vu* didn't already have.

"We were totally against *So Far* coming out," says Nash. "I mean, to make a great-est-hits album from two records was absurd."

Nevertheless, Atlantic patched together the record, put a Joni Mitchell watercolor of CSN&Y on the cover, and threw it to the hungry fans. *So Far* quickly rose to the top of the charts. CSN&Y had never been hotter.

And the relevance of the band's lyrics, particularly "Long Time Gone," "Ohio," and "For What It's Worth," had not changed, particularly when Nixon resigned during CSN&Y's Roosevelt Raceway stadium show and Neil broke the news to the crowd. "Whether what they said was right or wrong," says Bill Graham, "I always sensed that people listened to CSN&Y very closely. It's like their lyrics were important, beyond the melodic content. And besides this, CSN&Y had *talent*, which is more than I can say for a lot of groups."

The climate within CSN&Y throughout the summer of 1974 was generally sunny. There were no major conflicts. And in most of the interviews they granted along the road, the various members talked about being "less sensitive," about having "grown," and about not letting "infantile ego problems" interfere with the music. Stills, in particular, seemed to have mellowed the most, and when he wasn't on stage with CSN&Y, he pursued his favorite hobby—jamming. One night, after a Minneapolis show, he and Tim Drummond spent four hours in a hotel room with Bob Dylan—who played them every song that would eventually end up on *Blood on the Tracks*. Stills walked on at Eric Clapton's Denver show and, in California, sat in with the Jerry Garcia Band. Crosby sampled various hedonistic delights. And Nash, who in one interview was portrayed as being very depressed and emotionally sullen away from the gigs, now says, "The writer just caught me at a bad moment. Doesn't everybody have them? I had a good time traveling and seeing lots of sights." But nobody saw the sights of America better than Neil Young, who chose not to fly between shows with the rest of the group; instead, he traveled separately in a Winnebago with a couple of friends. "Neil wanted to maintain his own universe between shows," says Nash. "It was probably best that he did that. He was in a good frame of mind on that tour, and into playing." Bill Graham reveals, "There were a couple of times, when we had to play some shows back-to-back, that I had to give one of my major speeches, like 'Let's do this one for the Gipper.' But CSN&Y never let an audience down. They delivered the goods on that tour."

It was not hard for Stills and Young to get up for the shows. Together in the Buffalo Springfield, they had never been able to grab the golden ring. Now, suddenly, they had a *handful* of golden rings and relished the feeling.

"I remember driving into the Kansas City ballpark," Stephen says. "Neil and I were together, and he said, 'Hey, remember a few years ago when we talked about playing baseball stadiums and everybody laughed at us?' We grossed eleven million dollars in one summer."

However, says David Crosby, "We really didn't make as much money as you might think. Without naming names, let's just say we got paid after everybody else took their share." Mac Holbert, a CSN&Y crewmember and current chargé d'affaires for Graham Nash, explains, "Eighty-six people were a part of the CSN&Y 1974 entourage. And *nobody* starved. Nash said it all in his song 'Take the Money and Run.'"

The final show of the tour, September 14, at Wembley Arena in London, found CSN&Y on the verge of exhaustion. The Band, Joni Mitchell, and Jesse Colin Young opened. And even though they were suffering from jet lag, Crosby, Stills, Nash & Young rallied one more time and traded songs until past midnight. A British reviewer from *New Musical Express* summed up the show, and perhaps CSN&Y's entire 1974 tour, in one line: "They finished as they had begun—powerful, unified, and genuinely impressive."

CSN&Y: Studio Breakdown (1974)

After the Wembley show, CSN&Y took some well-deserved time off. Young bought a Rolls-Royce "woody" in London, and he and Nash, with a couple of friends, drove to Holland. Stills headed to Paris, where he played bass in Veronique Sanson's backing band. Only Crosby flew back to America. And when he arrived in Mill Valley, he was just in time to witness the birth of his daughter, Donovan Ann, by his lady at the time, Debbie Donovan.

"Deliverin' a kid," says David, who had taken some Lamaze classes before the CSN&Y tour, "that was the hottest single thing in my life. The best magic trick ever. Death's defeat. My life force passed on."

A couple of months later, CSN&Y met at the Record Plant in Sausalito, with the intention of recording a new studio album. Crosby's "Homeward Through the Haze" was cut, as was Nash's "Wind on the Water." A CSN&Y album was in view, and Crosby recalls, "It would have been the best one, man. You should have heard us. 'Wind on the Water,' 'Human Highway'. . . . We cut 'Homeward Through the Haze' . . . Stephen and Neil playing guitar, Nash on organ, me on piano, Russ Kunkel on drums, Leland Sklar on bass. We smoked and *burned!*"

Then hassles started setting in. Elliot Roberts's assistant, Leslie Morris, remembers, "They were sitting on the floor arguing like kids, wasting costly studio time. When they realized they weren't accomplishing anything, someone suggested, 'We might as well go to Graham's house. We're not getting anywhere here.' Everyone walked outside."

Crosby says, "I could feel the pendulum swing right then. And Neil goes, 'Well, see you guys tomorrow.' And he never came back."

"Neil utilized CSN as a springboard for his own career," says Graham Nash. "It was a very deliberate move and well done. As soon as CSN didn't suit him, he sloughed us off like an old snakeskin. That's part of my relationship with Neil that's a little tender. Because it was so blatant. He would always find excuses to disappear." Graham pauses before adding, "But I love Neil dearly, and I'm sure there were points when our scene was driving him nuts."

When Cameron Crowe asked Young about the inner workings of CSN&Y, he responded, "Well, everybody always concentrates on this whole thing that we fight all the time among each other. That's a load of shit. They don't know what the fuck they're talking about. It's all rumors. When the four of us are together, it's real intense. When you're dealing with four totally different people who all have ideas on how to do one thing, it gets steamy. And we love it, man."

Asked specifically about the Sausalito CSN&Y sessions, Young said, "We were really into something nice. But a lot of things were happening at the same time. Crosby's baby was about to be born. [She had in fact been born already.] Some of us wanted to rest for a while. We'd been working very hard. Everybody has a different viewpoint and it just takes us a while to get them all together. It's a great group for that, though. I'm sure there'll come a time when we'll do something again."

Film producer Larry Johnson, a close friend of Young's, says, "Neil has always liked playing with those guys. But as soon as the hassling starts, he doesn't want to deal with it. He doesn't *need* to deal with it. So he splits."

Without Young, CSN attempted to resume recording with Sklar, Kunkel, and Grateful Dead drummer Bill Kreutzmann. But, as Crosby recalls, "There was doom in the room." Nash explains, "Stephen and I got into an argument over a part, a harmony part that involved fitting a major progression through a minor chord on this jazzy thing of Stephen's . . . 'Guardian Angel.' Everything in my musical soul rejected it . . . and back then I felt like I was being manipulated and that my opinion wasn't being listened to. David's opinion was the same as mine, as it happens, not that it was important. So that broke it . . . and I remember Stephen going at the master of 'Wind on the Water' with a razor blade, he was so pissed at me. It was madness."

"For the first time," says Stills, "we pointedly did not attempt an idea, not fully understood by everyone, on faith in musicianship. Think about Cros, 'Mr. Dissonance,' objecting to a dissonance. He hadn't heard the root clearly enough and I definitely felt it had been short-circuited.

"The razor blade business was a joke. But nerves were too taut. It was sheer frustration. I got drunk and made some nasty cracks. Nash threw me out of his house. And I was ill-mannered enough to deserve it."

CHAPTER NINE

More Solos and Duos (1975–1976)

Crosby & Nash: "Wind on the Water" (1975)

CSN&Y seemed like a dead issue in early 1975. Graham says, "I'd decided that I'd had enough of this bullshit and that David and I were just going to concentrate on David and I." The two of them moved into a bungalow at the Chateau Marmont, in Los Angeles, and began plotting for the future. Before they came to any firm conclusions, the phone rang. It was James Taylor. He wanted Crosby and Nash to sing harmony on a couple of tracks on his *Gorilla* album.

"James invited us up to his house in Coldwater Canyon," says Nash. "We spent a couple of nights learnin' these two songs, 'Mexico' and 'Lighthouse.' *Great* sound, with me, David, and James. We went into Warner Bros. studio, then James had a record."

And Crosby and Nash had the boost in confidence that they needed. Having parted ways with manager Elliot Roberts, they were now relying on their own professional instincts, with the support of Roberts's former assistant, Leslie Morris. She served as a manager, adviser, and friend.

"There was no one else they trusted or who knew their business like I did," says Leslie. "So we worked as a team out of my house in Mill Valley."

Graham says, "Leslie was there when we needed her, and I'll never forget that."

Before David and Graham launched into their duo project, however, Crosby engaged in an "experiment" with Grateful Dead bassist Phil Lesh and electronic musician Ned Lagin. The LP project, called *Seastones*, also featured Jerry Garcia, Grace Slick, David Freiberg, and several other Marin/San Francisco musicians. Crosby recalls, "I was just trying to push back the

Leslie Morris, manager for Crosby and Nash, 1975.

walls, go past the boundaries, and explore new stuff. I did a lot of sub-speech, proto-speech vocal lines. We also did a few live concerts that were real outrageous. Mickey Hart came and played a bunch of percussion. Garcia was there. He and I talked back and forth—Jerry with his guitar, me with my voice. It sounded like a couple of Martians talking. Very weird, but great, man."

By May 1975, Crosby and Nash had wiggled out of their contracts with Atlantic and signed a new record deal as a duo with ABC. They entered the studio with a sterling corps of friends—Kunkel on drums, Sklar and Drummond on bass, David Lindley and Danny Kortchmar (a.k.a. Kootch) on lead and slide guitars, and Craig Doerge on keyboards. Also present adding their harmony support, were James Taylor and Carole King.

"We'd helped sing a couple songs on Carole's album [*Thoroughbred*]," says Nash. "So we went over to Carole's house . . . then David and I sat next to Carole at the piano, sang three-part harmony, and gave Carole King the famous Crosby–Nash 'ear fuck,' which consists of one of us on either side . . . singing directly into the ear."

"Those were peak times," says Crosby. "We were really singing well. And we were comin' up with some great stuff. It was an intense period of creativity for both of us."

During one afternoon at Village Recorders, in West Los Angeles, C&N recorded "Carry Me," "Wind on the Water," "Mama Lion," "Bittersweet," and "Margarita."

At the time, as Crosby told Cameron Crowe, "Graham and I wanted to make a record—a *pushy* record—that came out and collared you."

They succeeded. The album, called *Wind on the Water*, was released in September of 1975 and created an immediate stir. Critic Stephen Holden wrote in *Rolling Stone*: "If *Wind on the Water* shows Crosby and Nash at the height of their musical powers, it is also suffused with melancholy,

David Crosby and Graham Nash, 1975. (Photo by Joel Bernstein.)

resignation, and anger . . . *Wind on the Water* is not an album made by or about kids, but the work of men who face being beached like whales on a sandbar by the youth culture and who are determined to survive. They will."

The sentiments were clear. Crosby and Nash were not simply "retread folkies," but an effective, vital entity as a duo. In 1975, this was important to them. As Nash said, after *Wind on the Water* was released, "I'd rather play as Crosby and Nash than any other combination."

When C&N hit the road in support of *Wind on the Water*, they managed not only to retain the musical power they had created in the grooves, but to *add* to it. Also, they became one of the first rock acts to blend video with live performance. In conjunction with their support of the Greenpeace/Save the Whales organization, Crosby and Nash would screen a film showing how whales were being brutally slaughtered and, in other scenes, what beautiful creatures they were. The soundtrack to these visuals would be, first, "Critical Mass," wordless harmony by Crosby, followed by Nash's "Wind on the Water." The combination was the centerpiece of a show that was augmented by the presence of Kunkel, Drummond, Kootch, Lindley, and Doerge—nicknamed "The Mighty Jitters."

"Nerves of steel," jokes Crosby, "and a *mighty* band."

A series of tours all over America proved this emphatically. There were CSN chestnuts, such as "Teach Your Children" and "Long Time Gone," juxtaposed with the new material, including Crosby's barreling "Low Down Payment" and Nash's "Love Work Out," featuring the "warpath guitars" of Crosby, Kortchmar, and Lindley.

"Those tours cooked, man," says Kootch. "That was the first band I was in where I was actually encouraged to turn up. I remember being on stage and Crosby walked over to me and said, 'Play louder!' No one had ever told me that before. I loved it."

Rock critic Dave Marsh, in his review of one of the C&N shows in October 1975, said: "What we have here is a pair of old pros, secure in their stature at last. . . . If Crosby and Nash have finally grown up—as their new material seems to suggest, they also seem to have rediscovered the charm that drew them (and us) to rock in the first place."

Carole King was a frequent onstage visitor to these shows, prompting one writer to joke, "Crosby, Nash & King." This led to follow-up questions about the future of CSN&Y. Nash commented sincerely, "I really want to make a break from Stephen and Neil. That's not to say I won't be right there for them—but they have to be right there for *me*. . . ."

"His state of mind was such," says Stephen, "that I wasn't allowed to be there for him."

Stills: New Solos Lead to an Old Partner/The Stills–Young Band (1975–1976)

"It was obvious I had to do something," says Stephen Stills. "Here I was with a solo album I'd really taken my time on. I was really proud of it. So I didn't want to just turn it in to Atlantic and watch it die."

Stephen adds, "In the early and mid-seventies, when CSN or CSN&Y wasn't happening, they could give a shit about my solo stuff. It happened to all of us. They seemed to think that they could force us together by ignoring what we did on our own. And if I ever had some success it was like, 'Great, great . . . shit, he got a hit.'"

Stills decided to go label-shopping. Columbia Records turned out to be the most interested. But jumping from one record company to another required a little doing. Stephen told *Crawdaddy* in 1975, "I had to convince one side I was totally together and the other side I was totally crazed, right? And it worked like a charm."

Stills signed with Columbia, and in June 1975 they released *Stills* (containing much of the material recorded for *As I Come of Age*). The album drew together a collection of tracks Stephen had been working on over the preceding several years, including "As I Come of Age," with CSN vocals.

Stills admits, "I was *real* happy when a lot of that music was made. My marriage was goin' great, I had a son . . ." In his bright acoustic "To Mama from Christopher and the Old Man," Stephen sang, "So my love do the things you got to do/ Never have to be afraid, I'm always with you/Believin' in me and you like Christopher does/Believin' is the magic that makes one from the two of us." Is this the same man who wrote "4 + 20"? Stills talked with Cameron Crowe in the mid-seventies about this turn toward positive lyrics. "I'm basically a blues singer. And blues singers are supposed to suffer. I almost feel guilty. [But] I'm trying harder than I have in years . . . I want to be good."

When Stills hit the road in early July, he *was* good. Stephen kept telling his audiences, "This is the best band I've ever played in." That statement seemed a little strong, but Stills's enthusiasm was refreshing. With Donnie Dacus on rhythm and second lead guitar, George "Chocolate" Perry on bass, Tubby Ziegler on drums, Rick Roberts on vocals and guitar, and Joe Lala on percussion, the unit thundered behind Stills and gave him freedom to roam into extended jams on "Turn Back the Pages," "Wooden Ships," and an electrified version of "Suite: Judy Blue Eyes."

In the middle of these shows, Stephen would plop down on a stool in front of a large semicircle of acoustic guitars, a banjo, and a dobro. He'd reach back for the blues and find it every night. He also delved confidently into folk territory on a couple of new songs.

Stephen was working hard and he was trying, he said at the time, "to make *Stills* [the album] number one." It never got close. But this did not cause Stills to lose his cool. He stayed tight with his band. And Stephen announced to one reporter, "I ain't the asshole everybody wants to make me out as."

Of course, Stills had not abandoned his "take charge" mode of operation, and Rick Roberts explained to *Rolling Stone* in 1975, "Stephen's the sergeant, a real sarge. He has to control everything—on a musical level. But we accept it and can handle it. It's the way Stephen does things best."

"I was tired of being in this role," Stills says. And he was not totally committed to staying solo. He repeatedly talked about his desire to make some music with one of his old partners.

"Neil Young," he said to reporter Barbara Charone after a summer 1975 show, "backs me up better than anyone in the world. He understands what I'm going for. Neil allows me to explore my chops. What I want to do is make an album with Neil. We'd terrorize the industry."

Young, who had made similar comments to the press about Stills, was recovering from a throat operation in the summer of 1975. And even though he had to refrain from talking for several weeks, he could still play his guitar. When Stephen's show hit the University of California's Greek Theater in mid-July, Neil appeared backstage with his black Les Paul electric guitar. A jubilant onstage reunion occurred, with Stills and Young trading licks, rather than dueling with their volume knobs. And, as if to seal the sincerity of the pairing, Stills performed Young's "The Loner" *twice* (once with Neil on stage, and once before he arrived), then launched into Young's "New Mama" and "On the Beach." "From now on," Stephen announced to the crowd toward the end of the three-hour show, "I'm gonna put at least one Neil Young song on all of my solo albums."

Stills solos during an electric version of "Black Queen," Maples Pavilion, Stanford University, October 1975. (Photo by Dave Zimmer.)

Stills and Young jam together, Maples Pavilion, Stanford University. October 1975. **(Photo by Dave Zimmer.)**

For an afternoon, Stills and Young seemed like old pals. But how long would the good vibes last? The answer to that question came four months later, when Stills played a show at Stanford University's Maples Pavilion. Once again, Neil showed up, this time with two guitars *and* his voice. In the middle of Stephen's acoustic set, Neil walked on and the two paired up on Fred Neil's "Everybody's Talkin'," Young's "Long May You Run" and "Human Highway," and Stills's "Do for the Others." When the electric music commenced, Neil trotted back out with his Les Paul. The playing got even hotter the next night, when Young visited Stills's UCLA Pauley Pavilion show. After a particularly astonishing stretch of jamming, Stills shouted from the stage, "The spirit of the Buffalo Springfield is back!"

On January 3, 1976, the following item appeared in Herb Caen's column in the *San Francisco Chronicle:* "New Year's Eve, the phone rang at Alex's nightspot on Skyline behind Woodside, and a voice twanged to co-owner Tom Stafford, 'Hey, can I come over with my guitar and bring a friend?' And that's how Neil Young and Stephen Stills, one half of the celebrated Crosby, Stills, Nash and Young team, entertained there for free, far into the night."

Before Young left for a lengthy tour with Crazy Horse and Stills resumed work on another solo album, the two men agreed to meet at Criteria Studios in Miami in April to begin, at long last, a duo project. But a lot could happen in four months, so no word was leaked to the press.

Jumping between Caribou Ranch Studios in Colorado, Criteria in Miami, and Cherokee in Los Angeles, Stills finished an album called *Illegal Stills* by March. "I worked my *can* off makin' that record," says Stills. And that effort can be heard in the multilayered "Buyin' Time" (expanded from the live acoustic version), the authentic Latin piano/congas mix of "No Me Niegas" (with Stills's Spanish lyrics), and the sprightly acoustic guitar line in "State-line Blues," a great gambler's theme song. But Stephen admits, "The stuff I did at Caribou isn't as good as it could have been. That part of my life . . . I don't know, I lost it a little bit. There was some personal shit going on with my marriage, and nothing I tried seemed to turn out right. It was just a bad time for me. I got cabin fever. I drank too much and couldn't pin anything down for myself. Colorado became a little too isolated for me."

A song that evoked this feeling on *Illegal Stills* was Stills's cover of Young's "The Loner." It worked as a hopeful prelude to what might occur when Stills and Young got down to business together in Miami.

Right on schedule, the two guitarists met at Criteria in April. At the time, Stills said, "Whenever we play together, I teach Neil a little more about being polished. He

Neil Young and Gary Burden, 1975.

teaches me a little more about being real." Stephen also once related, "Neil and I have this passing joke between us, that I rush and he drags. I mentioned this to Robbie Robertson [of the Band] and he said, 'Wait a minute, that's no joke, that's true.' Robbie said to me, 'Stephen, when you play alone you play too fast, and Neil plays too slow alone.' Neil and I kinda looked at each other and said, 'But when we play together it's all right.'"

This cooperative attitude was evident during the initial sessions in spring 1976. One of Stephen and Neil's roadies at the time, Gerry Caskey, recalls, "Everybody had heard that Stills and Young never got along. But they were acting like real buddies in Miami."

Stills and Young worked feverishly for a couple of weeks. However, as productive as these sessions were, there seemed to be a lack of genuine collaboration going on. All of the backing players were Stills's—Lala, Perry, Vitale, and Aiello. And Neil and Stephen never really took the time as they had on stage the previous year, to *explore* together. It was either Stills playing on a Young track, or Young playing on a Stills track, but never Stills and Young playing on *their* track.

The quality of songs such as Stills's

"Black Coral" and Young's "Long May You Run" could not be denied, however. And during a break in the sessions, Young suggested they expand the project to include David and Graham.

Crosby & Nash Meet Stills–Young (1976)

Made for years to feel like leftover parts—like the George and Ringo of CSN&Y—David and Graham were anything but that in the spring of 1976. As Nash explained vehemently to a tactless radio interviewer, "Let's get this straight. David and I are not one half of anything." Crosby remembers, "Me and Nash had something solid, just scrumptious, man. There was no bullshit, no weird trips, just *us* . . . making music."

The Crosby and Nash team had been operating steadily for a year. The only solo project undertaken was Nash's production of an album called *Seed of Memory*, for English folk-rocker Terry Reid. The success of C&N's *Wind on the Water* bolstered their confidence as a team; and their live shows, whether acoustic or electric with the Mighty Jitters, were warm and exciting affairs. Also, in the studio, David and Graham were preparing songs for another album, to be called *Whistling Down the Wire*.

"We were having fun and we had a lot of musical integrity," says Nash. "We got off, just the Jitters and us, *jammin'*. We came up with some delicious outtakes with obscure titles like 'Howls on Dog Mountain.'"

Bassist Tim Drummond reveals, "A tape exists called 'The Dirty Thirty,' with a lot of great Jitters tracks that never got released. They all came about very spontaneously. And Crosby came up with this one great song called 'Drop Down Mama,' real funky boom-chicka-boom-chicka-like. I've been on him to do it for years. Every time I see him, I say, 'Come on, Crosby.' And he'll say, 'Oh, man, I can't.' He thinks it's too funky for him, but I say bullshit, he should just sing it. And Graham wrote this song called 'Taxi Ride,' with a Bo Diddley rhythm, that we learned but never went back and worked on."

Drummer Russ Kunkel adds, "I tell ya, Crosby and Nash thrived on the thrill of the moment. Nothing was very preplanned. We'd just *smoke* it and start playin'."

The "keepers" from these sessions were generally more folkish and subdued than a lot of the music on *Wind on the Water*. "It was a peaceful time for us," says Crosby. And into this sea of calm came a call from Neil Young.

"I must tell you, I was surprised to hear from Neil," says Graham. "But I was intrigued by what he was telling me about this project he was doing with Stephen. And when Neil came by my house here in San Francisco and played me and David a tape of some of the things they'd done— 'Black Coral,' 'Midnight on the Bay,' 'Human Highway'—they sounded *great*. Then Neil said, 'Isn't there somethin' missing?' Crosby goes, 'Yeah, *us*,' meaning me and David. So the next morning we were on a plane to Miami."

Right away, Crosby and Nash went to

Russ Kunkel. "We'd just smoke it and start playin'."

work and wrapped their harmonies around Stills and Young's vocals. Also recorded was a CSN&Y version of David and Graham's "Taken at All," which included the lines, "We lost it on the highway / Down the dotted line / You were going your way / I was going mine." Now this time, Crosby says, "Everything was happening so fast, I don't think anybody had time to invent hassles. I thought we were really gonna nail it."

But when Crosby and Nash were forced to leave the project and return to Los Angeles to complete *Whistling Down the Wire* on time, the energy in Miami shifted. Stills and Young were committed to a tour, set to begin in June. The possibility of turning it into a CSN&Y tour was discussed, but with the first show only a couple of weeks away, questions arose. How could they rehearse if David and Graham weren't there? How could they work up their songs for the album before leaving? Stills recalls, "Neil and I were almost finished with the album. When David and Graham had to leave, we had to get on with it. We couldn't wait." As Stephen also confided to Cameron Crowe, "we just had to do it ourselves this time. No Richie Furay, no David and Graham, nobody between us."

With this decision made, Stills and Young had a discussion. "It was Neil's idea," says Stephen, "to take David and Graham's vocals off our tracks. So we made safeties of the CSN&Y versions then removed Crosby and Nash's vocals from our songs."

When this obliteration of their work got back to David and Graham, they were livid.

"Fuck 'em," Nash told a reporter from *Crawdaddy*. "They're not in it for the right reasons. They're in it for the bucks. . . . I will not work with them again. The reason they fuckin' wiped our voices had nothing to do with music. It had to do with whether they could have an album in time to support their tour."

Stephen didn't attempt to deny that timing was a factor. But even when the project reverted to Stills–Young, it wasn't completed before the road beckoned. There were some hasty rehearsals—with Stills's backing players filling out the parts—before Stephen and Neil began a tour as the Stills–Young Band in late June 1976. They followed a path through Northeastern cities that had been plotted out months earlier for Young and Crazy Horse.

On stage, the Stills–Young Band was a bit ragged at first, but reached emotional peaks on old Buffalo Springfield songs such as Stills's "Bluebird" and Young's "Mr. Soul," a bevy of CSN&Y standards, solo songs—like Manassas's "The Treasure" and Young's "After the Gold Rush"—and the new Stills–Young material, the most effective of these songs being Stills's "Make Love to You" and Young's "Long May You Run."

To finish mixing the Stills–Young album, on off-days between dates, Neil flew down to Miami. Before long, he returned with tapes of the finished product. This seemed to inject some life into the machine and, following a hot show in Cleveland, highlighted by fantastic Stills–Young guitar fireworks, this band seemed as though it might run forever. Cincinnati, Pittsburgh, Charlotte—the buses rolled on and the tunes flowed. "There was definitely some magic happening out there," Stephen remembers. "It got to the point where we were tight enough so we could really cut loose."

Following one such show in Greensboro, however, Young decided to *physically* cut loose. The next stop on the tour was Atlanta, but Neil never arrived there. Instead he sent everyone in the band telegrams. Stills's wire read: "Dear Stephen, funny how some things that start spontane-

ously end that way. Eat a peach. Neil."

The reason given for Young's sudden departure was that a throat ailment had acted up and required another stretch of rest. Young has never gone on record about this incident. And skeptics conjectured that Neil simply wanted out, that he was bored and just moved on.

Stills offers an insight: "I was firm about sticking with one show and one song list until the band got tight and not so nervous. Neil was impatient and wanted to throw in new material. We could have been more flexible."

Regardless of the reasons, Stills was shaken, and when asked what he was going to do next, Stephen responded at the time, "I have no answers for you. I have no future."

Somehow, though, Stephen managed to pull himself up off the mat. "I found myself a replacement organization," he says, "with Flo and Eddie [former Turtles Mark Volman and Howard Kaylan] and George Perry, so I could save a couple of promoters' hides. At least I was a trouper."

Upon returning to Colorado, however, more bad news awaited him. His wife, Veronique, was filing for divorce.

"Colorado was just a little remote for her," Stephen now says. "Also, my French never quite got over the hump, you know? And she just couldn't get used to America. She just couldn't. So the situation got more and more frustrating and the marriage died of natural causes, I suppose."

Stills was not capable of such rational thought in the middle of the breakup, however. He wanted to get away and nurse a broken heart. He cleared everything out of his house in Colorado and moved to Los Angeles.

In August 1976, the Stills–Young Band's *Long May You Run* was finally released (on Young's old label, Reprise). The LP had a few moments of fire, but the feeling was generally casual. The startling peaks that Stills and Young had produced as a pair on stage were not evident. Had the two guitarists actually done some collaborative writing, with Young penning some words to Stills's music or vice versa, this might have been a more powerful record.

Stephen reveals, "Neil wrote almost all of his songs while we were there, as if he didn't want to waste anything special. He was very supportive on the 'Black Coral' and 'Guardian Angel' arrangements. But it came and went. Neil seemed preoccupied sometimes.

"Basically, Neil had his attitude about the record and I had mine. We were close, but we really could have concentrated a little harder. To me, it was a question of, for expediency or whatever, cheating the songs. The road to hell is paved with good intentions. And it never got beyond the intentions."

Crosby & Nash: "Whistling Down the Wire"/A Visit from Stills (1976)

And the Bluebird over my head
 is waiting for the sea to dry
And the farmer standing on the bridge
 is hoping that the fish will fly
And the boat on the bay
 is waiting for the cloud to cry
Mutiny
On Sailboat Bay

Those words, from Nash's song "Mutiny," were written after the Miami sessions had aborted and another attempt to get CSN&Y off the ground failed. "I was feeling like there was room for CSN&Y," Graham says. "But there was always something that would pull it apart. It all looks like so much foolishness now. Yet it sure seemed real then." Graham wrote, in "J.B.'s Blues," for

Joel Bernstein.

friend/photographer/musician-in-a-pinch Joel Bernstein, "You've been looking through the glass at shooting stars/ And all you ever wanted was for them to see/ Who they are, it's not 'so far'/ So forgive me if I ever disappointed you." Joel says, "Graham was talking about CSN&Y, and the 'so far' referred to was *So Far*, CSN&Y's greatest hits [album]. He understood the need to get on with it. But he was only one voice."

Following the erasure of Crosby and Nash's tracks from the Stills–Young album, David and Graham finished *Whistling Down the Wire* (which included "Mutiny" and "J.B.'s Blues"). Released a bit before *Long May You Run*, it actually outsold the Stills–Young Band. A relatively meaningless fact, except insofar as it proved that the talents of Crosby and Nash could not be overshadowed by the work of Stephen and Neil.

Whistling Down the Wire was a gentle album. There was lots of harmony and melody and there were several shared writing credits, between Crosby and Nash, and with guitarists Danny "Kootch" Kortchmar and keyboardist Craig "Degree" Doerge. But, unlike *Wind on the Water*, there were no full-blown rockers.

"We were a little amped-out for a while," admits Nash. But after *Whistling*

Down the Wire was released, C&N broke into new regions on stage with the Jitters. "Déjà Vu" became a lengthy "space jam," in which David Lindley and Danny Kortchmar let their guitar licks fly. Kortchmar says, "We had an enormous amount of freedom to roam on stage. It got *very* experimental. I remember in New York, me and Crosby went to see John McLaughlin play and immediately David went, 'Man, he plays so *fast*. I wonder if we could ever do things like that?' We came damn close in a lot of ways. Some of the Crosby and Nash shows left the ground, man."

While this was happening, unknown to anyone in the Crosby and Nash camp, Stephen Stills was in Los Angeles, barricaded in the studio, pouring his battered emotions into his music. When he now thinks back to those sessions, he says, "All I can remember is the broken heart and the futility of the situation. I can't remember how the songs evolved, just that they did. There's a point where you just . . . you suck it in and say, 'I'm gonna take the hill.' If there is something to the mythology of a star, I'd like to think I set some kind of example with that kind of courage, because it took everything that I had. But I'll be *damned* if I'm gonna let something stop me."

Crosby and Nash were set to play a concert at the Greek Theater in Los Angeles. Stills was moving between the studio and the house of a friend, Ken Weiss of Gold Hill Publishing. "It was a very dark period in Stephen's life," says Weiss. "When I saw David and Graham were going to be at the Greek, I told him, 'You gotta go.' He said, 'They don't wanna see me. Not after what happened in Miami.' But I went ahead and arranged for Stephen to get into the show."

"My life was in a shambles," Stills says. "I was getting divorced and trying to save my career at the same time. So I took a big gulp and went to see David and Graham."

When Nash saw Stills backstage at the Greek, he remembers, there was "lots of heart-thumping and dry mouths, but it was okay. It was good to see him."

In the next instant, as Graham told *Rolling Stone*, "I hugged him. And it amazed me, 'cause I realized in the middle of the hug that the last time we'd met, he'd wiped some very valuable work of David's and mine . . . but it didn't matter. We're all incredibly changeable people, God knows, and Stephen had come with his hat in his hand. So fuck it, I hugged him." Then Crosby lunged toward them and made it a three-way hug. Later, on stage for the show's final encore of "Teach Your Children," Crosby, Stills & Nash was together once more.

After the show, it was Graham's girl friend, Susan Sennett (she eventually became his wife), who suggested that Stephen come back to her house with them. "Since I'd known Graham," Susan says, "all I'd heard was what a monster Stephen Stills was. I figured anybody Graham could hate this much, he must really love. And when I met Stephen, here was this shy man who didn't seem so terrible. I liked Stephen. And I thought he and Graham should get together and talk."

Graham remembers, "That night, Stephen and I got drunk and decided *one more time* to get this ship asail."

First, however, Crosby & Nash played a few more shows together, and Stills went on a solo acoustic tour. After a benefit show in San Jose for David Harris's congressional bid, Stills admitted to *BAM* magazine's Miles Hurwitz that hitting the road alone "was a question of finances. It's a question of what people want to hear. And I'm certainly not unwilling to please my audience." There was no mention made of what his audience *really* wanted to hear. But during his set on this night in October of 1976, Stephen performed the Crosby & Nash song "Taken at All." He cried the lines, "We lost it on the highway/ Down the dotted line/ You were going your way/ I was going mine." Then he repeated the words, "Can this road be taken, taken at all?"

"Every once in a while," says Ahmet Ertegun, "the group gets back together. It's like an institution. Just when you think that it's all gone, that they can never reconcile their differences, somehow they always do. The spirit of CSN is much stronger than any of its members. I've often heard them say, 'I've got this great song for me to record, but it's not strong enough for CSN.' I've heard that from each of them. They have a reverence toward the group that is larger than their concern for themselves."

In December 1976, Crosby, Stills & Nash met with engineers Ron and Howard Albert at Graham's house in San Francisco. Howard recounts the scene. "It was just the lads and us. They sat down in Graham's living room and sang 'Blackbird.' It was their 'let's show you how good we are' song. And it definitely captured the essence of what CSN is all about. Those three voices together, with one acoustic guitar—the chemistry was chilling. If there ever was a moment in our careers when we weren't recording, but *should* have been, that was it."

CHAPTER TEN

CSN Again (1976–1978)

Crosby, Stills & Nash: Together in Miami / CSN on Vinyl (1977)

Crosby, Stills & Nash celebrated their new friendship at the Record Plant in Los Angeles a week before Christmas in 1976. They gathered around one microphone, tilted their heads back, and took a vocal run through Stills's "See the Changes." Ron Albert, in the engineering booth with the tapes rolling this time, says, "I knew right then that *no one* could sound quite like Crosby, Stills & Nash." A few more tracks were cut, including Nash's "Just a Song Before I Go."

"I'd written that when I was in Hawaii with Leslie Morris," says Graham. "We were at a friend's house in Maui, waiting for the rain to stop so we could go somewhere. So this guy said to me, 'You've got half an hour, why don't you just write a song before you go?' He was being totally flippant, but you can't say that to me. So I sat down at this piano and wrote the song. His words were the opening line and everything else fell into place. Took about twenty minutes."

The initial CSN sessions were moving easily. Everyone was happy, and it carried over into the music. Before getting down to the business of making a record, though, they took some time off for the holidays,

then regrouped at Criteria Studios in Miami. The promise of the second CSN album hung in the air.

"With it being just the three of us," Crosby says, "the whole vibe was different. It was more like it had been the first time around, without Neil. And me and Nash didn't *have* to do it. Crosby and Nash was in good shape. But Stephen came to us, man. And I gotta say, of all the combinations, Crosby, Stills & Nash is the best one. Nothing else touches it. So, when Stephen showed up, I was ready. And when we started doing it, it was *real.*"

They stayed together in a large rented house that resembled an Old World villa, with its stucco walls and Spanish tile. A short drive from the studio, it was a perfect Miami oasis.

"What a lazy, easy time," says Nash. "I took this piece of alabaster down there and, I swear, it looked like Crosby! So I sculpted away at this bust of Crosby in the late afternoons while waitin' for David to wake up and Stephen to come down."

A typical day for CSN at this time was the opposite of a "normal schedule." The group would work in the studio from 8:00 P.M. until about 4:30 A.M., then sleep most of the day. Such a routine apparently agreed with them, because production level and time efficiency in the studio were running at an all-time high.

CSN in Miami, 1977. (Photo by Joel Bernstein)

Stills says simply, "Everybody was into working, everybody was *cooperating,* and we all had the songs."

"That's the key," says Crosby. "We've always had this reality rule—we don't record *anything* that we don't feel is a good song. We had *great* songs in 1977."

The words to "Shadow Captain" had come to Crosby in the middle of the night on his boat. He scribbled them out as fast as he could write, painting a surreal scene that would eventually be sung to a syncopated melody and piano progression written by Craig Doerge. "Who guides this ship/ Dreaming through the seas/ Turning and searching/ Whichever way you please?" The answer comes in the last two lines: "Shadow captain of a charcoal ship/ Trying to give the light the slip."

Stills's new songs were more direct and literal. The pain he expressed throughout "Run from Tears" and "I Give You Give Blind" were like personal exorcisms. In "Dark Star," Stills came right out and said, "Forgive me if my fantasies might seem a little shopworn/ I'm sure you've heard it all before/ I wonder what's the right form/ Love songs written for you have been going down for years/ But to sing what's in my heart seems more honest than the tears."

Stills maintained a strong creative drive throughout these CSN sessions. And Ron Albert says, "I couldn't remember him going for it that hard since the first Manassas album." Nash says, "Stephen works best when he has support. We all do, really. But I remember at those 1977 sessions, he'd stopped drinking. He was in great spirits

Graham sculpting marble bust of Crosby. (Photo by Joel Bernstein.)

[and] when Stephen's on it and he's clear, there's nobody better."

Toward the middle of February, Nash left for about a week to visit his mother in Manchester, England. While there, Graham says, "It was snowing and I went and stood on the very street corner where Allan and I had waited for the Everly Brothers years before. And goddamn if everybody didn't look exactly the same. The same little bundled-up people, the same charcoal-gray suits and overcoats and red noses against the cold. I was so thankful that I'd had the instinct to want to get out of there and experience something my father never experienced. He never left England. But I had been around the world a couple of times already. I had escaped."

When Nash returned to CSN in Miami, his mind wandered back to the Manchester streetcorner, while he was watching Walter Cronkite on the news. By the time he got to the evening's sessions, he'd written a new song, "Cold Rain."

Wait a second, don't I know you?
Haven't I seen you somewhere before?
You seem to be like someone I knew
He lived here, but he left when he
Found that there was more

"I love it when emotion comes out like that," says Nash, "and you have no choice but to follow it."

A similar experience of being overwhelmed by emotions beyond his control had happened three years earlier in England and climaxed with the writing of "Cathedral." Nash explained the experience that sparked the song to Anthony Fawcett in *California Rock, California Sound:* "The incident was: getting up in the morning about six o'clock, getting in this old Rolls-Royce that we'd hired for the day, going over to this dealer's in London and picking up some acid, dropping the acid and then going through Richmond Park with the ultimate goal of ending up in Stonehenge—and we went through Winchester on the way. We were with Leo Makota and another friend. And the experience in Winchester Cathedral was probably my favorite acid trip I've taken—I haven't taken that many, perhaps a couple of dozen. It was an amazing space—the feeling of the sunlight pouring in through the windows, in fact, when the sunlight hits, it definitely make a *bbhhrr* sound, the pillars turn to ivory white. So much feeling inside it, I'm sure I didn't need the acid. I was walking down the aisle, one of the aisles, there were graves on the floor and one of them attracted my attention and my legs started to waver, not shake, but just waver, you know, like a divining rod—it was real strange. I looked down and this guy had died on February second [Nash's birthday] in—I think the actual date was 1798, but poetic license made it 1799 for the rhyme scheme—and it was very interesting that I would be attracted to a thing I hadn't seen, with my eyes six feet above the ground."

After this, says Graham, "I began to write a piece of music with no lyrics that was the *feeling* of what it was I wanted to say. But trying to hone down the overwhelming series of feelings I had into some cohesive form that was understandable to other people was a *long* process." But the result, finished in time for this CSN album, was well worth the wait. The words depict Nash's personal experience and take a swipe at the hypocrisy of religion. It stood out as the only even remotely political comment that came out of these sessions. In *BAM*, Stills was asked about the disappearance of overt political comments in his songs, and he responded, "[That] doesn't mean I'm any less political. I am an American and I reserve my right to speak. Since then, I have learned the art of lobbying, you see. So I don't discuss it in public forum. I use the telephone."

Ten years singing right out loud
I never looked—was anybody listening?
Then I fell out of a cloud
Hit the ground and noticed something
    missing

Those were Stills's words, from "See the Changes." Crosby's penchant for singing and speaking out had also mellowed a bit by this point. But in an honest appraisal of his personality, in the song "Anything at All," David admits, "Anything you want to know, just ask me, I'm the world's most opinionated man." Later in this song, Crosby says that he never admits to "having the key to the instruction booklet." He sings, "You see, just beneath the surface of the mud/ There's more mud here [Crosby chuckles] . . . Surprise."

It was Crosby, more than anyone, who missed the musical and emotional exchanges and camaraderie that CSN and CSN&Y held. Never fond of being alone, he admits, "My greatest joy in life is makin' music with other people." In one of the songs he brought to the 1977 CSN sessions, this one called "Dreams," he sang, "Two or three people fading in and out like a radio station that I'm thinking about but I can't hear."

Two of the people were with Crosby in 1977 and *not* fading in and out at all. Crosby, Stills & Nash had not been so unified and tight since 1969; no single member screamed out over another. It was an evenly distributed team effort with help from a small group of backing players— Doerge, Vitale, Kunkel, and Perry. And the CSN harmonies were in top shape. When "See the Changes" or "Shadow Captain" boomed over the monitor speakers, that *sound* was there.

Howard Albert remembers one evening of high harmony toward the end of the sessions: "We were all in the studio, when I saw somebody outside in the bushes. I thought this guy was trying to steal something from one of the cars. He had a big hat on, so I couldn't recognize who it was until he walked into the studio. It was Neil Young."

Nash laughs, "Neil was out there pissing in the bushes. When he came in, he said, 'I was just down here in Florida, man, and thought I'd pop in.' We played him some stuff. And it was great. You see, we never hold any grudges. There's a certain unspoken family tie."

Crosby, Stills & Nash, 1977. (Photo by Joel Bernstein.)

As Stills told a radio interviewer, Jim Ladd, in 1977, "I never had any brothers, but I got two, actually I got *three*, but the other one, he's just a loner, you know?"

So, as the summer of 1977 approached and the album *CSN* hit the stores, Crosby, Stills & Nash prepared for the first time to go on the road as a threesome.

CSN: Three for the Road (1977)

"We really wanted to get out there as CSN," Nash says, "because we'd done some fine work, I felt. We'd communicated some sincere sentiments. And we were ready to sing on stage."

But who would be out in the audience, this time around? Would there be aging hippies waving the Woodstock banners? Would the thousands who'd flocked to the stadiums for CSN&Y in 1974 be back? Had the various solo and duo ventures sustained the fire? Would the new album bring new fans? Young kids?

Answers to these questions were complicated by the state of popular music in 1977. The disco craze was just beginning. Punk music was about to rear its spiky-haired head. The impact of Peter Frampton's pop-metal explosion could still be felt. The Eagles were filling ballparks. Where would CSN fit in?

Crosby insists, "We didn't think about it that much. If we had, we'd have been fucked. We never worried about coming together because of external forces that we had no control over. We've just tried to concentrate on the *music* and let everything else fall where it may."

In 1977, Cameron Crowe asked Crosby if even the most ardent CSN fans might have grown weary of waiting for another taste. Crosby responded, "It'll depend on [whether] music was the issue, or [whether it was] the fantasy characters the media tried to create. If it was the music that moved them, I'm sure that the on-again, off-again rest of it isn't that relevant. If, on the other hand, they were more concerned with the psychodrama of the group trips . . . and flashed by the bullshit star thing, then maybe they've moved on from that to something else, like gas stations and Parcheesi."

When *CSN* started zooming up the trade charts, along with the single, "Just a Song Before I Go," it was obvious that a lot of people hadn't moved on and that some new people had moved *in*. And CSN met these record buyers in person in June 1977, when their American tour began (with Perry on bass, Vitale on drums, and Craig Doerge on keyboards).

Crosby, Stills & Nash sold out Madison Square Garden in a matter of hours. The night of the show, a reviewer from *Rolling Stone* reported, "After two encores, audience *and* band went home happy, having learned how easily dormant passions can be rekindled." A week later, CSN performed at the Forum in L.A. *Los Angeles Times* pop music critic Robert Hilburn observed: "The crowd gave the band a standing ovation when it came on stage and additional ones at almost every opportunity. The group played with an earnestness and intensity that kept the adoration from being part of a simply hollow, nostalgic exercise."

CSN had refurbished such golden oldies as "Love the One You're With," "Long Time Gone," "Wooden Ships," "Teach Your Children," and "Pre-Road Downs." But the cheers from the crowd were just as loud for the newer material, such as Stills's "Dark Star" and Nash's "Just a Song Before I Go"—now rising into the Top Twenty.

Throughout the first leg of this tour, it became clear that Graham Nash was emerging as CSN's gentle guiding light. Both Crosby and Stills had quieted down their stage raps and musical excesses. Consequently, when Nash stepped forward, the trio locked in with more equality than ever before.

Ron Stone, who had spent hundreds of hours with CSN and CSN&Y over the years, observed, "Nash was always the strongest person in the group. But it took him a long time to realize that. The others made him feel he wasn't heavy, but I think Graham finally realized, 'Hey, wait a minute, I'm the one who wrote all the hits—'Marrakesh Express,' 'Teach Your Children,' 'Just a Song Before I Go'—'I'm the one who's *feedin'* this outfit.' It's true. They were enjoying the success that he gave them. Without Nash's songs, CSN or CSN&Y would have been a big underground success, but they wouldn't have sold many records. Graham has always been rapped for writing simplistic songs, but that's the very reason they're so big. Graham's got the ability to touch the largest group of people."

The absence of Neil Young on stage with CSN in 1977 was only brought up when some voice in the audience would periodically scream, "Where's Neil?" To which Crosby would invariably respond, "You tell us." From the start, Young had insisted that he should never be looked upon as "Neil Young from CSN&Y." He wanted to remain separate. And this time he wasn't around at all. But his absence didn't create a void. CSN was functioning as a complete unit. And Stills, in particular,

CSN at the Forum, Los Angeles, 1977.

seemed more relaxed and technically fluid on lead guitar without Young looming an amp away. Also, the CSN vocal blends, always tighter than CSN&Y anyway, came off truer than ever before. And Crosby, Stills & Nash, like CSN&Y in the past, still had the ability to walk on stage and draw a deafening ovation before a single note had been struck.

With *CSN* about to turn gold, and with a triumphant tour just ended, it was clear that Crosby, Stills & Nash were in demand. Out in the audience there had been a motley cross-section of fans: youngsters (many of whom had been toddlers when *Crosby, Stills & Nash* came out in 1969), old faithfuls, and middle-aged fans with babes in arms, and a lot of college-age kids. The warmth of the CSN concerts was still invit-

ing, it seemed, to anyone who loved a dose of harmony. No longer as musically radical as they had once been, CSN still projected a sound and a personal feeling that was unique. They chatted with crowds of twenty thousand as if they were all in a living room. This was a special concert experience that no other group had duplicated.

In the heat of this rekindled enthusiasm for the band, ABC started making plans for the release of a Crosby & Nash live album. "If I'd had more control, that record would never have come out," says Nash. "ABC obviously just wanted to cash in on CSN's popularity. It was an obvious corporate move. And I didn't have a good enough relationship with the president of the record company to straighten things out. So David and I decided to put it together ourselves, rather than let somebody else do it. Because it was going to come out either way. I'm a little ashamed we didn't have more freedom to halt the project."

Crosby–Nash Live, released in the fall of 1977, was not a bad record. In fact, it captured C&N and the Mighty Jitters at some of their highest moments, particularly during "Déjà Vu" and "Immigration Man." The entire LP served as a nice coda for the Crosby & Nash/Jitters combination and helped appease the musical appetites of CSN fans. While this was happening, David, Graham, and Stephen took a two-month break.

CSN: Stills Jams/Nash Marries/CN&Y at Benefit (1977)

During this period, Stills tried to patch his marriage back together, and began work on another solo album at Criteria

Studios in Florida. One night, when Peter Frampton played Miami, Stephen showed up at the backstage door with his electric guitar and wound up jamming with Frampton during an encore of "Jumpin' Jack Flash."

Nash, who had gotten married May 4, returned to Los Angeles with his new wife, Susan Sennett, formerly in the TV series "Ozzie's Girls." Graham recalls the courtship: "I met Susan at Schwab's on Sunset Boulevard in 1976. We hit it off immediately. At the time, David and I were staying at the Chateau Marmont. And while we were rehearsing, Susan would be outside sculpting this piece of marble. One afternoon, I walked down into the courtyard, put my hand on Susan's shoulder and said, 'I love you.' Right at that moment, she misstruck the marble and the head of this bird she was sculpting flew off. That inspired the song 'Broken Bird' that I wrote with Crosby."

Susan remembers, "It was the first time he had told me he loved me, and at the same instant I destroyed this piece. But it was a piece that I'd been doing during the period after I'd left my first husband. So it was filled with a lot of pain.

"Most people didn't think I'd last a year with Graham," Susan continues. "And I was looked upon as the Yoko Ono of CSN. Everyone thought I was trying to break up the group. But it's always been just the opposite. I've always encouraged Graham to work things out with David and Stephen. I've always been for them."

Crosby, meanwhile, made plans for a solo accoustic benefit show for the United Farmworkers at the Santa Cruz Civic Auditorium in August 1977. A local paper circulated a rumor that Stills and Nash might show up. Graham did walk on partway into the proceedings, but Stills never appeared. Instead, Crosby and Nash introduced "a local picker who's been playin' some good

music around here." This "picker" turned out to be Neil Young, who was in fact playing guitar and singing in a Santa Cruz bar band called the Ducks. With David and Graham, Neil was laughing, smiling, and extremely talkative. He dedicated his song "New Mama" to Graham's wife, Susan, and his own woman friend at the time, Carrie Snodgress, and their son, Zeke. Before beginning "Only Love Can Break Your Heart," Neil said, "I wrote this song for Graham. I would have written it for Crosby, but he was just too happy."

While this was going on, Stills was down in Los Angeles, playing a benefit in order to raise money for the family of Jerry Aiello, his former keyboardist, who had died of a liver ailment (some reports said a heroin overdose) in July. With singer Bonnie Bramlett, bassist Felix Pappalardi, and the entire Little Feat band, Stills drew a sellout crowd to the Whisky nightclub in West Hollywood. It was a loose but emotional evening.

Toward the end of the summer, with the next leg of CSN touring about to begin, Stills was busy arranging a surprise for his cohorts: a visit with the President of the Unites States.

CSN: In the White House (1977)

It was a difficult image to conjure up—Crosby, Stills & Nash in the Oval Office, standing face to face with President Jimmy Carter. CSN and CSN&Y had spent so much of their careers denouncing the policies of the United States government, it seemed inconceivable that they would ever enter the White House grounds, let alone the Oval Office.

"I loved Jimmy Carter," says Stills.

Crosby, Stills & Nash meet the President, 1977. (Official White House photo.)

"And I think history will be very good to the man. I can't say that about many of the other presidents our generation has seen. But Jimmy was cool. And since we had all been into pretty heavy political stuff, I thought everyone should go meet the boss. So I arranged it. I'd paid my dues as a good party member. I knew who to call. And when we were with Jimmy, I thought, 'This is reality. This is it, pal. Right here in this room is where all the shit goes down.'"

Crosby remembers, "It was funny, man. One of us, and I will not say who, lit a joint in the Oval Office just to be able to say he'd done it, you know? But I remember looking at Jimmy Carter's eyes and seeing that they were shrouded and concealed . . . there wasn't much of anybody home, and who *was* home was not overly bright. You know, it was funny, but also frightening, because I could see all around me all of the people that were ultimately running the country and I didn't see anybody bright *anywhere!* That was scary. Because you can be sure the Russians have some bright people somewhere."

"Ah yes, the White House," Nash sighs. "I was very nervous. I didn't feel at home there. And here was the President of the United States coming through the door and walking toward me and looking at me and holding his hand out . . . it was quite an interesting experience. I got a nice feeling from the man, but of course, very quickly, in true politician fashion, he tried to get us to commit to doing a concert for him."

CSN: Tension Breaks on the Road (1977)

Before CSN launched into a series of fall 1977 concerts, keyboardist Kim Bullard, formerly in Veronique Sanson's band, replaced Craig Doerge, who was on the road with Jackson Browne. Besides this minor personnel change, something in the chemistry of Crosby, Stills & Nash had shifted. They were still very much together, the voices sounded strong, but the free-and-easy air on stage had turned to business-like, sometimes forced execution. Nash remembers, "David and Stephen were arguing about the *length* of a guitar chord and I grabbed both of them, threw 'em up against the wall, crying and saying, 'Don't you understand what you're fucking blowing here? You're arguing about the length of a chord and we've got to go out there and face twenty thousand people and be *good.*' This was the beginning of my feeling that

David and Stephen, to a large degree, were not facing the responsibility of the force that CSN could and *should* be."

When they played the Oakland Coliseum in late October, there was an awkwardness on stage. And in the middle of Crosby's "Lee Shore," Stills suddenly opened up with a howling lead guitar break. Both Crosby and Nash glared in his direction, but Stephen just shrugged as if to say, "What did I do wrong?" One writer from a Bay Area newspaper headlined his review of the concert, "Crosby, Stills & Nash Produce Tense Vibes at Show."

Stills explains, "I lost control of my amp and volume pedal, and it took sixteen bars to find out where the breakdown was. I

Young, Crosby, and Nash harmonize at the Santa Cruz Civic Auditorium, August 1977. (Photo by Steve Gladstone.)

just shrugged to try and get them to let it pass. But they *didn't* let it pass."

Something had to come to a head. Kim Bullard remembers, "There was all kinds of tension that was making *everybody* uptight. Then one night, after a day off, everybody headed to this hotel bar and got drunk. And I'm talking knee-walkin' drunk. This led to everybody jumping in the pool without any clothes on . . . buck naked. Graham and Susan [Nash] started it. Eventually everybody joined in. It was great to see Stills, Crosby, Nash . . . *all* of 'em drunker'n skunks, singin' and carryin' on in the pool at two in the morning. That cooled everything out. From then on, the tour was smooth sailin'. "

By mid-November, though, everyone was ready to retreat and reflect. The year 1977 had been a good one for Crosby, Stills & Nash, a *great* year in many respects. But it was clear that another spark would have to come from somewhere to keep the flame alive.

CSN: Sessions Abort/CSN's Hollywood Star/Stills's Solo Dance (1978)

When Crosby, Stills & Nash regrouped at Criteria Studios in early 1978, everyone was ready to work. But during rehearsals, the energy began to fade. One of the Mighty Jitters, Danny Kortchmar, was called in.

"When I got there, everybody was going insane," says Kootch. "I had a Les Paul Standard, set up in D tuning. So I just started foolin' around, moanin', 'Can't get no booty!' It was hilarious. I was really tryin' to cheer those guys up, 'cause they were at each other's throats. So I went, 'Here's this song,' and started playin' it. Stephen goes, 'That's *great!*' And we sort of worked it out together. I don't know

whether I'd want 'Can't Get No Booty' carved on my tombstone, but it's a great dance record."

As it happened, with that song, Kortchmar and another super sideman, keyboardist Mike Finnigan, succeeded in bringing some life to the CSN sessions. Several more "Latino Stills" numbers were recorded, as was Crosby's raucous "I Needed to Drive My Car," a song out of the "Almost Cut My Hair" mold, with Stills and guest David Lindley adding guitar solos. A Crosby–Nash song, titled "Jigsaw," came out of these sessions. Then there were two new Nash tunes—"Helicopter Song," about learning how to fly a helicopter in Hawaii, and the haunting "Mirage."

There were no serious "bummers" at these CSN sessions. But neither was there a feeling of great enthusiasm. Crosby recalls, "Something was missing and it was like we were all *there*, but everyone was thinking about other things and getting dangerously close to the old Wurlitzer effect. You know, you put the key in, turn it, and the same thing comes out every time. That isn't how CSN is supposed to work . . . *ever.*"

Nash adds, "We didn't have enough material for a whole album yet. And everyone's energy level was down. The timing just wasn't right."

Of particular interest to Graham was the imminent birth of his first child, Jackson. And as this event approached in February 1978, the CSN sessions ground to a halt. Nash flew home to be with his wife, Susan, and captured the experience of welcoming his son into the world with a sensitive ballad called "Magical Child."

Crosby drifted off to sea in his sailboat, then returned to his secluded home in Mill Valley. When his old Byrd mates Roger McGuinn, Gene Clark, and Chris Hillman played a couple of club dates at the Boarding House in San Francisco, David showed up to sing with them. But he did not make any attempt to launch another Byrds reunion project. There was some talk about the possibility, but the result was the McGuinn–Clark–Hillman Band, a unit that forged straight into the heart of dance music, right on the fringe of disco.

This was something that Stills was also flirting with. When Crosby and Nash split from Miami, he stayed behind and continued to record with Vitale, Perry, Finnigan, and Lala. "Can't Get No Booty," the song Stephen had written with Kortchmar, was a kind of parody of the 1978 disco/pickup scene. But then Stills started writing songs like "You Can't Dance Alone" and "What's the Game." These were nightclub fare, good nightclub fare, but songs that CSN would never attempt.

It wasn't until June 21, 1978, that Crosby, Stills & Nash were scheduled to join forces again. The occasion was the official unveiling of the CSN star on Hollywood Boulevard's Walk of Fame. But when June 21 arrived, only Stills and Nash showed up.

"Crosby fucked me up that day," says Nash. "He was too lazy to come to Los Angeles and left me and Stephen to deal with the crazies on Hollywood Boulevard on a *hot* day."

The CSN star was placed right between ones awarded to Marty Robbins and Guy Lombardo, in front of the old Peaches record store. John Lockhart, the store's manager at that time said, "Graham and Stephen stayed there signing autographs for hours. They didn't just split after the ceremony."

Nash says with a smile, "Getting a star was nice. I was walking by there one day a while ago and I saw a girl dancing on it. When she turned around, there I was. She just froze. It was a nice moment. But when she turned to tell her friends, I walked into a store. So, when she turned around again, I wasn't there. She must have thought she

Graham and Stephen at the official unveiling of the CSN star on Hollywood Boulevard's Walk of Fame, in front of the old Peaches record store. (Photo by Andy Zuckerman.)

was hallucinating. Funny. But in a way it was like she was dancing on our graves."

Crosby, Stills & Nash were far from dead in July of 1978. Following a few rehearsals, they went on the road once again and performed roughly the same sets they had presented in 1977. An hour's worth of electric music, a break, group, duo and solo acoustic numbers, a break, more electric music, then an encore of "Teach Your Children." Flashes of CSN euphoria rose up througout the shows—often sparked by Stills this time around. A new Nady wireless guitar setup allowed Stephen the freedom to wander all over the arena if he chose. One night, in the middle of "Turn

Back the Pages," Stills jumped off the stage in the middle of his guitar solo and started racing through the crowd. The spotlight followed his path down one aisle and up the next. Stills never stopped playing, and leaped back on stage just in time to pick up the beginning of the chorus vocals. All the while, Crosby and Nash were anchored to their amplifiers by guitar cords. Yet Crosby still bobbed his head enthusiastically while chopping out rhythm chords and laying in some purring harmonies. Nash, the proud father, was also extremely animated, bouncing from guitar to piano, then to the microphone, smiling broadly.

When the CSN show chugged into Madison Square Garden in late July, some of this freshness had waned, but Joni Mitchell was cheering from the sidelines and pushed "the boys" over the top. Then Joni trotted on stage and joined CSN for the "Teach Your Children" finale. After this show, David, Graham, and Stephen walked into a joke cooked up by their road crew.

"We'd invented these nicknames for 'em," says CSN roadie Jeffrey Husband. "Orca, Orbit & Ozzie. Orca was Crosby, because he was always talking about the whales. Orbit was Stills, because he went into orbit a lot and we'd have to keep waiting for him to come down again. Ozzie was Nash, because he's always been the Ozzie Nelson of the group. Graham can walk down a street and no one will recognize him. So . . . we had these nicknames printed up on T-shirts, in the same logo design as Crosby, Stills & Nash. When they came off stage, the entire road crew was wearing these Orca, Orbit & Ozzie T-shirts. It stopped the guys for a moment and we just laughed our heads off."

This air of levity trailed off as CSN swung easily through the rest of the tour, then split up. The next big "family" event occurred on August 14, 1978. Besides being Crosby's thirty-seventh birthday, it was also the day that Graham Nash became an American citizen. He was sworn in along with fifteen hundred other people at the Dorothy Chandler Pavilion in Los Angeles. When they sang " 'The Star-Spangled Banner,' " Graham says, "I was very moved, singin' that song with all those people, I must confess." In true American style, Graham, Susan, and Stephen Stills then went and had a "banquet" of hot dogs and hamburgers.

During the rest of 1978, Nash threw himself into his home life, sharing the duties of parenthood with Susan. He also devoted a lot of time to his ever-expanding photography collection. Over the years Graham had purchased and found some of the greatest photographic images that have been printed, some of them over a hundred years old. With the help of his photography curator, Graham Howe, Nash began to present many gallery showings of his photos and also published a book, *The Graham Nash Collection*, in 1978. "These images have moved me," he says, "and I wanted them to move lots of other people in the same way."

Crosby, a few hundred miles to the north, burrowed away in his home in Mill Valley, then went on a couple of sailboat cruises. He admits, "I wasn't paying as much attention to my music, on a daily basis, as I had in the past. I was still writing some, but I got a little lazy. And compared to the classical composers, *all* pop musicians seem like they're cruising sometimes, and I'm no exception."

Stills was the only member of the CSN crew who kept producing his music at a high rate. Over Labor Day weekend, he performed an acoustic solo set at the Bread and Roses Music Festival at Berkeley's Greek Theater, which culminated in an encore of "For What It's Worth." In the first part of October, Stills turned up at L.A.'s Troubadour and jammed with the Knack—

Stephen plays timbales at the Roxy, Los Angeles.

then the hottest "power pop" act in town. A few days later, *Thoroughfare Gap*, the Stills solo album that had been almost two years in the making, was finally released. Rock critics, seldom on Stephen's side to begin with, really dug their claws into this one. This was mainly because there were several percussion-and-string combinations that screamed that "evil, trendy style"—*disco!* For this, Stephen was crucified.

"There are elements of disco I really like—the percussion, the guitar," Stills told *BAM* magazine in 1979. "I've played on so many Bee Gees songs, I don't know which ones I played on and which ones I didn't— 'cause Barry Gibb is an old friend of mine and I just sat in and played chickum-chit, chickum-chit, a little wacka-wacka guitar."

Howard Albert, who produced most of *Thoroughfare Gap* with his brother Ron and Stills, sums up the effort: "There was a lot of emotion happening during the making of

this record. But the sessions stopped and started so much, it was hard to sustain some of the grooves Stephen was going for. And CBS seemed to want to sell Stephen as this slick, classy artist, when Stephen was really just down-home."

Stills was thinking along similar lines when he started cutting some new tracks in the basement of his Bel Air mansion, using a remote recording truck outside, backed up by Dallas Taylor, Joe Lala, Mike Finnigan, and Bonnie Bramlett. A couple of the best new songs, "Streetwise" and "Precious Love," were aggressive, surging rockers that Stephen drove with his guitar.

"My instrument is the electric guitar with an amplifier," Stills told *BAM* in 1979. "That's what I play best and that's what gets me off. I *like* to play acoustic, but that's kind of the Crosby, Stills & Nash thing. My thing is more R&B-oriented."

These words were backed up by a riot-

Left to right: **Gerry Tolman, Dallas Taylor, Bonnie Bramlett, George "Chocolate" Perry, Stephen Stills, Carl Pickard, Mike Finnigan.**

ous couple of shows at the Roxy nightclub on the Sunset Strip in late January 1979. Taylor, Finnigan, Lala, Perry, Bramlett, guitarist Gerry Tolman, and old Manassas guitarist Al Perkins made up Stills's playing unit. The intimacy of the club situation lit a fire under Stephen as he performed a bundle of new songs and several fairly obscure old ones, such as "Go Back Home" and "Cherokee," from his first solo album, and a large chunk of Manassas material. During these Roxy shows, a recording truck was outside with the tapes rolling.

On February 7, Stills went into the studio and became the first musician to cut an album with the then-revolutionary digital recording system. Pleased with the technique, but not totally sold on it, Stephen nonetheless captured some of the sound he was searching for. These sessions, combined with the Roxy shows, put him in an electric, confident mood. He announced at the time, "I'm not going to let CSN dominate my life. It's cost me in the past. But one does not preclude the other, and I'm always open." He went on to say, "There's a new song I've written with Chocolate [George Perry] called 'Dangerous Woman on the Loose.' That's kind of the way I feel now. I just want to get down and get bad and have a band and have my style evolve to the point where everybody forgets about all the other stuff.

"I feel like I'm a quarterback who has taken a team to the Super Bowl and wants to do it again with a different bunch of people. It's probably an impossible dream, I know, because people won't forget the past. Still, I'd like to equal what I've done with David and Graham with something just as significant and exciting and *new*."

CHAPTER ELEVEN

Alone . . . Together (1979)

Nash: "Nuclear Madness"/A Break with Crosby (1979)

"**W**hen Graham Nash is concerned about something, he doesn't just talk, he *does*. He takes action. Graham is an organizer. He's not a follower."

These words, spoken by rock promoter Bill Graham, rang true in early 1979, when Nash joined forces with Jackson Browne, and the pair performed a series of benefit concerts in San Diego, Los Angeles, and Oakland on January 26, 27, and 29. The shows were all sellouts, and $112,000 was raised for an antinuclear organization, the Abalone Alliance, which was trying to stop the construction of the Diablo Canyon and San Onofre nuclear reactors. In the middle of Nash's song "Military Madness," he screamed, *"Nuclear* madness is killing our country!"

"My history of antinuclear activism goes back to the late fifties," says Graham. "I remember seeing Lord Bertrand Russell walk with thousands of people from Aldermaston to London in protest of the deployment of U.S. nuclear submarines in England. But I, when I was sixteen or seventeen, didn't have any power to be able to do anything about it. Since then, as a musician and a human being, I've tried my best to make people aware of some of the things they might not be aware of. I've gleaned a

lot of information from Ralph Nader and Jacques Cousteau and have done a lot of studying and got more aware and more determined to do something about it.

"David and Stephen and I have always realized that the youth of this country is a very powerful and moving force. It was proven to us at Woodstock, it was proven to us during the civil rights movement, it was proven to us during the march on Washington for the Vietnam War. Just generally, if you get the youth of this country aware and annoyed enough at something that is actually killing them . . . they will respond."

These sentiments cut into Nash's songwriting, specifically the tune "Barrel of Pain," when he discovered the presence of barrels of low-level radioactive waste at the bottom of the Pacific Ocean off the coast of San Francisco.

"I take it very personally," Graham said in 1979, "when I think the people behind this nuclear madness are trying to kill me and my wife and my children."

Bristling with emotion, Nash decided to go into the studio. He and Crosby, with the help of the management team of Hartmann and Goodman, had severed ties with ABC and signed a new record deal with CBS. In February of 1979, recording sessions were behind schedule when Nash and Crosby met at Britannia Studios in Los Angeles.

Jackson Browne and Graham Nash, 1979.

Graham and Jackson with Bill Walton of the Portland Trail Blazers at San Diego No Nukes concert, 1979.

these sessions. He says, "It was not necessarily by choice, but out of necessity. David was not paying attention and often falling asleep. This led to a monstrous argument between the two of us. We just spaced out about a lot of things . . . *musically*, I didn't feel David was working hard enough. Far be it from me to say, but I don't think he was putting enough attention to music. I thought he was fucking off, so I told him that. You see, he's capable of being a brilliant artist, and it saddens me when I see him not realizing his full potential . . . as a person and as an artist. But I love him dearly and it's hard for me to be objective."

Crosby says, "I didn't have enough songs. And everyone was lookin' over my

Besides Nash's "Helicopter Song" and Crosby's "I Needed to Drive My Car," previously cut at the CSN sessions in Miami, the two singers worked on "Barrel of Pain," "Love Has Come," "Out on the Island"—all by Graham. Drummers Vitale and Kunkel, bassists Drummond and Perry, guitarists Lindley and Kootch, and keyboardist Doerge, were on hand for these recordings. Guitarist Joe Walsh was also called in.

"I wanted to see what this madman could do," says Nash. "So I got up the nerve and called him up. He came down and he played brilliantly."

It was Nash who was orchestrating

Graham Nash backstage at Hollywood Bowl Survival Sunday concert. Right: John Hartmann (manager).

shoulder, sayin', 'Well, he's gonna fail this week.' Then it turned into the longest goddamned psychodrama, man, this great big Mary Hartman scene. It was very strange. I didn't feel like I was doing anything to anybody. I just wanted to get high, me personally. I didn't ask anybody else to."

But David began internalizing more and more. His happy-go-lucky attitude about mixing drugs with music was not as carefree as it once had been. Cocaine was becoming an anchor that was tugging him down. He wouldn't admit this, but Nash says, "While we were at Brittania, I realized that David's problem was more of a problem than I'd thought it was. One night we were in the middle of an incredible jam, when his freebasing pipe fell and shattered into a thousand pieces. And he stopped the whole jam to pick up the pieces and that's when I lost it. That's when I realized David needed help."

When Crosby refused to accept the idea that he should change his lifestyle in any way, the C&N sessions stopped abruptly. Nash flew home to San Francisco and paid a visit to his neighbor, Joel Bernstein. Graham remembers, "Joel showed me this picture he'd taken of me on the edge of this volcano in Hawaii. It was so good . . . I decided that it was good enough to put an album between. So I took my songs—'Out on the Island,' 'Love Has Come,' 'Barrel of Pain,' 'Helicopter Song,' 'Magical Child'— and made the decision to start a solo album."

Stills: Havana Jam/"Costello Knock Out" (1979)

No American musicians had ever performed in Castro's Cuba when Columbia Records worked out a plan that would allow for a three-day "jam" in March of 1979 at the 4,800-seat Karl Marx Theater.

Stephen Stills says, "When they got everything worked out, I was the first rock 'n' roller they asked, because of my language, because I'd lived in Latin America and they knew I was politically astute."

In preparation for his appearance in Cuba, Stills tightened up his band, which now included Finnigan, Vitale, Perry, Bonnie Bramlett, and guitarist Gerry Tolman. Stephen also finished a song called "Cuba al Fin" ("Cuba at Last"), in Spanish, for the Cuban people.

"First of all," Stills said a few days before departing from America, "it's just music, you know? But it's also a chance to go down there and say that we, the American people, really don't give a shit about all this crap. We have to deal with these people, you know? And they're very proud of what they've done. So you have to give them due respect, because they have a unique form of socialism that's very significant in the scheme of world history. So, as long as you give 'em respect, you're cool. That's why I want to bring back this Cuban band, Irakere, when I tour in America."

Stephen was true to his word. After performing with other CBS artists, such as Weather Report, Billy Joel, Rita Coolidge, Kris Kristofferson, and Stan Getz, as well as many native Cuban players, Stills boarded a plane with his band and Irakere, an eleven-member Afro-Cuban outfit. When they touched down in the U.S.A., Stills had no political comment about his stay in Cuba. Instead, he said, "Being there with 174 of some of the heaviest jazz musicians alive—a lot of them from the generation of musicians I grew up listening to—has me feeling comfortable being in my mid-thirties and playing rock 'n' roll. While I've still got the energy, I'll rock 'n' roll. I'll be a folk singer later . . . when I'm forty."

Playing mostly medium-sized arenas and outdoor amphitheaters in the Eastern part of America, Stills and Irakere worked

California and shifted the personnel in his group. Finnigan and Tolman were still aboard, but Bonnie Bramlett had left ("to be an Allman sister with the Allman Brothers Band"), Lala had hit the road with the Bee Gees, Joe Vitale had done the same thing with the Eagles, and Perry had returned to session work at Criteria. In their places, Stills recruited singer Brooks Hunnicutt (through a friend in Lake Tahoe), drummer Bill Meeker (formerly in the Dudek, Finnigan, and Kreiger Band), and bassist Gerald Johnson (from Dave Mason's group). Percussionist Pete Escovedo sat in for Lala. This combination played a twenty-dollars-per-ticket benefit for Greenpeace June 9, 1979, at San Francisco's 2,200-seat Warfield Theater, on Market Street. Dave Mason was supposed to join

well. However, national attention focused on an incident that occurred offstage one night in Columbus, Ohio. Keyboardist Mike Finnigan recalls, "We were sittin' in this bar when Elvis [Costello] started givin' mouth. He had the *nerve* to call Ray Charles a blind nigger. I was about to send his teeth and eyeballs all over Columbus. But my mom was there. And she said, 'I didn't come all the way to Columbus to see you beat up some midget.' So Bonnie Bramlett stood up and goes *pow!* and sent Elvis *smell*vis twitchin'. Then she said, 'It's a good thing I stopped drinkin' or I mighta killed 'im.' That little bastard. He needed a beating by a woman and got one."

ELVIS COSTELLO PUNCHED OUT IN FRACAS WITH STILLS BAND. The headline showed up all over the country, and eclipsed what had been a sterling set of shows by Stills and Irakere.

By June 1979, Stephen had returned to

Stills plays for Greenpeace at the Fox Warfield, San Francisco, June 1979. (Photo by Dave Zimmer.)

Stills on stage, but tore up his knee in an accident the night before. So Stephen fronted his band alone and worked through a set that covered material from every part of his career. After the show, Stills mopped the perspiration from his face and slumped down on a couch in his dressing room. He talked about how "rock is where I belong, man." When asked about the future of Crosby, Stills & Nash, he sighed, "It'll happen when it happens. I'm having fun playing with my new group and not even thinking about it."

Stills in Roxy dressing room with Lyle Alzado of the Oakland Raiders and Steve Garvey of the Los Angeles Dodgers.

CSN: M. U. S. E. / A Cause Unites (1979)

A couple of days after Stills played the Warfield, he got a call from Graham Nash. And on June 14, 1979, Stills, Nash, Bruce Springsteen, Gary "U.S." Bonds, Bonnie Raitt, and a bevy of other performers turned out at the Hollywood Bowl in Los Angeles for Survival Sunday—a musical demonstration against nuclear power. MUSE (Musicians United for Safe Energy) grew out of this commitment, and as a board member, Nash became involved with coordinating the talent for more benefit concerts. All proceeds would go to grassroots antinuke groups from across America.

By September, such artists as Springsteen, the Doobie Brothers, Carly Simon, James Taylor, Tom Petty and the Heartbreakers, and Jesse Colin Young had agreed to join Nash, Jackson Browne, John Hall, and Bonnie Raitt for a five-night stand at Madison Square Garden.

"The MUSE people had asked me to get CSN together," says Graham. "And I totally refused. Because I didn't feel we had anything to contribute. Our music depends on our own personal feelings and love toward one another, and when it's not there, we can't perform. It's that simple."

But when Nash arrived in New York a few days before the shows were set to take place, September 19 through 23, he was forced to reconsider.

"I went to see Jackson in his hotel room," Nash explains. "And Jackson said, 'Hey, we're going to have to cancel the fifth night.' I said, 'What do you mean?' 'We don't have a headline act,' he said.

"I've done a lot of shows in my life, so I know that the first three nights cover expenses and the fourth and fifth nights are the gravy, the profit. So I was determined not to cancel that fifth night.

"Jackson looked at me and said, 'I know how you feel about it, but I'm going to ask you one more time . . . can you get David and Stephen, would you want to do that?'

"I thought about it for about seven seconds. And I went through all the changes by the microsecond. I went through *everything*. And I figured this cause was greater than whatever personal differences might exist between us. So I called them up. They were more than delighted to hear from me. And they were on the next plane—literally."

Crosby flew in from San Francisco,

Survival Sunday concert, Los Angeles, 1979. Left to right: John Sebastian, John Hall, Graham Nash holding his son, Jackson.

Stills from Los Angeles, and after a few brief rehearsals, CSN went on stage at Madison Square Garden and at an outdoor rally. Because the reunion came about so quickly, there was no time to work up any new material, so they played it safe with old reliables such as "Suite: Judy Blue Eyes," "Long Time Gone," and "Teach Your Children." The performances were a little rough, but the capacity crowd at the Garden cheered loudly.

At a MUSE press conference, a reporter asked, "Will the Crosby, Stills & Nash reunion last beyond Sunday night?"

Crosby piped up, "There have never actually been reunions and we've never actually been apart. It's always been that way, if you remember. It's always been like that."

David then recited the "we are not a group" rap. The absence of CSN for various lengths of time could always be chalked up to the fact that each of the three wanted to pursue his own personal projects. In the fall of 1979, personal interests were taking precedence over the group. After Crosby and Nash each played a solo set, then a brief duo set at the Bread and Roses Festival, they went their separate ways. Crosby took to the water and sailed toward Tahiti. Nash returned to Los Angeles, where he started polishing his solo album, to be called *Earth and Sky*.

Stephen had been on the road for most of the summer before joining David and Graham in New York. Back in California, he played a few solo shows, then he jumped into a new recording project with his touring group (known as the California Blues Band) and such guest artists as Herbie Hancock at Kendun Recorders, at the Record Plant, and in the basement (also known as "the pub") of his Bel Air home. These sessions were often marathon affairs.

"Stephen was going for a real authentic Latin sound," says drummer Bill Meeker. "We must have run every top percussionist in the country into the studio. He got some real great stuff going, real experimental-sounding. When Willie Bobo and Herbie Hancock came by, *that* was interesting . . . some percussion and keyboard combinations came about that just *jumped*. And we stayed up for a long time. Stephen was always trying to get everybody to translate what was in his head onto tape. He was always searching, trying different combinations. I think I spent twenty years of my life in the studio with Stephen Stills in a span of two months."

Across town, another marathon was stretching out. To get a three-disc album of the MUSE No Nukes concerts into the stores by Christmas, Nash, Jackson Browne, and a handful of engineers labored away inside Rudy Records (transplanted to Los Angeles) for seven straight days. During that time (from November 11 to November 17), Nash had two short naps. Browne was up the whole time. And Stills dropped by for the last seventy hours to help mix.

Don Gooch, one of the engineers, recalls, "You never knew, when you walked out of the control room, if it'd be light or dark. I remember watching Graham come out once, and he just froze when he saw the sun. He was firmly convinced that it was the moon and that there was no reason why it should be that bright."

"I was hallucinating, largely," Graham admits, "and I was amazed we were able to make such objective decisions. My greatest fear was that we would totally fuck it up because we were so out there, having been without sleep for so long. But it wasn't the case, obviously."

The three-LP set, *No Nukes* (later followed by a film of the same name) made it into the stores by Christmas of 1979 and contained three Crosby, Stills & Nash performances—"You Don't Have to Cry," "Long Time Gone," and "Teach Your Children," as well as Nash alone on "Cathedral" and in harmony with others. Of course, *No Nukes* also featured tracks by Springsteen, Browne, the Doobie Brothers, Bonnie Raitt, Ry Cooder, Nicolette Larson, and many of the other performers.

In reflecting on the task of producing this project in such an insanely short amount of time, Nash says, "I was higher after those seven days than I've ever been. The feeling was beautiful."

This glow of satisfaction and accomplishment carried Nash through the holidays and into 1980—a year that would bring frustration, growth, and change into the lives of Crosby, Stills & Nash.

CHAPTER TWELVE

Separate Journeys Cross (1980–1981)

"**I** can get off playing guitar by myself in an empty room . . . *heavily*," Crosby said in 1980. "But when I get to play with someone else in that empty room, the feelings get multiplied by four, by *ten* sometimes. Because you can catch another cat's lick and interlock with 'em in some exquisite way and make the hair on both your arms stand up, his and yours. Well, that's just heaven. It makes drugs look like kid stuff, *sex* even. And that takes some beatin'.

"So I didn't want to quit workin' with Graham; I didn't want to quit workin' with Crosby, Stills & Nash. That was the best music I made in my whole life. And because it's not happening, it's hurting so bad, man. But I gotta keep goin', I gotta keep making music, even if it's by myself, because it's still the main thing in my life. Whenever I ask myself, 'What am I supposed to do in this world?' I keep saying, 'Play and sing.' "

Crosby played a couple of acoustic solo shows at the Great American Music Hall in early 1980, and unveiled several songs the public had never heard before. One of them, called "Distances," had been written back in 1977, but the words dealt with the frustration of coping with "distances in my life"—which certainly applied to Crosby's situation in 1980. A new piano song,

"Delta," flowed like a beautiful poem. It was the best music Crosby had written in some time. But he was far from happy.

Stills, meanwhile, was playing occasional gigs, and he was also frustrated. Columbia didn't like the adventurous Latin/R&B/jazz compositions Stephen had recorded, and made him hire an outside producer.

Enter veteran Muscle Shoals producer Barry Beckett. "I was getting tired of wearing so many hats—singer, guitarist, band leader, producer, engineer—and I think I was losing a little perspective on my own music," says Stills. "Barry and I got along great. He was *real* efficient and allowed me the freedom to explore my musical chops more."

So Stills, Beckett, and a familiar corps of backing players went into the studio and got down to some serious recording.

By far the most visible member of the CSN camp in early 1980 was Nash. His third solo album, *Earth and Sky*, was released in February by Capitol. Nash had broken his contract with CBS when the company refused to remove a UPC code from the album cover. As silly as that might seem, Graham explains, "The bar [UPC] code *ruined* this beautiful photograph of Joel's." Rather than concede to CBS, he shifted to Capitol and *Earth and Sky* came out with no bar code.

"The music that goes inside is what this album cover shows," Nash said in late 1979. "It's light, it's airy, it's a little ominous in the darker areas. There's hope in it. There are rainbows, good feelings . . . being blown around."

Of the inside photo, a black-and-white portrait of Nash, he said, "It's much more direct, a *starker* image . . . which also reflects a certain amount of the music, too."

The sound of *Earth and Sky* was full and very direct, but Nash admits, "Some of the songs were a little lyrically abstract. It was a very personal album. A couple of the tracks felt tense to me, because it was a very trying time. I was going through enormous changes with David. So that made it tense. But when *Earth and Sky* came out, I was upset with its lack of acceptance."

In addition to poor sales, *Earth and Sky* was harpooned by certain rock critics. *Rolling Stone* published a particularly vicious review—with the reviewer arranging a series of Nash lyric excerpts, out of context, into a mocking, conversational scenario that signed off with the statement, "Even his best friends won't tell him."

"It hurt me," Nash admits. "Critics don't realize how fragile we all are. I can take constructive criticism, but for a writer to slough off a man's work with something so idiotic and nonsensical is ridiculous. I still don't know what the fuck he was trying to say."

"Graham Nash is a *friend* of mine," Stephen Stills said in 1980. "And *nobody* talks about a friend of mine like that. It's bullshit journalism. If that writer walked in here right now, I'd *deck* him."

The bad press had strained Graham's self-confidence, but when his thoughts turned to the road, he remembered that in August of 1979, he had drawn three sellout crowds in a row to the Universal Ampithea-

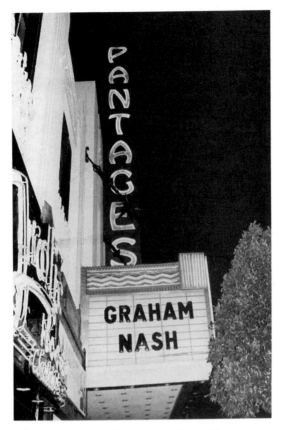

Hartmann and Goodman to Nash: "I only saw *your* name up on the marquee." Los Angeles, 1980.

ter in Los Angeles, "with no partners and no record." "I was rather pleased about the whole thing," Nash said at the time. "And John and Harlan [Hartmann and Goodman, Graham's managers at the time] really set me straight on opening night. They said, 'I only saw *your* name up on the marquee. I didn't see Stephen's or David's or Neil's, and look at 'em pouring in and filling this place. I guess they're just coming to see you, aren't they? So you better dig it.' And that was a really interesting perspective. I was totally shocked. Then I walked into the parking lot and heard this woman shouting, 'Get your Graham Nash T-shirts.' And it stopped me cold, because it was so odd to hear one's name, out there alone, with T-shirt sales . . . 'Get your Graham Nash T-shirts.' "

When Graham hit the tour trail in early March, he presented a largely acoustic show, backed up by Joel Bernstein on guitar and harmony and David Kessler on keyboards. "You can't forget Joe the Goldfish," says Nash roadie Jeffrey Husband. "The first show was in Seattle and we got Joe then. Every night, one of us would bring Joe, in his bowl, out on stage and that was the cue to bring the house lights down. Joe made it through forty-eight shows. He was interviewed with Graham on 'Merv Griffin.' That fish was a trouper, and we left him in Miami, after our last show, with one of the truck driver's girl friends, who had this big aquarium."

Part of the way into the *Earth and Sky* tour, Nash fired keyboardist Kessler and hired William "Smitty" Smith, who had been on tour with both Bob Dylan and Ry Cooder. "Graham taught me the show on his bus in three hours," says Smith. "And playing with Graham, I learned about pockets, I learned how to leave holes. His music is a lot more airy than Dylan's. Also, I was constantly amazed that all the kids in the audience knew the words to all the songs. To me, it was like someone going to a Coltrane concert and humming all the solos he'd done on his records. Now, with Dylan, he *expected* the crowd to respond and more. Graham was always *grateful* and sincerely touched by what he got."

"We played mostly small theaters," says Nash, "so it was very intimate with me, Joel, and Smitty. I learned a lot about myself on that tour. I learned *control*. I learned you don't need huge amplifiers to get people off. I learned to sing and play harmonica better. Those were nice shows."

Leah Kunkel, who opened for Nash on this tour, recalls, "A lot of the fans were half expecting one or two of the other guys to show up at the shows, but Graham carried

Graham Nash at the Pantages Theater concert, Los Angeles, 1980.

it off alone. He really is one of the greats."

There was almost a "walk-on" at the Pantages Theater in Hollywood. "David came the first night," says Graham. "But when I went to look for him to come out for the encore, he'd gone."

On May, 25, 1980, at the second Survival Sunday concert at the Hollywood Bowl, Crosby showed up to play with Nash. And this time Stills dropped in as well. The harmonies wavered in and out of key, but the audience greeted each song with reverential cheers.

"The chemistry that happens when the three of us are out there never ceases to amaze me," Stills said at the time. "We can be under-rehearsed, out of tune . . . just not very good at all. But the people are out there pulling for us, *behind* us. Our fans make us want to be good."

But after the Survival Sunday show,

CSN reunite briefly at the Survival Sunday concert, Hollywood Bowl, 1980.

which also featured a grand finale of Stills, Joe Walsh, Crosby, Nash, Timothy B. Schmit, and Don Felder all playing and singing together, the CSN combination did not stay together. Crosby went back to his home in Mill Valley. Nash returned to his family (which included now one more person, following the birth of his second son, Willie John), and Stills, as usual, went back to playing.

With producer Barry Beckett, Stills had put together an album. "We had a nice combination of songs," says Stephen. "Barry took his time and allowed me to play. I didn't have to wear the producer's hat. I didn't have to think with him. He knew what I was after."

There was a glossy R&B feel to much of this music. But the best songs of the lot

were rawer and bluesier, particularly "One Way Ride" and "Southern Cross."

"Kenny Weiss [Gold Hill Music publisher and Stills's manager at the time] played me a tape of this song called 'Seven League Boots' by the Curtis Brothers," says Stills. "There was something about the rhythm, a lick that I liked. So I asked 'em if I could play with it. I wrote a new set of words, added a different chorus, and turned it into 'Southern Cross.'"

Despite the strength of this song and some of the other material Stills had recorded in 1979 and early 1980, CBS, once again, felt that this was not the kind of music that would sell in the contemporary market. The record company made various demands. Stephen refused to cooperate. So the master tapes of this Barry Beckett-pro-

217

Stephen Stills and Ken Weiss, Los Angeles, 1979.

duced Stills music were impounded and have yet to see the light of day (except, that is, re-worked versions of "Southern Cross" and "You Are Alive"—which appeared on CSN's 1982 *Daylight Again* album.)

In the spring of 1980, however, Stills was antsy and wanted to play live with a new set of players. He'd been working closely with guitarist/songwriter Gerry Tolman. In fact, the pair had written some great material. But while in Lake Tahoe on a short vacation earlier in the year, Stephen ran into a young musician named Michael Stergis, who had played trumpet with Maynard Ferguson and guitar with Helen Reddy. Stergis immediately became Stills's new playing buddy. The two started trading licks and a playing unit began to take shape. Bassist Trey Thompson was suggested by drummer Meeker and keyboardist Finnigan—and in June, with the addition of Joe Lala, this Stills group, dubbed the California Blues Band, was ready for the road.

Ken Weiss managed to land Stills a spot on "Going Platinum," a cable-TV music program. Some interviews and a live appearance with the band were taped at the Concord Pavilion in Northern California. Then a short tour of Europe was booked.

Before leaving for the European tour,

Stills decided to "re-energize" for a couple of weeks in Hawaii. What he didn't know was that Nash was there already and about to call him. "In Hawaii, where I live with my family sometimes," says Graham, "this lady, thought to be a real mover and shaker, was running for mayor. She needed money. I offered to do a benefit for her. Then I thought about inviting Stephen. When I called Stephen, he said, 'Sure,' because he was already planning to go to the islands for a vacation. So we did this benefit. And with me and Stephen just singing and playing our acoustic guitars, it reminded me of all the stuff we did on the first CSN album. We sang really great together. And afterwards, I began to realize that there was a certain part of the CSN formula that had not been fully explored—me and Stephen. So we became musically close in a way we hadn't before."

Stills says, "Me and Nash hit some peaks that I think surprised both of us. I mean, we'd never really sat down, just the two of us, and sung quite like that. I got off, man. So I invited Graham to come with me over to Germany."

"I wasn't sure I wanted to travel from Hawaii to Europe to do four shows," Nash remembers. "But the more I thought about it, the more interesting the proposition became. So I flew to Munich with Susan [Nash], rehearsed in the afternoon with Stephen and his band, and that night walked on stage with them. We had a great time."

Back in Los Angeles, in August 1980, Crosby was laying down tracks for a solo album and, he recalls, "I was feeling lousy. Making that solo album had to be one of the strangest experiences of my whole life. I missed Nash. I missed Stephen. But I had to make some kind of record."

Working at Rudy Records and Brittania Studios, Crosby got musical support from keyboardist Craig Doerge and bassist

Lee Sklar. Guitarist Larry Carlton even dropped in for a while and played on a Crosby song originally called "Drowning Man." "It was too doomish," says David, "and I didn't dig it. It painted a really grim picture of someone in dire straits who would have to be snatched from the jaws of doom by somebody else. The music seemed to lend itself to a happier mood, so I changed the song to 'Flying Man.'"

Craig Doerge suggested that Crosby record "Might as Well Have a Good Time," written by Doerge and his wife, Judy Henske. "It was how I felt," Crosby says. "Even if things aren't like you want them to be, you might as well have a good time."

Another song, called "Melody," communicated the sentiment, "Melody . . . you are my reason for living."

Also recorded at this time were "Distances" and "Delta." The stream-of-consciousness lyrics of "Delta" included such lines as, "Thoughts / Like scattered leaves / Slowed in midfall / Into the streams."

"I wrote that stoned halfway out of my mind on my boat," Crosby said in 1981. "I finished it on Warren Zevon's piano. Jackson Browne was there. He helped me pull it through. He told me, 'Finish it or I'll break your arms.'"

To these songs Crosby added a couple of tracks from the past, a wordless scat number called "Kids and Dogs," written back in 1968 and recorded in 1970 with Jerry Garcia, and "King of the Mountain," a live take with Craig Doerge from a Crosby & Nash show in the mid-seventies. When they were put in sequence, "King of the Mountain" fell at the end of this prospective album and featured an impassioned Crosby repeating the chorus line, "He's the king of the mountain . . . alone."

By the time Stills and Nash returned from Europe in September, Crosby was out of Los Angeles and back up at his house in Mill Valley. There was little hope of a CSN

Stephen and Graham recording vocals at Rudy Records, Los Angeles.

project at this point, and Nash admits, "We had no intention of inviting David at first, because me and Stephen wanted to do an album. We wanted to take this duo combination and see what we could do in the studio."

Atlantic Records, however, was anxious to get some CSN product on the market by Christmas. So, rather than begin a Stills–Nash album right away, they were forced to piece together yet another greatest-hits collection. "It was insanity," says Graham. "But we had no choice."

Stills says, "I'd always wanted to recut 'Carry On' without 'Questions' on the second half. So this seemed like the right time to do that. I got Billy Meeker to lay in some new drums, and on the second half I cut a new rhythm guitar track, then cut loose on lead. I was happy about how it turned out."

But besides "Carry On," this compilation, appropriately called *Replay*, offered no new twists except for a version of *CSN*'s "I Give You Give Blind," remixed without the strings. The rest of the material was a motley selection of CSN tracks, all of them authored by Stills or Nash, with the exception of "Shadow Captain," co-written by Crosby and Doerge.

"I didn't even hear about the album until it was finished," says Crosby. "It was an obvious money trip. Nothing more."

Stills and Nash started recording with Stephen's backup band in October. Six tracks were cut, then sessions ground to a halt. "We didn't like how the music was sounding," Graham admits. "And there were some problems with the band." Bassist Trey Thompson was replaced by George Perry, who wanted to play with Vitale. So Bill Meeker was out, Vitale was in. But before this new assemblage could get down to some serious recording, Stills and Nash decided to knock off for Christmas. The next sessions didn't begin until February 1981.

"We were shuffling around for a while," says Stills, "waiting for each other to write some new songs."

Stephen, during this period, was very open to collaboration. He explains, "I find it much more exhilarating to write with other people than to write alone. It's fun to trade licks back and forth and come up with something as a team. Everyone has nice bits and pieces that are lookin' for homes."

When Nash was chopping around on his electric guitar one day, he kept going back to a four-chord cycle of changes. Stills overheard him, asked if he could "run with that music," and, two days later, after tossing some ideas around with Michael Stergis, came back with a completed song, "Turn Your Back on Love."

Stills and Stergis hung out quite a bit while this project was coming together. Stergis says, "A lot of times I'd get these calls at one A.M. from Stephen. He'd say, 'I have this idea for a song, but it needs a little something else. Wanna come up?' I'd never not go up to Stephen's house, even if it was two or three in the morning. We'd always end up with something, and Stephen's a monster lyricist with a magic ear. I really respect the guy. And I probably bought *ten* copies of *Déjà Vu*, I played it so much. I

Michael Stergis, 1982.

figure I probably paid for Stills's coffee table or something."

When Stills and Stergis had gone to Tahoe after one of their sessions, a year earlier, they brought along a tape of some of their new music. Stergis remembers, "When we drove from Tahoe to Graham's house in San Francisco, we put a tape player between us and put down about fifteen to twenty verses to this song, 'You Are Alive.' We actually finished it in front of Graham and his wife."

"You Are Alive," a tender ballad about finding life and love with a partner, was presented to Graham and Susan Nash as an anniversary gift.

"Susan Nash," says Stephen, "was and remains the best and strongest advocate of Graham and I working together. I'll never forget that it was Susan who wanted me to come back to their house in L.A. after that Crosby and Nash show at the Greek Theater show in 1976. She would always look at both sides of any disagreement between me and Graham and cool it before tension set it. She would always look at my point of view and remind Graham if he wasn't. I'll never be able to thank her properly and she remains one of my dearest friends and one of the few women 'buddies' that I have."

Graham wrote a piece of music that communicated his own feelings about his wife, "Song for Susan."

Graham, Susan, and Willie John at Zoetrope rehearsal, Los Angeles, 1982.

"I think, at times, we've all fooled ourselves about how to exist," says Nash. "I used to think staying in the studio for twenty-five hours a day was it. But Susan helped me see there was more. And having a family only added to that feeling . . . which I tried to express in 'Song for Susan.'"

In 1982, Nash said, "My center, from which I draw my strength, has been reinforced by my family life. I think one needs a strong center to work from, or you can become really scattered. If I didn't have an understanding partner like Susan, I wouldn't be nearly as effective as I am. She always encourages and supports me. . . . She also allows me the freedom to be as crazy as I am—in a good way."

When Nash reflected back to times when his craziness or inability to put up with other people's craziness had resulted in squandered energy and lost moments, he began stringing together words that grew into "Wasted on the Way." "I was thinking about CSN," Nash admits, "about how many times we wasted chances to really make some music that would not only bring joy to us, but to others too. I must tell you, 'Wasted on the Way' was also written from a feeling that I had as a teenager. I remember being at dances and being envious of all of the guys who would just go up to a girl and say, 'Wanna dance?' I could never do that. I was always afraid of rejection . . . that she wouldn't want to dance and that I'd be out there looking like a turkey. But, as I learned, you've got to just plunge ahead and take some chances. Because some things don't come around twice, and there's only so much time you can make up."

With a full head of steam built up, Nash and Stills were intent on not wasting any more time getting their project on track. They now had new songs to work with, and an eager band—Stergis, Finnigan, Vitale, and Perry. With engineer/producers Stanley Johnston and Steve Gursky behind the board in the studio, sessions moved efficiently. While, in the past, Stills had insisted upon overseeing and masterminding much of what went on in the studio, during these sessions he pulled back considerably.

"I couldn't have done it without Nash," says Stills. " 'Cause he can remember every little detail. Consequently, I can forget everything and just concentrate on my playing."

"He trusts me," Nash said at the time, "which is a primary force between us. He knows I'm not going to screw him around. He knows I only want the best from him. I believe I can get things out of Stephen that

Stephen and Graham at Rudy Records with Mike Finnigan and John Hall, who dropped by during recording, Los Angeles, 1982.

not a lot of people can get. I force him to work harder, and he does the same with me."

As hard as they worked, however, there were few marathon sessions. Stills, once the "marathon king," rationalizes a shift away from old habits: "I was younger then. I'd just keep going and sometimes some interesting things would happen. But I'm sorry, I can't do it anymore. After so many hours, your judgment just isn't that good. I basically found that it wasn't that productive."

The Stills and Nash sessions were *very* productive, though. And by May they were ready to record vocals. To escape the madness of Los Angeles, it was decided that all the vocal overdubs would be done at Sea West studios in Hawaii, on the island of Oahu. At this point, Nash admits, "I thought it would be nice if David would get involved. But I had a hard time gettin' hold of him. I made about forty calls, then just lost heart and we [Stills and Nash] decided to just keep on going."

Crosby tells a different story. "Graham came to one of my shows in Mill Valley and I was terrible there, I admit it. But it's like he didn't want to give me another chance. I wanted to go to Hawaii to sing with Graham and Stephen, but Graham and I had an argument on the phone. And all of a sudden I wasn't going."

Either way, Crosby was still by himself and very sensitive to criticism concerning his drug use. "I'm not ashamed of being stoned," Crosby said in 1981. "But when that's the reason people give for not wanting to work with me, I get real upset. I figure if I'm not hurtin' anybody or fuckin' anybody over, I should be able to do anything I goddamn well please. If I want to paint myself purple, blow my house up on Thursdays, I should be able to do that if it doesn't hurt anybody else. But I'm not allowed that freedom by my peers.

"Everybody's been on my case for so long, saying I'm so smashed, so stoned, strung out. But I was stoned for every bit of music I've ever played. Every record, every performance . . . I was stoned halfway out of my gourd. If they can match the music, let them criticize it. Anybody who can't, ain't got no fuckin' right to tell me nothin' about gettin' high."

When Crosby turned his solo album in to Capitol Records, they did criticize the music. In their opinion, the album was incomplete. There were too many songs without words, and no marketable singles. Crosby says, "All I know is that they didn't want to put my record out. They said they didn't like it. They felt it wasn't rock 'n' roll enough, wasn't like Devo or Elvis Costello. But they're dead wrong. They wouldn't know a song if it bit 'em in the ear."

Certainly, Capitol couldn't have expected Crosby suddenly to turn to new wave, especially in light of his view of the music form. "Shock rock, I call it," Crosby said in 1981. "It's just dumb. Those bands will do anything to get attention. 'I can be freakier than you can. Let's guillotine a chicken. Oh, I think I'm turning Japanese, I think I'm turning Japanese.' That isn't saying anything. Music is the most beautiful thing on the planet. It makes the distances

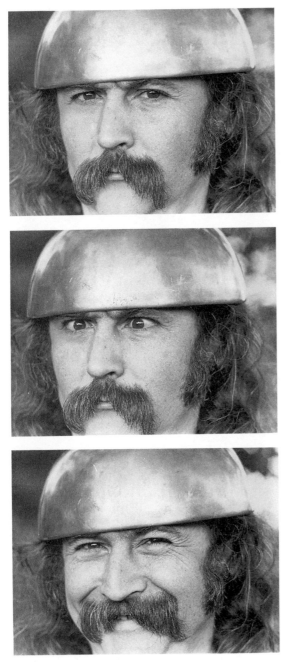

David Crosby, Mill Valley, 1981.

singing 'Teach Your Children,' music is bringing them together."

Unfortunately, Crosby's attitude was not getting him anywhere with Capitol or Stills and Nash. "I don't see where I need to change my record or my life," Crosby said in 1981. "I like my record. Maybe I could substitute one or two things with songs that might be a little more accessible, more rock 'n' roll-y. I don't *want* to. But it's being demanded of me and they have me over a barrel."

David did attempt to make minor changes in his album, but he never carried them through, and ultimately Capitol dropped him from its roster of artists. At this point, Crosby responded, "I've got to keep going, because I believe I have a future. I don't know, man, I've gotten myself deeper and deeper into this estrangement and isolation from everybody and all I want to do is make music and *play* music with other people."

Several of Crosby's closest friends— Paul Kantner, Grace Slick, Carl Gottlieb, and several others—attempted to draw Crosby closer to this goal in 1981 by literally ambushing him at his Mill Valley home and enrolling him in a drug rehabilitation program. But Crosby checked out after a couple of days.

"I *want* to get high," Crosby said in 1981. "I'm not ashamed of being stoned. But drugs are like a wrench. They will fuck with you and they can also give you moments of great pleasure. I have a lot of fun stoned. But freebase has a real bad name. I wouldn't recommend it to a neophyte, that's for sure. It's the most addictive drug I've ever seen. It's tougher than heroin, speed, *anything*. But it doesn't seem to have ruined my lungs or my throat."

David still sounded strong on stage and, in April 1981, he managed to piece together a backup band, comprised of bassist Tony Saunders (Merl's son), drummer

between people smaller. This new wave stuff doesn't do that. But at the end of a CSN concert, when the whole audience is

David Crosby and friend, Mill Valley, 1981.

Jay David, and Karl Schwindeman. Following a few rehearsals and a warmup gig at the Phoenix Theater in Petaluma, California, this group, called the David Crosby Band, toured all over America, playing mostly small clubs and some colleges. Being out there on his own, Crosby said in 1981, "made me get off my ass and do things I wouldn't normally have to do. I worked up material I'd never worked up before. With CSN, I just had to do so many songs. On my own, I had to have enough for two sets by myself. I played four or five new songs a night and they all got a good response from the audience, especially this a cappella one ["Samurai"]."

The electric set, highlighted by a funky version of "Long Time Gone," was spirited but not as thoroughly moving as when

Crosby went one-on-one with the audience.

"Playing by myself, with no band," David said in 1981, "it's fairly demanding. You really have to tell the tale. You can't depend on your partners to shuffle you out of a jam. So, when I was out there, I discovered I could *get* an audience on my own, and it made me a lot less insecure."

While Crosby was re-establishing his self-confidence, Stills and Nash were in Hawaii laying down vocals. "We worked a lot during the day and the early evening," says Nash. "I'll never forget looking out this window while we were singing in Sea West [recording studios]. There was a view of the ocean. So we could overdub and watch these beautiful sunsets at the same time. A pretty magical feeling.

"And we were working well. . . . What I

enjoyed about Hawaii was seeing Stephen get up at ten in the morning, go into the kitchen, drink orange juice, then go play tennis for a couple of hours, swim, then go into the studio—fresh and clear."

Stills admits, "There was a lot less pressure, being in Hawaii. No one was looking over our shoulders. And," he chuckles, "I was behaving myself."

When Stills and Nash got to the point where it became obvious that they needed a third harmony voice to blend into the mixes, Stephen says, "We talked about singing with a lot of people. At one point we were going to have Michael McDonald sing lead on one song. But he was working on a solo album and we didn't want to diffuse his career.

"It was my old buddy Michael Finnigan who really helped out," Stills continues. "That guy's pipes are so strong. He added real power to a lot of the harmony blends."

Ex-Eagle Timothy B. Schmit eventually came into the picture. Stills and Nash had harmonized with him on Joe Vitale's solo album before leaving for Hawaii, and had sung backups on Schmit's "I Can't Tell You Why" at Survival Sunday. "Tim has a great falsetto," Stills said in 1981. "So he was able to reach some real high harmonies." Also chiming in on choruses was Michael Stergis. But when it came time to do the vocals for a song called "Daylight Again," Stills started hearing a low-register harmony that none of the singers in the studio were capable of reaching. "Then we thought of Arthur Garfunkel," says Stephen. "I knew he had a smooth baritone that would sound really nice underneath me and Graham. I really wanted that song to sound special."

Graham, Joel Bernstein, and Timothy B. Schmit harmonize in the studio.

This isn't surprising, since it had taken Stills about seven years to mold "Daylight Again" into its final form. In the mid-seventies, at the end of each of Stephen's solo shows, he would break into a spontaneous tale about the Civil War and modern society, over a deliberate acoustic guitar pluck. This would segue right into "Find the Cost of Freedom."

"I used to make up these words nightly," Stephen admits. "And it had many more verses. Nash finally got me off my ass and I pared it down some and turned it into a real song. I'd always heard it as the introduction to 'Find the Cost of Freedom.' The setting is the Civil War, but the words fit what's happening today . . . this fight against nuclear madness. It's *our* war."

In contrast to the sentiments of the "Daylight Again"/"Find the Cost of Freedom" combination, the vocal harmonies Stills wanted had to be beautiful. Back in Los Angeles, at Rudy Records, Stills and Nash called Garfunkel in New York. "Arthur was very excited about singing with us," says Nash. "Because normally he gets asked to sing on a shitty song to make it better. But when we sent him a cassette of 'Daylight Again,' he realized we'd saved one of the best songs for him. And in the studio, he stepped right in and sang a beautiful part."

By August 1981, Stills and Nash had completed an album that needed only to be tinkered with a bit more and fine-tuned. But they were far from jubilant. As Graham explained in 1982, "From the start, Atlantic was not fantastically interested in a Stills–Nash album, because it was an unknown quantity. And in the particular economic climate of a year and a half ago, they were loath to come up with the money to make this album. So Stephen and I made a decision to finance it ourselves. We went into the hole about $400,000—out of our own pockets—and we were in danger of not having the record come out."

Over the next several months, the Stills–Nash album changed little, and neither did Atlantic's position. "They wanted a Crosby, Stills & Nash album," says Graham. "They knew that as a combination, CSN would sell more than anything me and Stephen might have together. And when I started listening, over and over, to the work that Stephen and I had done, I swear I could hear Crosby's voice in there. It was like his ghost was singin' on the tracks. Very weird. Then I would realize he really wasn't there and I started to miss him. I missed his vocal quality. I missed his unique musical contributions. And I missed David as a *person*."

At this point, Nash and Stills began discussing the possibility of turning their album into a CSN project. "Me and Stephen went through some incredible trips," admits Graham. "It took a while to make a decision."

During this time, Nash devoted a lot of energy to his family. Stills, meanwhile, regrouped his California Blues Band and played some shows at Caesar's in Lake Tahoe. "There's always been a certain stigma about playing in casinos," says Stephen, "but hey, everybody likes to gamble a little now and then. The halls are nice. There are real mixed crowds. You can ski or fish while you're up there. I had a hell of a time." And at these particular shows, Stills was in great form. Playing a forty-five-minute opening acoustic set, he reached back for songs and notes that were thought to be long gone. "Do for the Others," "Blackbird," "Everybody's Talkin'," "Helplessly Hoping"—he delivered them all with clear passion. The same feeling ran through his electric set, which featured a cameo appearance by Glen Campbell, who was playing next door at Harrah's. But when these live dates were over and Stills was back in Los Angeles, he remembers, "It was time to find out where David was at."

Nash says, "To make it musically bet-

Stephen Stills at Lake Tahoe, 1982.

ter and financially easier, we made a decision to ask David to come into the project." But getting hold of Crosby wasn't that easy. He was still touring with his band and was rarely home. By means of several phone calls, a letter, and a telegram, Nash finally got through to Crosby in mid-November 1981. Graham remembers, "I told him, 'The situation with me and Stephen is really screwed because we miss your part. If your voice isn't on the record, Stephen and I are going to be forever hearing it in our heads.' When you've heard what CSN can sound like, and you take one of the voices out, it's a drag."

Then Nash explained about the bind they were in with Atlantic, that CSN was the combination the company was holding out for. A short while later, Stills dropped into a David Crosby Band show at the Golden Bear nightclub in Huntington Beach. How did Crosby react to all of this sudden attention?

"I was hurt they hadn't called sooner," Crosby said in 1981. "And I coulda told Nash, 'Forget it.' My feelings were hurt pretty bad. But . . . I love those guys. It was nice to be missed, God knows. I've always wanted to play and sing with them. Even when we argue or disagree, there's a bond, on a certain level, that is undeniable to us. It forces your ego out of the picture. The music becomes larger than just one person. So, ultimately, love wins and music conquers."

CHAPTER THIRTEEN

"Daylight Again" (1981–1982)

CSN: Tracking Together / The Hollies Return / Crosby Arrested . . . *Twice* (1981–1982)

December 1981: Crosby, Stills & Nash were together once more. Well, *almost*. Before the three could head into the studio, Stills went South for several shows with his California Blues Band. In Baton Rouge, his father appeared backstage. Stephen remembers, "He looked at me and said, 'Son, you've done all right. You've got my respect.' That meant a lot."

Back in Los Angeles, Crosby was eager to regain the respect of his old partner Nash. When the two of them walked into Rudy Records together for the first time in almost two years, Nash said, "I missed ya, Dave." Crosby merely put his hand over his heart and made a thumping motion, his eyes glistening with tears.

After a few warmup vocal runthroughs, Crosby walked out into the recording chamber to add a harmony line to Nash's "Song for Susan." Swaying gently in front of the microphone, David slapped on a headset, glanced down at a lyric sheet, and sang softly. A slight nervousness col-

ored his voice. He stopped and took another pass at the chorus. In the control room, Nash had his back turned and was staring down at the carpet. After a few moments he looked up, pressed the intercom switch, and said, "I can still hear you readin' it, David."

Crosby smiled through his bushy mustache, chucked the lyrics aside, and tried the part again. This time his throat loosened and he sang a harmony that warmed up the entire chorus. The words may have been Nash's, but they seemed particularly meaningful to Crosby when he sang: "Fooling myself / About how to exist / All by myself / There was much I had missed / You came and showed me / What happiness is."

"I think he's got it," Nash whispered to engineers Stanley Johnston and Steve Gursky. After Crosby fired off another take, Nash bounded out into the recording chamber and said, "Sounds great, David. Why don't you come listen?" The two walked toward the control room together.

The mood in the studio remained positive and relaxed well into the early-morning hours. But after Nash played several more songs that he and Stills had recorded, Crosby frowned slightly and said, "That's nice work, really nice work. But I don't hear where my voice is going to fit in there.

You've already got harmonies in there where I usually go."

"Dave," said Nash, "we'll take 'em out, if you think we should."

Crosby frowned again. "Part of me says if this is going to a Crosby, Stills & Nash album, we ought to just wipe the tracks and start from scratch. But I don't know if I can deal with the guilt of wiping out those harmonies, after those guys put in all that effort."

Nash said, "Think about it. We've got lots of time."

When Stills got back to town, the three singers sat and listened to all of the tracks. After "Daylight Again" and "Find the Cost of Freedom" floated from the speakers in the studio, Crosby said, "Damn, Arthur really put his heart into that. That's just too fuckin' beautiful to wipe." On that note, David left the studio.

"We actually tried three new takes of 'Daylight Again' as Crosby, Stills & Nash," Stephen says. "But when we listened back, David collapsed into laughter because he could hear that it wasn't even close to the version with Arthur. So, we did try to make it CSN, but it simply wasn't as strong."

And Crosby, physically, was not that strong during these fall 1981 sessions. Because of his ongoing drug use, his stamina in the studio had diminished to the point where he could only work for short stretches of time. And his vocal quality, though still impressive, was often glazed with a hoarse edge. David obviously was not well, but he was making a determined effort to contribute.

One night in December, Ahmet Ertegun came by to listen to the Stills–Nash tracks that were being expanded into CSN. "Steve and Graham *had* to get Crosby in it." Ahmet now reflects. "Because without Crosby, it just wouldn't have had the same feel. As sick as David was, his very appearance made things whole again."

But Graham Nash admits, "The atmosphere was a little awkward. When he realized that a lot of the three-part was already locked in, he felt weird about taking out any of the voices. He didn't want that guilt of destroying another man's work. Especially when it was as beautiful as Arthur's or Michael's or Timmy's. And David was a little suspicious of us. He'd been alienated far too long. And I could feel that alienation. But, being the musician that he is, he finally threw himself totally into the project."

Crosby explains, "I really didn't have much choice. I wanted to sing with Graham and Stephen, so I just fit in where I could."

Crosby also brought in the tapes of songs from his solo album sessions. With "Delta," which Crosby had recorded with Doerge, Kunkel, and guitarist Dean Parks, there was little room for Stills and Nash. "My harmony stacks were so tight," David says, "we left most of 'em in. Graham and Stephen barely sing on that song." But on "Might as Well Have a Good Time," new CSN harmonies were added over the piano and organ lines. That was one of the few instances where that happened. There was to be little *pure* Crosby, Stills & Nash harmony anywhere on the album, which was now to be called *Daylight Again*.

"We decided this time there were not rules," says Nash. "There were a couple tracks David did not sing on. There were a couple of tracks I did not sing on. It was no big deal. We decided we'd sing with whoever the hell we wanted, as long as it sounded good."

Crosby admits, "They put me over a lot of the harmonies. So some things are doubled . . . a jumble and jangle of voices. But I didn't mind. It sounded good. That was the only rule. That the music sound good."

Toward the end of the sessions, however, Crosby did muse that "I wish I would have been involved sooner. I wish some more of my music was on there."

At the final song selection stage, Stills clearly dominated from a writing and singing standpoint. Seven of the album's eleven original tracks bore a Stills writing credit. And the only *new* CSN song that was cut after David got involved was a Stills–Stergis collaboration, "Since I Met You," recorded at a furious pace all in one night, with Toto drummer Jeff Porcaro sitting in with the rest of the CSN gang.

"Historically," says Nash, "Stephen has always had the most tunes. He's been the most prolific of us, the writer of the melodies we want on there. Even on the first CSN album, Stephen far outweighed me and David in terms of song contributions. You know why? It's because he never sleeps. I haven't seen Stephen sleep since 1968, so he just naturally has more time to write than the rest of us."

Stills says, "I've always got a song or two on the fire. It's a matter of playin' steady and searchin' for new ideas. I like to write on the road. And I've always been willing to take jobs we couldn't get as a group. I just work and play more than the other guys, it seems. But nothing's ever predecided before we go into the studio, as far as how many songs each guy is gonna have on a particular album. I mean, we try not to get it too out of balance. I co-wrote a lot of things on *Daylight Again*, and the songs we ended using were the ones we *all* thought were the best."

By the first part of February, *Daylight Again* was at the sweetening stage. As Nash said at the time, "When David got involved in December, what I envisioned was a four-month project to redo the vocals. But it only took a month and a half. David was not always in the best of shape, but he worked as hard as I've ever seen him work. He'd always say, 'Can I do more?' He put himself totally in our hands, and it was great."

When Nash took an overview of the entire project, which had actually begun in October of 1980, he sighed, "Two Super Bowls. Can you believe that since we've been working on this album, two Super Bowls have been played and we're still not finished yet? That blows my mind when I think about it."

In contrast to "the album that wouldn't die"—which is what *Daylight Again* became known as, among the band and its crew—Nash entered into another project in February 1982: a reunion album with his old band, the Hollies. A "Stars on 45" medley of the Hollies' hits had been released in England in August of 1981 and had become such a smash on British radio that the BBC's "Top of the Pops" television show wanted the original Hollies to appear. This, of course, would require getting Graham Nash. Old wounds had healed. But Allan Clarke admits, "When CSN became a success and there were articles on them in the paper, I never read them. I wanted to shut Graham out of my life completely. I could have ended up a very bitter man, if I hadn't had some degree of success myself and if I hadn't gone through a particular period of growth. As the years passed, Graham and I became friends again, and I was anxious to sing with him."

When Nash heard from his old band in early 1982, he consented to appear on the TV program and to record a couple of songs with them. "I figured, 'Why not?'" says Nash. "So I hopped on a plane to England with Susan, and then something very strange happened. When we hit that Hollies vocal blend again in Abbey Road Studios, I thought, 'What in the 'ell is this? Things haven't changed a bit. Did I really leave? Did I go to America or didn't I?' It was like I'd never left. That was the scary thing. And I had the same old fears. 'Am I moving backwards or forwards? Am I standing still?' But it all came down to, 'Yeah, it feels good to be singin' with the Hollies again.' "

Graham promised to record an album with the Hollies as soon as the CSN album was finished. "I couldn't help it," says Nash. "It was so much fun right away, cutting tracks with them again. Very energetic. We'd knock off a couple tracks in one day. This gave me an immediate sense of completion, which I needed. Because the CSN album had become such a marathon, never-ending thing, I wanted a little instant gratification."

After getting a quick rush from his past, Nash returned to Los Angeles and took a rather humorous look at his future.

Graham and Susan Nash singing "Our House."

Graham Nash's fortieth birthday party. Left to right: Graham, Mac Holbert, Stephen Stills, Margie Lala, Candy Finnigan.

In honor of his fortieth birthday, which had passed earlier in February, Graham staged a party where everyone who attended was "aged" at least thirty years, by means of makeup and costumes. Stills showed up in a U.S. military officer's uniform, his hair turned steel gray. Other guests wore white whiskers and leaned uneasily on canes. Nash looked at least seventy as he stumbled toward the piano with the help of his wife Susan. Together they mumbled through "Our House," Graham periodically dosing off and knocking his head into the microphone. The evening was a hearty laugh in

the face of Father Time, and Graham announced, "Thanks, friends, thanks for growing old with me."

Reality quickly replaced fantasy when the *Daylight Again* mixing sessions resumed and ran through most of March. "I can see the tunnel at the end of the light," Nash remarked one night. But the sessions rolled on. Graham took a break on March 20 to perform with Jackson Browne at a Sing Out for Sight concert in Santa Monica to help raise money for the Seva Foundation (a nonprofit organization to help cure preventable blindness in the Third World).

"Things haven't changed a bit." The Hollies in Los Angeles, 1982. Left to right: Bob Elliott, Graham Nash, Allan Clarke, Tony Hicks.

March 28, 1982, Crosby, Stills & Nash were set to appear on stage together at an antinuke rally in San Onofre, California. Stephen and Graham made it there, but David never showed. En route, traveling down the San Diego Freeway, he nodded off at the wheel of his rented car and crashed into a center divider. When police arrived on the premises, they conducted a complete search and discovered a .45-caliber pistol, a small amount of cocaine, and a freebasing pipe and butane torch inside the automobile. Reportedly, Crosby simply uttered John Lennon's name when police asked why he was carrying a weapon. "When I chew on Lennon's death for a while it makes me real angry," David had said earlier in 1982. "We didn't need to lose John. He was a good guy. He wasn't doing anybody harm. He brought an awful lot of beauty into this world . . . then some crazy just walked up and shot him. If that guy'd come after me, he'd have been a piece of fuckin' Swiss cheese."

Ever since his days with the Byrds, Crosby had maintained a collection of guns. So it was no surprise that he had a weapon in his possession in this instance. The court must have agreed, because David was charged only with reckless driving, to which he pleaded no contest. The judge then levied a $751 fine, put Crosby on three years' probation, and instructed him to enter a drug rehabilitation program. But more trouble would land in Crosby's life in mid-April.

Backstage at Cardi's, a Dallas nightclub where David was playing a solo show, police stormed in and searched his dressing room. Another gun was found, along with freebasing equipment and a quarter of a gram of cocaine residue. Crosby was promptly arrested, then released on bail. However, illegal drug and weapons possession are felonies in Texas and would haunt Crosby indefinitely.

CSN: A Record at Last / "Peace Sunday" (1982)

Back inside the control room at Devonshire Studios, Nash had put one of the tape players in reverse and the machine moaned, *"Grrrp, Wrrr, Grrrp, Wrrr."* "Group war," Graham laughed. "Maybe that should be the name of this album." Later on during this mixing session, though, Nash said, "People have always tended to place far too much importance on the nature of the personal relationships between us, instead of what is created out of these relationships. Because of the volatility of our chemical beings . . . I admit we've loved each other one day, hated each other the next, and that volatility comes out in our music. But it's not like we've ground each other into a flat disc."

Graham at Devonshire Studios mixing board.

In 1982, Stills said, "It might appear to some that we've been professional children. And though we have wasted a lot of time, over the years, bickering about certain things and letting personal shit build up . . . there's a certain amount of professionalism involved. We've never overly restrained each other. The press likes to accent our differences, but, really, we give an amazing amount of support and direction to each other's songs."

Putting it together at Rudy Records, Los Angeles. Left to right: Stanley Johnston, Jay Parti (back), Graham Nash, Stephen Stills, Steve Gursky.

On what was supposed to be the last night of mixing *Daylight Again*, there was still some tinkering going on. It had been decided that some hand-claps would be added to "Too Much Love to Hide"—a bristling, locomotive-like rocker that Stills wrote with guitarist Gerry Tolman in 1979. After a microphone was placed in one of the studio's bathrooms for that "natural echo effect," Nash playfully suggested, "Okay, let's go to the toilet and get the claps." He and Stills trotted off and did just that. Later, three different mixes of another song, "Turn Your Back on Love" were played. Nash spoke up first. "I like the 'ahhhhs' on the second one." Stills nodded. Then engineer Stanley Johnston said, "How about our idea for the 'Wizard of Ahhhhs?' Graham's got to play the Tin Man. We'd have to get Neil back to play the Scarecrow." "Crosby'd be Dorothy," added Stills. "No,

Crosby's the Cowardly Lion," Nash laughed. "*You're* Dorothy." Stills glowered at Nash, rose from the mixing board, and annouced in mock fury, 'I am the *wizard.*' "

Hours later, at about 3:00 A.M., all laughter and talk had died down. It appeared that *Daylight Again* might finally be ready for mastering. "We did it!" cried Stills as he embraced everyone in the control room. Nash picked up a half-empty bottle of champagne and cheered, "Here's to you, David, wherever you are." (He was still on the road, finishing up a few solo acoustic shows.) Engineer Steve Gursky leaned back and sighed, "Here's to CSN . . . I think we're finished."

But as Yogi Berra once said, "It ain't over till it's over." The next day, while Nash flew to Hawaii for a ten-day vacation with his family, a little controversy cropped up. It seems that one of Stills's songs, called

"Feel Your Love," contained a chorus melody that resembled, a bit too closely, the hook in a Rose Royce song, "Love Don't Live Here Anymore."

"It was one of those cases where something you heard in the middle of a busy day takes up residence in your subconscious and just floats to the surface," says Stills. "The similarity of the two songs had not occurred to me until Arthur Garfunkel brought it up. The minute he said it, I was just floored. I remembered the exact moment I had heard that Rose Royce song, some two years before in a motel room before a soundcheck. I wanted to strike a deal. Because the rest of 'Feel Your Love' in no way resembles the Rose Royce song. But greed set in on the other side, with their publishers, so I was stuck."

When no workable publishing deal could be settled upon, "Feel Your Love" was pulled off *Daylight Again* and replaced by Nash's "Into the Darkness," recorded months earlier for the original Stills–Nash project, containing such lyrics as, "All of your friends / Have been trying to warn you / That some of your demons / Are trying to drag you . . . away / Into the darkness."

"That was a song I wrote for a screenplay created by John Hartmann," says Nash. "David felt it was about him. And although I get twinges that maybe I am writing about David, it's that way with a lot of my songs. They're vague enough, yet direct enough, so they can be applied to many different situations. So, although David might be a little upset that 'Into the Darkness' is on there, it wasn't an intentional thing. We couldn't hold up the project any longer. We couldn't go back into the studio. All of the artwork had been done, the lyrics laid out. We had to act fast."

Crosby's reaction was, "That song didn't need to be put on there. I could tell it's about me, and I don't like it. They could have put one of my songs on there, like

'Melody.' That's good music *about* music. Why did that have to get left off?"

David was wondering the same thing about the billing for the Peace Sunday concert co-sponsored by the Alliance for Survival and the Ecumenical Council. Instead of Crosby, Stills & Nash, the posters for the event listed only Stills and Nash. "David's brushes with the law created an awkward situation between us and the churches," Graham said in 1982. "The weapons charges, in particular, forced us to hold off putting his name on the ad. It was done to appease the clergy. But we always intended to include David. We just had to wait to announce that CSN would be playing."

When Crosby caught wind of this plan, he simmered down a bit and arrived in Los Angeles the week before Peace Sunday. Almost as soon as he got to town, radio stations all over Southern California were told that Crosby, Stills & Nash would be performing at the event. This would mark only the third time the trio had shared a stage together in four years.

How were they going to sound? Many in the CSN camp wondered if Crosby was well enough to hold up his end of the harmonies. As strong as David's desire was to make it all work, his endurance was still well below normal and it had been a long time since he'd really shined on stage with his old partners. Would the magic still be there?

On June 5, CSN warmed up inside an empty Rose Bowl in Pasadena. Late-afternoon sun scattered across the football field as the vocal harmonies intertwined. Volunteers and crew members near the stage froze for a few moments during the choruses of "Wooden Ships." One roadie softly sang along, then nudged the guy next to him and said, "I must have heard them do this a couple hundred times. And I still get goose pimples."

Less than twenty-four hours later, a

Graham Nash and Jackson Browne, Peace Sunday, Los Angeles, 1982.

and Stephen Stills. A charge of applause whipped through the audience when Nash pounded the piano chords to "Chicago," then wailed, "Won't you please come to the Rose Bowl just to sing . . . We can change the world / Rearrange the world." But the biggest response of the set greeted David Crosby when he launched into "Long Time Gone," which had been written fourteen years earlier, to the day, when Bobby Kennedy was assassinated. Crosby's voice sounded strong and sure.

Peace Sunday. Left to right: Tim Sexton, Linda Ronstadt, Graham Nash, Patti Davis Reagan.

crowd of 85,000, then the largest number of people ever to attend a musical benefit, would be jolted by one emotional rush after another. The music of Bob Dylan and Joan Baez, Stevie Wonder, Tom Petty, Jackson Browne, Tierra, Linda Ronstadt, Stevie Nicks, Dan Fogelberg, and other artists framed the words uttered by ministers, rabbis, nuclear war survivors, and concerned speakers such as Cesar Chavez, Ed Asner, Michael Douglas, Jane Fonda, Patti Davis Reagan, and California governor Jerry Brown. It was a nonstop onslaught of energy that was encapsulated by a stadium-filling chorus of John Lennon's "Give Peace a Chance."

One of the first peak moments of Peace Sunday occurred when Graham Nash stood at center stage and called out David Crosby

"It was sheer *triumph*," Crosby said later. "Everyone thought I was going to fail, that I wouldn't be able to cut it. But I proved them wrong. The feeling was great."

When Peace Sunday wound to a close, far into the night, it was clear that Nash, as the talent organizer of the event, was feeling pretty great himself. In a trailer with David and Stephen, Graham exulted, "My dream came to life. The stage may not have been in the shape of a globe, but can you believe the number of people who were out there? It seemed like a broad, global spirit. And I could feel the power of everybody's concern. Now I just hope this unified demonstration for peace will inspire more people to find out about this nuclear threat that looms over our lives."

Crosby, Stills & Nash play at Peace Sunday concert.

More people did show their concern throughout the rest of Peace Week (dubbed "Seven Days in June"), timed to coincide with the United Nations' special sessions on bilateral nuclear disarmament. On June 12, 800,000 antinuke demonstrators marched near the United Nations. There was a lot of music and a series of speakers, and the message was clear. Back in Los Angeles, Nash stated, "People don't want to die. And they want a planet that will be safe for their children. Is that so much to ask?"

When Nash's mind cycled back toward music a few days later, he was sitting in the office at his Rudy Records studio, inspecting the cover artwork for *Daylight Again*, a haunting painting by Gilbert Williams, called *Celestial Visitation*, which showed three glowing flying saucers hovering near a temple in a surreal blue mountain range, bathed in the copper tones of sunrise.

"I was always drawn to the peace in the work," Graham said. "But I must tell you, I would have much preferred a picture of the three of us together, happy and healthy, looking good. But the three flying saucers say a lot about this project, in a way. There's Stephen, off and up to the left where he always is. Crosby's high on top, over everything. And me, I'm on the bottom, underneath all this shit again."

The fourth saucer never swooped in for a visit, this time around. The last time any member of CSN had been in Neil Young's musical orbit was when Crosby and Nash were on stage with him in Santa Cruz, back

CSN, Pasadena, 1982.

in 1977. Since then, Young had rambled through many changes, peaking with Crazy Horse and the "Rust Never Sleeps" shows in 1978. In 1982, he was experimenting with computers, and seemed removed from the CSN cycle.

"Neil is Neil and CSN is CSN," Nash said at the time. "It's always been that way. He comes and goes as he pleases. And he never has given us much warning. It wouldn't surprise me if he called up tomorrow and said, 'Hey, I've just written these new songs that would sound great with your voices.' It also wouldn't surprise me if he never talked to us again."

"Neil's one of the best songwriters on the planet," Crosby said in 1982. "Some of his stuff is sheer genius. And I love him. I also realize he looks out for his own best interests a lot and he's a classic no-show. Bernard Shakey . . . that's what everybody who really knows Neil calls him. And he's broken all of our hearts by taking off at the strangest moments. But I've been through too much with him not to want to work with him again. I'd love to sing with him . . . but I don't see it happening soon."

As Stills explained in 1982, "Neil and I are still friends, and when our imaginations have run parallel, we've gotten into some interesting stuff. I wish we could have done a lot more. I really miss playin' guitar with

him sometimes, you know? But I tell ya, Neil just has never liked being in a band. I mean, he's *always* gone after his own trip. Which is okay. But he just could have gone about it more aboveboard. Me, I've enjoyed my solo work, but I'm much happier collaborating and playing in a band situation. When Crosby, Stills & Nash is working right, I can really stretch in all kinds of directions."

A couple of days before *Daylight Again* was released in mid-July 1982, Nash reflected, "This was, by far, one of the most frustrating projects of my life. Sometimes it was hard to see the whole and get a sense of CSN as a unit. But we pulled it together. Stanley Johnston and Steve Gurksy were always able to make me see how great the music was. I'm very proud of this record. It took far too long to complete, but it was worth it."

When Nash tried to explain what the *feeling* of the album represented, he said, "It really starts and ends with people . . . how we relate to each other, how we are alienated from each other, how we are suspicious of each other, how we love each other—a lot of the songs on *Daylight Again* are about you and me. How are we going to coexist on this planet? How are we going to work it out?"

Nash did not feel that *Daylight Again* was simply a reminder of a bygone era. "We've always been open to new ideas," he said. "I don't think we've ever let our music get stale. At the same time, we've never followed fashion. We've always wanted to say things in the best way that expresses the feelings of the three of us. I think we're getting better as communicators, better as songwriters, and better as musicians. I think those factors have combined to make our music not boring, old hat, or run-of-the-mill."

Stills said, "It's got more balls than our other ones. And I think because popular music is in such a state of flux, I think we have enough of a bowling ball of an album to knock 'em all off."

This prediction proved to be fairly accurate. When *Daylight Again* was released, it rocketed up, with a super "bullet," into the Top Ten. The single, "Wasted on the Way," followed the same path of success.

Crosby was not surprised by this strong, immediate commercial showing. "The way I see it," he said in 1982, "there are millions of record players in the country. And a lot of record markets don't overlap. We're not competing with Devo. We're 180 degrees away from them. There's a whole other segment of the population that still likes harmony, melody, and words that count."

Joni Mitchell explained, a few months later, "I got a letter from a nineteen-year-old girl on the East Coast and she said something to the effect of, 'Oh damn it, you know, I missed all the good music. There's no music for me now. The only good thing I've seen is Crosby, Stills & Nash.' Then she said, 'I hear you're going out on the road. Way to go. Way to go.' So I think there are a lot of kids out there who are not ready to dye their hair orange or mutilate their bodies. There are a lot of kids who don't want to identify with the more radical cultural breakouts of the new wave. So there still seems to be a strong place for the music of CSN and me, despite the fact that the media would like to dismiss us."

Daylight Again was slammed by the rock press. One writer called it "regurgitated, post-hippie harmony clichés that should have been left in 1969." Stills shrugged and commented, "Critics have never liked what we do. They can't wait to rip us apart. And we're such a big target, it's like throwing mud pies at the side of a house. But, you know, when the mud dries and blows away, the house stays."

Joni Mitchell added, "If they were to make records now as an unknown band, I think they could generate some press enthusiasm. But because they've been around so long, they don't stand a chance. In a culture like America, which eats things and spits them out, things tend to devalue fairly quickly, even while they're still blooming. And us, it's like we're wallpaper and the press'll say, 'Oh, you've been up there too long. Let's tear it off and put up a new pattern.'"

David Crosby had tested the "live waters" earlier in 1982, when he toured America alone. "There were an awful lot of young kids out there," he recalled. "Young enough to be puzzling. Too young to have been around for Woodstock. Kids of the seventies and eighties. Yet they all seemed to know the songs. I'd look out there and see 'em singing 'Long Time Gone' and 'Wooden Ships' and wonder who turned them on to us?"

CHAPTER FOURTEEN

Back on Top (1982–1983)

CSN: On the Road Again/"Daylight Again" Video/Crosby Arrested...#3/"Allies"/The Hollies Come Around (1982–1983)

In mid-July 1982, Crosby, Stills & Nash were readying themselves for the *Daylight Again* summer tour. Rehearsals were being held inside a huge soundstage—the size of an airplane hanger—at Zoetrope Studios in Hollywood. One afternoon, Stephen, with his wireless electric guitar hookup in his back pocket, roamed behind the newly constructed stage and unleashed a vicious guitar solo that howled up toward the ceiling. Then he trotted back to a row of three microphones set up on a tattered oriental rug, and locked into harmony with Graham and David on the chorus of "Love the One You're With."

Later, Stills slumped down on a couch in the lounge area and speculated, "I think new people, old people, young people, all *kinds* of people are turning on to us again because this music stands up. That's the crux of it. You know, we've got a lot of songs that just haven't died, that are still appropriate and *mean* something. There aren't many bands that can build a catalogue of songs over a fourteen-year period and still

have the chops to do 'em all justice. The Stones and the Who have done it. Now we're doing it again. You see, we ain't about to let our rock 'n' roll die just yet."

At the same time, there was still great concern about David Crosby's health. During rehearsals, he would often only play for a couple of songs before having to take a break. This worried Nash: "Here we are just a few days away from going on tour and David's just not well at all. Frankly, I don't know if he'll survive out there on the road."

Crosby had little doubt that he could withstand the rigors of a national tour. "I've been on the road a lot the last couple years," he said. "But everybody seems to think that I won't make it this time. I promise you, I won't let anybody down." But when he surveyed the 1982 CSN back up band—Vitale, Perry, Finnigan, Stergis, keyboardist Michael Hanna, and percussionist Efain Toro—David was certain that no one believed him. He felt that Stergis was being kept in the band "as an insurance policy, because everybody thinks I might fuck up on the road." But Stergis said, "Once David realized I was on his side, that I wasn't out to steal his parts, it was cool." By the end of rehearsals, Crosby and Stergis were joking around like old pals. David announced, "Crosby, Stills & Nash has always operated like a family. And now the family's just a little larger."

Crosby, Stills & Nash, Zoetrope Studios, 1982.

CSN, 1982.

CSN rehearsal at Zoetrope. (Michael Stergis, far left.)

Rehearsal at Zoetrope with Michael Hanna, Michael Stergis, Efrain Toro, and Joe Vitale in the background.

The night before CSN left for the road, Graham Nash's family got a little larger. His wife had a baby. During the final stages of Susan's pregnancy, it had been deter- mined that her baby would be a boy. So at the moment of birth, everyone in the oper- ating room was rejoicing about the Nashs' new son, until, amid the shouting, Graham

CSN '82 tour cast and crew.

An hour before the show somewhere in the Midwest, 1982 tour.

said softly, and with much love, "It's a girl!" The scan had been wrong! The Nashes had a new daughter, Nile Ann.

"Little Nile," says Graham, "she's a very important person in my life. She helped make this family whole."

When the CSN tour commenced July 31 in Hartford, Connecticut, the band's family out in the audience had also increased. When the *Daylight Again* show hit the Nassau Coliseum on Long Island, the sellout crowd that filtered in was largely under eighteen years old. A reporter from *Good Times*, a regional New York and New Jersey music newspaper, wrote, "This might as well be an Aerosmith concert. CSN might be old-timers, but they sure are connecting with the kids. And they proved it for two and a half hours, as they brought the kids to cheering, stomping, fists-in-the-air elation with an immaculate performance."

For three more weeks, CSN criss-crossed America and drew ecstatic crowds everywhere. Bill Graham commented, "That they were received so well is a testimony to the way they left. They didn't outstay their welcome. They left with quality and they came back with quality. I wish we had more sounds like Crosby, Stills & Nash create. When their sound is in the air and people are sitting there on the side of a hill, totally absorbed . . . that's one of the all-time great feelings I've experienced.

"A lot of groups stop playing and say, 'We're retiring,'" Graham continued. "But when a group retires, it means, 'We can't draw anymore. But why should we say we can't draw anymore? So we're quitting. We're tired of the public.' No, the public's tired of *you*. Well, the public's not tired of Crosby, Stills & Nash yet. They put out a good product and went out and performed. I give credit to David and Stephen for get-

Crosby, Stills & Nash, 1982 tour.

ting healthy. Graham's always been Mr. Wheaties. That guy's ridiculously healthy, both in body and mind. I wish I had an anchor that was always that healthy. If we were all as balanced as Graham Nash, we'd need no buttons to push."

Rolling Stone seemed ready to push the "destroy button" where CSN was concerned. "You mean *Rolling Poot-butt?*" asked Mike Finnigan. "It's like *National Crapsheet*. All they talk about is bullshit." One item claimed that Stills was waiting for Neil Young to show up on the tour so that they could re-form Buffalo Springfield. "Total horseshit," Stills said. "I think Neil was touring in Europe when we were on the road in America. I admit, a while back,

Neil, me, Dewey, the original guys in the Springfield, got together in a hotel room and *talked* about maybe getting something together, but then Neil had to split to get some award in Canada and I had to get back to CSN. So maybe that's where that came from. I really don't know, though."

Young, himself, levied some criticism at his old mates before leaving for Europe. He told David Gans of *The Record* that "Neil Young from the sixties and early seventies is like Perry Como. That's the way I look at it. If I was still taking that seriously, I'd be where Crosby, Stills & Nash are today." Ron Stone, CSN&Y's former management assistant, had this to say about CSN's 1982 live work: "I was embarrassed for

Mike Finnigan and Stephen Stills during tour-bus poker game, 1982.

David, Graham, and Stephen. They were a shadow of their former selves, putting on nostalgia shows like the Beach Boys."

"I keep hearing this about us," Nash said in 1982, "and don't understand it, especially coming from Neil. He seemed to imply that we're just old fuddy-duddies, then he goes out and does seventy-five percent old stuff, but no one criticizes him. That confuses me. But I forget about it all when I see how our audience is reacting. We can *see* and *hear* the kids out there. That's the only important comment about what we do. Did we get the audience off? That's why we're playing. All the other stuff is just silly shit I can't waste my time worrying about."

CSN sloughed off the dissension rumors the rock press trumped up. It was true that each member traveled in a separate bus between gigs, but Stills said, late one night en route to Minneapolis, "Why does everyone think we're not getting along, just because we're not always holding hands when we're off stage?"

After the *Daylight Again* summer tour finale on September 6 at Irvine Meadows in California, David Crosby squealed, "What great fun we had, man. Me, Nash, and Stephen, we really got 'em goin' out there. You shoulda seen us in Oklahoma City. The audience wouldn't let us leave. They were

goin' fuckin' nuts. These little girls were screaming. This is 1982, man, and we're not gonna let anything stop us now."

Not ten minutes after Crosby had made that comment, however, police walked into his dressing room and arrested him. Two Culver City women claimed that Crosby had "roughed them up" in 1981. Assault

Graham on his bus somewhere in Minnesota, 1982 tour.

charges were later plea-bargained down to disturbing the peace. But Crosby had to spend a night in jail when his defense could not muster up the $100,000 bail. Once free, David hung out in Los Angeles for a while. But this matter has lingered on and has still not been completely resolved.

One night in early October 1982, CSN

Stephen writing lyrics on his bus somewhere in Iowa; Michael Stergis wearing wastebasket, 1982 tour.

CSN, 1982 tour.

huddled together inside Rudy Records. They were watching television and Grace Slick suddenly appeared on the screen as a guest on "The Merv Griffin Show." "Hey, why don't we give Grace a call?" suggested Nash.

"I was all by myself, watching MTV," remembers Grace. "Then CSN's video for 'Southern Cross' came on. And I thought, 'Jesus Christ, they sure can sing good!' I hadn't heard them in a while. Then the phone rang and this voice went, 'Hi, this is Willie. I'm sittin' here with David and Stephen, watching you on the tube.' And I said, 'Well, I'm watching *you* guys right now, too!' It was quite a moment."

Grace goes on: "The fact that Crosby, Stills & Nash have lasted as long as they have is because, for lack of a better word,

they are perfectionists. They've never put out anything sloppy. They've taken care of their music. It's like having an animal or a child. Some people mistreat animals, don't feed 'em, leave 'em out in the cold. Well, CSN has never left their music out in the rain. I've watched them all work. And they want their music to *shine!* In the middle of listening to a CSN record, I always know I'm going to start crying. Real good music always makes me cry. And when I hear that CSN *sound* . . . there come the tears. And I'm not being paid to sell their records. I just like 'em. I also like the Clash. So it's not a matter of just hanging onto the old shit."

When the CSN fall tour of 1982 kicked off in mid-October, "Wasted on the Way" was slipping down the charts, but "Southern Cross" was heading for the Top Twenty,

CSN trying out harmonies backstage, 1982 tour.

and the album was about to turn platinum.

The mood within the band was loose and easy. In fact, everyone from the lowliest roadies to the three principals began talking in a special "road code" that had grown out of "Family Feud," the TV game show. Mock routines would fly back and forth:

VITALE: "Hey, Finnigan, name a tooth in your head."

FINNIGAN: "Richard, we're gonna have to say 'front.' "

STILLS: "Good answer."

These kinds of comments would turn up spontaneously. Backstage at a concert hall in Minneapolis, Stills was presented with a huge Minnesota Vikings football jersey. Finnigan chuckled, "Richard, we're gonna have to say 'Interior Lineman!' "

Dave Zimmer (in chair) and Henry Diltz (in mirror) do their thing as Graham looks on in dressing room at Iowa State University gym, 1982 tour.

Stills was presented with a huge Minnesota Viking football jersey, 1982 tour.

On a long bus trip from Minneapolis to Cedar Rapids, Iowa, Finnigan reflected on his role in the 1982 model of CSN. "I block and tackle," he said. "I am *on the line!* I don't mean that in any fuckin' bullshit way. I'm in the band, in the machine."

Earlier in the summer, Neil Young had

Stephen warming up in the shower at Iowa State University, 1982 tour.

criticized CSN and CSN&Y for never really committing themselves to a band format. He said, "It was always the four of us, then a couple guys who were *hired*. There was never a band feeling with them."

"That's crap," said Finnigan. "We all cook together. We turn all the burners on. And it's *real*. It's not like some of those shows where the act is like, 'Zookeeper, bring on the monkeys! Man does handstand on pig!' A lot of poot-butt musicians hide behind jive theater.

"CSN," Finnigan concluded, "represent real class. Nash is a classy dude. Stills is as crazy as the day is long, but I love him and

Crosby finds his niche. Chicago dressing room, 1982 tour.

he's got a heart. Crosby . . . he may be the most soulful one of the bunch. He still has something burnin' in there. They *all* do."

On stage at the Four Seasons auditorium in Cedar Rapids, before a capacity crowd, CSN delivered a riotous show that reached one chilling peak after another. "Southern Cross" and "Wasted on the Way" drew gleeful screams from an amazing number of teenaged girls. When Crosby finished "Delta" on piano, the biggest roar of the night swelled toward him. He stood center stage, smiled, and thumped his hand over his heart. Then came the solid classics: "Wooden Ships," "Long Time Gone," "Chicago," "Suite: Judy Blue Eyes," "Guinnevere," "You Don't Have to Cry," "For What It's Worth," "Carry On," and "Teach Your Children."

Graham's wardrobe case with framed slogans: "It's not starting power that counts . . . it's staying power" and "Many players are not complete players because they cannot force themselves to bear down except when they have the ball or when their man has the ball." 1982 tour.

One young fan, seated ten rows back, was in tears at the end of the concert. "I didn't want it to end so soon," she sniffled. "I drove here—five hundred miles from Wyoming—it's the first time I've ever seen them. *God*, did they make me feel great. Now I know what my brother was talking about when he told me, 'Seeing Crosby,

CSN, 1982 tour

Stills & Nash live is like, you know, sitting by a campfire and hearing magical stories.' "

Hours later, in his hotel room in Cedar Rapids, an exhausted Stephen Stills was watching the sun rise. Since the show, he'd been up all night, working on three new songs. Now he cradled a Hasselblad camera in his hands and was snapping pictures of the sunlight glancing off the snow-covered town below. He looked like a young boy, completely enchanted by nature.

"This is such a great sight," Stephen murmured. "Everything's real calm and fresh." Moving from the window, he smiled and said, "You know, this life of mine has

been really something, so far. And now, with Crosby, Stills & Nash happening again, we're out here embracing these musical forms and addressing things that concern us and connecting with our audiences. I feel like the luckiest man in the world right now."

A few doors down the hall and a few hours later, Nash theorized, "Sometimes I think it's all an illusion, an ephemeral form of energy. CSN . . . it's been a very interesting chemical experience. A lot of magic. A lot of pain. Some funny times. Some *intense* times. I wouldn't change anything we've done."

On his bus, Crosby commented, "I knew

Crosby, Stills & Nash harmonize on 1982 tour.

we would be good this time. That's why I wanted to mend the fences so badly. When CSN is going great and really working together on stage, I'm in heaven, man. The feeling is unbelievable. And our music has made an awful lot of people feel good. And hardly anything does these days. These are not easy times. So we've always just tried to bring a little joy and a little hope into people's souls."

On Thanksgiving weekend, 1982, Crosby, Stills & Nash played three shows at the Universal Amphitheater in Los Angeles. All of the performances were taped and filmed for a two-hour MCA/Showtime special produced by Neal Marshall and directed by Tom Trborich. The three shows rose and dipped as the cameras and the tapes rolled. Crosby was not in the best of shape for the performances. He'd been in animated form and in strong voice throughout the fall tour, but before the L.A.

shows he got nervous. Nash explains, "David's always suffered from a little more stage fright than he lets on or projects. We *all* have our moments. But before this videotaping, he got *real* nervous and just got too high."

On camera, David looked stiff and his eyes were either frozen wide open or almost closed. But even though he wasn't in his best operating mode, David and the rest of CSN still managed to lift the spirits of everyone in the theater. One reporter from the *Daily News* wrote: "Crosby, Stills & Nash's first local appearance in a number of years was a real event, covered by the local television stations and given a reception befitting rock royalty. Yet, somehow this fits. Bands like this—with the ability to inspire, move, and entertain so profoundly—are rare now. Crosby, Stills & Nash are a vital treasure."

But after these Universal shows, the

CSN Universal Amphitheater concert, Los Angeles, November 1982.

trio scattered for the rest of the year. There was talk of regrouping for an album early in 1983, but there were no firm promises. This made Mike Finnigan a little anxious.

"CSN should quit this fuckin' around, get down in the alley, and really raise some sand," he said in the fall of 1982. "There's been *talk*, but, talk is cheap! We should go into the studio while the iron's still hot, instead of this two–Super Bowl crap. We should work up a sweat *now*. It's time to get down and really do some work. There's a word—*work*—which is something I don't think these motherfuckers know anything about. It's time they learned to forget about thought. Just go on *instinct*. It might be *important*. That's why I'm stickin' around. I'm a team cat. I'm loyal to a fault. But if a CSN album doesn't jump in six months, it ain't gonna jump and I'll be a very disappointed young white man."

After the first few months of 1983, it was clear that no new CSN studio album was going to be happening soon. Crosby

was out on the road by himself. Stills and Nash were in the studio, editing the soundtrack for the CSN video. This was an arduous task because, said Stills at the time, "We had to get all of the music in sync with the video, which multiplied the time factor in the studio by about four."

But work on this video carried right into the compilation of a CSN live album,

Stephen Stills, Universal Amphitheater, 1982.

David Crosby and Graham Nash, Universal Amphitheater, 1982.

drawn mostly from the performances taped at the Universal shows. "We figured, 'Why not?' " said Stills. "It was a logical thing to do. And we tried to choose material that hadn't been released much." "Dark Star," "Blackbird," "For What It's Worth," "Barrel of Pain," "Turn Your Back on Love," and "Wasted on the Way" were included, as well as two Crosby performances that had been recorded live in Houston in 1977—a cover of Joni Mitchell's "For Free" (listed as "He Played Real Good for Free") and his own "Shadow Captain."

"David was not in good voice at the Amphitheater shows," Nash said in early 1983. "And he wasn't around to do any repairing." Stanley Johnston recalls, "When David had me isolate his vocals on a couple of tracks, he couldn't listen to them. He said, 'Turn it off.' Then he left." Nash added, "But we wanted more of David on the album, so we listened to some earlier live tapes and picked out two where David was really singin' great."

Nash and Stills also recorded two new songs in the studio. One was a fierce, metallic rocker by Stills called "War Games," written for, but ultimately pulled out of the John Badham film of the same name. The other song, "Raise a Voice," was a Nash–Stills collaboration with words that urged everyone to speak out and be aware.

The instrumental tracks for both of these songs were cut in one day by Stills on his own, with a backup group that was composed of guitarist Danny Kortchmar, bassist Perry, drummer Jeff Porcaro, and keyboardists Craig Doerge and James Newton Howard.

"I was pissed at Stephen for doing those tracks without me," says Nash. "I was in Hawaii and thought he was just making demos. But he made complete tracks. I

Stephen and Graham unwind between mixes driving golf balls in the studio, Los Angeles, 1983. A handwritten sign on the door said: "Devonshire Country Club and Sound Studios. New driving range now open. Ask about our night putting facilities."

wish he'd just told me that's what he was planning to do. But the results were great. So I didn't get uptight. On 'Raise a Voice,' Stephen took a funny set of changes of mine that were written in three-four time, recognized a different groove, and made the song better. I let him do it and it was marvelous. In the past, whenever I've tried to stop Stephen, everything has turned to a piece of shit. So I've given Stephen his head a great deal now. He needs to know his partners support his madness."

"I just want room to create, without being told to simmer down," Stills said in the spring of 1983. " 'Cause sometimes I need to experiment a little bit before really nailing something. This 'let's go with the first take' is just jive. Sometimes you can get it *better* and you can always go back. So I need the freedom to try what I *hear*, and I've got that with David and Graham."

Stephen didn't have to worry much about interference from Crosby during these sessions, because David was rarely around. In fact, Stanley Johnston flew up to San Francisco, with tapes of "War Games" and "Raise a Voice," so that Crosby could overdub his parts. In the final mixes, though, he's hardly audible.

"I don't consider *Allies* a CSN record," Crosby said in early 1983. "A lot of it was put together when I was on the road. When I got back, it was almost finished. Stills and Nash did that one. I don't even know why it was made."

Crosby had withdrawn into his own world since the fall 1982 CSN tour. This troubled Nash. "I don't know where David's at right now," Nash said while mixing *Allies*. "I used to know how he'd react to certain things and how he'd handle most situations. But I just don't know anymore. I haven't been with David on a twelve-hour-a-day basis for a long time. When the Crosby–Nash combination was at its peak, we used to spend most of the day together,

So I used to know and understand his inner workings. I've lost that thread of contact with David. But that's the way it is and the way David wants it for now. It'll come around again."

When Crosby removed himself from the video and *Allies* sessions, it was as if he didn't want to be reminded of those concerts. He wanted to move on to something else. When the CSN video was shown on Showtime in May of 1983, David's role was de-emphasized. He showed a few glimmers of magic, particularly during "Delta." But they were rare. Stills, with some steamy guitar licks and grainy blues vocals, came off well. And Nash, bouncing about the stage, leading the energy with his liveliness and clear vocals, shot off enthusiastic sparks. The two-hour *Daylight Again* video was one of the longest musical extravaganzas ever shown on a cable-TV network. "That show," says Nash, "is CSN in 1982, a frame of time, a fraction of our musical lives."

In April 1983, Nash had completed another fraction of his musical life when he wrapped up work on the Hollies' reunion album for Atlantic, *"What Goes Around . . ."* The Hollies' vocal blend worked on a variety of songs—none of them written by Nash or any other member of the band.

"The Hollies were always a great interpretive band," Nash says. "And for this album we decided to choose songs we liked to sing and that had a certain space for vocal harmonies."

Several compositions were written by Paul Bliss, a keyboardist/synthesist who had been working on the road with the Hollies the previous couple of years. He also added a synthesizer sparkle to most of the songs on this Hollies album, which included a remake of their earlier cover of Doris Troy's "Just One Look." But the tune that best exemplified the Hollies' vocal sound was their spirited rendition of the

The Hollies, Los Angeles, 1983. Left to right: Tony Hicks, Bob Elliott, Graham Nash, Allan Clarke.

Supremes' "Stop! In the Name of Love." When that single was released in May 1983, it moved up into the Top Forty. Nash even committed himself to a tour with the Hollies, after he returned from a European CSN tour, set to run from mid-June until mid-July.

"The Hollies are unfinished business with me," Nash told the *Los Angeles Times.*

"It's the same guys I worked with in the sixties. It's a chance to go back to my roots. I like Hollies music. It's pleasant pop music, you know, but it's not like CSN music. CSN music means more to me. CSN music is like a god, a sinister god. It haunts me. No matter what I do, I have to go back to it."

CHAPTER FIFTEEN

CSN's Last Stand? (1983)

CSN: Live in Europe / Crosby Gets Five Years (1983)

Stephen Stills was on a roll. During a break in rehearsals for the CSN 1983 tour of Europe, he was circling a pool table inside his Encino home. Methodically he pumped his cue stick, grinned, then pocketed one ball after another. He was also talking, *loudly*, about CSN.

"This time it's cool," he barked. " 'Cause Graham and I have it sorted out. And David's back into it. As far as who does what and when . . . leave the ego shit behind, gimme a break." Stills thwacked another ball into a side pocket. "Now I can actually fulfill my role with some dignity, without feeling like I'm going to get interrupted by those backbiting games we used to play, that Neil was so adept at. I adore Neil, but that shit used to drive me nuts."

Stills paused for a moment, then went on: "There's a little unwritten law now. If anybody tries to quit the group, they get *this*." He clenched his fist. "This time you get taken out on the fuckin' spot, right now . . . *boom!*" He took a wild swing at his own shadow. "You're not gonna cost me a fuckin' fortune with your goddamned egocentric bullshit trips. You're not gonna take food off my baby's plate. It's as simple as that, goddammit! You want a reality rule? There's a reality rule." With that, Stephen

struck a pool ball so hard that it ricocheted back and forth across the table six times.

Rehearsing at Zoetrope Studios in Hollywood once more, CSN had realigned their band again. James Newton Howard was tied up with sessions; Joe Vitale and George "Chocolate" Perry were out with Joe Walsh. So keyboardist Kim Bullard arrived on the scene, as did drummer Rick Jaeger (formerly in Dave Mason's band) and bassist Kenny Passarelli. Kenny had never forgotten his two missed opportunities to tour with CSN&Y, in 1969 and in 1974. Since his solo work with Stills in 1974, Passarelli had played with Elton John and Dan Fogelberg, among others. Then, in April 1983, Kenny got a call from Stills.

"Stephen's always been like my big brother," Passarelli said in May 1983. "When I worked with him before, he taught me a lot about the bass, more than anybody, as far as balls, feel, space, and *time*. So this is my chance now. After all these years, I get to play with CSN. I can't tell you how much this means to me."

Initially, Crosby was not at the CSN rehearsals. He had just finished some more solo touring and had recorded one show live at San Francisco's Old Waldorf, for possible use on a live album. At this Waldorf show, Crosby was presented with a platinum album for *Daylight Again*. But he shrugged off the moment. "Can someone

Kenny Passarelli, Zoetrope, 1983.

Despite these fiery words, Crosby was preoccupied, and on June 3, 1983, he appeared in court in Dallas. He was in poor shape and dressed haphazardly. He even dozed off a couple of times. This kind of behavior, of course, didn't go over too well with the judge, who found Crosby guilty on both the drug and the weapons charges. This meant that he could face a maximum of thirty years in prison. But official sentencing was put off until July 15—after CSN returned from Europe. Armando Hurley, who had been at Crosby's side during these proceedings, immediately phoned this news to the band in Los Angeles. This is how Graham Nash's end of the conversation sounded:

"Armando, how're ya doin'? No! Guilty on both charges? Did he sentence him? How's David going to do that? We'll be in Europe. So David's not going to jail today? He's with you? Fantastic! Get out of Dallas, baby!"

And Armando and Crosby did just that, arriving back in San Francisco just in time to take a taxi to Mill Valley, pack, and make some final arrangements before flying to London to rehearse with CSN.

This European tour was a rocky, erratic few weeks. A couple of shows in France and all of the dates in Spain were canceled, Nash said, "because the promoter made the mistake of overpricing the tickets." Also, some of the shows in Italy were rained out. These mishaps were preceded by several generally high shows in Germany. However, says Nash, "When it got toward the end, when we were about to play in England, the more David panicked, knowing that it could be his last gig, and that it could very possibly be the end of CSN. So that feeling loomed over the last few shows and we played better because of it. David really came out of his shell, not that he didn't try during the first part, but he, *all* of us, put a little extra into the last

take this and put it in my garage?" he asked. Never one for awards, Crosby has a garage in Mill Valley filled with dusty plaques and gold and platinum records that he's never displayed in his house. From the Waldorf stage, David told the audience, "When my dad got an Academy Award, he used it for a doorstop."

When Crosby finally arrived in Los Angeles for the last several CSN rehearsals, he exuded nervous uncertainty. His felony charges on drug and weapons possession in Dallas were due to be judged in court soon. "They're really playin' hardball," Crosby mused in late May 1983. "But ever since getting arrested in Dallas, I started doin' 'Almost Cut My Hair' again. I'm *not* giving in an inch to fear!"

shows. Because there was this unspoken thing that we might be seeing the last of CSN."

Such news was not what a lot of CSN fans in America were ready to hear. *Allies* was selling at a good clip, and the single, "War Games," was a few notches from the Top Forty. But the band was not paying attention to sales figures at this point.

Before the CSN tour ended at Wembley Arena on July 13, Crosby's defense attorney had managed to move back his day of sentencing until August 5. Theoretically, this was because CSN had talked of making up the Italian dates after playing at Wembley. But when the final chords of "Teach Your Children" faded into the night on July 13, that was it. There would be no more shows. Stills headed to Scotland to play golf. Nash had been planning to go to Hawaii, but his children came down with chicken pox, so he and his wife returned to their Los Angeles home. Crosby, while in England, had talked of heading for Tahiti in his sailboat. But more rational thought prevailed and he flew back to California instead.

"It doesn't look good for Dave," Nash said in late June 1983. "And it's a fuckin' drag, man. All the time that me and David were together in the seventies as a duo, we swore to each other that we would not . . . we'd *never* become victims of rock 'n' roll. We wouldn't be beaten by the system. What had happened to a lot of our friends and compatriots would not happen to us. We would not lose it. We would not get drugged out. I still cling to that . . . but David, somehow he went overboard. I, all his friends, tried to help . . . we've been whispering at David, we've been shouting at David, but in the end, a man must choose his own path."

On August 5, 1983, Crosby's path led to a Dallas courtroom. He showed up looking weary and downcast. Standing before Texas State District Judge Pat McDowell,

David heard his sentence: five years for possession of cocaine, three years for illegally possessing a firearm. The sentences would be served concurrently. Crosby's defense attorneys immediately announced they would appeal the decision on grounds that the search of Crosby's dressing room had been illegal. Released on $8,000 bond, David flew back to the Bay Area and secluded himself in his Mill Valley home. His phone remained disconnected.

Nash had written a letter to the court that read in part, "I truly believe that what David needs at this juncture of his life is help, guidance, and professional supervision. I believe that a confinement in prison would probably kill him."

On August 6, Nash wasn't sure how to take Crosby's sentencing. "I didn't expect five years. But he's got a big name and this judge no doubt wants to make an example out of David. And this is complicated by the fact that Culver City could still trounce him. And if he's facing *two* sentences, it's just a matter of time before he has to do time. And David won't do time, according to David . . . he'll either run or blow himself away."

Nash had found some escape from such thoughts a week earlier. When Neil Young played a couple of concerts down at Irvine Meadows in Orange County, Nash showed up for both of them. He even went on stage and sang "Ohio" with his old partner. "Singin' with Neil was a rush," Graham admits. "That was almost as exciting as playing with CSN in Europe. Because, I don't know, maybe I'm tired, physically and psychically tired. I'm just tired of carrying their weight. I enjoy the music tremendously, but I've had it with CSN for now. I've had it for as long as I need a rest, even if David, God bless him, somehow stays out of prison."

CHAPTER SIXTEEN

Where Do They Go from Here? (1983)

CSN: Crosby in "People"/Nash in Hawaii/Stills Keeps Playing/Young Raises a Voice/The Open End (1983-   )

CSN's future looked dark in August 1983. It was impossible not to view Crosby's fate as the proverbial nail in the band's coffin. As many times as these three men had endured tragedy and separation before, in this instance, it seemed like the glimmer of harmony that would always linger in their hearts was about to go out.

Ensconced in his Mill Valley home, Crosby brooded about the turn his life had taken. He felt he'd been treated unfairly by the Texas justice system. And in an effort to communicate his displeasure to the public, David allowed a couple of reporters from *People* magazine to visit his home on August 14—his forty-second birthday. Little did he know that, two weeks later, the publication would run a story on him headlined, "Cocaine Casualty." And on the *cover* of this August 29 issue were the words: "How Cocaine Ruined the Life of Rocker David Crosby."

In the article, Crosby's pitiful pleas for help and the grim description of his life as a freebase addict made for painful reading. Carl Gottlieb, a longtime friend of Crosby's, was quoted heavily in the story and he offered comments like: "I think you can safely say David has smoked up everything he owns—all the cars, everything. It is frightening. In the days when he was more in control, he was a connoisseur of quality objects. His houses were full of good paintings and art objects he had acquired over the years. Now it's all gone."

Crosby was understandably devastated by the publication of this article. He had always tried to keep his ongoing habit discreet and now it was being trumpeted from the magazine racks inside every supermarket in America.

"Nothing's sacred anymore," Crosby snapped. "I know I need to clean up. I know I can kick this thing. I just need some help, and money. But what good does printing all of this dirty laundry do?"

In an attempt to soothe David's anger, Carl Gottlieb flew from L.A. to Crosby's home. They were able to mend their friendship. "David was pretty upset," Gottlieb admits. "I didn't realize my comments would be used so prominently. I'd like to be able to say I was misquoted. But the sad fact is, most of what I said is true."

By mid-October, Crosby had entered a drug rehabilitation program in Philadelphia. But he was only able to endure the treatments for a few days. "The people who run these programs aren't out to cure people," David contended. "They're out to take your money. If I had enough money, I'd take my boat and some friends that cared and kick this thing on some island—where the support systems would be natural."

A couple of weeks before Christmas, Crosby was still in California and still discouraged. Slouched on a chair in his dining room, he mused, "I can't, for the life of me, understand what I've done to deserve this. I've never intentionally hurt anybody. All I've ever done and want to do again is sing and make music with my friends."

But Crosby could not make his problems disappear with words. The Dallas sentence was still hanging over him, pending appeal. There was a good chance he would have to do some time in connection with the Culver City conviction. Then, as if he didn't already have enough problems, the IRS was after Crosby, demanding thousands of dollars in back taxes. It looked like a miracle would have to occur for David to slip out from underneath this mess.

"In this world," says Graham Nash, "when you open Pandora's box and you jump in there and wash around in Pandora's shit, you can't help but have some of it stick.

"It's really tough for David, now," Nash said in November 1983. "We all want him to get past this. But David's got to be willing to put himself in another person's care and stick with a strict program. What it comes down to is this: David's got to want to help himself. Until he does, all his talk is only so much hot wind. I've tried to help, I've given him money. I've given him support. But there's only so much his friends can do."

In contrast to the depressing turn Crosby's life took in 1983, Nash's life shined

Nash family portrait (left to right): Susan, Jackson, Willie John, Nile Ann, and Graham, Hawaii, 1984. (Photo by Don Hudson)

brighter than ever before. After completing a short Hollies reunion tour of Eastern America in September, he returned to L.A., gathered together his family, and flew to the Hawaiian Islands. In the late seventies the Nashes had bought a home in Hawaii. Since that time, they had managed to enjoy only brief, periodic stays. But in the fall of 1983, Graham and Susan decided they would settle in there for a good while.

"It had been six years of virtual non-stop activity and I felt our children needed us as parents," said Susan in November. "I didn't want the money to always be buying us out of a normal family life. In rock 'n' roll, too many people let others do parenting for them."

Susan added, "I look at Graham and know he really blooms when he tunes in to his career as a father. Nobody applauds a good father. They don't give them gold records. But there are other rewards."

In Hawaii, the Nashes maintained a simple life, living with their children in a small, wood-filled bungalow in a tropical forest. It was a perfect environment for living peaceably and raising children.

Seated on the beach near his home, watching his three children frolic near the water, Graham said, "I've never felt more youthful or more centered. It's like, I've had a double beginning with the Hollies and, in the middle, this journey with CSN.

"Now I can start anything I want at this time in my life. I'd love to make some music with George Harrison. I think we've always run on parallel lines creatively. It would be an exciting musical combination. George would be able to sing the melodies. And whatever he'd do, I'd sing above it."

A few hours later, under the soft lamp glow in his living room, Nash sighed, "Whatever form of energy is responsible for our little trip here has smiled on me from the moment I was born." The instant Graham said this, his sixteen-month-old daughter Nile waddled toward him and he scooped her up in his arms. "Primarily my time here is taken up as a father and a husband," Nash said. "I get snatches of time for music, sculpting, and my photography collection."

After the children were put to bed, Nash walked back out into the living room and began fingering some patterns on a portable keyboard. "I don't think CSN is finished," he said, while playing some chords. "I can't let what David's horizon looks like interfere with my vision of the music I feel CSN still has the ability to make. My intention is to write enough songs to be able to make another CSN album in 1984."

Back in Los Angeles, in November of 1983, Stephen Stills was also in the middle of writing some new songs. Since CSN's tour of Europe, he had spent some time in England playing with former Led Zeppelin guitarist Jimmy Page. Stills had also taken the CSN backup band on the road for a series of dates in the Western and Midwestern United States. Having signed a new contract with Atlantic as a solo artist, Stills was anxious, with the onset of fall, to head into the studio and cut a new solo album. But Atlantic was not fully behind this decision.

"Stephen has a solo deal with us in principle," said Ahmet Ertegun in December 1983. "But frankly, I would rather see him go in and cut another group album. CSN should not be allowed to peter out."

David Crosby was thinking along similar lines in December. He said, "If I could be anywhere in the world right now, I'd be in the studio singing with Graham and Stephen. I mean, that's a feeling I *need* now. And Neil has said he might want to work with us again."

Crosby was telling the truth. In November, Young had appeared on "Rockline," a syndicated rock radio talk show. One caller asked him about Crosby's situation and Neil responded: "Everybody's concerned about David. He's a unique person and has a lot of problems that are unique to him. He's having a rough time. He really took a bad turn. I hope he gets himself together. I've told him that if he does get himself together and straightens up, that I'll join the group again and we'll do something together. And that's all I can do, you know?"

When the talk show host pressed for more details regarding the possible CSN&Y reunion, Young said cryptically, "The building's still standing. It didn't burn down or anything."

Graham Nash confirmed the idea of another CSN&Y project: "Neil told me he'd like to set aside some time for it. But it all depends, ultimately, on what happens with David. I can continue writing songs. We can *talk* about playing together. But if David goes to jail or he's not in good enough shape to work, then it won't happen."

A few weeks before Christmas, Crosby's future was still clouded. But his spirits were being lifted by thousands of letters from fans. Sentiments like, "Hang in there, David," "We've never stopped loving you," and "We're behind you" lightened his dark moods.

On the night of December 11, Stephen

Stills played a couple of political benefits solo at a tiny, 175-seat club called the Palms, located in Davis (fifteen miles west of Sacramento). In the middle of his first set, a fan in the audience politely asked Stephen, "How's Dave doin'?"

Stills looked down for a moment and continued to tune his guitar, then he said softly, "Did you see that movie, *Richard Pryor Live on Sunset Strip?* Well, everything he said about that [freebase] pipe is true. But David'll be okay. He's got a lot more strength than people give him credit for."

And therein lies the key to this whole story—*strength*. It's a quality that every member of the CSN gang has exhibited.

Stills said earlier in 1983, "All of us have had our share of hard times and we've always made it through them. God knows how, sometimes. But the fact is, we've *done* it. My survival instincts are very strong. David and Graham are troupers. It's like, once 'the show must go on' attitude gets in your blood, you don't ever lose it."

With the dawning of 1984 right around the corner, Ahmet Ertegun offered this assessment of Crosby, Stills & Nash: "They test themselves, but they never give up. CSN can always get back together and make a great record as long as they're alive."

David Crosby.

Stephen Stills.

CHAPTER SEVENTEEN

The Legacy Continues

The last Crosby, Stills, Nash & Young reunion of the twentieth century was marked by the October 26, 1999 release of *Looking Forward* on Reprise Records. Over thirty years had come and gone since the musicians first made music together as a band, yet there, in the songs on this album, were new lyrics offering fresh takes on the human experience, a kaleidoscope of glistening guitar tones, and those unmistakable vocal harmonies, delivered with renewed strength.

The idea that CSN, let alone CSN&Y, would still be creating meaningful new music together at the turn of the century would have been greeted with major skepticism back in the mid–1980s. Even though CSN, at that time, was still managing to tour and fill arenas, the band's future was tenuous as Crosby's alarming drug addiction continued to be the dominant force in his life. He was more obsessed with getting high on freebase cocaine than creating music. Friends desperately tried to convince him that he was destroying himself. But nothing—not interventions, not drug treatment programs, not even grand mal seizures, the threat of prison, or death—deterred him from his free-fall descent. By November 1985 Crosby had hit rock bottom. He was a ravaged, confused, strung-out drug addict and a certified fugitive after failing to appear at a bond revocation hearing in Texas stemming from another drug and weapons arrest. He'd already spent two months in a Dallas County Jail. He was determined not to spend any more time behind bars. He was, in fact, on the verge of hitting the high seas with his wife-to-be and then fellow addict, Jan Dance.

David Crosby.

"We were ready to leave the country to avoid going to jail," Crosby said in 1986. "But I couldn't handle it. Neither could she. I just couldn't do it. I love it here, man. And I love playing music. I couldn't leave all that behind. I finally just said, 'I can't be this guy. This is not who I promised myself I would be.'"

On December 19, 1985, Crosby surrendered to authorities in West Palm Beach, Florida. Shortly thereafter, he was placed in solitary confinement at the Dallas County Jail. "They were afraid somebody else would kill me," David says. "Being in solitary was flat awful. So I told them to send me to prison, because I had to get out of solitary."

Crosby entered the Texas Department of Corrections in Huntsville on March 5, 1986. When not suffering unimaginable pain and nightmares while kicking his addiction to drugs, "with no help. . . no tranquilizers. . . no medicine. . . no nothin'," says Crosby, he sang and played guitar—but only in the prison music room, not in his cell. He explains: "They [prison officials] were afraid I'd hang myself with the strings or use 'em to cut through the bars, pick the lock. That would have been some trick."

Making the most of the musical outlet afforded him, David became the star of the prison band. "There were some good musicians in there," he recalls. "Some were excellent, like this guy, a guitar player named Billy Jones, who was in for murder. We did some shows. That helped a lot."

What also helped raise Crosby's spirits were letters from fans and friends, and, most importantly, letters from his partner, Jan Dance, who was successfully completing a drug detox and rehabilitation program while David was in prison. "Jan," says Crosby, "was my shining light when there wasn't much light to be found."

Since he was prohibited from playing music in his cell and had no access to a tape recorder, when it came to songwriting, Crosby says: "I just wrote a whole lot of lyrics, *sheaves* of lyrics, man. Then I would try and put some music to 'em when I got in the band room. But there were usually twenty other guys in there. So it was real hard. One of the first songs I completed was called 'Alexander Graham Bell.' It's kind of like a country tune about the telephone—which was my main contact with the outside world. I wrote some other songs. The best one was 'Compass,' which begins: 'I have wasted ten years in a blindfold/Ten fold more than I've invested now in sight.'"

In his 1988 autobiography, *Long Time Gone*, co-authored by Carl Gottlieb, Crosby wrote, "When I saw the lyrics to 'Compass,' I realized that, even though I was still suffering and things were not fun, there was obviously more of me awake than had been in a long time. It was the turning point. It was when I realized this was actually going to happen. I was going to wake up and somehow this long nightmare was going to end."

On August 8, 1986, Crosby was paroled from prison in Huntsville, Texas. David remembers: "It felt great. It also felt strange. It felt sort of like coming back from a war. . . alive. . . and surprised to be alive." He was initially released into a halfway house called New Directions in Houston, where he stayed until August 22. The night before leaving Texas behind, Crosby performed at a Houston nightclub with Graham Nash. "Thinking about this, about playing music with my friends, is what kept me going," Crosby told the audience.

When Crosby's drug dependency, subsequent arrests, and prison time threw CSN into disarray in the mid '80s, both Stills and Nash had pursued individual projects. Stills toured regularly on his own and recorded a solo album called *Right By You*. Released by Atlantic Records in July 1984, the record peaked at #75 on the *Billboard 200* album chart. Among the songs were "50/50," co-written with Joe Lala; "Stranger," co-written with his

Crosby, Stills, Nash & Young at the Arlington Theater, Santa Barbara, February 1987.

son Christopher; and a cover of Neil Young's "Only Love Can Break Your Heart" (featuring additional lyrics by Stills). Guests on the record included Graham Nash, Mike Finnigan, Chris Hillman, and Jimmy Page. "Pagey and I hit some nice grooves over in England," Stills said in 1985. "We didn't have to talk about it much. I played the songs for him a couple of times and he was off."

Nash's fourth solo album, *Innocent Eyes*, was released by Atlantic Records in March 1986 and reached only #136 on the *Billboard 200* album chart. There was a decided electronic pulse to much of the material. Nash now says: "I think that album was a panic. It was me thinking I had to do something to be more contemporary."

In the fall of 1986, another old friend, Neil Young, agreed to fulfill a 1983 promise. "If

you get yourself together and straighten up," Young had told Crosby, "I'll join the group again and we'll do something together." That something turned into the making of the first Crosby, Stills, Nash & Young studio album since 1970.

In February 1987, after two CSN&Y acoustic concerts in Santa Barbara to benefit Greenpeace, Young told *Rolling Stone*: "There's a very strong chance of the group being better and stronger and perhaps bigger than it ever was before. There's a lot more depth and rawness and a lot more funk and soul in this band than has ever been heard on record." Young added, "We see ourselves as being able to do this for another twenty years. With us, we can go away for four or five years and come back and our audience is still there. We don't have to stay with what's happening.

David Crosby, Jackson Browne, Graham Nash, Stephen Stills, and Neil Young backstage at the Palace in Hollywood, November 1988.

Because *we're* happening. We're not in that race. We're in our own slot."

Recording sessions for the CSN&Y album, ultimately called *American Dream*, were held at Young's Northern California ranch studio, Redwood Digital, at various points from February 1987 to September 1988. This twenty-month stretch of time was eventful in many other ways as well.

On May 16, 1987, David Crosby was married to Jan Dance at a simple ceremony in Los Angeles at the Hollywood Church of Religious Science on Sunset Blvd. At the same ceremony, Graham and Susan Nash celebrated their tenth wedding anniversary by reaffirming their vows. Stills was also married seven months later in Washington, D.C., to an *Elle* fashion model named Pamela Ann Jordan. They've since divorced, but she and Stephen

became proud parents of a baby girl named Eleanor in 1988.

Crosby, Stills & Nash completed two long tours in '87 and '88. After the band's August 8, 1987 concert at Irvine Meadows in Southern California, a reviewer for *The Los Angeles Times* wrote: "After eighteen years (plus or minus) of togetherness (more or less), Crosby, Stills & Nash have pretty much become rock's million-mile Volkswagen. Just when you think they've sputtered their last breath, they're off and running again."

Meanwhile, Neil Young recorded two albums—one with Crazy Horse (*Life*, released by Geffen Records in '87) and one with the Bluenotes (*This Note's For You*, released on Reprise Records in '88). Neither record reached the Top 20, though Young embarked on tours with Crazy Horse, then the Bluenotes.

After the May 1987 Crosby/Nash "double wedding" in Los Angeles: (left to right) Jan Crosby, David Crosby, Susan Nash, Graham Nash.

Despite all of this activity, the four musicians were continually drawn back to the CSN&Y album sessions at Young's ranch studio. "Neil was a champion," Nash said in 1988. "He's a natural leader. It's difficult to have an entire scene that has three or four madmen at your home. Neil was the quarterback—but you still need the rest of the team."

When Atlantic Records released *American Dream* in November 1988, music reviewers did not rave. In the January 12, 1989 edition of *Rolling Stone*, critic Anthony DeCurtis wrote: "Despite pleasant melodies, the occasional interesting song, and the signature harmonies, *American Dream* is, for the most part, a snoozefest." In retrospect, Stills says of *American Dream*: "The personality the album took on was not particularly in keeping with who we

were then. The project became contrived and I think the music paid for it." Crosby adds: "The whole thing, the recording of *American Dream*, it just got stretched out. And we did not have, really, the best group of songs to work with. I only had two songs anybody really liked. Neil and Nash had good songs. I don't think Stephen did. I love the guy and he's one of the best songwriters there is. But at that particular time he was not blessed with really top-notch material. I didn't like any of his songs that much. So that put a serious strain on the project. Then, even though we did not have enough good songs, we ended up putting 14 of them on the album! I think that was stupid."

Nevertheless, *American Dream* ultimately sold over one million copies and rose as high as #16 on the *Billboard 200* album chart. And

Graham, Susan, David, and Jan cool off in the Nashes' pool.

while there was to be no CSN&Y tour in support of the release, the group did appear on November 12, 1988 at The Palace in Hollywood as part of a benefit dubbed "Graham Nash's Children of the Americas Radiothon." The event raised enough money to innoculate over 300,000 children. Performing as an acoustic quartet with no rhythm section, CSN&Y's spirited set included vintage group and solo material as well as songs from *American Dream*.

With the dawning of 1989, the memory of CSN&Y quickly faded as Young and Stills took to the road with solo bands and Crosby & Nash began laying down tracks for a possible duo

Stephen Stills with his daughter, Eleanor,
Beverly Hills, 1992.

Crosby, Stills, Nash & Young during the recording of *American Dream* at Neil's ranch studio, Redwood Digital, in Northern California, 1988.

album. In addition, David Crosby's *Oh Yes I Can* solo album, featuring a mixture of new songs and older material, was released by A&M Records in February. Crosby reflects: "There was some new excitement when that album came together because I still had something to prove to myself and a lot of other people: that I could still create meaningful music. The most important thing was—I was out of jail and I had the chance to do it."

On stage in '89 with a solo electric band, Crosby's live show crackled with fresh, unbridled emotion. The April 8, 1989 performance at the Tower Theater in Philadelphia was taped for broadcast on the nationally syndicated radio program, The King Biscuit Flower Hour, and eventually released on CD in 1996 by King Biscuit Flower Hour Records.

The original trio format of Crosby, Stills & Nash closed out the '80s in dramatic fashion. With the fall of the Berlin Wall imminent, they entered the studio and recorded a new

version of Tom Fedora's "Chippin' Away," which Nash had included on *Innocent Eyes*, his 1986 solo album. At the sessions, James Taylor added harmony vocals. In November '89, as an acoustic trio, CSN ultimately performed the song at the Wall as it was in the process of being dismantled.

By 1990, the proposed Crosby & Nash duo album had turned into a CSN project. The resulting album, *Live It Up*, was released in June of that year and reached #57 on the *Billboard 200* album chart. Graham Nash remembers: "The *Live It Up* project was a little bit painful for me. I found it very difficult to be one of the guys. I produced the record with [drummer] Joe Vitale and [engineer] Stanley Johnston. And I found it very difficult to take a leadership role as a producer and maintain my friend/band vibe with David and Stephen. I couldn't separate myself."

During the *Live It Up* sessions, Nash admits, "Only once did we sing together on one mike. So in that sense, it was not really a true CSN record. At that time, we did not trust ourselves enough to let go, to accept each other's opinions or reject them. We did not let each other know how we really felt. David and I did. But that's not enough."

Despite the shortcomings of *Live It Up*, which was also referred to by some as the "hot dogs on the moon album" after the off-beat cover photo collage by David Peters, the record did feature several stand-out songs, including "Arrows," by Crosby and Michael Hedges, "Haven't We Lost Enough," by Stills, "House of Broken Dreams," by Nash, and "Yours and Mine," by Crosby, Nash and keyboardist Craig Doerge, with soprano sax master Branford Marsalis adding emotional solos to both "Arrows" and "Yours and Mine."

During the summer of 1990, CSN continued to tour extensively. In fact, the group performed more live concerts during the '90s than in the '60s, '70s, and '80s combined. They did it mostly with longtime supporting players, including keyboardist/vocalist Michael Finnigan,

Crosby, Stills & Nash publicity shot used to promote the *Live It Up* album, 1990. (Photo by Greg Gorman.)

bassist Gerald Johnson, and drummer Joe Vitale. CSN also toured as an acoustic trio.

"The acoustic thing works for us extremely well," says Crosby. "It stresses what we can do that other people cannot do. We give you the songs. There's a real joy there."

Of the CSN acoustic tour in 1991, Stills says: "It made me a much better guitar player. It really did a lot for my chops. When you're out there all by yourself, it sharpens up your technique a lot. It requires some finesse. Doing so many shows in that format—just the three of us, then our solo spots—you start playing licks you think of spontaneously. That's a pretty big milestone for any musician, to be able to instantly play what comes into your head."

"Just voices and acoustic guitar always brings us back to our roots," says Nash. "The living room was where we were born. When we bring back that feel in concert, it's still a rush for us and the audience after all these years."

In 1991, Nash's mind was definitely focused on "all these years" with respect to Crosby, Stills & Nash, as he completed the CSN box set with co-producer Gerry Tolman and engineer Stephen Barncard. Why the group decided to issue its career retrospective in '91—the twenty-second anniversary of their first record—rather than waiting until their Silver Anniversary in '94, is explained by Nash: "I knew we were headed into this veil of twenty-five years and it made us want to clear the deck and make a definite point from which to carry on. We wanted the project to mark a milestone, not be a headstone."

Pouring over reels and reels of tape was a Herculean task, one which Crosby and Stills gladly allowed Nash to undertake with their blessing. Crosby says, "I'd give Nash 90 percent of the credit for the box set." Stills adds, "The sheer volume of tapes was enormous. I remember me and David looking at this room filled with boxes of [record] masters, all

Stephen Stills at the Greek Theatre, Los Angeles, 1990.

stacked up. We both immediately turned to Graham and said, 'Start whittling.'"

The review and selection process, according to Nash, "made me re-fall in love with our music all over again. I had a fabulous time doing the box set. Because of the longevity of our careers, as a group, in various combinations and solo, I'd forgotten about how much fun we had, how much music we'd made and what kind of an impact we had and continue to have."

Among its seventy-seven tracks, the CSN box set ultimately featured a stunning array of musical gems—time-honored classics mixed with never-before-released tracks—which captured the essence of CSN and CSN&Y. Released in November 1991, the collection also delved into solo and duo projects.

Apart from the group dynamic in the fall of 1991, Stills released another solo album, *Stills Alone*. As the title suggests, the music was primarily Stills alone with an acoustic guitar, this approach producing a stark, intimate portrait of the man. Released indepen-

David Crosby, Graham Nash, and Stephen Stills at the Greek Theatre, Los Angeles, 1990.

CSN at show's end, Universal Amphitheatre, Los Angeles, 1992.

dently in October '91 on Stills's own Gold Hill Records (distributed by a Florida-based company, Vision Records, Inc.), the album featured a handful of new songs, new arrangements of some of his older solo material, and a song each by three of his favorite songwriters: Fred Neil, Bob Dylan, and John Lennon.

"The whole album took a week to do," Stills remembers. "I was in good voice at the end of a tour and took my guitar and sound system into the studio and just started singing. I didn't worry about anything and got the sound I was getting on stage."

Most of Stills's visibility apart from CSN in '90s was as a live performer. But rather than arenas and amphitheaters, he was playing mostly smaller halls, casinos, and clubs. "It feels good to be playing a little down and dirty," Stills said. "After performing in so

many big places for so many years, it's nice to get back to the venues where you can really feed off a crowd."

Another of Stills's activities of note in the early '90s was his recording of a new version of "Change Partners" with Flaco Jimenez, for the accordion player extraordinaire's 1992 album entitled, appropriately enough, *Partners*. Stills also expanded into the realm of writing and recording music for television, including penning the theme song for the short-lived early '90s series, *Second Noah*. He even tried his hand at acting, landing a small role in a 1992 Perry Mason made-for-TV movie. But Stephen admits: "Music still drives it all. At the beginning of '93, I cut the tip off this finger"—he holds up the index finger on his left hand—"which is like the most important finger for guitar playing. I had to cancel a gig,

Outtake from *Stills Alone* album cover shoot, Beverly Hills, 1991.

Nash remembers, "I felt I'd gotten all I wanted from the photographic images I'd collected and decided to sell them at auction at Sotheby's in New York to generate money to propel me into a new universe."

The April 25, 1990 auction of 2,400 of the photographs from the Nash Collection was the largest sale of a private selection of photos that Sotheby's had ever handled. The auction of images by the likes of photographers Ansel Adams, Paul Outerbridge, and Diane Arbus garnered $2.39 million.

Simultaneously, an exhibit of Nash's own photography was being shown at galleries in Tokyo and New York. Nash says, "I must confess that I was far more excited to sell one of

Graham Nash at O'Henry Studios, Burbank, 1994.

a real special, big money gig. While this finger was healing it gave me a completely new perspective on my gift, a full resonant appreciation for what I can do as a musician. So, yeah, music still pretty much drives everything."

Graham Nash diversified his creative pursuits considerably in the 1990s. "As an artist, I'm always looking for a new brush," Graham says. "I'm always looking for a new form of expression. At the insistence of Joni [Mitchell], I started to share my photographic images with people. I've been taking pictures since I was eleven, but I'd never shared them with anyone because I was too busy being a rock and roller."

While reconsidering his own private photography collection one day in early 1990,

Mac Holbert (left) and Graham Nash at Nash Editions gallery showing, Santa Monica, 1993.

my own prints than I was selling $2 million worth of prints I'd collected."

Much of the money Nash made from the sale of his collected photography helped finance a new printing process he developed with the help of friends Paul and Charlie Wehrenberg, David Coons, Jack Duganne, and R. Mac Holbert. The resultant large format 34-inch by 42-inch prints were described by one New York art critic as "combining the deep black available from silver, the tonal delicacy of platinum, and the richness of gravure." Holbert helped Nash turn the process into an ongoing fine art printing business, Nash Editions, based in Manhattan Beach, California, with artist David Hockney among the company's list of clients.

In 1992, Nash cofounded a venture called Manuscript Originals, which makes available to the public limited edition original manuscripts (and related fine art lithographs) of a wide variety of popular song lyrics, ranging from Nash's "Our House" to Peter Yarrow's "Puff the Magic Dragon," and from James Brown's "Papa's Got A Brand New Bag" to Grace Slick's "White Rabbit," handwritten, hand-doodled, and hand-signed by the artists themselves.

Nash also began merging his fascination with new technology with his life as a musician. Using such tools as PictureTel and the Integrated Services Digital Network (ISDN), with support from Silicon Graphics, Nash was able to create a revolutionary one-man show (with the help of musician/technician Rand Wetherwax) that he dubbed "Life Sighs"—a multi-media event in which Graham, using his voice, guitar, piano, a 30-foot

Nash Family: (left to right) Graham, Will, Nile, Susan, and Jackson.

by 17-foot high definition video screen, and a wireless mouse, presents his life and times live in a theater setting. "It's very interactive and very now," says Nash.

In addition to entering the world of television for a time with a music and talk show called *The Inside Track*, which aired on the Arts & Entertainment cable television network in 1990 and 1991, Nash kept writing new songs. Despite accumulating over forty tunes, Nash never revived his solo recording career. He did, however, rekindle his musical relationship with Crosby as a duo—mostly on stage at various benefits and on the records of others.

"Me and David singing together has always been a special, unique thing," Graham says. "The bond is so strong. . . it's scary sometimes. I recently put together a DAT (dig-

ital audio tape) comprised of me and David singing on some of our friends' records over the years. It starts with 'Doctor My Eyes,' with Jackson [Browne], 'Mexico,' with James [Taylor], 'Breakaway,' with Art Garfunkel, then 'Another Day In Paradise,' with Phil Collins, then us with Bonnie [Raitt], us with Joni, Neil, Kenny Loggins." Crosby adds: "We think it's some of the best harmony work we've ever done." This music is scheduled to be released in the year 2000 on an album to benefit the Children's Defense Fund in Washington, D.C.

And while Crosby & Nash failed to release a new studio album in the '80s or '90s, they unearthed *Another Stoney Evening* with the help of longtime friend and engineer/producer Stephen Barncard. The CD is a pristine recording of Crosby & Nash live, with just their voices, acoustic guitars, and a grand piano, at the Dorothy Chandler Pavilion in Los Angeles on October 10, 1971. The tape was discovered in the wake of the making of the CSN box set and serves as a kind of companion—of far superior audio quality—to the once popular early '70s bootleg album, *A Very Stony Evening*, made from an audience tape of another fall '71 C&N show. Barncard, who produced and mixed (with Nash) *Another Stoney Evening*, doggedly shepherded the project from inception to its eventual release on Grateful Dead Records in 1998. It was worth the effort. The rapturously funny between-song patter and magical melding of voices and acoustic instruments encapsulates the special connection that Crosby and Nash had and still have on stage and in life.

In the '90s, David Crosby was the most prolific member of CSN—in terms of musical projects. In 1990, he spent time working on a Byrds box set, released by Columbia Records in November of that year, featuring a plethora of classic tracks as well as several new Byrds songs Crosby recorded in Nashville with old bandmates Roger McGuinn and Chris Hillman. In January '91, the Byrds were inducted into the Rock and Roll Hall of Fame. "The Byrds was my first band," Crosby said at the time. "And your first band is like your first love; you never forget it and you never quite feel the same way about any other band."

In '92 and early '93, Crosby cut new tracks for a solo album in studios in Los Angeles and England. The best of these sessions—featuring bassist Leland Sklar, late drummer Jeff Porcaro, drummer Jim Keltner, guitarist Jeff Pevar, as well as guests Phil Collins, Graham Nash, Jackson Browne, and Kipp Lennon—

Crosby & Nash share a humorous moment on stage.

David Crosby, Los Angeles, 1993.

can be heard on *Thousand Roads*, Crosby's third solo album, released by Atlantic Records in May '93.

One fact that distinguishes *Thousand Roads* from Crosby's other solo work is that a majority of the songs he recorded were written by others. "Not that I didn't think I had enough good songs of my own," Crosby says. "I just wanted to sample a wider palette of colors and stretch in some new directions with other people's material." Crosby put his special musical brand on songs by the likes of John Hiatt, Jimmy Webb, and Marc Cohn. He also did some collaborating with Joni Mitchell and Phil Collins.

Crosby had first met Collins at the Atlantic Records Fortieth Anniversary party in 1988. They kept in touch. Then Crosby sang on Collins's *...But, Seriously* album, specifically the song, "Another Day in Paradise" (which Crosby also performed live with Collins at the Grammy Awards in 1991). Their next collaboration resulted in the song "Hero," which Collins also produced, and it became a moderate radio hit for Crosby. "We've really only just scratched the surface," David says. "Someday Phil and I would like to do some very strange harmonic work. That's when the fun will *really* begin."

Crosby's collaboration with Joni Mitchell yielded "Yvette in English" (which she also eventually recorded for her 1994 album, *Turbulent Indigo*). "I ended up finding some meter and cadence to some of the lines David wrote," Mitchell remembers. "And the music came easy. I'm wondering now... was it the first time I'd written a song like that? I hadn't done that much collaborating before."

Crosby had always wanted to write a song with Mitchell and says, "Maybe we'll do it again. I hope so. She is, without question, one of the greatest songwriters on the planet."

Crosby performed periodically throughout 1993, including a magical night at the Whisky in West Hollywood. The December 7 show, featuring guitarist Jeff Pevar, with guest appearances by Graham Nash, Kip Lennon of Venice, and Chris Robinson of the Black Crowes, was recorded and eventually released by Atlantic Records in January 1995. The CD was produced, engineered, and mixed by Chris "Hoover" Rankin, and its title, *It's All Coming Back to Me Now. . .*, was a direct reference and response to the title of Crosby's first solo album, *If I Could Only Remember My Name*—a title suggested by CSN&Y guitar roadie John Gonzales.

Beyond his busy music agenda, Crosby also began exploring another creative avenue—acting. "I wanted to be a character actor when I first started out," Crosby says. "Music is just a side track I got off on, really. So I did this part on *Shannon's Deal* as an alcoholic songwriter—a bit of a stretch," David chuckles, "I saw that I could do it and started soliciting parts. I got lucky and one part just led to another." Since becoming a periodic visage on television and the big screen, Crosby says, "It's a lot of fun to have some kid come up to me in an airport and say, 'Aren't you the guy who was in *Hook?*'"

But Crosby was still first and foremost a musician. And in 1994, twenty-five years after the release of their first album, Crosby, Stills & Nash recorded *After the Storm*. During a break in the making of that record in May '94, Stills admitted, "The old spirit of collaboration is back and it's high time, too. There are so many old wounds that have sometimes gotten in the way. But this year it's been really cool."

Crosby added: "The chemistry that happens between three people that work together can be fleeting. A couple of years ago, due to the breakdown of relationships—particularly between me and Stephen—it came to the point where I didn't trust that chemistry and wouldn't commit to it. For one reason or another, one of them being [producer] Glyn [Johns], I got past that. And Stephen and I have managed to be friends to each other again, and not just on a surface level."

Released by Atlantic Records on August 16, 1994, *After the Storm* effectively captured the spirit of Crosby, Stills & Nash's twenty-five years on such tracks as Nash's "Find a Dream," Stills's "It Won't Go Away," Crosby's "Camera," and a cover of the Beatles' "In My Life." With Stills's "Only Waiting For You" sent to radio as the single and emphasis track, *After the Storm* entered the *Billboard 200* album chart at #98, then all but disappeared from view, despite the fact that CSN made appearances on television talk shows, were touring, and had performed at Woodstock '94: Three More Days of Peace & Music.

CSN's decision to be part of Woodstock '94 was not an automatic one. "Over the last twenty-five years we have tried to fight the effort of people to continually lump us in with Woodstock," Nash said in the spring of '94. "Because, obviously, we've created a lot of good music since that concert. So when we were asked, I thought, 'We can look at it two ways: 1) We can decline, thinking they just need us old farts to validate the Woodstock reunion vibe trip or 2) We can celebrate it and take part in a great rock and roll concert.' I decided that because we cannot deny that we played Woodstock and because we cannot deny that we recorded the song, 'Woodstock,' I decided that we should do it. It would have been very easy to intellectualize ourselves out of participating. But I think it's kind of charming and exhilarating that twenty-five years later, in my mind, we're still kicking ass." Then Nash added: "If we're bad at Woodstock, it's over. If we're good at Woodstock, it's just the beginning again."

Crosby, Stills & Nash were good at Woodstock '94. But their performance did not define the spirit of the festival as it had in '69. Along with Bob Dylan, Joe Cocker, Santana, and other veteran artists who performed at the '94 concert, CSN represented the enduring power of word and melody-based music. Bands such as Nine Inch Nails, Green Day, Cypress Hill, and Metallica hammered out a new, edgier brand of rock that some were calling "the musical voice of Generation X." Not all of the musicians agreed. B-Real of Cypress Hill snarled from the stage: "They say we're Generation X. I say we're Generation Fuck You!"

Violent Femmes lead singer Gordon Gano called Crosby, Stills & Nash "Woodstock '94's Mount Rushmore." That kind of designation reinforced CSN's standing as the enduring emissaries of Woodstock Nation. But the three musicians were also busy creating new chapters in their careers.

When Crosby paused for a moment amidst a particularly high level of productivity in early 1994, he reflected: "There's an effect that happens to you when you get sober. You have all of this time and the consciousness that you want to do something with it. Before, I was too busy getting loaded. Now, I wake up in the morning and think, 'So, what are you going to do today?' Crosby added: "Kicking [drugs] is still the hardest thing I've ever done. It will probably always rank as the single hardest thing in my life."

Little did Crosby know that he would be in for another fight for his life a few months after making that comment. David had been experiencing pain in his stomach and abdomen since the spring of '94, but discounted

Crosby, Stills & Nash on stage at Woodstock '94, Saugerties, New York, August 1994.

it until early summer when he was forced to miss a CSN show in Salt Lake City (the only time he has ever done so). A week later, doctors at Johns Hopkins Medical Center in Baltimore ran a series of tests on Crosby and discovered he had liver disease. His deteriorating liver was linked to a case of Hepatitis C that had gone undetected for as many as fifteen years.

"The hepatitis could have been connected to my drug problems—though I can't be certain of that," David said. "But it was exacerbated by the years I spent trying to turn myself into a chemical dumping site. Hence, I wound up with a liver that looked like the surface of the moon."

Crosby had been advised to leave the CSN '94 tour in July, but he refused. "I was broke and needed the money, having squandered it on drugs and losing even more because of bad tax advice," David said. "And I was having fun on stage."

He was also often in great pain. When CSN performed at Woodstock '94 on August 13, Crosby said, "I lay in our tour bus screaming because of the horrible cramps in my legs—a side effect of the medicine I was taking to reduce the fluids accumulating in my abdomen because of my malfunctioning liver. I'd also begun suffering diminished mental capacity due to hepatic encephalopathy [a brain condition caused by toxic substances accumulated in the blood]. Later [in August], Stills and Nash cornered me backstage after a gig. 'David, you were a quarter of a beat behind all night,' they said. 'What the hell is wrong?' I burst into tears. Graham and Stephen knew about my liver problem, but only then did I tell them how bad it was. 'David, you have to take care of yourself,' they told me. 'You have too much to live for.'"

In early November, two and a half months past his fifty-third birthday, Crosby was admitted to the UCLA Medical Center with hopes that a liver donor would materialize soon. While in the hospital, Crosby endured intense pain and horrible nightmares. During this tough period, his wife Jan discovered she was pregnant. David reflects: "It's as if God said, 'Look, you're going to go through this hard ordeal or else you'll die. But I'm also giving you this little prize.'"

Even with Jan right by his side, David admits, "I was very afraid—of the procedure and of dying. Jan and I meditated and held each other—whatever helped me believe I was going to be fine."

The first liver that became available for Crosby turned out to be cancerous. Then, on November 20, a thirty-one-year-old Southern California man who had been involved in a traffic accident was declared brain dead. This young man matched Crosby's blood type and body size. His liver was about to give Crosby hope for prolonging his life.

As David was wheeled to the operating room, he and Jan held each other and sang "Amazing Grace." Upon reaching the operating room doors, Jan gave David a kiss and said, "See you in a minute."

A seven hour operation ensued. Dr. Ronald W. Busuttil, Director of the Dumont-UCLA Liver Transplant Center and the principal surgeon during the transplant, issued a statement following the lengthy procedure: "As with all transplant patients, we will watch his progress closely for several days, and I am optimistic that he will do well."

Stephen Stills also issued a statement to the media that was read on many television newscasts that night and printed in newspapers the following morning: "I could not be happier. Although I recognize the fact that the next few days and weeks are going to be crucial to David's recovery, I just wanted to express my joy over the news that my dear friend and partner has completed this operation. It is the best Christmas present I could have hoped for."

Following several post-surgery complications, Crosby was allowed to go home—51

David Crosby, Graham Nash, Neil Young, and Stephen Stills in Nash's backyard, Los Angeles, 1995.

days after the transplant operation. "My prognosis is good," Crosby said in early 1995. "I have to be careful for awhile because I don't have an immune system that can fight even the simplest of germs, but if I mind my P's and Q's I stand a very good chance of having a happy and productive life. So I'm basically taking the next year off to get healthy—I plan to diet and exercise—and to help Jan have our miracle baby."

In April 1995, Graham and Susan Nash hosted a shower in their Los Angeles home for a very pregnant Jan Crosby. "Neil brought his whole family down," David remembers. "Stephen was there, too. That was the first time all four of us had seen each other in one place since Bill Graham's wake [in November 1991]. It was a wonderful, happy afternoon. Everybody was in good spirits and very com-

fortable. Neil especially. It was very kind of him and [his wife] Pegi to come and be there."

A month later, on May 9, Django Dance Crosby was born. His name represents a kind of fusion of David and Jan's names and pays homage to legendary jazz guitarist Django Reinhardt. "I think I'm extremely fortunate," Crosby said in June '95. "I think it's incredible that I'm even alive—considering all of the time I nearly wasn't. So for me to be able to have a new baby with Jan. . . I don't know how to say this without sounding corny, but I somehow feel like I've been blessed with this child. 'Cause he's a stunner, a wonderful little kid. And he rejuvenates me. I was feeling pretty old when I walked out of the hospital. And I don't feel like that today. Django is an incredibly enlivening force. He's so full of life it rubs off on you."

Crosby was also spending more time with his daughter, Donovan Ann. "She's a wonderful artist," David says, "a really good painter, a fine animator, a good writer. Donovan is full of talent and she's one of the closest people to me in my life. She's a very generous spirit, a wonderful young woman. And I finally found the right bait to get her to come hang out with me. . . Django. She loves my little boy."

Another son entered David's life in 1995. "Almost thirty years ago, I was going with this girl and she got pregnant," Crosby says. "I was very young and didn't know what to do. She didn't know what to do either; so she put the kid up for adoption. Over the years, I'd been thinking off and on about this kid, wondering if he or she was all right and feeling badly about having run out. To now find out that he's not only all right but that he is a really

fine human being and a musician is another stunner for me."

When the parents of James Raymond, a singer-songwriter and keyboard player, learned in late 1994 that Crosby was in the hospital for a liver transplant, James's adoptive father wrote a letter to David that read, in part: "We know you may not make it, and we think it would be a shame if [James] never knew his biological father."

James was "blown away" when he discovered that Crosby was his biological father, and admitted, "while I was more inspired as a kid by Elton John and Stevie Wonder. . . this connection made me more aware of my musical heritage and I began wondering how similar David and I were musically."

When Crosby and James finally met, David says, "I felt a little awkward and nervous that

Jan and Django Crosby backstage at the Palace, Hollywood, California, 1997.

David and Donovan Crosby at a '60s party at Nash's house, Los Angeles, 1988.

he might feel resentful. He could have, but he wasn't. He was very generous, very kind. And as if there wasn't enough emotion in the air, the day after he met his genetic father, James had his first kid (Grace Isabella). So it was a pretty eventful twenty-four hours."

Crosby and Raymond soon connected as musicians. "I sent him off some lyrics I'd been playing around with," David remembers. "And James came back with music that sounded like Steely Dan! That song was 'Morrison.' I knew right then and there we should work together more, and we did." They eventually teamed up with guitarist Jeff Pevar, who remembers, "From day one, the sparks really flew. In addition to the instrumental synergy, we also found a nice vocal blend." This association would come to be known as

CPR—"a very apt acronym considering my medical history," Crosby said—with more live shows and recording sessions looming on the horizon. But Crosby admitted to writer Matthew Greenwald: "I haven't quit my day job." Indeed, CSN was very active as a touring band in '96 and '97.

On May 6, 1997, CSN was inducted into the Rock and Roll of Fame at the Renaissance Hotel in Cleveland—joining the Bee Gees, Buffalo Springfield, the Jacksons, Joni Mitchell, Parliament-Funkadelic, the Rascals, Mahalia Jackson, Bill Monroe, and Sydney Nathan as "The Class of '97."

When David Crosby stood at the podium that night to say a few words, he began, "I'll be damned. . . I too am very honored to be here. I feel like a very lucky man. For a guy

CPR: (left to right) Jeff Pevar, David Crosby, and James Raymond, Santa Monica, 1998.

who was supposed to be dead a couple of years ago, I'm doing pretty well." Having survived a liver transplant operation, years of severe drug addiction, and prison time in Texas, Crosby had become an American folk hero, rising from the depths of self-destruction to get a second and third chance at life; and he was still making music with his friends, Stills and Nash.

Graham Nash, seated on a couch in the music room of his Los Angeles home in early 1997, commented: "When I look at my life, this kid from Manchester that grew up idolizing Elvis and the Everly Brothers and Gene Vincent—to be honored in the Rock and Roll Hall of Fame with the very people who helped shape my life, I'm thrilled beyond belief."

As a member of CSN and Buffalo Springfield, Stephen Stills became the first musician ever to be inducted into the Rock and Roll Hall of Fame twice in the same year. "I'm tickled pink to be part of this," Stills admitted via the Hall of Fame website a week before the induction dinner, "and you could never have convinced me that they'd both happen in the same year. I thought they would cancel each other out. I thought that half the voters would vote for Buffalo Springfield and half would vote for Crosby, Stills & Nash, and it wouldn't be enough to get either one in. Now that they're both in, I'm just going to say thank you and get

off stage before they figure out I shouldn't be there!" Stills laughed, then added: "It's cool with me. You're going to watch one bedazzled kid on his diplomatic best. . . We're really looking forward to being there, and, like I said, I'm flattered beyond measure. I'm just hoping Neil shows up with a guitar."

As it turned out, neither Neil Young nor his guitar would make it to the Twelfth Annual Hall of Fame Induction Dinner. Young boycotted the event because he objected to the $1,500-a-plate fee for additional guests and how the festivities were being taped by VH1 and edited down into a two-hour television special. While Crosby, Stills & Nash shared Young's grievances, they nevertheless participated in the event with pride. Young simply sent the Hall of Fame Foundation a fax, which read, in part: "Although I accept the honor, in the name of rock and roll, I decline to take part in this TV presentation and be trotted out like some cheap awards show."

In making this stand, Young not only skipped the Rock and Roll Hall of Fame event, he also missed the opportunity to join Crosby, Stills & Nash for the band's first-ever performance at Kent State on May 4, 1997—twenty-seven years after four students were slain and Young's reaction to the event had sparked the creation of the CSN&Y song, "Ohio."

Though periodically aligned with Crosby, Stills & Nash since 1969, Neil Young has mostly charted his own course, maintaining a solo career that has yielded over thirty albums. Embraced by a new generation of alternative rock bands as the "Godfather of Grunge," Young continued to raise his rocker quotient in the '90s with explosive tours and albums with Crazy Horse, and an album and live appearances with Pearl Jam. Neil also showed his softer, gentler side on the gold album, *Harvest Moon*, on *MTV Unplugged*, and solo acoustic live shows. No one could predict the next time Young would team up with CSN.

Crosby says of Young: "He's like a river man—sometimes he wanders close to you,

David Crosby (holding son Django), Graham Nash, and Stephen Stills backstage after CSN was inducted into the Rock and Roll Hall of Fame, May 6, 1997, in Cleveland. (Photo by Taro.)

sometimes he wanders away from you. And that's how it is." Consequently, it is CSN that has stood as the most enduring combination. "I feel better about the three of us than I have in years," Nash said in 1997. "The main reason is that Stephen and I are getting on extremely well now. I am, and Stephen is, as open as possible to new ideas."

Nash continued: "My relationship with David is a little more distant because of the physicality of our homes. He lives two hours north of here. When he used to live just around the corner, we used to see each other almost daily. I kind of miss not seeing him around so much. And I miss not being able to work on new musical ideas with David at a moment's notice."

Looking at CSN's basic mode of operation, Nash explained: "There's been a game-plan on my part to change the way CSN dynamically always operated. Over the years it kind of became. . . me and David on one side and Stephen on the other. I recently decided that I would try to almost get back to the way it was on our first album. I want Stephen to feel that he can be Captain Manyhands again—not in terms of him playing everything, because we've got some great musicians with us, as you know—I just want Stephen to feel trusted. I want him to feel supported. In that setting, Stephen is at his best —in the studio and on stage."

In a review of CSN's 1997 concert at the Universal Amphitheatre, *Los Angeles Times*

CSN at Kent State University, Ohio, May 4, 1997. (Photo by Dave Zimmer.)

writer Steve Hochman wrote: "Stills, in particular, has been the revelation of the group in recent years, adding fire and grit to both his vocals and guitar playing. Trim and spry, he performed with child-like enthusiasm, hopping with glee as he ripped out a stinging solo on 'Wooden Ships.'"

Rolling Stone ranked Crosby, Stills & Nash's six-night stand in September 1997 at the Fillmore in San Francisco among "The Greatest Concerts of the '90s." Neil Young made a surprise walk-on appearance toward the end of one of the shows, but this was clearly CSN's time to shine. The trio mixed re-energized classics with several new songs, including Nash's "Half Your Angels" (written in the wake of the April 1995 Oklahoma City fed-

Neil Young delivers a nonverbal message.

Stephen Stills at home with his White Falcon and other Gretsch guitars, Beverly Hills.

eral building bombing) and "Lost Another One" (written after the August 1995 death of Jerry Garcia), Crosby and Raymond's "Morrison" and Stills's "No Tears Left." The group's new material had been sparking periodic recording sessions since the fall of 1996. Unlike most of their past studio work, the musicians were not following a schedule, instead recording when the time was right and when the songs "felt ready."

Stills told the *Denver Post*: "I think it's a more reasonable way to go about [making a record], and more efficient. . . I could make a whole album of songs I wished we'd recorded better."

Crosby, Stills & Nash have been in the position to do whatever they wanted with their music since separating from Atlantic Records—a process which began in 1996, with the dissolution of the partnership finalized in early 1997 and officially announced on March 11, 1997.

A week before the announcement was made public, Nash commented, "Back in 1994, when we did *After the Storm*, the last CSN record for Atlantic, we played all of the gigs. We did *Larry King Live*, we did Letterman and Leno, we did all of the radio shows, we did interviews 'round the clock. We did Woodstock. We reached about 150 million people in 1994. Then we sold about 40,000 albums. That's because Atlantic threw *After the Storm* out there and did not work it. As a creator of the music, that hurts. Because your heart and soul is in this piece of music and to just have them throw it into this ocean of sharks, with no protection, no promotion, it was heartbreaking to us. From that point on, we began thinking about getting off Atlantic Records, and now we're finally doing it.

"Our decision to leave Atlantic had nothing to do with [Atlantic Records Chairman Emeritus] Ahmet Ertegun; we still love him dearly as a person. But the truth is, Ahmet is not as hands-on, at seventy-five years old, as

he was twenty years ago. That makes a big difference. We ended up having to deal with guys at the label that didn't really know who we were, and frankly didn't care. This was the impression we were given."

Nash added: "We'd sooner be on a smaller label that was thrilled to have Crosby, Stills & Nash. We want a label to say, 'Fuck, man, we've got CSN! Let's go!' In that kind of an atmosphere we would thrive. But to be discounted is not nice—it's not right; you can not count us out at all."

CSN's loyal and ever-growing fan base has never discounted the group. With the computer age in full swing, it was only a matter of time before fans of CSN would make use of technology to connect and communicate.

An ongoing, fan-driven e-mail list dedicated to discussions and topics involving or related to the music and lives of Crosby, Stills & Nash was launched in 1995 by Australian Mick Anderson. He conceived of the idea while communicating with fellow CSN fan Harlan Thompson, a Hawaii resident. Mick recalls: "The lack of a focal point on the Net for CSN was the main motivation behind the creation of the Lee Shore" (named after one of Crosby's finest songs). Interestingly enough, among the early subscribers to the Lee Shore list was Crosby himself, a big fan of online communication.

"When I first logged onto the WELL (Whole Earth 'lectronic Link) and looked in the music conference," Crosby told writer Steve Silberman in 1995, "here were these people talking about me! It was great ego food. I'm a raving egotist. So I sat back and dug what they were saying. It was neat, because it was uncensored. Uncensored data is a pearl beyond price, because usually people tell you what they think you want to hear. On the Internet, they tell you what they think."

Currently administered by Anderson and Dean "Doc" Dunn, "The Shore" has become a kind of global "safe home" for a broad spectrum of individuals around the world. With CSN as touchstone and springboard, discussions range from how and why the group's music has touched members so deeply, to detailed analysis of concerts and recordings.

Hans Velduizen's excellent CSN website is another destination for fans to find and share information. The website once even helped organize a fan song "request line"—at the urging of Crosby—which resulted in CSN frequently revamping their set lists to reflect what fans wanted to hear. "We're giving 'em a show that's different from every show we've ever done," said Crosby, "and we really have a helluva lot of fun playing stuff that we haven't played. Giving your audience what they want to hear. What a concept."

During a break in CSN's 1997 summer tour, Crosby turned his attention back to CPR. The band entered a studio in Santa Monica in August and recorded an album in only twenty days. "There were so many great moments that captured honest and spontaneous energy," says Jeff Pevar. "Many of the takes on the record are first takes. Even some of David's lead vocals were done on the fly."

Simply entitled *CPR*, the album is a stunning amalgam of vocal harmony, rock, jazz, and folk, and was released in mid–1998 on Samson Records. CPR also released two other albums in 1998: *Live at Cuesta College*, a double-CD of the band's January 18, 1997 show as a trio in San Luis Obispo, California, and *Live at the Wiltern*, a double-CD capturing CPR's November 7, 1998 concert at the venerable Los Angeles venue. The Wiltern show featured CPR with bassist Andrew Ford and drummer Stevie DiStanislao, as well as special guests Graham Nash, Phil Collins, and Marc Cohn.

In addition to working with CPR, Crosby also found time to conduct interviews for a book and multi-media documentary called *Stand and Be Counted*. Along with Stills and Nash, Crosby has participated in hundreds of benefits over the years, as well as humanitarian and civil rights causes. He decided to cre-

Kristen and Stephen Stills, Beverly Hills, 1996.

ate a written and audio-visual record of what inspires him and his many artist friends to put themselves on the line.

Stills, meanwhile, was continuing to embark on occasional solo tours and devote time to his family, having married former recording studio manager Kristen Hathoway on May 27, 1996 in West Palm Beach, Florida. In October of that year, Stephen and Kristen celebrated the birth of their son, Henry, named after Henry Diltz.

In September 1997, Stills was inducted into Hollywood's Rock Walk, his handprints placed alongside the likes of Eddie Van Halen, Dick Clark, and Willie Dixon. Stills's ongoing reverence for and picking brilliance on Martin

Stephen Stills's young son Henry.

acoustic guitars was forever etched into history when C. F. Martin & Company announced the creation of the D–45SS Stephen Stills Signature Edition in the fall of 1998. Priced at $19,000 each, there were the same number of 91 D–45SS instruments offered for sale as the highly coveted original D–45 guitars Martin produced in the pre-World War II period between 1933 and 1942. Martin was continuing its tradition as "the Stradivarius of American musical instruments," says Stills, who wrote the foreword for the book, *Martin Guitars: An Illustrated Celebration of America's Premier Guitarmaker*, by Jim Washburn and Richard Johnston.

Stills spent stretches of time in 1998 at Neil Young's Broken Arrow ranch, helping his old friend compile an historical Buffalo Springfield box set. "We had a wonderful time listening to old material and revisiting our childhood," Stills said in late '98, "alternately laughing and crying."

Stills's most revered Buffalo Springfield song, "For What It's Worth," was revisited by rap group Public Enemy in 1998, serving as the driving pulse of the title track for the Spike Lee film, *He Got Game*. "I was flattered beyond measure," said Stills, who ended up playing guitar and singing on the chorus of the reworked version, and appearing in the song's video.

When Stills considers how CSN appeals to a generation of music fans who weren't even born when the trio first came together, he isn't sure "if all of the hard-edged, triangular-clothed people get our music. Sometimes I wonder what's up with them. Sometimes the things they do are really insightful. I don't know. The kids I've met go back and forth, from being really enlightened, wonderful people to the great *illiterati*. They used to call our generation 'The Great Unwashed.' Maybe the kids today should go camping more and watch less television." Then Stills adds, "I know we draw a lot of Generation X kids. I see them out there. Some of them are fourth generation."

Speaking of generations, there is Stephen's daughter, Jennifer, who performs and records her own brand of folk/rock music, and his son, Chris, whose debut album, *100 Year Thing*, was released by Atlantic Records in January 1998. While there are echoes of his father, in acoustic guitar and vocal mannerisms, Chris crafted a distinctive blend of alternative folk, rock, and blues. "He's a complete artist now," Stephen says with pride. "He sings, he plays, he writes, plays rhythm and lead guitar, plays piano. My only advice to him has been. . . grow eyes in the back of your head and never sell your [music] publishing."

Chris Stills told *MOJO* magazine in 1998: "My father inspired me like he inspired millions of other kids. . . I remember someone playing me 'For What It's Worth' and I thought it was the most amazing thing I had ever heard. I asked what it was and I was told it was my dad. . . That song was an epiphany for me. I played it over and over again. . . I don't mind sounding like my old man at all. I don't want to stray too far from that era. Those are the records that I still love the best."

Nash, as the group's ongoing curator, is mindful of the public appetite for CSN's archival recordings and the need, for the sake of history, to establish a complete documentation of what they've accomplished over the years. "With the CSN box set," he says, "we spanned the history of this band in four CDs. There is another CD that we're planning of stuff that wasn't in there. There are 48 demos

of our most famous songs that we found in the process of listening to this mountain of tapes. One idea we've discussed is. . . we'd have the 1968 Crosby demo of 'Wooden Ships,' without words, then follow it with the CSN version from our first album; have my 1968 demo of 'Teach Your Children,' then follow it with the recording of 'Teach Your Children' from *Déjà Vu*. . . and so on. So, there's a bunch of stuff we still have in the vaults and, I'm fairly certain, we will release as much of it as we can before we're through."

In January 1999, CSN was not ready to tackle another historical project just yet. Instead, the trio was determined to finish a new album, having cut new renditions of the Byrds' "Turn Turn Turn" and one of Stills's Buffalo Springfield songs, "Rock and Roll Woman," as well as several new songs, including Stills's "No Tears Left" and Nash's "Heartland." This new CSN music attracted a curious listener: Neil Young.

Stills recalls: "I'd asked Neil to come down [to Los Angeles] to play on a song of mine ('Acadienne'). So Neil calls and says, 'I'm on my way.' I said, 'Cool. When's your flight? What do you need?' He said, 'No, you don't understand. I'm in the car. I've got my Gretsch [electric guitar] and my acoustic. I'll be there in about six hours.'"

"Neil came to play on one song, and he stayed," Crosby told writer Matthew Greenwald after appearing on the nationally syndicated radio show *Rockline* in February 1999. "Ya know, I love the guy, and I love playing music with him. He is about going after all of the things I think are really valuable, the soul of the song, the storytelling quality. . . His effect on us has been to pull the best out of us. He's got us singin' around one microphone, getting air blends and stuff."

What was initially going to be a CSN record soon become a full-fledged Crosby, Stills, Nash & Young album. This fact had an immediate impact on the landscape of the project. According to Crosby: "Well, you know, CSN is a very

Jennifer and Chris Stills, Santa Monica, 1998.

full thing. CSN&Y is seven pounds of stuff in a three pound bag, [so] you have to make room. It's a lot of give and take. It's a different thing." Crosby adds: "Stephen is more comfortable with Neil there, because Neil and Stephen are deep buddies. With Neil there, it strengthens Stephen. He doesn't feel threatened and he's much more open and giving."

Stills himself admits: "Neil brings the best out in me and I bring the best out in him. He breathed life back into me. With Neil there, it's like there's no question, you know? 'I'm right behind you pard,' and the same with him."

"When Neil joins us," says Nash, "we know the edge that it brings. We know the slight ruggedness that it brings, and it's very attractive."

After Young added guitar and vocal parts to songs CSN had been recording, he brought in his "Looking Forward," "Slowpoke," and

"Out of Control," songs which he had previously slated for an unreleased solo album. Stills remembers: "He brought three of his best songs from what he had been working on and we did vocal harmonies and I played guitar on all of them. . . I made myself part of those and he made himself part of ours."

In addition, Young and Stills rekindled some of their old dual guitar muscle in a "live in the studio" setting, creating fresh sparks, particularly on Crosby and Raymond's "Stand and Be Counted." "If you listen to that song," Young told writer Dave DiMartino, "the way Stephen and I are playing is very similar to what we did in the Buffalo Springfield. . . Stephen and I are standing by each other, watching and listening to each other play, and interweaving what we do.

"When I first joined with Crosby, Stills & Nash," Young continues, "Stills was the musical force in the band, and I think that his music and his vibe and his energy is very important to what we're doing now. And I think there's a kind of resurgence of his talent on this record."

Most notably, there are Stills's ringing Martin acoustic guitar runs percolating through Young's "Looking Forward," his spiraling electric leads during Crosby's "Dream For Him," and the guitar fireworks and vocal growls throughout his own "No Tears Left." In "Seen Enough," Stills unleashes a torrent of timely words, with the music and measured rhymes inspired by Bob Dylan's 1965 classic, "Subterranean Homesick Blues."

Writer/director Cameron Crowe once described Crosby, Stills, Nash & Young in the studio: "To see them all together in one dimly lit room was an incredible sight—like watching four big old gray timber wolves circling." Observing CSN&Y working on a new album in 1999 evoked a similar feeling, with the four fifty-something musicians still exuding a unique aura and personal chemistry only enriched by the passage of time. Nash told *Rolling Stone*: "I don't think the feelings between the four of us have ever been better. With experience, we treat each other with much more compassion and understand each of our own madnesses."

Rumblings about a CSN&Y tour had a promoter reportedly offering the foursome more than $500,000 per show. A 1999 summer/fall tour was even mapped out. Dates, cities, and venues were leaked to the Internet in May. Ultimately, though, the tour was postponed. Crosby, ever active with CPR in the studio and on the road, offered this explanation in late May to CSN fans via the Internet: "As far as I know from Neil, Stephen, and Graham, the tour is still very much on. It was delayed due to health issues with one of our kids, and they come first. As soon as we know what's up with the tour timing, we will tell you here. I promise."

The CSN&Y album, initially titled *Heartland*, after Nash's song of the same name, was

scheduled for a July 17 release; but it kept getting pushed back—first to August, then to October. In late June, Nash received a phone call from Young, who wanted to talk about the album. Rather than discuss a release date, however, Young wanted to talk about going back into the studio. "We had an album that was basically finished," Nash recalls. "I mean, I had mastered it with Joe Gastwirt, who does all our stuff. Then I get a call from Neil, and he thinks. . . it's a great start, [but] he doesn't think we covered enough musical bases."

"We did think we were finished [with the album]," Crosby admits, "and Neil, who is a perfectionist and great record maker, saw some ways to make it better. He sent a jet and we were off to the ranch. It was fun and there was no acrimony among us. We are having an unbelievable time working together."

The July 1999 CSN&Y sessions at Young's ranch studio yielded recordings of Nash's "Someday Soon," a moving acoustic song written as a musical letter to the parents of a fourteen-year-old girl dying of leukemia, Young's quirky pop-rocker, "Queen of Them All," and a new Stills composition called "Coming to the Rescue." Now with over twenty recorded songs to choose from, CSN&Y had to make a final decision about which of them to include on the album. Nash remembers, "We had to figure out if it was going to be a 10, 11, 12, 13, or 14-song album. We thought we had made a mistake with *American Dream*, putting fourteen songs on there. We weren't sure, at that point, eleven years ago, whether kids had the attention span to deal with fourteen songs, and [listeners' attention spans] have only gotten worse to me."

The CSN&Y album, re-titled *Looking Forward*, ultimately included twelve songs—from Stills's opening blast of rhythm and percussion, "Faith in Me," to the closing, gently swaying "Sanibel," written by band friend Denny Sarokin.

Among the tracks left off the record were Stills's "Acadienne" and "Coming to the Res-

Crosby, Stills, Nash & Young outside Conway Studios, Los Angeles, 1999.

cue," Crosby's "Climber," and Nash's "Half Your Angels." Nash admits, "I wish there had been room, musically, for 'Climber' and 'Half Your Angels.' It wasn't a question of whether they were good enough songs, it was a question of, 'How do they fit?'" Stills adds: "We didn't worry about what to take out, we worried about the flow [of the album], and if we were too long on mellow, basically." Crosby concludes: "The selection process was probably the toughest part of it. All of us really love our songs, but all of us knew we couldn't make it a twenty-song album. In the end, I think we wound up with a great record. And that's what counts."

Crosby ponders how the music on *Looking Forward* will strike listeners in the twenty-first century: "There's a thing they used to say about us, when we first came out [in 1969], which was that we were speaking for our generation. And I think we still have our finger on the pulse of ourselves and the people that we

speak to. And I think we're talking about stuff that people really want to hear. They've been hearing a lot of music that's about rage, frustration, anger, struggle, loneliness, alienation. . . not much that has to do with what we're singing about—hope, relationships, love, forward motion, growth, change. I think [*Looking Forward*] speaks to something in our generation of people, and, in the people from succeeding generations of people who love our music [I think] that's going to ring their bell big time. I really do."

Neil Young offers his perspective on CSN&Y: "What people think of us is totally up to them. I don't think we can ever live up to the myth that surrounded us in the first place. There's no way that any record we make now would please everyone. So we just tried to please ourselves."

In early September '99, Nash commented to a CBS reporter about what he feels the new CSN&Y music brings to their audience: "I think they can expect what they've always loved about us: four people who are human beings that have their weaknesses and their strengths, writing songs from their heart to your heart, and playing them and singing them with as much emotion as possible."

A short time after making that statement, Nash was with family and friends on a boat in the ocean off the Hawaiian island of Kauai. A forceful wave suddenly jolted Nash into the air, and as he was coming down the boat surged up atop another wave. The impact broke both of his legs and one of his ankles. He ended up with pins in his legs and a plate in his ankle.

While Nash's convalescence was speeded by his optimistic spirit and "healing beams" from his family, friends, and fans around the world, several planned CSN&Y activities for the fall of '99 were cancelled or postponed. But a CSN&Y2K tour was still very much on the minds of the band members, particularly Neil Young.

"I'm looking forward to playing with Stephen [on stage]," Young told writer Dave DiMartino. "I'm looking forward to extending what Stephen and I started in 1966 . . . just picking up that ball. We've always had a unique thing going on between the two of us, as far as being guitar players and singers and everything goes, and I would like to develop that a little further during this next tour. And we'll see if there's gonna be another [CSN&Y] record. . . and develop it there, too."

When Nash looks at the current specter of CSN and CSN&Y, he says, "I'm thrilled about where we are right now. We have a clean slate and a lot of stuff that's ready to be written on that slate, in terms of new songs. And that's the engine that drives our entire business. If we don't write and create songs that touch people's hearts, then we don't have a business—we're not in the business."

"It all comes down to the music," says Stills, "and whether or not we can still deliver it. Some people—mostly journalists—have written us off so many times over the years that I've stopped paying attention. All I know is. . . our fans keep coming to our shows and we're all having a roaring good time. When I see those kids in the front row smiling and singing along, that's the only review I need."

With such a high level of enthusiasm and drive still running through the band, no one is talking about closing the book on these musicians just yet. The longevity of CSN and CSN&Y has already crossed into the musical frontier territory occupied by the Rolling Stones and a select few other rock bands. It's hard to draw an analogy between their musical lives and the careers of, say, boxers or baseball players who don't know when to quit, and hang on past their prime to fight one more fight, or play one more season—because CSN and CSN&Y are still capable, amazingly enough, of creating timeless musical magic. Yet one can't help but wonder how their legacy will ultimately play out.

"We never think about it, really," Crosby says. "You don't sit there in 1969 and say, 'I wonder how long this is going to last?' And you don't look back. We've been lucky. . . none of us has died. . . you know, I came close. . . but we haven't died. And you know, we've just followed the music, and we write songs about things that have lasting value. I believe that's what's kept us in people's hearts."

Discography

CROSBY, STILLS & NASH

Crosby, Stills & Nash (Atlantic) 1969
CSN (Atlantic) 1977
Replay (Atlantic) 1980
Daylight Again (Atlantic) 1982
Allies (Atlantic) 1983
Live It Up (Atlantic) 1990
CSN (four-CD box set) (Atlantic) 1991
CSN Carry On (two-CD French import version of
     CSN box set) (Atlantic) 1991
After the Storm (Atlantic) 1994

CSN SINGLES (not featured on any albums):

"Chippin' Away," CSN with James Taylor (1989);
"Chuck's Lament (A Child's Dream)," written by
     CSN and Joe Vitale, heard over the closing
     credits of the 1988 Columbia/TriStar film,
     Amazing Grace and Chuck, released as the B-
     side of the single "Live It Up" (1990)

CSN ON OTHER ALBUMS:

Woodstock (1970); *Woodstock II* (1971); *Stills* (1975);
     No Nukes (1979); *1969* soundtrack (1988); *Nin-
     tendo: White Knuckle Scorin'* (1992); *Woodstock
     Diary* (1994); *Woodstock '94* (1994); *Woodstock:
     25th Anniversary* box set (1994); *Red, Hot &
     Country* (1994); *Flipper* soundtrack (1996); *Rock
     and Roll Hall of Fame—1997—The Twelfth An-
     nual Induction Dinner* (limited edition CD); *At-
     lantic Records 50 Years—The Gold Anniversary
     Collection* (1998)

CROSBY, STILLS, NASH & YOUNG

*Déjà Vu (*Atlantic) 1970
4 Way Street (Atlantic) 1971
So Far (Atlantic) 1974
American Dream (Atlantic) 1988
Looking Forward (Reprise) 1999

CSN&Y ON OTHER ALBUMS:

Woodstock (1970); *The Strawberry Statement*
     soundtrack (1970); *Woodstock II* (1971); Neil
     Young: *Journey Through the Past* (1972); *Zuma*
     (1975); *Decade* (1977); *The Wonder Years*
     soundtrack (1989); *My Girl 2* soundtrack
     (1994); *Best of Woodstock* (1994); *Woodstock:
     25th Anniversary Box Set* (1994); *Bye Bye Love*
     soundtrack (1995)

CROSBY & NASH

Graham Nash/David Crosby (Atlantic) 1972
Wind on the Water (ABC) 1975
Whistling Down the Wire (ABC) 1976
Crosby-Nash Live (ABC) 1977
Crosby & Nash Greatest Hits (ABC) 1978
Another Stoney Evening (Grateful Dead Records)
     1998

C&N ON OTHER PARTNERS'
     ALBUMS:

Young: *Time Fades Away*; Stills: *Stephen Stills,
     Stills*

C&N ON OTHER ALBUMS (selected):

Joni Mitchell: *Court and Spark* (1974), *The Hissing of Summer Lawns* (1975); James Taylor: *Gorilla* (1975), *In the Pocket* (1976); Carole King: *Thoroughbred* (1975), *In Concert* (1994); Art Garfunkel: *Breakaway* (1975); Dave Mason: *Split Coconut* (1975); Jackson Browne: *The Pretender* (1976); Elton John: *Blue Moves* (1976); Gary Wright: *Headin' Home* (1979); *Bread & Roses Acoustic Music Festival* (1979); Bonnie Raitt: *Nick of Time* (1989); Michael Hedges: *Taproot* (1990), *Torched* (1999); Marc Cohn: *Barcelona Gold* (1992), *The Rainy Season* (1993); Kenny Loggins: *Return to Pooh Corner* (1994), *December* (1998); Dana Promfret: *Soul Cottage* (1998); *Sing Out for Seva* (1999)

THE STILLS-YOUNG BAND

Long May You Run (Reprise) 1976
On other albums: Neil Young: *Decade*

SOLO PROJECTS

David Crosby

If I Could Only Remember My Name (Atlantic) 1971
Oh Yes I Can (A&M) 1989
Thousand Roads (Atlantic) 1993
It's All Coming Back to Me Now (Atlantic) 1995
King Biscuit Flower Hour Presents David Crosby (King Biscuit) 1996

Crosby on other partners' albums:

Stills: *Stephen Stills, Stephen Stills 2, Stills, Still Stills*; Nash: *Songs for Beginners, Wild Tales, Earth and Sky*; Young: *Harvest, Time Fades Away, On the Beach, Zuma*

Crosby on other albums (selected):

Jefferson Airplane: *Crown of Creation* (1968), *Volunteers* (1969); Joni Mitchell: *Joni Mitchell* (a.k.a. *Songs to a Seagull*) (1968); The Flying Burrito Brothers: *The Gilded Palace of Sin* (1969); John Sebastian: *John B. Sebastian* (1969); Paul Kantner/Jefferson Starship: *Blows Against the Empire* (1970); Paul Kantner/Grace Slick: *Sunfighter* (1971); Cyrus Faryar: *Cyrus* (1971); Bob Gibson: *Bob Gibson* (1971); Jackson Browne: *Jackson Browne* (a.k.a. *Saturate Before Using*) (1972), *For Everyman* (1973), *World in Motion* (1989), *I'm Alive* (1993), *Looking East* (1996); Rick Roberts, *Windmills* (1972); Hot Tuna: *Burgers* (1972); Grace Slick: *Manhole* (1973); Paul Kantner, Grace Slick, and David Freiberg: *Baron von Tollbooth & the Chrome Nun* (1973); Roger McGuinn: *McGuinn* (1973), *Back to Rio* (1991); Phil Lesh and Ned Lagin: *Seastones* (1975); John David Souther: *Black Rose* (1976); Art Garfunkel: *Watermark* (1978); *Bread & Roses Acoustic Music Festival* (1979); The Section: *Fork It Over* (1979); Kenny Rankin: *Hiding in Myself* (1988); Phil Collins: *...But Seriously* (1989); Bob Dylan: *Under the Red Sky* (1990); Dan Fogelberg: *The Wild Places* (1990); Indigo Girls: *Rites of Passage* (1992); Willie Nelson: *Across the Borderline* (1993); Jack Tempchin and The Seclusion: *After the Rain* (1993); Jimmy Webb: *Suspended Disbelief* (1993); *Grammy's Greatest Moments Live, Volume 1* (with Phil Collins) (1994); Hootie & the Blowfish: *Cracked Rear View* (1994); Stevie Nicks: *Street Angel* (1994); Bonnie Raitt: *Longing in the Hearts* (1994); Nicolette Larson: *Sleep Baby Sleep* (1994); Chris Hillman: *Like a Hurricane* (1998); *Return of the Grievous Angel: A Tribute to Gram Parsons* (with Lucinda Williams) (1999)

Crosby songs recorded
by other artists (selected):

"Triad," Jefferson Airplane, *Crown of Creation* (1968); "Wooden Ships" (co-written with Stills and Kantner), Jefferson Airplane, *Volunteers* (1969); "Guinnevere," "Long Time Gone," "Song with No Words (Tree with No Leaves)," Paul Horn, *Visions* (1974); "Guinnevere," Miles Davis: recorded in 1970, released on *Circle in the Round* (1979) and *Complete Bitches Brew Sessions* (1998); "Eight Miles High" (co-written with McGuinn and Gene Clark), Leo Kottke: *Mudlark* (1971), Roxy Music: *Flesh & Blood* (1980), Crowded House (with Roger McGuinn): *I Feel Possessed* (1989), Golden Earring: *The Naked Truth* (1991); "Long Time Gone," Galliano: *The Plot Thickens* (1994);

"Yvette in English" (co-written with Joni Mitchell), Joni Mitchell: *Turbulent Indigo* (1994); "Almost Cut My Hair," "Déjà Vu," Fareed Haque: *Déjà Vu* (1997)

CPR (Crosby Pevar Raymond):

CPR (Samson) 1998
Live at Cuesta College 1998
Live at the Wiltern (Samson) 1998

CPR on other albums:

Live on the Mountain 3 (1997)

Stephen Stills

Stephen Stills (Atlantic) 1970
Stephen Stills 2 (Atlantic) 1971
Manassas (Atlantic) 1972
Down the Road (with Manassas) (Atlantic) 1973
Stills (CBS) 1975
Stephen Stills Live (Atlantic) 1975
Illegal Stills (CBS) 1976
Still Stills: The Best of Stephen Stills (Atlantic) 1976
Thoroughfare Gap (CBS) 1978
Right By You (Atlantic) 1984
Stills Alone (Gold Hill/Vision) 1991

Stills on other partners' albums:

Nash: *Earth and Sky*; Young: *After the Gold Rush, Harvest, Zuma*

Stills on other albums (selected):

Mike Bloomfield • Al Kooper • Steve Stills • Super Session (1968); Judy Collins: *Who Knows Where the Time Goes?* (1968); Joni Mitchell: *Joni Mitchell (a.k.a. Songs to a Seagull)* (1968), *Blue* (1971), *For the Roses* (1972); Cass Elliot: *Dream a Little Dream* (1968); The Monkees: *The Birds, the Bees and the Monkees* (1968), *Head* soundtrack (1968); Joan Baez: *Any Day Now* (1969); John Sebastian: *John B. Sebastian* (1969); Jefferson Airplane: *Volunteers* (1969); Eric Clapton: *Eric Clapton* (1970); Timothy Leary: *You Can Be Anyone This Time Around* (1970); Doris Troy: *Doris Troy* (1970); Rita Coolidge: *Rita Coolidge* (1971); Jimi Hendrix: *Cry of Love* (1971); Bill Withers:

Just As I Am (1971); Mickey Hart: *Rolling Thunder* (1972); Loggins & Messina: *Loggins & Messina* (1972); Humble Pie: *Smokin'* (1972); Elvin Bishop: *Juke Joint Jump* (1974); Veronique Sanson: *Le maudit* (1974); Dave Mason: *Mariposa de Oro* (1978); Bee Gees: *Saturday Night Fever* (1978); *Havana Jam* (1979); Chicago: *Closer to You* (b-side single) (1979); Hoyt Axton: *A Rusty Old Halo* (1980); Joe Vitale: *Plantation Harbor* (1980); Michael Schenker Group: *MSG* (1981); Ringo Starr: *Smell the Roses* (1981); Firefall: *Break of Dawn* (1982); Flaco Jimenez: *Partners* (1992); *Love: John Lennon Forever* tribute (1997); *Prefontaine* soundtrack (1997); *He Got Game* soundtrack (with Public Enemy) (1998); "Love Shouldn't Hurt" (CD single, with Chris Stills) (1998); The Jimmy Rogers All-Stars: *Blues Blues Blues* (1999)

Stills songs recorded by other artists (selected):

"Sit Down I Think I Love You" (single), The Mojo Men (1967); "For What It's Worth," The Staple Singers (1967), Sergio Mendez and Brazil '66 (1972); "Bluebird," The James Gang: *Yer' Album* (1969), Bonnie Raitt: *Bonnie Raitt* (1971), Steve Lukather: *Luke* (1997); "Everydays," Yes: *Time and A Word* (1970); "Special Care," Doris Troy: *Doris Troy* (1970), Fanny: *Charity Ball* (1971); "Love the One You're With," Aretha Franklin: *Live at Fillmore West* (1971), Percy Faith & His Orchestra: *I Think I Love You* (1971), Bob Seger: *Smokin' O.P.'s* (1972), The Isley Brothers: *Live* (1973), Joe Cocker: *Live in L.A.* (1975), Ian Cussick: *Treasure Island* (1989), The Neville Brothers: *Live on Planet Earth* (1994), Luther Vandross: *Songs* (1994); "To a Flame," *Astrud Gilberto with Stanley Turrentine* (1971); "So Begins the Task," Judy Collins: *True Stories and Other Dreams* (1973), Rice, Rice, Hillman & Pederson: *Out of the Woodwork* (1997); "Go and Say Goodbye," Poco: *A Good Feelin' to Know* (1972); "Four Days Gone," Alex Taylor: *Dinnertime* (1972), Rick Roberts: *She Is a Song* (1973); "Open Up," REO Speedwagon: *Ridin' Out the Storm* (1973); "The Witching Hour," Chris Hillman: *Slippin' Away* (1976), McGuinn, Hillman & Clark: *Three Byrds Land in London* (1997); "It Doesn't Matter" (co-written with Chris Hillman and Rick Roberts), *Firefall* (1976), Dan Fogelberg: *Exiles* (1987); "As I Come of Age," The Pointer Sisters: *Energy* (1978); "Closer to You" (co-written with Donnie Dacus), Chicago, b-side of 1978 single and included on *Group Portrait* (Chicago box set, 1991); "Helplessly Hoping," J. D. Crowe & the New South: *Straight Ahead* (1983), Richie Havens: *Live at the Cellar Door* (1990), Eden: *Eden* (1998), Taxi: *A Walk on the Moon* soundtrack (1999); "Livin' on Rock and Roll" (co-written with Thomas Jefferson Kaye), Thomas Jefferson Kaye: *Not Alone* (1992); "Treetop Flyer," Jimmy Buffett: *Banana Wind* (1996); "Carry On," "4 + 20," "Everybody I Love You" (co-written with Neil Young), Fareed Haque: *Déjà Vu* (1997)

Graham Nash

Songs for Beginners (Atlantic) 1971
Wild Tales (Atlantic) 1973
Earth and Sky (Capitol) 1980
Innocent Eyes (Atlantic) 1986

Nash on other partners' albums:

Crosby: *If I Could Only Remember My Name, Oh Yes I Can, Thousand Roads, It's All Coming Back to Me Now, Live at the Wiltern* (with CPR); Stills: *Stephen Stills, Stills, Still Stills, Right By You*; Young: *Harvest, Time Fades Away, Zuma* (Nash also recorded "War Song," a single, with Neil Young, released on Reprise in 1972)

Nash on other albums (selected):

John Sebastian: *John B. Sebastian* (1969); Rita Coolidge: *Rita Coolidge* (1971), *Nice Feelin'* (1971); Paul Kantner/Jefferson Starship: *Blows Against the Empire* (1970); Paul Kantner/Grace Slick: *Sunfighter* (1971); Grin (featuring Nils Lofgrin): *1 + 1* (1972); Dave Mason: *Headkeeper* (1972), *It's Like You Never Left* (1973); David Blue: *Nice Baby and the Angel* (1973); Dan Fogelberg: *Souvenirs* (1974); Joni Mitchell: *For the Roses* (1972); Terry Reid: *Seed of Memory* (1976); Waylon Jennings: *Are You Ready for the Country?* (1976); Steve Gillette: *A Little Warmth* (1979); James Taylor: *Flag* (1979), *That's Why I'm Here* (1985); *Bread & Roses Acoustic Music Festival* (1979); *No Nukes* (with James Taylor &

Carly Simon, with Jackson Browne, with CSN, and solo) (1979); Leah Kunkel: *I Run with Trouble* (1980); Joe Vitale: *Plantation Harbor* (1980); Dwight Twilley: *Scuba Divers* (1982); Jimmy Webb: *Angel Heart* (1982); Warren Zevon: *The Envoy* (1982); *Fast Times at Ridgemont High* (Nash contributed his "Love Is the Reason" to this film soundtrack) (1983); Donovan: *Lady of the Stars* (1983); Marc Jordan: *Talking Through Pictures* (1987); Nicolette Larson: *Sleep Baby Sleep* (1994); *Not Fade Away: Remembering Buddy Holly* (with the Hollies, on "Peggy Sue Got Married") (1995); Anastasia & John: *That's About You and Me* (1997); Modern Folk Quartet: *Wolfgang* (1997); Allan Thomas: *Coconut Culture* (1997); Paul Williams: *Back In Love Again* (1997); *Shake, Rattle & Roll* original soundtrack (1999)

Nash songs recorded by other artists (selected):

"Teach Your Children," *Country Gazette* (1973), Richie Havens: *Collection* (1987), Suzy Boguss, Alison Krauss & Kathy Mattea (with Nash and CSN): *Red, Hot + Country* (1994), Modern Folk Quartet: *Highway 70* (1995); "Simple Man," Barbra Streisand: *Butterfly* (1974); "Wasted on the Way," William Jansen: *String Fever* (1995); "Teach Your Children," "Our House," Fareed Haque: *Déjà Vu* (1997)

Neil Young

Neil Young (Reprise) 1969
Everybody Knows This Is Nowhere (with Crazy Horse) (Reprise) 1969
After the Gold Rush (Reprise) 1970
Harvest (Reprise) 1972
Journey Through the Past (Reprise) 1972
Time Fades Away (Reprise) 1973
On the Beach (Reprise) 1974
Tonight's the Night (Reprise) 1975
Zuma (with Crazy Horse) (Reprise)1975
American Stars 'n' Bars (Reprise) 1977
Decade (Reprise) 1977
Comes a Time (Reprise) 1978
Rust Never Sleeps (with Crazy Horse) (Reprise) 1979
Live Rust (with Crazy Horse) (Reprise) 1979
Hawks and Doves (Reprise) 1980

Re•ac•tor (with Crazy Horse) (Reprise) 1981
Trans (Geffen) 1983
Everybody's Rockin (with the Shocking Pinks) (Geffen) 1983
Old Ways (Geffen) 1985
Landing on Water (Geffen) 1986
Life (with Crazy Horse) (Geffen) 1987
This Note's for You (with the Bluenotes) (Reprise) 1988
Freedom (Reprise) 1989
Ragged Glory (with Crazy Horse) (Reprise) 1990
Arc/Weld (with Crazy Horse) (Reprise) 1991
Lucky Thirteen (Geffen) 1992
Harvest Moon (Reprise) 1992
Unplugged (Reprise) 1993
Sleeps with Angels (with Crazy Horse) 1994
The Complex Sessions (with Crazy Horse, special EP-length CD featuring video versions of tracks from *Sleeps with Angels*) 1994
Mirror Ball (with Pearl Jam) (Reprise) 1995
Dead Man soundtrack (Vapor) 1996
Broken Arrow (with Crazy Horse) (Reprise) 1996
Year of the Horse (with Crazy Horse) (Reprise) 1997

Neil Young on other partners' albums:

Crosby: *If I Could Only Remember My Name*

EARLY RECORDINGS

David Crosby

Les Baxter's Balladeers: *Jack Linkletter Presents a Folk Festival* (Crescendo) 1963
Early L.A.: Archive Series Volume IV (Together) (Recorded in 1964, released in 1969)
with the Byrds (all on Columbia, except *Byrds*):
Preflyte (Recorded in 1964, released in 1969 on Together, then on Columbia in 1973); *Mr. Tambourine Man* (1965); *Turn! Turn! Turn!* (1965); *Fifth Dimension* (1966); *Younger Than Yesterday* (1967); *The Byrds' Greatest Hits* (1967); *The Notorious Byrd Brothers* (although Crosby left the Byrds before this album was released in 1968, the album contains several songs he co-wrote. When the album was reissued in 1997, it included Crosby's "Triad" among the bonus tracks); *Byrds* (Elektra/Asylum) (1973); *The Byrds Box Set* (1990)

Stephen Stills

with the Au Go-Go Singers: *They Call Us the Au Go-Go Singers* (Roulette) (1964)
with Buffalo Springfield (all albums on Atko):
Buffalo Springfield (featuring Stills's "Baby Don't Scold Me" on original 1966 version, re-released in 1967 with his "For What It's Worth" replacing that song. Special *Buffalo Springfield* re-issue in 1997 included both original mono mix and subsequent stereo mix of the group's debut album) (1967); *Buffalo Springfield Again* (1968); *Last Time Around* (1968); *Retrospective* (1969); *Buffalo Springfield* (greatest hits collection, featuring nine-minute extended version of Stills's "Bluebird") (1973)

Graham Nash

with the Hollies (selected):
(Released in America) *Here I Go Again* (Imperial) (1964); *Hear! Here!* (Imperial) (1965); *Beat Group!* (Imperial) (1966); *Stop! Stop! Stop!* (Imperial) (1966); *The Hollies' Greatest Hits* (Imperial) (1967); *Evolution* (Epic) (1967); *Dear Eloise/King Midas in Reverse* (Epic) (1967); *The Hollies' Greatest Hits* (Epic) (1973); *"What Goes Around..."* (Atlantic) (1983); *30th Anniversary Collection* (box set) (1993); *Archive Alive!* (1997); *The Hollies at Abbey Road • 1963–1966* (EMI) (1998); *The Hollies at Abbey Road • 1966–1970* (EMI) (1998)
(Released only in Great Britain) *Stay With the Hollies* (Parlophone) (1964); *In the Hollies Style* (1964); *Hollies' Greatest Hits* (Parlophone) (1968).
While in the Hollies, Nash appeared on the Everly Brothers' *Two Yanks in England* (Warner Bros.) (1966)

Special thanks to John Einarson (author *of For What It's Worth: The Story of Buffalo Springfield*, among other books), Johnny Rogan (author of *Crosby, Stills, Nash & Young: The Visual Documentary*, among other books), Hans van Netburg, Hans Velduizen (and his CSN website), and the Lee Shore discussion group for information provided during the compilation of this discography.

For links to Internet websites related to Crosby, Stills & Nash, go to the World Wide Web and type *http://www.crosbystillsnash.com*, home of the Crosby, Stills, and Nash Pages.

HENRY DILTZ

Henry Diltz was born September 6, 1938, in Kansas City, Missouri. He developed an ear for music as a child while traveling overseas with his parents (Henry's father worked for the State Department). During the late fifties, Henry divided his time between college in Munich, the U.S. Military Academy at West Point, and the University of Hawaii—where he studied psychology and started getting serious about his music. In 1963 Henry became a founding member of the Modern Folk Quartet. This seminal folk-pop harmony group played numerous clubs and colleges all over America, recorded two albums for Warner Bros. and a Phil Spector-produced single. While in the MFQ, Henry met Stephen Stills and David Crosby, and also became interested in photography. This opened up a whole new career for him. He took photographs of his friends—first the Lovin Spoonful, the Hollies, and the Buffalo Springfield; then Crosby, Stills & Nash, Joni Mitchell, Neil Young, James Taylor, the Doors, Linda Ronstadt, Jackson Browne, the Eagles, America, Dan Fogelberg, and over a hundred other artists in the '60s and '70s. Many of Henry's photos were featured on these artists' album covers, designed by Henry's longtime friend and associate, art director Gary Burden. Henry was the official photographer at Woodstock and the Monterey Pop Festival. In ensuing years, Henry photographed many other artists, including Garth Brooks, Tom Petty, and Ringo Starr, while continuing to record and perform with the MFQ. His work has appeared in such magazines as *Rolling Stone* and *Life*, and in such books as *Shooting Stars* (a Straight Arrow book published in 1973 that featured rock's greatest photographers), *California Rock, California Sound* (with text by Anthony Fawcett, published by Reed Books in 1978) and *The Innocent Age* (a retrospective collection of Henry's photos, published in Japan by Switch in 1990). In addition, a CD-ROM titled *Under the Covers* offers extensive insights into Henry's album cover photography, while the film and DVD version of *Under the Covers* provides a fascinating guided tour through these album cover sessions, from CSN to the Eagles to Jimmy Webb, featuring a running commentary by Henry and Gary Burden, along with exclusive interviews with the artists. Henry has a website (www.henrysgallery.com) that opens up another window into the world of his distinctive images. Throughout the years, Henry has continued to photograph CSN and CSN&Y. The best of these photos appear in this book.

Crosby, Zimmer, Stills, and Nash at Zoetrope Studios, Hollywood, July 1982. (Photo by Henry Diltz.)

DAVE ZIMMER

Dave Zimmer was born January 13, 1953 in San Jose, California. Baseball was his first love; music and writing came next. Dave was more interested in Giants games at Candlestick Park and Willie Mays's home run totals than the action on San Francisco's Fillmore concert stage and the rise of flower power in the Haight-Ashbury. After graduating from Palo Alto High School in 1971, Dave entered the University of California at Davis and, by 1975, had earned a B.A. degree in English/Writing. It was during this period that Dave turned toward the music of Crosby, Stills & Nash, Neil Young, and Joni Mitchell. Songs such as "Wooden Ships," "Carry On," and "Teach Your Children" sparked creative inspiration, and led to Dave's career in music jour-

nalism. A majority of his reviews and feature interviews, with artists such as Tom Petty, Chrissie Hynde, Robbie Robertson, Tom Waits, k.d. lang, Todd Rundgren, and Grace Slick, as well as CSN and Neil Young appeared in *BAM: The California Music Magazine*, where he was an editor from 1979 to 1990. Since 1990, Dave has worked as a writer and communications executive, first for MCA Records and later for Universal Studios and Seagram. He is married to the love of his life, Claudia, and they have one son, Casey. Dave's many conversations with Crosby, Stills & Nash (individually and collectively) and close friendship with longtime CSN photographer Henry Diltz led to the creation of this book.